Capitalism, socialism, and serfdom

Capitalism, socialism, and serfdom

Essays by
Evsey D. Domar
Massachusetts Institute of Technology

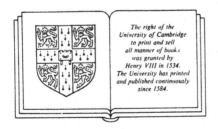

The right of the
University of Cambridge
to print and sell
all manner of books
was granted by
Henry VIII in 1534.
The University has printed
and published continuously
since 1584.

CAMBRIDGE UNIVERSITY PRESS
Cambridge
New York   Port Chester   Melbourne   Sydney

CAMBRIDGE UNIVERSITY PRESS
Cambridge, New York, Melbourne, Madrid, Cape Town, Singapore, São Paulo

Cambridge University Press
The Edinburgh Building, Cambridge CB2 8RU, UK

Published in the United States of America by Cambridge University Press, New York

www.cambridge.org
Information on this title: www.cambridge.org/9780521370912

First published 1989
This digitally printed version 2008

A catalogue record for this publication is available from the British Library

Library of Congress Cataloguing in Publication data
Domar, Evsey D.
Capitalism, socialism, and serfdom : essays by Evsey D. Domar / by
Evsey D. Domar.
p.   cm.
Bibliography: p.
Includes index.
ISBN 0–521–37091–4
1. Comparative economics.   2. Capitalism – United States.
3. United States – Economic policy.   4. Communism – Soviet Union.
5. Central planning – Soviet Union.   6. Soviet Union – Economic
policy – 1917–   7. Economic history.   I. Title.
HB90.D66   1989
338.947 – dc20   89-31498

ISBN 978-0-521-37091-2 hardback
ISBN 978-0-521-07020-1 paperback

To Tupa

Contents

List of tables and figures   ix
Foreword   xi
Acknowledgments   xxi

Part I. Economic systems
1 Reflections on economic development   3
2 Poor old capitalism: a review article   15
3 The blind men and the elephant: an essay on isms   29

Part II. Economic growth and productivity
4 On the measurement of technological change   49
5 On total productivity and all that: a review article   73
6 Economic growth and productivity in the United States,
   Canada, United Kingdom, Germany, and Japan in the
   post-war period *(with S. M. Eddie, B. H. Herrick, P. M.
   Hohenberg, M. D. Intriligator, and I. Miyamoto)*   91
7 An index-number tournament   107
8 On the measurement of comparative efficiency   126

Part III. Soviet economics
9 Special features of industrialization in planned economies: a
   comparison between the Soviet Union and the United States   143
10 The Soviet collective farm as a producer cooperative   176
11 On the optimal compensation of a socialist manager   202
   Special appendix: The effect of a proportional subsidy or
   a tax on the quality and quantity of output   218

Part IV. Slavery and serfdom
12 The causes of slavery or serfdom: a hypothesis   225

13 On the profitability of Russian serfdom
    (with M. J. Machina)   239

14 Were Russian serfs overcharged for their land by the 1861
    Emancipation? The history of one historical table   280

    Index   289

Tables and figures

Tables

6.1.	Rates of growth of output	94
6.2.	Rates of growth of labor input	96
6.3.	Rates of growth of labor productivity	97
6.4.	Rates of growth of capital input	99
6.5.	Rates of growth of capital productivity	100
6.6.	Rates of growth of value-added arithmetic Residual	102
6.7.	Ratios between annual rates of growth of Residual and output	104
7.1.	Values of inputs and outputs in the base year	111
7.2.	Indexes or relative rates of growth of inputs and outputs between the base and given years	111
7.3.	Relationships between the indexes S, H, and V expressed in terms of B and the covariance between u_i and X_i	118
7.4.	A comparison of index numbers	120
7.5.	A further comparison of index numbers	122
8.1.	Real national income per unit of factor inputs, selected countries, 1960	136
9.1.	Relative magnitudes of capital formation, USSR and U.S.	148
9.2.	Price movements of components of gross national product, USSR and U.S.	151
9.3.	Rates of growth of principal economic indicators, USSR and U.S.	154
9.4.	Rates of growth of principal productivity indexes	156
9.5.	Percentage distribution of employed persons by economic sectors, USSR and U.S.	160
9.6.	Distribution of the stock of fixed capital, USSR and U.S.	162
9.7.	Percentage distribution of gross fixed investment in USSR and U.S., 1950–59	163
9.8.	Relative distribution of capital and labor, USSR and U.S.	166
9.9.	Relative distribution of engineers in industry, USSR and U.S.	168

9.10. Rates of growth of labor productivity in the USSR,
    1928–1960   172
10.1. Effects of an increase in p_i on the magnitudes of outputs
    and inputs   182
10.2. Effects of changes in rent, tax rates, and prices on the
    employment of labor by the co-op   190
13.1. Effects of the growth of the serf population on the
    variables in the second model   251
13.2. Prices of serfs obtained by different methods   262
Appendix Table 13.1. Nominal prices of serfs and of populated
    land   276
Appendix Table 13.2. Real prices of serfs and of populated land   278
14.1. The basic data   281
14.2. The quantity of allotted land   282
14.3. An estimate of the overcharge   286

Figures

3.1. The firm's position under monopolistic competition   33
10.1. The effect of an increase in rent   180
10.2. The effect of a rise in price of output   181
10.3. The supply curve of labor   185
10.4. The excess supply of labor   188
11.1. The movement toward the optimum with declining
    elasticity of demand and rising marginal cost   206
11.2. The movement toward the optimum with declining
    elasticity of demand and falling marginal cost   206
11.3. The movement toward the optimum with increasing
    elasticity of demand and rising marginal cost   213
13.1. The subsistence isoquant   243
13.2. The Master's income under freedom and in First and
    Second Models   253
13.3. The two constraints: the subsistence isoquant and the
    Z^* ray   255
13.4. The relationship between the nominal prices of serfs
    and the prices of grain   269

Foreword

The essays in this volume have been written since the publication of my first collection, *Essays in the Theory of Economic Growth,* in 1957.[1] Although all but two of them (Essay 3 and the Special Appendix to Essay 11) have appeared in print before, I hope that, being collected in one place, they may still be of some use to my fellow economists and even to a few historians (Part IV).[2]

A number of minor changes and corrections were made in the original texts.

Unlike the earlier essays which had a definite focus – the theory of economic growth – this book appears to lack one. Actually, most of the essays in the first three parts do have a common theme: the comparative performance of different economic systems, particularly of American capitalism and Soviet socialism (at least as it had existed before Gorbachev's *perestroika*).[3] My ventures into Soviet economics have not been sufficiently deep or frequent to claim the title of a sovietologist, but they have continued to be a rich source of ideas. They have also aroused my interest in the history of serfdom and slavery, which led to the three essays in Part IV.

Let me now describe the origin and nature of each essay and end with a few brief comments on the *perestroika,* to the extent that these essays are relevant to it.

The first three essays (Part I) are discourses. They are rather general and nontechnical with one formula and one diagram for all three. Essay 1 was written over twenty years ago. As I reread it, I found very little to change (a matter for pride or for shame?), except for rejecting Oscar Lange's suggestion that non-fully-competitive markets should be subject

[1] *Essays in the Theory of Economic Growth,* New York, 1957.
[2] Several papers were omitted from both collections. The most important of them are "Proportional Income Taxation and Risk Taking" (with Richard A. Musgrave), *The Quarterly Journal of Economics,* Vol. LVIII, May 1944, pp. 388–422, and "Kahan on Russian Economic History," a review article on *The Plow, the Hammer and the Knout: An Economic History of Eighteenth-Century Russia* by Arcadius Kahan, *The Journal of Economic History,* Vol. XLVII, September 1987, pp. 769–74.
[3] *Perestroika* means restructuring. By now it has entered the English language.

to permanent price control. Unless we were dealing with a true monopoly (like a public utility), I would rather take my chances with monopolistic competition. Essay 11 shows how to limit its potential harm, and Essay 3 claims that it might even do some good. The other recommendations I would make stronger. In particular, I would emphasize two: first, that underdeveloped countries do not rush into communism (or socialism); and second, that we do not treat as our enemies those of them who disregard this good advice. The obsession with communism has already cost us much blood, treasure, and prestige. Our political right must have very little faith in the viability of our economic and political system if its members become hysterical every time some little country goes communist or even veers slightly to the left. Actually, our *national* interests suffer very little, if at all, from such moves, unless, in our anger, we push that country into Soviet arms, as we did with Cuba. Even if Mexico turns communist, which it may do some day, the sun will continue to shine. (In *My Fair Lady*, Eliza expresses a similar idea much more vividly than I can.) I doubt that citizens of West Germany lose much sleep because they have two communist neighbors. More sleep is probably lost on the other side.

Chances are that we will have to live in a world where some countries are capitalist, some communist, some in a transitional state from one system to another and back again (like China is today and, perhaps, the Soviet Union will be tomorrow). We may not like this kind of world, but we will have to get used to it, just as Catholic and Protestant governments in Europe, after a good deal of warfare, finally learned not to love but to tolerate one another and even to choose allies and enemies across religious lines. Look at the cooperation that has developed lately between the two Germanies, which China and Taiwan are beginning to imitate. And it was communist China that, not so long ago, fought undeclared wars against communist Soviet Union and communist Viet Nam. Surely, the Soviet government must have regretted many a time that it supported Mao Tse-tung against Chiang Kai-shek in the Chinese Civil War.

Essay 2 is a review article. It was written in response to an attack on capitalism launched in a book of readings edited and partly written by three young radical economists.[4] I do not harbor any particular love for capitalism (to paraphrase Churchill, I regard it as the worst economic system, except for all others that have been tried), but I feel that even the devil should have his day in court. The authors/editors charged American capitalism with a number of ills, many of them true, but forgot to inquire whether these or similar ills were found in socialist countries as well. Many of them were. Why then pick on capitalism?

[4] Richard C. Edwards, Michael Reich, and Thomas B. Weisskopf, *The Capitalist System: A Radical Analysis of American Society,* Englewood Cliffs, N.J., 1972.

The title of Essay 3 was taken from an old and familiar Indian tale, the meaning of which, I trust, is obvious. In the spirit of that tale, I confined my comparison between capitalism and socialism to only two criteria – the distribution of risk and power between producers and consumers – and disregarded the traditional themes of the ownership of the means of production and of class struggle. I argued that, under capitalism, producers bear most of the risk while consumers enjoy most of the power because of the prevalence of monopolistic competition. Friends of capitalism welcome this state of affairs and call it "market discipline" while its enemies, the socialists, deride it as "market tyranny." The excess demand prevalent in most (or all) socialist countries protects workers from this tyranny by transferring the power from consumers to producers. The latter do not retain all of it either: much of it passes on to the bureaucrats who perform the allocative functions of the market.

In the last part of the essay I discussed the bias introduced into international comparisons of welfare by our exclusive acceptance of the consumers' point of view.

In Part II, all essays except Essay 7 deal with the so-called Index of Total Factor Productivity, which, for brevity's sake, I call the "Residual."[5] It has been given various names, and it has been expressed in many forms; the form that I favor now is the weighted mean of the productivities of land, labor, capital, and intermediate products, if their presence is recognized.[6] Usually, it is not: in most studies, intermediate products are excluded from both the input and the output sides in order to avoid double counting. (I have always marveled at the economist's ability to produce potato chips without potatoes.) This exclusion, which distorts the magnitude of the Residual, is not absolutely necessary, but without it integration of industries and sectors creates problems. After a lot of tedious algebra, I found a method for dealing with them, though I have to admit that it is likely to interest only the specialist. But while searching for it, I discovered that the Residual is mathematically equivalent to Leontief's Index of Structural Change (with corrected weights), published by him as early as 1953, and probably well forgotten by the profession.[7] Its resurrection was worth all that algebra. It offers a better understanding of the process of technological change by expressing it in a disaggregated form (obtained from two or several input-output tables). It shows that

---

[5] It is usually calculated as a residual after the contributions of labor and of capital have been accounted for.

[6] Hence, the name "Index of *Average* Factor Productivity" would be more appropriate for it than the commonly used "Index of *Total* Factor Productivity." In any case, the word "Total" is out of place because of the exclusion of intermediate products.

[7] Wassily Leontief et al., *Studies in the Structure of the American Economy*, New York, 1953, pp. 27–35.

the Residual is composed of a great many small changes in input coefficients. Both proponents and opponents of central planning would benefit from studying it.

Essay 5 is merely a review article on John Kendrick's magnum opus.[8] It concentrates on his methodology in obtaining the Residual and criticizes him for having omitted intermediate products. I think I owe him an apology, because, in the very next essay (6), statistical necessity forced us (five graduate assistants and me) to do exactly what he had done. We calculated the Residual by his method for five countries in the 1948–60 period. This was one of the early comparative studies; its main accomplishment was the disaggregation of the data into eleven sectors. Among other things, we found that agriculture in all but one country must have gone through a virtual revolution.

"The Index-Number Tournament" (Essay 7) is exactly what its title says – a contest between the Federal Reserve Index of Industrial Production based on value-added weights and a Soviet index with value-of-output weights. My interest in this dismal subject (index-number theory) was aroused by the nearly unanimous acceptance of the Federal Reserve index and the condemnation of the Soviet one by our sovietologists because the Soviet weights involved double counting, while the Federal Reserve weights supposedly did not. I have always been suspicious of unanimity among economists (only economists? see Essay 14): it usually indicates that a result obtained by one researcher has been accepted uncritically by others. In this case, my suspicions were justified: both indexes were found to be defective, and neither had a clear advantage over the other, but the moral victory clearly belonged to the Soviet underdog. Of course, the latter had to be of the "pure" variety. An "impure" Soviet index is not worth discussing.

The last essay in Part II (8) was presented at a symposium held at the University of Michigan in 1968. It began as a comment on Bergson's paper, "Comparative Productivity and Efficiency in the Soviet Union and the United States," and eventually acquired a life of its own.[9] Bergson's paper consisted of three parts: (a) the theory of interspatial comparisons, (b) the calculation of the interspatial Residual, and (c) an explanation of Soviet inefficiency. I was particularly interested in part (a) because of the work I had done in Essay 4. The substitution of comparisons in space for those in time involves few methodological changes: the less developed

---

[8] John W. Kendrick, *Productivity Trends in the United States,* National Bureau of Economic Research, Princeton, N.J., 1961.

[9] Abram Bergson, "Comparative Productivity and Efficiency in the USA and the USSR" in Alexander Eckstein, editor, *Comparison of Economic Systems: Theoretical and Methodological Approaches,* Berkeley and Los Angeles, 1971.

country (the Soviet Union, in this case) corresponds to the early year, the more developed one (the United States) to the late year. Unfortunately, the index-number problems bedeviling comparisons in time do not disappear when time is replaced by space, because these problems have no definite solutions. Bergson's principal findings were sufficiently robust, however, not to be affected by the choice of a specific index form or of a set of weights: the Soviet–American interspatial Residual remained far below unity.

Why? Two hypotheses may be offered: first, the Soviet Union is at an earlier stage of economic development; second, the Soviet economy is simply less efficient than ours, presumably because it is socialist. The two explanations are not mutually exclusive: Bergson seemed to lean to the latter, and I suggested the former, at least as a partial alternative, because similar results had been obtained from comparisons of the United States with other capitalist countries. Since neither Bergson nor I presented much evidence (in this exchange) to support our respective views, the question was left open at the time, but lately, in the light of recent Chinese developments and Soviet revelations, I have moved closer to his view.

Essay 9 went through quite a transformation from its original design to its final form. My assignment called for a comparison between the industrialization patterns of planned and nonplanned economies. To make the task manageable, I started by reducing the number of countries to two – the Soviet Union and the United States. Next came the choice of the criteria for making the comparison. My old growth models notwithstanding, I believe that a country's most important factor of production is not its physical capital but its human one – the able, educated, and trained manpower – and that its economic performance depends heavily on the use made of it. For the United States, there are some data on the distribution of its labor elite by occupation, but for the Soviet Union I could find none. This forced my investigation into more conventional and less exciting grooves, but at the end I stumbled into two interesting problems: first, should a country bent on rapid economic development concentrate its best resources in a few key industries, like machine building, as the Soviets seem to have done, or should it follow the American pattern of advancing on a broad front (as reported by Kendrick)?[10] Second, should the machine-building industry concentrate on mass production of standard machines with infrequent model changes, or should machines be produced in small batches, even custom-made, with frequent model changes to take advantage of recent technological advances? My preliminary results suggested that the former policy was appropriate for a less

[10] Kendrick, op. cit., p. 146.

developed country, and the latter for an advanced one. The data hinted that something like that had actually taken place in the two countries, respectively, an outcome that appeared to me too good to be true. But if it was true, perhaps the perpetual scolding that the Soviets have received from us and from themselves for their slow introduction of new models has been overdone?

I intended to come back to these problems, but, alas, I have not. Perhaps by now they have been worked out by others.

Essay 10 was inspired by Benjamin Ward's pioneering work on the theory of producer cooperatives.[11] It generalized his results for any number of inputs and outputs and established that, contrary to his findings, a perverse reaction by a co-op to a rise in the price of a particular output was unlikely. If it thus disposed of one puzzle regarding the nature of a producer co-op, it reemphasized another: the co-op is supposed to be democratic, it should appeal to its worker-members and call forth increased efforts on their part; it should avoid the endless labor-capital conflicts characteristic of capitalist firms; in a word, the co-op form of business enterprise should grow and spread, and yet in countries where it is not imposed from above (as in Yugoslavia) producer co-ops are hard to find. Has Tugan-Baranovsky's pessimistic prognosis (of 1921) been vindicated?[12] Does co-op democracy interfere with efficient management?

Although my model of a producer co-op was supposed to apply to the Soviet *kolkhoz* (collective farm), I have to admit that its relevance to it is only marginal. Soviet *kolkhozes* have performed badly not because they are co-ops but for other well-known reasons. If and when these reasons are removed, the specific problems created by their cooperative character can be addressed.

The last essay in Part III (11) should have been dedicated to Mr. Kosygin, then the Soviet premier, because it was suggested by his famous speech inaugurating the Soviet economic reforms in 1965.[13] (How much that speech resembles Mr. Gorbachev's pronouncements of our day!) Two aspects of Kosygin's speech caught my eye: first, that prices should be set to secure every functioning enterprise a profit rather than to equate demand and supply; this implied that the separation between production decisions and price setting – a clumsy and inefficient method – would continue, to the detriment of quality and technological progress. Second, that enterprise managers (directors) would be instructed to maximize (more or less) some

---

[11] Benjamin Ward, "The Firm in Illyria: Market Syndicalism," *The American Economic Review,* Vol. 48, September 1958, pp. 566–89.

[12] M. I. Tugan-Baranovsky, *Sotsial'nyia osnovy kooperatsii* [The Social foundations of cooperation], Berlin, 1921, pp. 237–56.

[13] Kosygin's speech was published in *Pravda* and *Izvestiia* on September 28, 1965. Several English translations are given in a footnote to this essay.

function of profits and revenue (sales), a strange objective if managers were facing parametric prices. I found, however, that this objective made excellent sense if the managers were permitted to set their own prices, because a bonus based on a proper combination of profits and of revenue could induce the managers to equate these prices to the corresponding marginal costs, as required by the Pareto optimum. But since I wrote Essay 3, I have begun to doubt the wisdom of this prescription.

So much for economics proper. We now turn to economic history.

The first essay in Part IV owes its genesis to the great Russian historian V. Kliuchevskii.[14] It provided an analytical explanation for his masterful description of the development of Russian serfdom. The explanation, which is applicable to (agricultural) serfdom and slavery in general, is unbelievably simple: both institutions are caused by an abundance of land relative to labor. An abundant factor of production does not bear rent. If landowners are to derive an income, it must come from the ownership of some other factor that *is scarce* – in this case from labor.

But as I look at this essay today, I am far from satisfied with it. Its empirical foundation is rather weak. (A job for historians?) It failed to distinguish between slavery and serfdom, two quite different institutions: a slave (usually) works for his master full-time and is paid in subsistence; a serf works part-time and *is paid in land*. I also failed to bring out the basic contrast between the Russian (or east European) and west European types of serfdom: in Russia, the master was free to set and to change the serf's land allotment at his discretion; in the West, the serf's holding was protected (more or less) by law and custom. Since its value was likely to increase with economic development and population growth, the master's inability to reduce it made serf labor ever more expensive for him; eventually, he would wish to get rid of his serfs, provided he could keep the land. In Russia, on the other hand, serfdom reached its peak as late as 1801 (the end of Emperor Paul's reign) and lasted until 1861. The reasons for its abolition are discussed in Essay 13.

This essay attacked the widely held (particularly among the Marxists) notion that Russian serfdom had become unprofitable *for the masters* before the Emancipation. It developed several rather elaborate theoretical models (for the various kinds of serfdom), but, once again, on a weak empirical foundation. Lacking data on the profitability of serf estates, we (my coauthor Mark Machina and I) tried to estimate serf prices on the presumption that their persistent decline, if it occurred, would indicate the fall in the profitability of serfdom. For this, time series were required that we did not have. Instead we used cross-section data, and of doubtful validity at that. (Our respect and sympathy for historians who face such

---

[14] V. Kliuchevskii, *Kurs russkoi istorii* [A course of Russian history], Moscow, 1937.

obstacles daily increased by the hour.) In the end, we did not find that, except for Lithuania, serf prices had fallen close to zero before the Emancipation. (We did find that they were closely correlated with regional prices of grain.) So Russian serfdom, just as American slavery, was not dying out for economic reasons. In each country, it had to be terminated by political action, in which the Russians showed much more sense than we did.

Essay 14 again attacked unanimity, this time regarding the magnitude of the overcharge allegedly imposed on former Russian serfs for the land allotted to them by the Emancipation. Since land valuations are notoriously inexact, such unanimity naturally aroused my suspicion. Indeed, I discovered that several historians (I counted five before ending the search) simply reproduced the same sloppy estimate that had been published in St. Petersburg in 1906.[15] My calculations indicated that the overcharge might have been much larger than that estimate; at the same time, there was a small chance that the peasants had not been overcharged at all.

Beware of unanimity in the social sciences!

Now for a few words about Mr. Gorbachev's *perestroika*. None of these essays bears on it directly because all had been published or worked out before it was introduced. However, a few relevant ideas can be found in essays 1, 3, 4 (the last pages), 10, and 11.

It has become rather obvious that Mr. Gorbachev has a hard job before him because neither of his economic objectives – the improvement in the quality and assortment of Soviet goods and services and in the speeding up of the technological progress – can be achieved without the market, and the market cannot function properly in the presence of excess demand. When a producer of ten units is besieged by eleven customers, each willing to pay the fixed price, he has little incentive to improve his product (or service) or to introduce a new model, nor does he know which of the eleven to leave out because he cannot judge the relative intensity of their needs. If he is to remain honest, he must receive instructions from above, that is, from the bureaucracy, which returns it (if it ever left) to the driver's seat. I am not sure that Mr. Gorbachev realizes how destructive of his objectives excess demand is.

In any case, its elimination is difficult because of the active or potential opposition of large segments, perhaps even of a majority, of the Soviet populace: the greatest long-run beneficiaries of the change, the consumers, fear the expected rise in prices; the bureaucrats object to the inevitable reduction of their functions and hence of their power; many of them will lose their jobs; the producers, both managers and workers, may see in

---

[15] A. Lositskii, *Vykupnaia operatsiia* [The redemption operation], St. Petersburg, 1906.

the reform the return of the market tyranny, just like under capitalism.[16] (See Essay 3.) Since the protection of workers' interests is supposed to be the primary function of socialism, how far can Gorbachev go without destroying the very essence of that system?

But if not the *perestroika,* then what?

Concord, Massachusetts
August 1988

---

[16] For a very interesting description of the attitudes of several groups to the *perestroika,* see a summary of a seminar on the subject described in *The Current Digest of the Soviet Press,* Vol. XL, June 22, 1988, pp. 18–19.

Acknowledgments

Even when the title page bears a single name, it is a rare book that was *not* created by a collective effort. These essays are no exception to this rule. As a longtime member of the Economics Department at M.I.T. and of the Russian Research Center at Harvard, I have greatly benefited from the participation in my ventures, even if unwitting, of their members. I am particularly indebted to Abram Bergson, the father of our Soviet studies, and to two former M.I.T. students, now renowned economists: Michael Manove of Boston University and Martin L. Weitzman, now at Harvard. I should also thank my students, graduate and undergraduate, at M.I.T., Wellesley, Brandeis, and several other schools, members of numerous seminars, and many friends for allowing me to try out my ideas on them.

I appreciate the permission granted by several journals, publishers, and organizations to reprint a number of my papers published by them: *The American Economic Review, The American Economist, The Economic Journal, The Journal of Economic History, Journal of Political Economy, The Quarterly Journal of Economics, The Review of Economics and Statistics,* International Economic History Association, JAI Press, and the University of California Press.

From time to time I have received financial support from the American Council of Learned Societies, the Center for Advanced Study in the Behavioral Sciences, the International Research and Exchange Board, the National Science Foundation, the Organization for Economic Cooperation and Development, the RAND Corporation, and the Sloan Foundation. I am grateful to all of them.

Of course, none of these persons or organizations bears any responsibility for my conclusions or for my errors.

Theresa Benevento and Shirley Sartori assisted me in the final preparation of the manuscript; Shirley Kessel (of Primary Sources Research) made the index; Lindsey Klecan (a graduate student at M.I.T.) read the proofs and, in the process, corrected a few of my mistakes and made a number of other improvements. I greatly appreciate the splendid job that each of them did.

My greatest debt, as always, is to my wife (to whom this book is dedicated) for her help, her patience and her sense of humor.

PART I

Economic systems

Reflections on economic development

> I have tried to analyze the friendship of my Friday Niters. I trace it back thirty years to the time when I came to Wisconsin and had given up my first ideas of teaching. I began simply to tell my classes personal stories of my mistakes, doubts and explorations, just as they happened to occur to me, injecting my generalizations, comparisons and all kinds of social philosophies....
>
> John R. Commons, *Myself*

If the establishment of the John R. Commons Lecture is a new experiment for Omicron Delta Epsilon, so is its preparation for me.* For these "Reflections" are not a research paper but a discourse. They contain no formulas, mathematical appendixes, statistical tables, and footnotes, the indispensable props of my other efforts. I believe that it behooves an economist between ages of maturity and senility to engage in such a discourse occasionally, and Commons' words give me the courage to try. But they do not remove my fear that this discourse, like many such, will be trivial.

I

In a game of free associations among economists, the expression "economic development" is likely to be followed by "model" and "plan." A plan usually aims at maximizing the rate of growth of consumption or income either by solving an explicit system of equations (and inequalities), or by selecting a preliminary target rate and adjusting it by iteration. In either case, a so-called bill of final goods (or its equivalent) is customarily drawn up and is combined with a matrix of input coefficients to find the required inputs (labor, capital, materials, foreign exchange), and the resulting outputs. Soviet planners prefer to begin with a target list of several important outputs (like steel, fuel, power, etc.), rather than with that of final products, and even though their use of input-output techniques, at least until recent years, has been less explicit and elegant than

Reprinted by permission from *The American Economist*, Vol. 10, Spring 1966, pp. 5–13.
*Originally presented as a John R. Commons Lecture to Omicron Delta Epsilon, the Honor Society in Economics, on December 29, 1965.

ours, the difference in approach, from the point of view of this lecture, has been slight.

Obviously, a reliable matrix of input coefficients is the heart of this planning process, and clearly the change in the coefficients, that is the saving on the various inputs over time, must constitute an important ingredient of growth. Since I have promised to avoid formulas, let me merely state that the average relative change in the coefficients named by Leontief the "Index of Structural Change," and similar to Solow's "Index of Technical Change," and to Kendrick's "Index of Total Factor Productivity," accounts for a large fraction of the rate of growth of income in advanced countries: some 40 or 50 percent of the total rate of growth, and perhaps some 70–80 percent of the rate of growth of income per capita. We know less about the behavior of such indexes in underdeveloped countries, but it stands to reason that a similar, though possibly less pronounced, phenomenon must exist there as well.

Now the remarkable fact is that the planner usually takes the changes in most input coefficients as given, that is as determined outside of the plan itself. This attitude is a tribute to his common sense: he knows that the planning organization can do little to achieve the proper reductions. The Russians have indeed tried, both by appeal to socialist patriotism and by direct command, to regulate thousands upon thousands of coefficients, which they call "norms" (of which an enterprise may have as many as five hundred). The truth is that Soviet planners (by their own admissions) simply do not know which norms should be reduced in what enterprise and by how much, and are loath to allow any increases, however necessary they may be. Their attempts to regulate norms from above have produced little more than straight jackets for their managers, who try to escape from them by misreporting and cheating. The French have done more explicit planning than other Western countries; but even they, to my knowledge, have not tried to prescribe specific norms to firms.

In contrast, most governments of advanced Western and of socialist countries have been quite successful (depending of course on your standards) in achieving a reasonable degree of macro-equilibrium. The Russians, for instance, have had no serious inflation since their monetary reforms of the late nineteen-forties, and mass unemployment has been unknown in the West for a quarter of a century.

This success in macro-planning, combined with the obvious inability of a government, even as strong and as dedicated to all kinds of planning as the Soviet, to enforce, and even to know, the correct micro-decisions, strongly suggests that at the present state of economic knowledge governments should concentrate their activities in the macro-sphere. And they should promulgate some general rules and incentives to insure that the correct micro-decisions are made, as they should be made, in a decentralized manner, on the spot, by those who have the necessary detailed information. There is no clear dividing line between macro- and micro-decisions; the existence of externalities, increasing returns, monopolies, large risks, and ignorance reduces the effectiveness of decentralized decisions and calls for government interference, particularly in underdeveloped countries where markets are small (see below) and many investment decisions have important external effects. I cannot suggest any simple general rules for the division of functions; much depends on the historical setting in particular countries and on the *relative* ability, efficiency and honesty of government functionaries. But I do suggest that a government begin its planning activities in the macro-area and move into the micro-area only if and when clearly necessary, with the burden of the proof for each such move being placed on the government.

It is this optimal and ever-shifting division between centralized and decentralized decision-making that is, in my opinion, the central economic problem of today, rather than the question of private versus public ownership of the means of production. It was Oscar Lange who clearly perceived the problem in his classical essay on socialism, and not Karl Marx.

Following Lange, the managers of enterprises, private or public, should be instructed to select the least expensive method of production and to equate marginal cost with price (as a general rule subject to proper qualifications and exceptions). But I do not know of any practical way of enforcing this instruction except by ordering the managers to maximize profits, with prices set by the market under competitive conditions, and by the government or some other body under monopolistic ones. The maximization of profits, though under certain important restrictions, has now become the declared policy of the Soviet government.

I fully realize how abstract my simple suggestions are, and I do not imply that the quest for profits in the real world will indeed result in a Pareto optimum. There is no shortage of studies showing the limitations of this method of resource allocation, particularly in underdeveloped countries. It is only that I do not know of any better method for enforcing economic discipline and preventing wholesale waste. The future may present us with a wider choice.

Economic efficiency is served by the pursuit of profits no better than the acquisition of knowledge is by the pursuit of good grades. Neither method is esteemed by intellectuals. A student can get good grades by choosing easy courses, flattering teachers, and even by cheating on examinations. With a small, highly motivated group of students better stimuli are available, as they are in the economic world. But what are we to do in the age of mass education and of mass production? Should we prescribe the Soviet-type norms to our students, that is the exact number of hours to be spent (by each student individually or by all?) on each subject, with their study hours policed by a horde of proctors, supervised in their turn by super-proctors? And what is to prevent a student from spending the prescribed number of hours looking into the assigned book and thinking of something else?

In the privacy of our faculty lounges we discount the significance of students' grades, and stress instead their intelligence, imagination, creativity, research ability, and other attributes not necessarily reflected in grades. But if a student with a poor record is to claim these attributes, the burden of the proof must be on him.

Similarly, planning agencies, investment banks, international lenders, and foreign donors will have plenty of opportunity, in the privacy of their well-appointed offices, to re-examine the submitted projects (particularly when externalities are involved or the price system is defective) and rank them not necessarily in order of the expected rate of profit; nor should a manager's performance be judged on that basis alone. But the burden of the justification for an unsatisfactory profit rate, actual or expected, should rest with enterprise managers and project sponsors.

So far I have tried to bypass the question of private as against public ownership of the means of production, or of capitalism versus socialism, and concentrate instead on the making of economic decisions under either system. I have no general solution to this complex question independently of time or place. I wish (though I do not hope) that this question could be discussed with less passion, and that our government would not try to force capitalism on unwilling people, even though my own advice to the underdeveloped countries is to try capitalism first. Their governments are simply not yet ready to undertake the very complex and difficult task of managing their economies. Few governments are. Can you imagine the mismanagement, waste and corruption which would accompany an attempt by the government of my own Commonwealth of Massachusetts to take over its economy? A sharp movement toward socialism in an underdeveloped country invariably antagonizes and frequently destroys the class of capitalist owners and managers who are so scarce there to begin with; their replacement by socialist administrators is a slow and painful process involving much waste. And when all is said and done, it remains true, particularly in underdeveloped countries, that a capitalist owner has a stronger attachment to *his own* resources than a state-appointed official has for the *public* wealth. As President Johnson once remarked, "The best fertilizer for land is the footprint of its owner."

II

I have little hope that my advice to the underdeveloped countries – to experiment with an essentially market-oriented capitalist economy – will be welcome to most of their intellectuals and to many government officials. Since my advice is strikingly unoriginal and is likely to be joined by the majority of American economists, it is worthwhile inquiring into the reasons for its rejection. Let me list several.

1. The market mechanism strives to satisfy effective demand for goods and services which depends on the existing distribution of income and wealth. Granted a lopsided distribution, which is true of many underdeveloped countries, how can one justify the resulting production and importation of luxuries (including sojourns in Miami and on the Riviera) for the few rather than food and shelter for the many? Of course, the distribution of wealth can and should be corrected by taxation, wider access to education, and other measures, but what underdeveloped government is strong enough to attack the holders of wealth? And what is the use of running an efficient economy for a wrong purpose?

2. As a disciplinary device (this being its main function) the profit criterion can be harsh and unfair. It can punish the most well-intentioned and hard-working person and throw riches to the unscrupulous speculator. It is easy to forget this and to join Schumpeter in extolling the selection process supposedly rewarding the able and bankrupting the weakling, but how would we enjoy being on the receiving end? No wonder that the current Soviet reforms oriented toward the market and profits are opposed by many Soviet managers, who would gain freedom but lose security. And who are we to complain, being, as most of the members of this assembly undoubtedly are, either holders of tenure positions or aspirants for them?

3. The next objection is directed not so much against the market economy as such, as against its capitalist incarnation. To put it bluntly, capitalism is an unappetizing system. It runs not on the higher human motivations, but on the lowest – selfishness and greed, which are regularly denounced by the keepers of our conscience on Sundays (and Saturdays), and put to good use the rest of the week. It is hard to love an economic system in which public welfare is merely a by-product of the pursuit of private gain.

Perhaps I am making a virtue out of necessity, but there is a great advantage in propelling an economic system by greed because greed is so abundant. No civilization, to my knowledge, has ever suffered from a shortage. The Russians have tried to run their economic system on much higher fuels – patriotism and social consciousness – but when they run out of these precious propellants, as they invariably do, they resort to brute force. Lately they have talked more and more about "material self-interest" of the managers and workers in a language reminiscent of the testimony of our business men at congressional tax hearings. But I have to admit that by running our economy on greed we fail to develop moving forces of higher quality, and we suffer from their shortage in our political and social life.

We know that the pursuit by each person of his selfish ends, under proper restrictions and conditions, can result in a reasonably efficient allocation of resources and a good deal of personal freedom, because selfishness need not be forced. On the whole, the practice of *modern* capitalism may be better than its theory (while the opposite may be true of socialism), but it is the theory that attracts intellectuals, and the theory of capitalism is difficult to explain to a person not versed in economics, and particularly to one from an underdeveloped country whose impression of *its* capitalism (symbolized, I imagine, by a picture of peasants devoured by a horde of landowners, money-lenders and tradesmen) is altogether different. In a growing economy like ours where national wealth, roughly speaking, doubles every generation, and where abject poverty is relatively rare, one may be tolerant of other people's making fortunes. Not so, however, in a country with a long history of stagnation (even if no longer present) where the gain for one implies the loss for another. If, to borrow an historical term, our present economic system may be named "Enlightened Capitalism," one would not so honor its predecessors, nor the capitalist or semi-capitalist systems found in most underdeveloped countries today.

4. The less enlightened phases of capitalism, through which most Western countries passed in their own time, were long remembered for their exploitation of women and children, miserable wages, high profits, repressive taxes, and other ills, which, however horrible in themselves, were nevertheless conducive to capital accumulation and economic development *and were permitted to exist by the ideology of the time.* Many underdeveloped countries are more backward today than Europe was on the eve of the Industrial Revolution, but the ideology of their intellectuals, largely imported from the advanced countries, has little tolerance for such a process. Impressed as we are with the skills and knowledge which underdeveloped countries can obtain from the advanced ones, we may forget that one such import – medical knowledge – has inflicted upon them a growth of population which Europe has not experiencd in all her history. Similarly, many ideological imports, appropriate for our state of economic development, are not at all suited for theirs. Besides, they lack the immunity to ideas which we, from long association with them (and

with TV commercials), have developed. Hence the tendency to carry ideas to the extreme. If we are bored with the profit motive, they are apt to reject it altogether. If the pensions paid under our social security system are modest, in Uruguay (according to the *New York Times*) one can retire with a full income at the age of fifty-five. Marxism, I would venture to suggest, as a protest against the social and economic conditions of the working classes of the nineteenth century, has done the Western countries much more good than harm. (How mild does the Communist Manifesto of 1848 sound to-day!) But when exported to Russia and China it started a conflagration. One cannot embargo ideas, and it is the import of Western ideas into the underdeveloped countries that contributes to the rejection of capitalism.

5. The last reason for this rejection which I would like to offer (there must be many others) is *impatience*. As seen by the intellectuals from the underdeveloped countries, what does this system have to offer? First, the development and export of agricultural and mining products, with all the uncertainties of the world demand for them. Then, a gradual expansion of light industries, beginning with food, textiles, and the like, and the refining of minerals. All through this period they will be threatened with inflation to which a market economy easily succumbs when it tries to move fast, and their dependence on advanced countries for technical help, machinery, spare parts, materials, and foreign exchange in general, will continue and even increase. And finally, after a long period of apprenticeship during which their rich are likely to get richer, and the poor poorer (at least for a while), they will eventually reach our present standard of living from which we, at the time, will be miles away.

Realistically speaking, perhaps there is no faster method. But how unexciting this prospect is! Soviet economic literature of the nineteen-twenties, reflecting this feeling, was obsessed with speed. Capitalist countries must be overtaken not in generations, but in ten–fifteen years. No other promise could have satisfied the Soviet leadership of the time, nor the Chinese leaders of today.

Suppose, while driving to a very important appointment (or a final examination) you suddenly have a flat tire. Twenty minutes later you are ready to go on, but you know how long the trip takes, and you know that you will be terribly late if you follow your usual route. What are you to do? Presently, stopping for a traffic signal, you notice a left turn which you have never taken before. It is in the generally correct direction, but it may lead nowhere and delay you even more. In desperation, you make the turn. You will probably fail. But – who knows – perhaps you will discover a new and faster route and make your appointment after all. You *know* that otherwise you are bound to be late.

According to what I call the "Gerschenkron Law" (which is a bit tauto-logical, but interesting nevertheless), the more backward a country is, the greater are the tensions arising in it and the more radical are its indus-trialization methods. England got along without any special innovations; France, and particularly Germany, developed the investment banks. The big push in Russia and Japan in the last century came from the govern-ment. Russian innovations since 1928 and Chinese since 1949 have been most radical, and yet one wonders what Africa will do in her time. We may disapprove of these costly, even if heroic, methods of development, but we must understand the preference for them by many intellectuals in underdeveloped countries.

III

I suspect that you are becoming impatient with my superficial sketch and want to hear the answer to the basic question – what can we do about all this? My first suggestion is not to get excited. Economic development is a difficult and complex process, hard to deal with, because contrary to some of our favorite models, it is essentially not a capital but a human problem. I cannot prove this, but I can illustrate. Take Colombia and Japan. In 1958 the per capita income of Japan ($285) was, according to the U.N. sources, a bit below that of Colombia ($301). By now it is prob-ably twice as high. But Japan must be making better use of its capital, so its capital per person is perhaps only some 50–70 percent higher than that of Colombia. Imagine now that the Colombian capital is suddenly increased to the Japanese per capita level. The standard of living of (at least some) Colombians will rise, and even their balance of payments may improve, but no economic miracles will happen. Now reduce the Colom-bian capital to its original level, but replace the seventeen million Colom-bians with seventeen million Japanese. Need I continue?

The human problems in economic development and in our War on Poverty at home are similar: in both cases the victim must acquire the middle-class mentality, so much abused by intellectuals: ambition, will-ingness to accept discipline, ability to work hard and efficiently, to learn, to save and invest, to exercise foresight, and so on. It is curious that most of these virtues would please both a good New England puritan (if any are still left there) and a good Russian communist. Indeed, the human ideal of the two creeds is strikingly similar, and for good economic rea-sons, though the puritan would naturally stress one's responsibility to God, and the communist to socialism.

So far this looks not like an economic, but a psychological problem which might best be left to our colleagues on the other floor or in the other building. But our colleagues have proved singularly ineffective (or much wiser than we are); hence the operationally-minded economist must do what he can do. We cannot increase human happiness directly, but we can increase a person's income and his choice of occupations, improve his health and widen his horizon, in the hope that these changes will make him happier. Similarly, we cannot change the human beings and the society in the underdeveloped countries directly, but we can suggest some reasonably practical measures with helpful direct and indirect effects. Here are a few:

1. Education (including technical assistance). This is the most direct way of transforming both individuals and societies – witness the Soviet and Chinese efforts and recall the striking achievements of the Jesuits in the past. Statistics of the number of souls saved by Christian missionaries in Africa are unfortunately unavailable, but how often one sees the phrase "educated in missionary schools" in the biographies of African leaders. To be sure, education contains risks – dissatisfied intellectuals, Ph.D.'s refusing to return home, barely literate youngsters rejecting manual work, and others – but these risks must be taken. We cannot hope to educate the millions in underdeveloped countries, but we can train teachers, help finance selected areas, set standards of excellence, and hope for the "demonstration effect." At present, aid to formal education comprises only some two or nine percent (depending on the denominator used) of our foreign aid. Why should it not be magnified ten or twenty times? Surely it will do much more good and much less harm than military aid.

2. Birth control. Hardly any comments are needed here. Perhaps future historians will ridicule our concern with a population of *only* three billions in the presence of empty spaces in much of the Americas, Africa, Australia and Northern Asia, just as we, until recently, ridiculed Malthus. But what matters now is not the opinions of future historians but the growth in the number of mouths to feed, children to educate, and men to be provided with jobs.

3. Economic integration. By area and population many underdeveloped countries look large. For instance, Colombia is larger than France, West Germany, and Italy combined; and it contains 17 million people. But her GNP in 1963 was hardly $5 billion, about a third of that of the state of Massachusetts, and less than the GNP generated by the Boston Metropolitan Area. International income comparisons are notoriously inexact, and perhaps Colombia's income is understated. But a part of her population is still engaged in subsistence farming and is therefore almost outside of the market. Even with a generous correction, Colombia is small by market size, and there are of course many smaller countries.

For that matter, the GNP of *the whole of South America* was estimated (by the parity method) at some $45 billion in 1963, much less than the $67 billion of New York State alone. All of Africa was rated at some $40 billion with $11 billion generated by the Union of South Africa. Without the latter, the African GNP was below that of the state of Ohio. But New York and Ohio are parts of a larger economic entity, while neither South America nor Africa comprises one.

We should persuade, push and even bribe the underdeveloped countries into forming free trade areas and common markets. Only then will they benefit from economies of scale and of specialization and will be able to reduce the risks inherent in foreign trade. The argument that their economies are similar to one another and that they therefore trade more with the advanced countries than among themselves makes just as little sense as a similar argument that might have been presented to our Founding Fathers in regards to the thirteen American states.

4. Emergency assistance in case of natural calamities, famines, epidemics and the like. The humanitarian reasons for such aid require no comments.

Beyond these four obvious suggestions, foreign aid policy becomes rather complex. It is certainly most proper for us to help the less developed countries to accelerate their development (particularly if we recognize that we are partly responsible for their predicament), and it is in our own interest to do so. The problem is how to help these societies to change themselves rather than to hinder the change, since it is difficult to aid a country without adding strength to its ruling classes and to its government, however unenlightened both may be. It may also not be easy to avoid the creation of the patron-client relationship between the donor and the recipient, which is most unhealthy for both sides. It is very tempting to force reforms on the recipient by the promise of aid. But such reforms can remain on paper, and our insistence that they be carried out according to the agreement made is apt to cause mutual animosity. Besides, seldom is our knowledge about the country sufficient to assure us of the correctness of our stand.

If I have run out of simple positive suggestions, let me make a negative one: that military aid be given only under exceptional circumstances. The sight of Indians and Pakistanis fighting each other with American and British tanks is a good example of the harm that our good intentions can cause. And let us not forget that Trujillo rose to power in the Dominican Republic on the shoulders of American-trained constabulary. In our obsession with fighting communism we tend to over-emphasize the effectiveness of military means; we seem to have forgotten Lenin's dictum that it is not the rifle that fires but the man who pulls the trigger.

IV

Above all, let me repeat, we should not get excited every time a riot, a coup, a revolution or a counter-revolution sweeps some underdeveloped country. Economic change without political change is impossible, and the latter does have a nasty habit of not always proceeding in a nice, evolutionary and democratic manner. What the present-day advanced countries have accomplished over generations, the underdeveloped ones must do in a few decades, and usually with weak and inefficient governments. If France has gone through five republics, four major revolutions and several near-revolutions in less than two hundred years, surely each underdeveloped country is entitled to its quota of political upheavals concentrated into a short span of time.

During this process many underdeveloped countries will enjoy spells of democratic rule interspersed with military, rightist, leftist, tyrannical, benevolent, and all sorts of dictatorships. It is altogether possible that *in the middle* of their developmental process some will go communist. I would venture to suggest that communism is an experience (some would say a disease) of adolescence. No advanced country has yet succumbed to it (except by foreign force, like East Germany and Czechoslovakia), while Russia and other East European countries are beginning to recover from it as their economies develop. The Chinese are not entirely wrong in questioning the purity of the present-day Russian communism, and perhaps the Africans will question the Chinese variety some day. It was comfortable to think that communists could seize power only after a long and exhausting war (Russia, China, Yugoslavia), or under foreign pressure (the rest of Eastern Europe). Cuba has destroyed this pleasant belief, and the state of Kerala in India has shown that communists can win even a reasonably fair election. Some day they may repeat this feat in a whole country, and it will be particularly galling to us if that country has grown to adolescence with our aid, and if the communist leaders were trained in American-organized or aided schools.

I do not wish communism on any country, advanced or underdeveloped, but we must realize that the chances for our *effective* interference are small. If we only knew how to save a country during those critical years some action might be recommended. But our performance in Russia and China in the past, and in Viet Nam and in the Dominican Republic at present has revealed a striking degree of ignorance and ineptitude. Indeed, it is likely that in our anxiety to permit only an orderly change we may inhibit any change, and thus create the most favorable conditions for a communist victory. The recent House resolution authorizing our intervention in Latin American countries to save them from communism which was, by the way, opposed by the would-be victims of our benevolence – the irony of it! – is a rare example of political stupidity, to put it mildly. At best it will be ineffective; at worst, it will give the respective regimes a false sense of security and lead them into traps from which we will be unable to rescue them when the time comes.

For her role in defeating Napoleon, Russia enjoyed a brief spell of good will from other European countries. But Russian opposition to every popular movement which threatened the existing order in Europe eventually made her the most hated country on that continent. We also enjoyed a period not only of international good will but of real affection at the close of World War II. Need I belabor my parallel?

Poor old capitalism: a review article

I

For a teacher of comparative economic systems, the publication of *The Capitalist System: A Radical Analysis of American Society,* by Edwards, Reich, and Weisskopf, is a windfall: it presents him with 540 pages of radical attack on capitalism all in one place, including passages from Marx and Engels, Polanyi, Dobb, Baran and Sweezy, Mumford, Gintis, Fromm, Bowles, and others.[1] The three editors wrote brief introductions to each chapter and to each selection and contributed several articles of their own. Most of the material is nontechnical and well written; it should be accessible to any intelligent undergraduate and lay reader.

An ordinary book of readings is essentially a pedagogical tool. Its editor need not agree with, or be held responsible for, the views and conclusions presented in it. But this is no ordinary book of readings. It presents almost exclusively the radical point of view. The introductions written by the editors gave them ample opportunity to state their disagreements, if any, with the contributors.[2] Hence, the reviewer has the right to treat the book as an integrated work and to hold the editors responsible for its content.

Nevertheless, if the book's subtitle were *A List of Evils of the American Economy,* or something like that, I would not quarrel with it; I might even suggest a few extra ones. But what provoked me was the word "Analysis" in the subtitle. Now, I thought, our radicals will analyze the causes of American evils and show that they are indeed produced by capitalism. Unfortunately, my high hopes were disappointed.

II

American capitalism is charged with six principal evils: inequality, alienation, racism, sexism, irrationality, and imperialism, plus a number of

Reprinted by permission from *The Journal of Political Economy,* Vol. 82, November–December 1974, pp. 1301–14.
[1] Richard C. Edwards, Michael Reich, and Thomas B. Weisskopf, *The Capitalist System: A Radical Analysis of American Society* (Englewood Cliffs, N.J., 1972).
[2] Their disagreement with a passage from Baran and Sweezy was duly recorded on p. 309.

lesser ones. But before discussing them, let me make a few general comments.

An analysis of capitalism, like any analysis, can be expected to consist of two parts: first, a logical formulation of a hypothesis showing how this or that evil is caused by capitalism; and, second, an empirical testing of the hypothesis against the reality of capitalist and noncapitalist systems.[3] There is no shortage of logical formulations, of different degrees of plausibility, in the book. But there is almost a complete absence of empirical verification.[4] Since the evils are both complex and not easily quantifiable, the authors (that is, the editors and the contributors) could not be required, at least at this stage, to come forth with a battery of regression equations, but surely, as a first step, they could have made an attempt to examine historical trends and to establish the presence or absence of each evil in other capitalist and noncapitalist countries. In particular – most fortunate for this attempt – there are now several socialist countries, some of them quite advanced and most of them sharing our common cultural background. On one of them – the Soviet Union – there exists a large literature in English, while the others have not been neglected either.

But no comparisons of any importance are made in the book. We discover that there is not a single socialist country in the world! The Soviet Union and the other East European countries are referred to as "state socialism" (pp. 4, 277, 281, 362, 524–25) or as "so-called socialist" (p. 277). They are treated with disdain and together with the state-capitalist countries (England, France, or Sweden) are declared not to be "model societies of socialism to be emulated" (p. 4). Worse than that, "The state socialist countries of the Soviet Union and Eastern Europe are to true socialism what 'the monsters of the paleolithic era are to present animal species: clumsy, abortive, prototypes'" (p. 4).

If countries which have been regarded by themselves and by others to be socialist have turned out to be something else, surely an explanation is in order. Since none is provided in the book, let me suggest two alternatives. (1) Lenin, Stalin, and, by implication, all other socialist leaders – including Tito and Mao – never intended to build socialism. (2) They

---

[3] It seems that there is no disagreement between the authors and myself on methodology, as the following quotation taken by them from a paper by Baran and Hobsbawm testifies: "It suggests the necessity of an interpretation of theory and concrete observation, of empirical research illuminated by rational theory, of theoretical work which draws its life blood from historical study" (p. 55).

[4] The three papers by Reich and Weisskopf, respectively, discussed below in Section III, do contain, or are based on, empirical data. Some data are also given in the interesting paper "The Negro Worker in the Chicago Labor Market" by Harold Baron and Bennet Hymer, pp. 297–305. There are also scattered statistical data elsewhere in the book.

did try, but failed miserably, ending up with "paleolithic monsters," in fact.

I will leave the choice and the consideration of the sad implications of each alternative to the reader.[5]

Terminological arguments are, of course, fruitless, and I would not have started this one if our authors were consistent. But they are not. Thus, we read in the book about "a powerful socialist sector of the world" (p. 55) and about "opposition from the socialist world" (p. 409). There are "successful socialist revolutions" (p. 418), "development of socialism" (p. 418), and "rise of socialism" (p. 424), and there is the "military strength of the socialist camp" (p. 425). Of course, the several authors need not agree among themselves, but the failure of the editors to clarify this rather important issue in their introductory comments leaves the reader with the impression that socialism does and does not exist at the same time and place, depending on the need of the argument.

But whatever these countries are, they are not capitalist. Our authors' failure to investigate whether capitalist evils exist there as well places every statement in the book under suspicion of being a half-truth at best, like a savings bank's claim that it pays the highest rate of interest allowed by law. This difficulty is not removed by the editors' statement that "it is not our intention to imply that *all* forms of oppression are a result of capitalist institutions" (p. 5), and by their assertion that "the elimination of basic capitalist institutions is necessary, though not sufficient, to eliminate the oppressive problems of the modern world" (p. 5). At best, such face-saving afterthoughts leave the question wide open. At worst, they are grossly misleading.

III

The six evils cover so much ground that only a few comments on each can be made in my limited space. I will try to avoid factual disputes – there is not much serious factual information in the book in any case – and will concentrate instead on the analysis of the arguments presented and on comparisons, whenever possible, with socialist countries and particularly with the Soviet Union.[6]

[5] If existing socialist countries are not really socialist, could not the proponents of "real" capitalism declare all existing capitalist countries not capitalist? After all, none of them has perfect competition and complete laissez faire. It would be particularly pleasant to exclude Franco's Spain and the colonels' (or was it the generals'?) Greece, among others. Then we would be comparing completely imaginary systems!

[6] I concentrate on the Soviet Union because of its large size and the relative abundance of Western studies on its economy. Also, I am more familiar with its economic system than with those of other socialist countries.

Alienation

In simple English, this word means that workers are dissatisfied because they neither own nor control the means of production, do not participate in decisions, and are compelled to perform repetitive and meaningless-to-themselves tasks. Since this dissatisfaction is a state of mind, it is not easily quantifiable, and sources differ on its importance and extent.[7] Our authors are sure that it affects very large numbers of workers. If so, it is rather strange that labor unions have shown so little interest in mitigating it. Perhaps they find that dissatisfied workers make better union members. In any case, one would expect that a book of this kind would devote at least one long chapter to the analysis and criticism of union policies. But, except for a few scattered remarks, little criticism of unions and even of the racial policies practiced by some of them is found in the book.[8]

With the exception of Yugoslavia, workers do not own and do not control the means of production in the socialist countries, either. With similar technology, they are also engaged in repetitive and uninteresting work. Socialist enterprises are also organized in a hierarchical manner, with the managers (directors) wielding great power. That some dissatisfaction exists among Soviet workers as well is confirmed by the recent publication of at least two serious Russian books on the subject (Osipov 1966; Zdravomyslov, Rozhin, and Iadov 1970).

Nevertheless, I would expect Soviet workers to be less alienated than ours, basically because of the chronic existence of excess demand. The

---

[7] According to the Survey Research Center of the University of Michigan, as cited by Jencks et al. (1972), the majority of workers seem to be quite satisfied. Thus, 63 percent would recommend their job to a friend; only 27 percent would hesitate to take the same job, and 9 percent would not take it; as many as 49 percent would choose the present job if they could have any job they wanted. A Gallup poll reported in the *New York Times* (December 6, 1973, p. 24) says that 79 percent of workers were satisfied with their jobs. This, however, was a decline from 85 percent recorded in 1963. On the other hand, a government report, *Work in America* (1972), gives the impression that the dissatisfaction among workers is much greater. Unfortunately, the data are presented in this report so sloppily that it is difficult to judge whether dissatisfaction affects many or few workers and whether it is becoming better or worse. Whatever the present situation is, it seems to me probable that dissatisfaction will increase as a result of rising educational and aspirational levels of workers as suggested by Bowles in the reviewed book (pp. 492, 498). Also, the strict hierarchical control to which workers are subjected contradicts the spirit of our time. Finally, previously satisfied workers may become dissatisfied from mere discussion of the subject, as happened in the Goldthrope experiment described by Andre Gorz in *The Capitalist System* (pp. 479–80). Workers' management or at least participation in decision-making has been suggested as a remedy; see, for instance, Hunnius (1973) and Jenkins (1973).

[8] See, however, pp. 273, 315, and a few others. In another radical book (Hunnius 1973), the reasons for the unions' attitudes are discussed and the unions are severely censured.

producers (including workers) are less concerned with pleasing their customers by the proper assortment and quality of goods. They are also less concerned with profits. Hence, there is less pressure on the workers and greater job security, reinforced with usage and legislation. From his own experience with shortages, the worker may derive a feeling of accomplishment from increasing his output without endangering his job. The enterprise's welfare and cultural activities, particularly important in an economy of scarcities, create an additional bond. And of course he is told time and again that profits, far from enriching capitalist exploiters, are put to social use.

But these are a priori considerations, which may or may not be true. Strangely enough, Herbert Gintis, one of the contributors, has already decided that the "so-called socialist" worker is not any better off than his capitalist counterpart because of the similarity of their basic economic institutions (p. 277).

In any case, much of what the Soviet man gains as a worker he loses as a consumer. It would be possible to eliminate alienation in any society by the simple expedient of allowing each worker to produce whatever he wants, irrespective of consumer desires. Our authors do not suggest this extreme solution: in their ideal society (see Section IV below), workers' and consumers' preferences are reconciled by some unspecified mechanism, but their sympathy, like that of socialists in general, is for the worker. For the consumer they show little more than contempt (see below). But it is curious that in the university – one of our few organizations where at least some of the workers, namely, the professors, do make decisions – our radicals call for more power to students, that is, to consumers! It is also strange that our authors show little interest in, and no sympathy for, the one country – Yugoslavia – where workers have more decision power than in any other. It seems that Yugoslavia cannot be forgiven for her use of the market mechanism and of profits (pp. 483, 525–27).

Irrationality

This big word means that our economy produces the wrong assortment of goods and services. To the extent that this assortment is determined by the existing distribution of income and wealth, I believe that our authors have a good point, as they have regarding the composition of government expenditures (although neither they nor I can claim that our views are shared by the majority of the American electorate). But here our ways part.

If in the old days (and even in days not so old) capitalism was blamed for unemployment and for the exploitation of workers (pp. 50, 71, 465–67), now it is accused of depriving workers of any joy from work and thus forcing them to become addicted to consumption as the only pleasure in life. This phenomenon is called "consumerism." It is treated with so much disgust (pp. 22, 369-70) that the old-fashioned exploitation might have been a lesser evil.

Consumerism exaggerates the importance of material things; the addicted workers buy millions of useless objects that they do not need and do not even enjoy (pp. 362, 376, 391, 404). Unfortunately, the lists of these useless objects and of the consumers who buy them are not provided. (Presumably our authors are innocent of these offenses.) It takes a remarkable intellectual arrogance, reminiscent of the old aristocratic contempt for the "lower orders," to hold this position (pp. 20-21, 268, 376). We may expect that after the revolution, the production of objects of which our authors disapprove will cease.

The mechanism that creates artificial desires to be satisfied by useless objects is advertising (pp. 283, 362, 369, 376, 378, 381).[9] But advertising is merely an instrument. The real cause of irrationality (and of many other capitalist ills) lies in the profit motive (pp. 90-91, 99-106, 274, 363, 383-86, 410-11). Goods are produced for profit, not for use.

A few years ago, a Soviet manager of a trucking firm was publicly castigated for using plan fulfillment as the criterion for ranking his shipments. The manager recognized his error and promised to mend his ways. But neither he nor his critics ever indicated how he, a mere trucking boss, could possibly rank his shipments in order of their marginal social utility, as his critics (implicitly) demanded.

The literature on the defects of profit maximization as an allocational device can fill a library, and yet through some 50 years of searching, the socialist countries have not discovered a better alternative.[10] Nor do our authors offer any. They are completely unconcerned with the problem of transforming a given social objective into microdecision rules.[11] It does not even occur to them that if their publishers, a good capitalist firm, had

---

[9] In insisting on the effectiveness of advertising, our authors merely repeat what the advertising industry advertises about itself. Actually, as Schmalensee (1972) has discovered, there is not much reliable information about its effects; see, however, Taylor and Weiserbs (1972).

[10] Since income distribution in the socialist countries is closer to their ideal than ours is to our ideal, and since managers are confronted with parametric prices, profit maximization by socialist managers might be more appropriate than by capitalist managers, provided, of course, that prices were correctly set.

[11] In an amusing little book, Soviet engineer Antonov (1965) gives many examples of antisocial behavior by Soviet managers. His solution is not to induce them to behave altruistically, but to set such success indicators as would make them behave in a socially desirable manner while maximizing their own objective functions. The tone and the title of the book (*For All and for Oneself*) suggest the need for Adam Smith's "invisible hand."

tried to maximize social welfare according to their own capitalist lights, rather than to make profits, they would not have published this book.

Inequality

The facts are not in dispute: American income distribution is highly unequal, and that of wealth is even more so, as confirmed by several standard tables in the book. For some reason, none of the well-known tables by Simon Kuznets (1953) (partially reprinted in the *Historical Statistics of the United States*) showing a considerable improvement in income distribution between 1913 and 1948 is presented. But the book does contain a table (10-H, p. 445) indicating a more equal distribution of income in this country than in a number of others.

The authors missed a good debating point by their failure to compare income distribution of capitalist and socialist countries: according to two recent studies, in the latter it is more equal.[12]

Granted that, the practical question is whether the effective functioning of the capitalist system requires as much inequality as is actually observed. Only social experimentation can definitely answer this question, but judging by the experience of other advanced capitalist countries, a considerable movement toward equality is not likely to ruin us. Rather unexpectedly, the book arrives at the opposite conclusion: "The capitalist mode of production is characterized by a serious conflict between income equality... and economic efficiency.... A high degree of income equality could be attained in a capitalist society only at a very high cost in productive efficiency" (p. 128). A number of such passages are found in the book (pp. 127-28, 208, 249). Soon they will be quoted by business speakers. Imagine the delight of their audiences when they learn the source!

There are two common objections to the concentration of income and wealth: (1) if the rich have more, the poor have less, and (2) wealth conveys power. It is not quite clear why our authors should be concerned with the first objection. They emphasize the diminishing utility of income (pp. 284, 381) and the lack of connection between income and happiness (pp. 284, 362); they oppose economic growth (pp. 284, 371); they deplore

---

[12] The comparison of income distribution among different economic systems is, of course, a very complex and difficult task. Among other problems, nonmonetary incomes play a more important role in the socialist than in the capitalist countries. Nevertheless, Wiles and Markowski (1971) have found that income distribution is more equal in Poland than in the United Kingdom, and more equal in the latter than in the United States. Also, the distribution of Soviet nonagricultural income is more equal than the American one. Pryor (1972, 1973) reports that income distribution in socialist countries is more equal than in capitalist ones, even when agricultural income is included. In recent years, the position of Soviet peasants has improved considerably.

the interest in material things and consumerism in general.[13] If higher incomes for the poor will merely increase their addiction to consumption without making them any happier, why bother about it at all?

It should be possible to eliminate the power of the rich by depriving them of their riches, but it would be much more difficult to diffuse their power. The absence of large stockholders would enhance the power of corporate managers, and the nationalization or public control of corporations would transfer the power to the government, even to one headed by a Nixon and worse, a familiar problem in the socialist countries.

Racism

Again, the facts are not in dispute. Only the blind would deny the existence of racism in this country.

In my limited space, it is difficult to say much about this complex problem without repeating the trivial and the obvious. A narrow definition of racism would single out three countries: the United States, South Africa, and Rhodesia – all capitalist. But there is much less racism in capitalist Latin America, and particularly in Brazil. On the other hand, it is present in semisocialist India and in precapitalist Africa. If the definition of racism is to include the dominance of specific national or ethnic groups as well, there is no shortage of it in the Soviet Union, Rumania, Yugoslavia, and probably in China. Competition for jobs, particularly in periods of unemployment, should make capitalist countries more vulnerable. On the other hand, if capitalists are as determined to maximize profits as they are described in the book, why should they bother to discriminate? Indeed, The Netherlands, the most money-minded country in the seventeenth century, was also the most tolerant. The Dutch had discovered that discrimination interfered with business.[14]

Perhaps it would be more fruitful to leave these generalities and inquire instead into the beneficiaries of discrimination.[15] Traditional wisdom, speaking through Gary Becker (1971), names white workers and black capitalists (such as there are). Edward Reich, in a refreshingly interesting paper on "The Economics of Racism" (pp. 313–21), by far the

---

[13] Our authors' attitude to material wealth resembles that of the early Jesuits; see Harney (1941).

[14] Jews were allowed by Cromwell to return to England, and were emancipated in France by the Great Revolution, as they were in other countries with the development of capitalism.

[15] In this discussion, the gain or loss from discrimination is merely relative. The country as a whole would, of course, gain from equal treatment of all citizens because of the resulting improvement in the use of resources.

best in the book, blames white upper-income groups.[16] Paradoxically both may be right.

If white capitalists refuse to hire black workers, as Becker assumes, his conclusion follows. But most blacks in the labor force are employed. They are employed, however, in low-paid occupations.

Let us assume that all occupational differences between whites and blacks are caused by discrimination. When that is gone, the occupational structures will (eventually) become identical. Then the low-paid white workers will gain because of the upward movement of many of their black competitors, while the high-paid white workers will lose. If our assumption covers the distribution of wealth as well, black capitalists will gain at the expense of the white. Thus, it is the high-paid white workers and capitalists who gain from discrimination, as Reich suggests.

But all this after many years. In the meantime, the burden of equalization will fall on white semiskilled and even some unskilled workers, long before it reaches high-paid professionals and capitalists. Thus, the current, if only temporary, beneficiaries of discrimination are neither at the top nor quite at the bottom of income distribution, but somewhere below the median, as confirmed, more or less, by the intensity of racial prejudice among these groups.[17]

But if Reich is to be commended for a useful contribution, he may be reproached for failing to explain how the alleged interests of the capitalists as a class are promoted by everyday actions of individual capitalists. Are the latter so devoted to their class that they are ready to forego larger profits to be derived from hiring blacks? Reich might have also said more about racist behavior of white workers (and of some unions), unless he thought that their motivation was too obvious to require a lengthy explanation.

Sexism

Since the problem is similar to racism, there is no need to go over the arguments again. But it would be only fair to record that in socialist countries women's participation in the labor force is greater than it is in ours.

[16] Reich found a correlation (in a multiple regression) between the degree of income concentration among whites and racism defined as the ratio between black and white median incomes by metropolitan areas. Since only a summary of his work (a doctoral dissertation) is presented in the book, I cannot comment on his data and methods.

[17] That these conclusions are strongly affected by the nature of assumptions made can be seen by comparing them with Barbara Bergmann's (1971) findings. She assumed that the elimination of discrimination would reshuffle workers only in each educational group and found that the greatest losers would be low-educated whites.

They are active in medicine, engineering, science, construction, administration, etc. But the performance of two sets of duties is anything but easy.[18]

Imperialism

If it is defined as "the internationalization of capitalism" (pp. 408, 417), then everything is conveniently settled by definition. But if imperialism means a directed expansion of an economic system beyond the boundaries of a particular country that intervenes and acquires control over other areas, as the book further elaborates (p. 408), then between the American and Soviet imperialisms there is little to choose. To preserve its position and power at home, one ruling group invades Vietnam; the other, Hungary and Czechoslovakia – not to mention their other aggressions. Whether capitalism is more likely to pursue imperialist policy than socialism is a subject on which many arguments and counterarguments can be made without settling much, particularly in a limited space.[19] Let me turn instead to Weisskopf's two papers, "United States Foreign Investment: An Empirical Survey" (pp. 426-35) and "Capitalism and Underdevelopment in the Modern World" (pp. 442-57). Both look like interesting articles with analytical and empirical content, but both turn out to be little better than lawyer's briefs.

Thus, Table 10-B (p. 429) is supposed to demonstrate that in 1950-69 the rate of return on American foreign investment – 13.3 percent – was much higher than the overall one of 7.7 percent. But these rates are net of taxes. A simple recalculation based on Weisskopf's own assumptions reveals that the pretax rates differ little; they are 14.8 and 14.2 percent, respectively.[20] Profit rates are notoriously inexact and subject to manipulation, so I would rather abstain from conclusions, but what was the

[18] Several years ago, the Soviet literary journal *Novyĭ Mir* [New world] published a story named "Nedelia" [Week] in the form of a diary by a young married professional woman, with two children, describing her activities during 7 days. According to her, holding a full-time job and taking care of her family was extremely difficult. If more American women enter the labor force and earn incomes, would not consumerism increase? See the story about the female employees of the telephone company on pp. 20-21 of the book under review.

[19] Those who are sure that socialist countries are not imperialist might ponder on the likely Soviet behavior if the Soviet supply of oil were threatened.

[20] Without examination, I took Weisskopf's estimate of the average tax rate on foreign investment as 10 percent. For the overall rate I used 45.6 percent. The gross profit rates so obtained are simple averages calculated from Weisskopf's data. Since profit from foreign investment constitutes a small part of total profit, the small difference in the pretax profit rates stated in the text implies considerable difference between foreign and domestic rates. It is puzzling that Weisskopf used the overall, rather than the domestic, rate for his comparison.

purpose of presenting this table? To show that income from foreign investment is taxed lightly?

Table 10-G (p. 444) is supposed to illustrate the uneven character of capitalist development. Indeed, among the nonsocialist countries, the ratio of per capita income of the rich to the poor is 12 to 1. But for socialist countries (here they are called "socialist"), this ratio is as high as 10 to 1, certainly high enough to proclaim a new "Law of Uneven Socialist Development." It seems that India and Egypt are placed in the nonsocialist category. As both regard themselves semisocialist, perhaps the honor of their company should be shared by both categories. I wonder what the two ratios will be then.

Still another table, this time 10-I (p. 455), shows a widening gap between the per capita incomes of rich and poor nonsocialist countries. But the fact that population growth in the poor countries is faster than in the rich (as given in that table) is not mentioned in the text, although, in the spirit of Weisskopf's discussion, population growth hardly contributes to the growth of output.[21] It seems that population growth is still a forbidden subject among many radicals. Now that even China has embarked on population control, should not this taboo be lifted?

According to Weisskopf, the poor capitalist countries are doomed whatever they do. They gain little from investment because the latter merely increases labor productivity instead of alleviating unemployment (pp. 449–50), as if it would be difficult to make investment less labor-saving if only someone was willing to pay the cost. Industrialization merely raises incomes of industrial workers, already above the average, and thus increases inequality (p. 456); evidently low-earning peasants never move into industrial jobs. His own data (Table 10-H, p. 445) show that advanced capitalist countries enjoy greater income equality than the underdeveloped ones. I wonder how the former have ever managed to achieve this?

IV

Poor capitalism

As the old saying goes, a glass of water can be described either as half full or as half empty. Our authors never tire of playing this game. Poor capitalism! It is damned if it does, and it is damned if it does not. Thus, a change in the relative positions of white- and of blue-collar workers is described as a loss for the former rather than as a gain for the latter (pp. 180,

---

[21] Actually, the total income of poor countries was growing faster (at 4.6 percent per year) than that of the rich (4.4), but the population of the former was growing at 2.4 percent, as compared with only 1.3 percent for the latter.

256–57). Federal policies for economic stability and growth are blamed for leading "to the survival of inefficient business, and hence, in the long run to the need for more subsidies" (p. 197). What a surprising piece of social Darwinism! The United States is scolded for imposing a brain drain on the poorer countries (p. 447). But if we forbade the entrance of their nationals, the same authors would accuse us of racism, since many of these immigrants are nonwhite. A quotation from *The Communist Manifesto* deplores the fact that "labor of men [is] superseded by that of women" (p. 71) – a rather strange idea for sympathizers with Women's Liberation. Even minimum-wage legislation is bad because "it can serve the interests of organized labor at the cost of overpricing and hence underutilizing unskilled labor" (p. 453). Milton Friedman would agree.

Our educational system is severely criticized for, among other things, preparing people for productive jobs, for being "more or less firmly tailored to the needs of 'economic rationality'" (p. 124). Shall we train economically useless graduates instead? Compulsory education is described as being "basically coercive. . . . In many parts of the country, schools were literally imposed upon the workers" (p. 221). Why not repeal it, then?

These are a few examples. I have run out of space.

The promised land

To condemn capitalism is easy, to present a superior practical alternative is difficult, particularly for our authors: their rejection both of the market and of bureaucracy as instruments for resource allocation would require a truly ingenious substitute. Unfortunately, none is offered.

The "Visions of a Socialist Alternative" is given only 20 pages at the end of the book, plus a number of scattered suggestions. Here is a brief summary.

People will live in communities based on "geographical contiguity" (p. 527). The communities consisting of a "variety of functional groups" (p. 527) will control productive wealth and make economic decisions. They will be "unoppressive, nonexploitative . . . where individuals are encouraged to lead creative lives" (p. 347). Their members will be motivated by "a cooperative ethic of recognizing people's responsibility to each other" (p. 520). They will work for the joy of working and not for income or profit (pp. 520–28). This wonderful transformation in human behavior will come about because people are not "inherently greedy, acquisitive, selfish, competitive or aggressive" (p. 4). "Changes in the environment can interact with changes in the individual to usher a new era of human cooperation" (p. 5).

The economic mechanism that will be used to make decisions within the communities, and – more important – to allocate resources and to organize exchange among them, is not described. But with human nature so good and pliable (in the right hands, of course), who needs formal organizations, markets, prices, plans, and all other economic paraphernalia? So the end result is just another utopia, recognized by the authors as such (pp. 392, 530). It is an old-fashioned anarchist utopia that would delight Kropotkin and Proudhon (and Furier), but hardly please Marx, if he remained true to his own spirit. In its treatment of economic problems, it is not superior to Thomas More's original creation, and it is greatly inferior to Edward Bellamy's *Looking Backward* ([1888] 1960), now nearly 100 years old. And Bellamy was not even an economist!

There is no harm in describing utopias if one does not take them seriously. But what is the use of criticizing capitalism, or any other existing economic system, in a supposedly scholarly and analytical manner, by comparing it with an ideal, which can be made as wonderful as the authors' imagination allows? Surely more effective methods can be found. The ineptitude shown by the contributors and the editors (well-trained young economists of known ability) merely damages their own cause: it makes capitalism look better than it is. Instead of winning converts, they are more likely to repel even those who have no love for capitalism and are searching for better alternatives.

References

Antonov, O. K., *Dlia Vsekh i dlia Sebia* [For all and for oneself], Moscow, 1965.

Becker, G. S., *The Economics of Discrimination,* 2d ed., Chicago, 1971.

Bellamy, E., *Looking Backward,* New York, 1960.

Bergmann, B., "The Effect on White Incomes of Discrimination in Employment," *J.P.E.* 79 (March/April 1971): 294–313.

Edwards, Richard C.; Reich, Michael; and Weisskopf, Thomas B., *The Capitalist System: A Radical Analysis of American Society,* Englewood Cliffs, N.J., 1972.

Harney, M. P., *The Jesuits in History,* New York, 1941.

Hunnius, C.; Garson, G. D.; and Case, J., eds., *Workers' Control: A Reader on Labor and Social Change,* New York, 1973.

Jencks, C., et al., *Inequality: A Reassessment of the Effect of Family and Schooling in America,* New York, 1972.

Jenkins, D., *Job Power: Blue and White Collar Democracy,* Garden City, N.Y., 1973.

Kuznets, S., *Shares of Upper-Income Groups in Income and Savings,* New York, Nat. Bur. Econ. Res., 1953.

Osipov, G. V., ed., *Industry and Labor in the U.S.S.R.,* London, 1966.

Pryor, F. L., "The Distribution of Nonagricultural Labor Incomes in Communist and Capitalist Nations," *Slavic Rev.* 31 (September 1972): 639–50.

———, *Property and Industrial Organization in Communist and Capitalist Nations,* Bloomington, 1973.

Schmalensee, R., *The Economics of Advertising,* Amsterdam, 1972.

Taylor, L. S., and Weiserbs, D., "Advertising and the Aggregate Consumption Function," *A.E.R.* 62 (September 1972): 642–55.

U.S., Bureau of the Census, *Historical Statistics of the United States: Colonial Times to 1957,* Washington, D.C., 1960.

Wiles, P. J. D., and Markowski, S., "Income Distribution under Communism and Capitalism: Some Facts about Poland, the UK, the USA, and the USSR," *Soviet Studies* 22 (January 1971): 344–69; (April 1971): 487–511.

Work in America: Report of a Special Task Force to the Secretary of Health, Education, and Welfare, Washington, D.C., 1972.

Zdravomyslov, A. G.; Rozhin, V. P.; and Iadov, V. A., eds., *Man and His Work,* White Plains, N.Y., 1970.

The blind men and the elephant:
an essay on isms[1]

> A certain Prince commanded several blind men to examine an elephant and to
> describe to him what the elephant was like. Each blind man examined one part
> of the elephant's body and reported accordingly. And the blind men fell into
> quarreling among themselves, each insisting that only he was right.
>
> – an old Indian tale[2]

The comparison between capitalism and socialism presented in this essay
was made by one blind man.

[1] Since some thirty-eight years passed from the inception of this essay to its completion
(in July 1988), a brief history of it may be called for. The basic idea was suggested by a
silly old movie, *Born Yesterday*, around 1950. One of its principal characters is a successful junk dealer whose business operations have become so vast as to require the services
of a public-relations expert. He hires an ex-senator (who must have failed his last reelec-
tion) at the then fantastic salary (in 1950) of $100,000. Both the junk dealer and the ex-
senator know that in no other employment could the latter command such a salary. As a
result, the senator finds himself in the power of his employer, who treats him worse than
the proverbial dog. The movie taught me that money (or income) and power can be ex-
changed for each other.

Scholarly integrity requires that due credit be given to as many of the author's predecessors as possible, particularly to those whose works he consulted when writing his own.
My attempt to honor this good custom resulted in a huge pile of notes and references (the
literature on socialism and related subjects being so vast) that could not possibly be included in this essay. A separate paper, or even a book, would be required. I have decided,
therefore, to express to their respective authors my sincerest gratitude and apology and
to mention here only those who have influenced my thinking directly.

I start with Oscar Lange's classical essay (*On the Economic Theory of Socialism*, Min-
neapolis, 1938), proceed to Janos Kornai's first book (*Anti-Equilibrium: On the Economic Systems Theory and the Tasks of Research*, Amsterdam, 1971, though I disagree
with his explanation of the demand deficiency under capitalism; see pp. 33–35), then to
some unidentified paper by Burton Weisbrod (which neither he nor I could find again),
and to ideas propagated by the American radical movement expressed in, among other
places, *The Capitalist System: A Radical Analysis of American Society*, edited by Richard C. Edwards, Michael Reich, and Thomas B. Weisskopf, Englewood Cliffs, N.J.,
1972 (see Essay 2). The two very important sources that I should have read at the time,
but did not until recently, long after the second draft of the essay was completed, are
Albert O. Hirschman's *Exit, Voice and Loyalty: Responses to Decline in Firms, Organizations, and States*, Cambridge, Mass., 1970, and an unpublished manuscript of my colleague Robert L. Bishop, *Microeconomic Theory*, 1956, Book II, Chapter 3, pp. 32–42,

I   Introduction

According to an old custom, sanctified by Marx, an essay on isms should deal with the struggles between two classes: in our time, between the capitalists who own the means of production and the workers who do not. I intend to violate this custom for two reasons: first, I do not regard the question of ownership, by itself, to be so critical; second, it has been discussed and debated to the point of boredom.[3] Instead, I propose to divide the populace into producers and consumers and to inquire how each group fares under capitalism of the American type and under socialism of the Soviet variety, at least as it still existed in the middle 1980s. This does not imply that the people suffer from split personalities, but only that each person performs several roles and has different

which presents the clearest explanation of the existence of excess supply under monopolistic competition.

I am very grateful to him, to Michael Manove, and to Martin L. Weitzman for their excellent comments on an earlier version of this essay. My membership in the Harvard Russian Research Center has been invaluable.

Over the years, I have presented this essay orally in my classes and, since 1972, in numerous seminars and lectures. The ideas spread. They were reflected in Martin L. Weitzman's well-known book *The Share Economy: Conquering Stagflation*, Cambridge, Mass., 1984, and in a paper by Tibor Scitovsky, "Pricetakers' Plenty: A Neglected Benefit of Capitalism," *Kyklos*, Vol. 38, 1985, pp. 517-36.

2 The person who identified this little tale as Indian was Padma Desai. The more I think of it, the more I am struck by its depth. Consider how many religious disputes, persecutions, and wars might have been avoided if its spirit had prevailed. It seems to have prevailed among the thirteenth-century Mongols, who practiced remarkable religious tolerance in the belief that every religion had something to contribute. See René Grousset, *The Empire of the Steppes: A History of Central Asia*, New Brunswick, N.J., 1970.

3 Public (or social) ownership of the means of production is regarded by almost all socialists as a necessary condition of socialism, practically by definition. But few regard it as sufficient. Among their additional demands we find democracy, nonbureaucratization, workers' self-management, abolition of workers' alienation and of commodity production, the end to markets and to the profit motive, and so on. Richard Crosland forms an exception: he does not attach much importance to the question of ownership. A whole section of his book *The Future of Socialism*, New York, 1963, pp. 35-42, is entitled "The Growing Irrelevance of the Ownership of the Means of Production." By now he must have company.

Perhaps the importance of class struggle, which to Marx embodied the essence of human history, should also be reevaluated. In our times, the sight of business and unions lobbying hand-in-hand for protective tariffs and government regulation for their industry does not point to an intensive class conflict. In the 1970s and early 1980s, business generously granted union wage demands exceeding the growth in labor productivity and then recompensed itself by passing the higher costs to the public. Arthur M. Okun found a close relation between wage and price increases but not between their reductions. See his *Conflicting National Goals*, Brookings Institution, General Series Reprint 320, Washington, D.C., 1977, p. 80.

interests.[4] Originally, I had hoped to bypass the question of ownership entirely, but, alas, as the reader will see, it came back because privately owned firms usually derive all or most of their revenues from sales and therefore must please their customers or go bankrupt, while firms owned by the government, even if they sell their products and services in the market, are seldom denied access to government subsidies and credit.[5] But to avoid unnecessary argument, I am willing to recognize the importance of ownership and even to offer it the honorable position of the elephant's head, while retaining that of the tail for my suggestion. In the elephant, this organ is short and insignificant, but it must perform *some* function. Will the reader not wish to examine it, if only to satisfy his or her curiosity?

Two criteria will be used in our comparisons: economic power and risk. A person or a firm X will be said to have power over Y if X's actions can affect Y's economic welfare.[6] Risk means the possibility of a loss. The meaning of both criteria will become clearer as the argument develops.

---

[4] This suggestion is not particularly original. Already in 1921, G. D. H. Cole wrote that "It is no longer necessary to deal with the argument that, because producers and consumers are the same persons, there is no need for distinct organizations to represent the respective points of view." (*Guild Socialism,* New York, p. 82.) However, he also stated that "... because consumers and producers are practically the same people ... there can be no real divergence of interest between them." (Ibid., p. 29.) Perhaps he could not make up his mind. Other divisions have been suggested:

> ... To Saint Simon the antagonism between the third estate and the privileged classes took the form of an antagonism between 'workers' and 'idlers.' The idlers were not merely the old privileged classes, but also all who, without taking any part in production or distribution, lived on their incomes. And the workers were not only the wage workers, but also the manufacturers, the merchants, the bankers.

From Friedrich Engels, "Socialism: Utopian and Scientific," in Robert C. Tucker, *The Marx-Engels Reader,* New York, 1972, p. 610.

A Danish Professor, Joergen Dich, "has propounded ... a theory that the members of the new ruling class in the welfare state are public servants, and that the Marxist conflict between labor and owners of capital has been succeeded by a conflict between those who work in the private sectors and those who work in the public sector." (*The New York Times,* February 12, 1976, p. 16.)

This quotation suggests that my division of the populace into consumers and producers who (under capitalism) work for firms deriving all, or most, of their funds from sales may be too restrictive. Government employees are also producers, but they do not have to please the users of their services, at least not directly. The same holds true for employees of nonprofit organizations.

[5] In reality, the distinction is not as sharp as the text implies. Private firms have been known to receive credit and subsidies from the government, as the Lockheed and Chrysler examples demonstrate. So have American farmers and many others. On the other side, Mrs. Thatcher has been closing down unprofitable government-owned mines, and Mr. Gorbachev has insisted that public enterprises should pay their way. See *Pravda,* June 27 and July 1, 1987.

[6] The source of this power is the absence of perfect substitutes. Perhaps it will amuse the reader to reflect that true romantic love, so glorified by the poets, can be a perfect

II   Power and risk under capitalism

Tradition demands that we start with the case of perfect competition. This exercise is purely theoretical because no consumers and very few producers operate in perfectly competitive markets. It is not the number of participants that matters here – there are certainly plenty of consumers and quite a few producers in most markets – but the rarity of standardized products.[7] Even a bottle of Gordon gin bought in one store is not exactly the same as a bottle sold by another: location, appearance, atmosphere of the store, and the manners of the sales clerks are not identical, not to mention home delivery, credit, and so on. In the labor market are many similar, but few identical, jobs, and among the workers pairs of identical twins are rare. The near absence of perfect competition (except in agriculture and in organized exchanges), however, has not prevented us from dreaming about it. What attracts us is not only the promise of a Pareto optimum but the virtual elimination of power: the availability of perfect substitutes guarantees that no seller or buyer and no employer or worker will be in anyone's power. Yet for all its virtues, perfect competition is incompatible with the introduction of new products, as Schumpeter observed some forty years ago.[8]

The participants in this market would face three kinds of risk: first, the timing of sales and of purchases amid frequent (or even continuous) price fluctuations; second, the production and the purchase of the wrong, even if standard, products, including the choice of the wrong occupation; third, various random events, like fires or hurricanes. The first kind of risk would be shared by both producers and consumers, with the former bearing the lighter burden because they can be expected to be better informed. The second should fall mostly on producers because production, and particularly education and training, take time, while consumers are protected by their knowledge of the standard products and by the diversification of their purchases. The third kind of risk, from random events, would also hurt mostly producers, particularly the capitalists, because they own the means of production. But at least they would be relieved of the need to attract and to please their customers.

instrument of enslavement because, by its very nature, it allows no substitutes. Reciprocity (if it can be induced) is the only known remedy.

[7] The rarity of standardized products has not prevented their use in most economic models. Often, no harm is done. But this assumption is certainly out of place in studies of technological change, consumer economics, comparative economic systems, and even taxation, to mention just a few. See the Special Appendix to Essay 11.

[8] "As a matter of fact, perfect competition is and always has been temporarily suspended whenever anything new is being introduced – automatically or by measures devised for the purpose – even in otherwise perfectly competitive conditions." (*Capitalism, Socialism and Democracy,* New York, 1942, p. 105.)

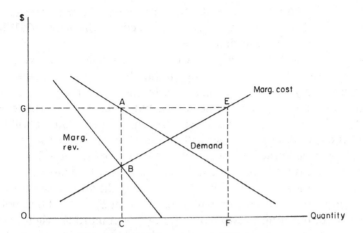

Figure 3.1. The firm's position under monopolistic competition.

So much for the case of perfect competition. The most common capitalist market structure has probably always been monopolistic competition.[9] It will be assumed that a typical capitalist firm operates under the following conditions:

1. The only, or at least the overwhelming, source of its revenue is derived from the sale of its products and services.
2. It tries to maximize profits.[10]
3. The demand curve for its products has the usual negative slope, but *its exact position and shape are known imperfectly.*
4. The marginal cost curve is positively sloped. This assumption is made because it *weakens* the argument. A constant or a falling marginal cost would strengthen it.

These assumptions are ordinary and widely used. Subject to them, the behavior of the firm will be depicted by the simple diagram (Figure 3.1) that we all learned in our professional childhood. (I use straight lines because they are easier to draw.)

According to the familiar story, the producer will find the point of intersection of the marginal revenue and marginal cost curves *B*, draw a vertical

---

[9] I tried to avoid the use of the clumsy expression "monopolistic competition" but could find no acceptable substitute. "Oligopoly" was vetoed by every reader of an earlier version of this essay. It is strange that we do not have a convenient term for the most common market structure under capitalism.

[10] As Peter Wiles said about a capitalist firm, "It may not wish, as in western economic textbooks, to maximize profit, but it will certainly be keen to avoid loss. For the basis of the market economy is that loss-makers cease to exist." (*The Political Economy of Communism,* Oxford, 1962, p. 20.)

line through it and settle down at point *A* where this line intersects the demand curve. Thus, he will sell *OC* units and charge the price *OG*. What else need be said about this diagram?

A good deal. It does not make clear the fundamental distinction between perfect and monopolistic competition. Under the former, the producer can sell any quantity he wants, but he cannot set the price. Under the latter, he can set any price he wants, but he cannot determine the quantity. Whether he can or cannot sell *OC* units depends on the willingness of his customers to buy.[11] Actually, he has no preference for point *C* and may not even know its exact location (because of Assumption 3): so long as his price is kept above the marginal cost, he will be anxious to expand his output and sales, that is, to move along the horizontal line *GE* until its intersection with the marginal cost at point *E*. Beyond that point he will not go, but if his position at *E* (or at any point to the right of *A*) appears reasonably long-lasting he will realize that he must have underestimated the demand. The new demand curve will be drawn (as it were) above the original one, and the story just told will be repeated once more. If the marginal cost is constant or declining, which it often is in the long run, the stopping point *E* may never be reached; a determined producer will always strive for a larger market and will always deplore its limitation. That a simultaneous attempt by many firms to expand output may run into a shortage of resources (such as labor) need not affect his microimage of the world.

Perhaps this image is the source of the belief that a capitalist economy suffers from a chronic shortage of demand, a belief held by Malthus, Marx, Engels, Hobson, and many other representatives of the so-called underconsumptionist school, long before the macrostatistics required for supporting this view became available. No statistics were needed for the 1930s, but when Keynes projected the then-existing situation into all of human history and portrayed the latter as a perpetual and usually unsuccessful attempt to escape from an excess propensity to save (recall his discourse on the blessings of Egyptian pyramids), his remarks were little more than amusing.[12] More recently, the existence of this shortage was reaffirmed by Janos Kornai.[13] That this shortage has not been uncommon

---

[11] This point was also made by Tibor Scitovsky in *Welfare and Competition: The Economics of a Fully Employed Economy,* Chicago, 1951, p. 247, and by Bishop, op. cit., Book II, Chapter 3, pp. 33–34.

[12] I wonder if Keynes ever realized that the principal assumption of classical economics that he rejected was that of perfect competition. It is its absence that forces most of the adjustments to demand to fall (at least in the short run) not on prices and wage rates but on output and employment.

[13] See his *Anti-Equilibrium,* op. cit., and his other writings. A particularly strong statement appears in his more recent paper "Pressure and Suction on the Market," in Judith Thornton, ed., *Economic Analysis of the Soviet-Type System,* Cambridge, Mass., 1976, p. 207:

under capitalism there is no doubt, but its presence cannot be deduced merely from capitalists' laments. The underutilization of capacity is a perfectly normal and, I would add, desirable characteristic of capitalism that is responsible for its remarkable flexibility.[14]

But to come back to our main theme. The nearly permanent excess of the price charged by the capitalist producer over his marginal cost is responsible for some of the most significant features of capitalism, both good and bad. As mentioned earlier, it drives him to try to expand his production and sales by any means, fair or foul, to search for new markets and to introduce new products – in a word, to innovate. It generates the remarkable dynamic force of capitalism admired even by Marx.[15] In the present context, it forces the capitalist to exert every effort to please his customers, in whose hands his final fate lies. He is in their power.[16] It also induces him to take advantage of his customers' ignorance and stupidity by adulterating his products, by misleading advertising (so familiar to TV watchers), and by millions of other deceptive tricks well-known to all of us. But if this endless pursuit of the consumer's dollar can be most annoying, would the consumer prefer to be met with indifference?[17] Thus a Victorian maiden with a pretty face and an ample dowry might complain that her numerous suitors never left her alone, but would she really prefer to be left alone?

The risk of timing, so important in the perfectly competitive case, now weakens because under monopolistic competition prices are not as unstable, but the immense variety of nonstandard goods brought forward by technological progress creates a great risk of producing and buying the wrong product. The consumer simply lacks the time and the ability to acquaint himself thoroughly with every new product, and often ends up with a poor one. But most of this risk falls on the producer because the invention, testing, and production of a novelty takes time, and the consumer's reaction to it is uncertain.

> ...Total purchasing power intended by the population for consumption is incapable of consuming the mass of commodities offered for consumption at any single moment.... In the final analysis, effective purchasing intentions lag behind commodity supplies as well as behind sales intentions based on potential production.

[14] To Edward Chamberlin this underutilization of capacity merely represented waste. See his *The Theory of Monopolistic Competition*, Cambridge, Mass., 1939, p. 109. I can see now why Schumpeter had so little use for this type of reasoning.

[15] There is no shortage of compliments in *The Communist Manifesto*. The best known of them reads: "The bourgeoisie, during its rule of scarcely one hundred years, has created more massive and more colossal productive forces than have all preceding generations together."

[16] The plight of some of our largest corporations in the last ten–fifteen years demonstrates the overpowering strength of the market. It also shows how wrong Galbraith has been in denying that. See his *The New Industrial State,* Boston, 1967, and his other writings.

[17] A few hours spent in Moscow should persuade anyone of the validity of this argument.

The power exercised by consumers over producers requires no police, no compulsion, and no letters to the editor of *The New York Times*. It works silently, like gravity. All the consumer has to do is not come back to the store, not buy the same product again. Most Western economists approve this arrangement. Was it not Adam Smith himself who said that "consumption is the sole end and purpose of all production; and the interest of the producer ought to be attended to, only so far as it may be necessary for promoting that of the consumer."[18] "Consumer sovereignty" is a sacred concept among us, our usual complaint being that it is not fully implemented because of labor unions, cartels, taxes, etc.[19] Perhaps it is not obvious to us that the same force which we lovingly call "market discipline" appears to the other side, that is, to producers, as "market tyranny." In our formal mathematical models, supply functions of labor (and of other factors) are given the same place and honor as the consumer demand functions for goods and services, but in reality we follow Adam Smith in expecting the producers to bend their knees to the consumers, rather than the other way around.[20] Bending their knees and subjecting themselves to the discipline or tyranny of the market places a great burden on producers. Schumpeterian "creative destruction" may sound like a heroic contest, reminiscent of knightly tournaments of old, yet how many economists, usually protected by tenure, civil service regulations or custom, would like to take part in it? Even Marx showed a bit

---

[18] *The Wealth of Nations,* The Modern Library Edition, New York, 1937, p. 625. But the same Smith expressed deep concern for the mental development of workers engaged in repetitive operations. He thought that, in this respect, members of "barbarous societies" pursuing varied occupations were better off. (Ibid., pp. 734–37.)

Alfred Marshall listed "The growth of mankind in numbers, in health and strength, in knowledge, ability, and in *richness of character*" (my italics) as "the end of all our studies." (*Principles of Economics,* 8th ed., London, 1936, p. 139.) He wondered (Ibid., p. 248)

> ...Whether the present industrial organization might not with advantage be so modified as to increase the opportunities, which the lower grades of industry have for using latent mental faculties, for deriving pleasure from their use and for strengthening them by use....

Many similar quotations from other nonsocialist writers can be given, but to all of them the satisfaction of consumers' desires was the paramount objective of economic activity.

[19] Of course, a strict interpretation of this concept would require the equality of all prices with their respective marginal costs and thus exclude monopolistic competition, which bestows so much power on consumers. Under perfect competition (with standardized products), producers would simply move to the point of equality of price with marginal cost and stay there. They would be interested only in cost-reducing technological change, if its appearance was consistent with perfect competition.

[20] The expression "worker sovereignty" is not seen very often, but it is not unknown. See, for instance, Abram Bergson, *Essays in Normative Economics,* Cambridge, Mass., 1966, p. 202, and Peter Wiles, op. cit., p. 97.

of sympathy for the poor capitalists.[21] Still, they can seek protection in the diversification of their holdings, but what protection is available for workers whose skills become obsolete and whose jobs disappear because of the dictates of the market? Few can hold several jobs simultaneously, and a skill not currently exercised quickly deteriorates. And even when employed, the worker has to produce not what pleases him but what the market commands – the source of alienation stressed by Marx and his followers.[22]

A simple expression of a person's welfare makes it a function of his income (consumption plus savings) and leisure.[23] This implies that the person is alive only before nine in the morning and after five in the afternoon. What happens to him between nine and five is immaterial, as if our work served no other purpose than providing us with consumables.[24] Surely, our work means much more than that.[25]

21 See his *The Economic and Philosophic Manuscripts of 1844*, New York, 1964, pp. 88–89, as reproduced in Paul Craig Roberts and Matthew A. Stephenson, *Marx's Theory of Exchange, Alienation, and Crisis*, New York, 1983, p. 49.

22 See Marx's "Alienated Labor" in his *Economic and Philosophical Manuscripts* as reproduced in David McLellan, *Karl Marx: Selected Writings*, Oxford, 1977, pp. 77–86 and his other writings; there exists a large literature on the subject. It has become very popular with American radicals.

23 Such a utility function was suggested by James J. Heckman in his "Estimates of a Human Capital Production Function Embedded in a Life-Cycle Model of Labor Supply," *Household Product and Consumption, Studies in Income and Wealth*, No. 40, NBER, New York, 1975, p. 229. A more sophisticated version would include the time pattern of consumption and saving, risk, etc.

24 The opposite point of view was strikingly expressed by Heinz-Otto Vetter, the head of the West German Union Federation: "I am not half helot, half man....The idea that I become a man when I go out of the factory is intolerable. I'm indivisible. I want to be a man in my whole life, at work and at leisure." (As quoted in *The New York Times*, March 25, 1976, p. 14.)

25 As a long-time (26 years) graduate placement officer in the Economics Department at M.I.T., I can testify that our new Ph.D.'s were much more interested in the quality of the academic environment, research facilities, courses to be taught, etc., rather than in their salaries. None of them ever asked their prospective employers whether the university was close to good shopping facilities. They were concerned with their careers, not with consumption.

For all their virtues though, they were hardly a good sample of the American population. However, in a study reported in *Work in America* (U.S. Department of Health, Education and Welfare, Washington, D.C., December 1972, p. 11) on the attitudes of American workers, "interesting work" commanded the first place, and "good pay" took the fifth. In a similar study made in Poland, "the atmosphere of the place" was in first place. Even though the respondents might have been embarrassed to stress their concern for money, it seems safe to conclude that nonmonetary aspects of their work were important to them.

My surprise witness on this issue is former president Nixon, who declared (or was made to declare) that "...The most important part of the quality of life is the quality of work, and the new need for job satisfaction is the key to the quality of work." (*Work in America*, op. cit., p. i.) Nixon – a socialist?

Actually, we affirm our allegiance to consumer sovereignty only in the classroom. Outside of it we think of ourselves first of all as producers (in this case, as economists), as does everyone else. If at a party you ask the host to identify the newly arrived guest, he will state his occupation – engineer, miner, teacher, sanitation worker (depending on the kind of parties you attend) – rather than describe him as the owner of a huge purple refrigerator. But if our work is of such importance to us why should we not try to transform an exertion for pleasing the consumers into an activity useful and enjoyable to ourselves?[26]

III Power and risk under socialism

According to the report of one blind person, this is exactly what socialism, particularly of the Marxist variety, tries to do. It does not forget that, after all, consumption is the aim of economic activity, yet it looks at the world from the point of view of the producers (or rather the workers, since capitalists are supposed to have been expropriated) and seeks to protect them from the tyranny of the market by shifting the risk to consumers while transferring the power to producers. I will suggest several ways of doing this. For some of them the nationalization of the means of production is necessary; for others, it may be merely convenient.

The most radical and direct method found in many utopias, including Marx's vision of the future communist state, would be to allow every person to produce what he (or she) wished.[27] It is assumed, of course, that normal, healthy people do desire to engage in some form of productive activity. If some workers enjoyed driving trucks or wagons or operating

The nonmonetary rewards (positive or negative) from work are called "psychic income," and most economists recognize its importance. But they don't quite know what to do with it. Those who assume that this income is already embodied in the wage rate, whatever that happens to be, may feel that it calls for no special recognition.

[26] A number of suggestions for relieving the monotony, boredom, fatigue, and, in general, for making work more attractive have been made, and some have been carried out, particularly in Sweden. To the extent that their adoption does not raise the cost, no problem arises. But if it does, who will bear it?

It is very strange that our labor unions have shown so little interest in this problem. Does it really exist, or has it been merely invented by intellectuals? Are our workers satisfied? Opinion polls have not given definitive results. Could it be that unions do not want their members to be satisfied with their work because dissatisfied workers make more loyal union members?

[27] Here is Marx's famous statement on this freedom: "...To hunt in the morning, fish in the afternoon, rear cattle in the evening, criticize after dinner." (*The German Ideology*, p. 22, as quoted in Roberts and Stephenson, op. cit., p. 31.)

pneumatic tubes, as in Bellamy's *Looking Backwards,* goods might be delivered to consumers' homes;[28] otherwise, consumers would have to make their own arrangements. There would be no general plan, no prices, and no wages.

The great virtue of this scheme lies in the elimination of workers' alienation, as defined by the Marxists. Unfortunately, the scheme itself is completely impractical. There is no evidence that a positive relationship exists between the social usefulness of a job and the pleasure of performing it. Even if consumers did not die from exposure and starvation, the existence of input–output relationships in all, except the most primitive, economies would make it impossible for every worker to do what he liked. I am told that in Berkeley, near the university campus, there are (or were) young people selling hand-carved leather belts of their own manufacture – a pleasant activity, useful to consumers and satisfying the creative urge of the producers. However, leather belts must be made out of leather, and leather is made from cow (or some other animal's) hides. I expect that in most societies a sufficient number of sadists, known as "hunters," willing to shoot the cows (without any danger to themselves) will be found, but who would want to mess with their hides? So this creative activity would have to be given up.

A more practical method would have the producers draw up a self-consistent plan. They might very well take consumers' wishes into account by consulting them or by studying past data, but the main requirement of the plan would be its acceptance by the producers. "Consumerism" would have no place here.[29] Prices and wages would exist, but firms would not be required to make profits, and losses would be made good by government subsidies. (Here the ownership of the means of production becomes relevant.) In a cruder version of this scheme, producers would not be particularly concerned with shortages in some markets and surpluses in others. (Let consumers worry about that.) In a more refined form, they would manipulate prices so cleverly that every market would always be in equilibrium. There would be no shortages and no queues. Consumers would retain complete freedom of choice among goods and services

[28] Edward Bellamy, *Looking Backward 2000–1887,* New York, 1960 (originally published in 1888).

[29] It is best to define "consumerism" by a direct quotation from the book of radical readings edited by Edwards, Reich and Weisskopf, op. cit., p. 369: "Consumerism derives from a fundamental tenet of capitalist ideology: the assertion that the primary requirement for individual self-fulfillment and happiness is the possession and consumption of material goods."

The importance attached to consumers and consumption differs greatly among socialist writers. A survey of their views cannot be undertaken here.

offered to them. Unless they had been abroad, they would never realize that they were enjoying only a part of consumer sovereignty.[30]

But even this seemingly moderate scheme would run into problems. First, such a skillful manipulation of prices, even with the help of computers, would be beyond the ability of any government, at least in the foreseeable future. Second, enough of bourgeois morality would probably remain, at least for some time, to make a manager of a firm suffering chronic losses feel humiliated when begging for a subsidy; for the same reason, the planners would feel uneasy observing the waste resulting from the production of unwanted goods. Even Soviet country stores, the usual dumping ground for unsalable goods, may object to receiving them. Hence, a better, easier, and more practicable scheme has to be found.

In this, the planners continue producing goods and services which, *in their opinion,* consumers ought to have, but instead of frequent manipulation of prices they keep them more or less constant and generate sufficient purchasing power to create a chronic state of excess demand in most markets. This can be easily done.

Whether or not the emergence of excess demand in the Soviet Union was intentional need not concern us here.[31] Perhaps its original appearance was simply caused by sloppy planning and lax financial discipline, but once it took hold its advantages were recognized, and it has been

[30] In Lange's classical essay, prices are also manipulated to equilibrate all markets (except for the highly competitive ones), but consumers do enjoy complete sovereignty. Among socialist writers, Lange is one of the few who look at the world from the consumers' point of view. He accepts the market allocation of resources and is not concerned with the protection of workers from the market. For a related view on Lange, see Paul Craig Roberts, "Oscar Lange's Theory of Socialist Planning," *Journal of Political Economy,* Vol. 79 (May/June 1971), pp. 562–77.

It is not clear to me why Lange favors the free distribution of as many goods as possible. Since, under socialism, income distribution is expected to be equitable, there is really little reason for not using the price mechanism. As soon as a good (or service) becomes free, its consumers lose all control over its quality, appearance, assortment, etc. On Peter Wiles's description of free army socks, see his "A Comment but Not a Rejoinder," *Soviet Studies,* Vol. XXII (July 1970), p. 41.

[31] In 1930 Stalin declared: ". . . In the USSR, the growth of consumption (purchasing ability) of the masses all the time overtakes the growth of production, pushing it forward, while with them, the capitalists, the growth of consumption of the masses (purchasing power) never catches up with the growth of production and all the time falls behind it, time and again causing production crises." (*Sochineniia (Collected works),* Vol. 12, Moscow, 1949, pp. 322–23.)

In 1956 Mikoyan repeated this: ". . . In a socialist society demand must be ahead of the supply of goods." (United Nations, *Economic Survey of Europe in 1958,* p. 28, note 72.)

Whether the two gentlemen were merely boasting or describing their actual policy I do not know.

permitted to thrive. Surely, after all these years of planning, the Soviet regime could have learned how to control demand if it really wanted to.[32]

In any case, the emergence and existence of excess demand have changed drastically the distribution of power and risk between producers and consumers. Waiting to be served, after a long stand in a queue, the consumer has lost all his power because his threat, implied or actual, to leave and not come back or not buy would be met not with regret but with derision. And if the goods or services were of the wrong quality or assortment, the excess demand would take care of that as well, at least most of the time. In any case, the risk would be borne by consumers.

Of course, excess demand, like any medicine, should be served in proper doses; too heavy a dose will disrupt the economy and reduce the desire of the populace to work and the willingness to obey. Since it is impossible to spread excess demand evenly over all markets, a moderate general application will bypass some markets and even leave an excess supply in others. Some firms will sustain losses because the prices for their outputs were set incorrectly, or because of mismanagement, or for other reasons. Losses are embarrassing, but so long as they remain moderate and the firms have access to the state credit or the state budget (as they usually do, being owned by the state), they will continue to function and their workers will keep their jobs.

The market for consumer goods, however, is only one of many. Its conditions are bound to affect the labor market and the markets for intermediate products and capital goods. With an excess demand for labor, independent labor unions could exercise tremendous power over their employers and demand and achieve ever higher wages. An endless inflation would result, disrupting the economy beyond control and making rational allocation of resources impossible. Hence, wages must be set by the government and not by collective bargaining. Unions may be permitted to engage in activities related to workers' welfare, fairness of treatment, and the like. Indeed, this is the actual situation in the Soviet Union and other socialist countries.

The knowledge that his employer needs him more than he needs his employer and that his job is virtually guaranteed places the socialist worker in a superior position, unknown under capitalism (except in wartime). He

---

[32] "Had the Soviet leaders wished to eliminate the disequilibria between supply and demand, they could have done so long ago. That they had not done so was a decision of economic policy." (Joseph Berliner, *The Innovation Decision in Soviet Industry,* Cambridge, Mass., 1976, p. 89.) The advantages of excess demand were also noted by Franklyn D. Holzman in "Some Notes on Over-Full Employment Planning, Short-Run Balance, and the Soviet Economic Reforms," *Soviet Studies,* Vol. XXII (October 1970), pp. 255–61. A number of references are given in his paper.

is not under pressure to perform; pleasing the consumers (or any buyers, with the exception of the defense and space establishments) is not among his duties, and the realization that by his efforts consumers are supplied with scarce commodities may give him a feeling of accomplishment, which the capitalist worker, concerned with the preservation of his job, may not have. For workers, acting as workers, socialism has important advantages to offer.

For the managers, however, the prevalence of excess demand creates a complex problem. Lords to their customers, they are slaves to their suppliers; helpless before the latter, they cry for help to the party and government functionaries (the "bureaucrats") with whom the ultimate power rests. This power is not derived from organs of compulsion, such as the KGB, the police, or the army. It arises because these functionaries perform the allocative functions of the market. They decide who shall and who shall not receive the scarce goods and services. If a chairman of a collective farm needs roofing iron for a new barn, he will seldom get it without the support of the local party secretary. And this support is given in exchange for obedience to the secretary's orders.[33]

The absence of open compulsion makes this exercise of power particularly effective and pleasant because compulsion, a poor method of governance, is frowned upon. No class or group willingly parts with power, and socialist bureaucrats would be no exception. When Western economists insist that the Soviet Union (and other socialist countries) should let the market allocate their resources (with a minimum of planning), they may not realize what a tremendous change they are advocating: the market cannot function properly without the elimination of excess demand; in its absence, the bureaucrats would lose an important source of their power.[34] Some of them may even become unemployed. And (reports one blind man), all this can happen without any changes in the ownership of the means of production.

To show that it is the existence of excess demand that is the key to the problem, let me invite the reader to join me in two experiments: the first is imaginary (a "thought experiment"); the second is real. Imagine that by some unspecified method (magic, perhaps) excess demand in the Soviet

---

[33] Excess demand creates power in all sorts of places. For instance, the prices of tickets to our popular athletic events, like the Rose Bowl, are set way below their market values. The power so created falls into the hands of the organizers, who decide who shall and who shall not get them. Do they use this power to obtain favors from the lucky recipients of the tickets? (I owe this observation to Steven N. Cheung.)

The existence of excess supply can also generate power for those who are given the right to allocate the scarce resource – this time, the customers. See Berliner, op. cit., pp. 209–24.

[34] They would still retain, however, other sources of power.

Union is suddenly eliminated. Examine now the changes in the behavior of a manager of some ordinary Moscow store. Usually, when he arrived to open his store in the morning, he was greeted by a sizable queue. Now there is no queue. Customers drop in at a leisurely pace, look (or sniff) at the merchandise; some buy, others do not. By the end of the day, and later by the end of the week, month, and quarter, he realizes that he has failed to fulfill his sales and profit plans. For the first time in his life he has been short of customers! What will he do to attract them? He may redecorate his store, rearrange his merchandise to make it more accessible, display the best of it in the window, demand the authority to order merchandise instead of passively accepting what is sent to him. He may even advertise (if he is permitted), and, finally, he will call his sales personnel and, paraphrasing a late World War II *New Yorker* cartoon, he will tell them that "under the new circumstances they are to proceed on the assumption that the customer may be *sometimes* right."

The second experiment consists in visiting one of the Soviet *Berezka* stores, which cater mostly to foreigners and accept hard currency only.[35] The visit will be a pleasure. The store is attractive, the goods are plentiful, of good quality, and tastefully displayed; the sales ladies are educated, well groomed, polite, and helpful.[36] Do these stores belong to some foreign capitalist? Not at all. They are state owned, just like other Soviet stores. But they do not suffer from (or shall I say "enjoy") excess demand.

Actually, it is not necessary to travel to Moscow to observe the creation of power by excess demand. My contemporaries can still recall how sales clerks treated their customers during World War II. The younger generation may still remember the adventures of finding gasoline in 1973 and 1979. The service stations had not changed owners, but the attendants suddenly became socialist functionaries. Those episodes, however, were short. We have in our midst two permanent socialist, or at least socialist-like, sets of organizations: the government, in all its numerous units, and the more prestigious universities.

That government functionaries of all countries have much in common is too well known to need elaboration. The explanation of their behavior is simple: they are not confronted with paying customers who can go elsewhere but with humble petitioners who do not pay (at least directly) for services received and therefore wield no power. The universities present a more interesting case.

---

[35] There are also bars operating on the same principle. I wonder if Soviet administrators are aware of the irony that West Germans are welcome to these exclusive places, but East Germans are not.

[36] This was my own experience.

The tuition in our leading universities is set sufficiently low to create an excess demand for available places. Its presence serves as evidence of high standards and is a source of pride; it also subjects the consumers (the students) to the power of the producers (the faculty), who derive additional power from assigning grades and writing recommendations. Students are helpless because they do not pay the market price for instruction and consultation. Often they pay nothing or are paid instead. Besides, universities do not try to maximize profits or revenues. Should a student decide to leave, no regrets would be expressed because his place would be quickly occupied by another. Fortunately, university teaching usually attracts nice (if I may say so), nonaggressive people who, on the whole, believe in noblesse oblige, like to be popular, and take pride in the performance of their students. But if the reader wants to understand the role of power in the university, let him compare the present arrangements with the following imaginary ones: professors would not be paid for teaching; those who desired to teach would sell (indirectly, to preserve their dignity) tickets to their lectures at rates established by themselves; consultations would be paid for in a similar manner.[37] Tests, grades, and degrees, if given at all, would be handled by some outside body.[38] Space forces me to stop here, but I am sure that the reader's imagination will be adequate for visualizing the resulting changes in human relations in the universities and in the quality of teaching.[39]

The distribution of power in our leading universities allows their tenured professors to lead double lives, as it were, enjoying the benefits of both socialism and capitalism without suffering from the defects of either: as producers, during working hours, say from nine to five, they live under socialism; after five and during vacations (and vicariously through their spouses), they become capitalist consumers. This remarkable arrangement may be responsible for the greater tolerance that professors usually display to both systems than is commonly shown by the society at large. If the society gains from this tolerance, as it probably does, perhaps it also loses, because those who play such important roles in the formation of public opinion lead such atypical, privileged lives.[40]

---

[37] A close friend of mine (now deceased) who taught at one of our leading universities set his office hours at eight in the morning in the hope that no students would ever come.

[38] As a long-time beneficiary of the present arrangements, I am not advocating these changes.

[39] These ideas were developed at greater length in my unpublished utopia *The Fall and Rise of the American Academic Establishment: The Revolution of 1960–2020*, written around 1970.

[40] On the other hand, they are, or at least regard themselves to be, underpaid. Hence, their true, or alleged, sympathy for the underdog.

IV   International comparisons

The urge to compare life in the United States and in the Soviet Union (or among other countries) is irresistible, and most students of comparative economic systems succumb to it. It involves methodological questions on which a vast literature exists. But on one aspect of the comparisons there is nearly complete agreement: whether they involve gross national product, national income, consumer expenditures, etc., they are made from the consumers' point of view.[41] Comparisons made by international tourists follow the same path. Indeed, how could it be otherwise, since a tourist, by definition, is 100 percent consumer. He (or she) does not take a job in a foreign country; if he does, he stops being a tourist.

Even before leaving the airport, an American tourist in Moscow begins picking up consumer horror stories, and by the time he departs for home he is likely to carry a whole bag of them, for the entertainment of his friends (and students). Most of these stories are true; for the consumer, life in the Soviet Union is very hard indeed. No doubt, the American consumer is immensely better off. A Soviet tourist visiting the United States comes to the same conclusion. He must be so overwhelmed by the fantastic quantity and variety of goods (including food) in our stores as to never be the same person again.

What about American and Soviet producers, or rather workers, since no capitalists are supposed to exist in the Soviet Union? Curiously enough, their welfare is usually excluded from these comparisons. Tourists do not get the information, and economists, even if they do, are at a loss to know what to do with it. Now, I do not claim that a Soviet worker, as a worker, is definitely better off than his American counterpart, but I do insist that the following symbolic inequality holds:

$$\frac{\text{Welfare of an American consumer}}{\text{Welfare of an American worker}} > \frac{\text{Welfare of a Soviet consumer}}{\text{Welfare of a Soviet worker}}$$

Surely, a comparison based only on the numerators of these fractions biases the result in our favor. Unfortunately, I do not know how to quantify this bias any better than my colleagues do. What is the value of job security or of absence of tension on the job?

If this bias works in our favor, there are a few others acting in the opposite direction. The low quality of Soviet merchandise and the lack of variety are well known, as is the excessive amount of time spent on

---

[41] This problem was recognized by Abram Bergson: "...A comparison of the total market value of the consumers' goods produced in the rival systems...already implies the acceptance of the principle of consumers' sovereignty." (Bergson, op. cit., p. 236.)

shopping.[42] What is less well known is the frequency with which Soviet shoppers have to accept a less satisfactory substitute because the desired object is not available.[43] How many percentage points could we add to our conventional measures of aggregate output if we followed the Soviet example? Probably quite a few, by drastically reducing the quality and variety of goods and services. To some extent, this happens automatically when we approach a state of full employment; hence, the statistical gain achieved at that time exaggerates the true improvement in consumers' welfare. Full employment is supposed to be welcome by all; actually, it is a friend to producers and an enemy to consumers.

If and when socialism arrives, the classical struggle between workers and capitalists, so dear to Marx, will cease because there will be no capitalists left to struggle against.[44] But the conflict between producers and consumers will continue. In the end, the elephant's little tail may outlive his big head.[45]

[42] See Frederic L. Pryor, "Some Costs and Benefits of Markets: An Empirical Study," *The Quarterly Journal of Economics,* Vol. XCI (February 1977), pp. 81–102.

[43] In an old story (or cartoon) in *Krokodil* (The Soviet satirical magazine), a young couple wishes to buy a pram for their baby. "There are no prams," says the salesman, "why don't you take a suitcase instead?" Suppose they did. In no statistics known to me would the true character of this transaction be recorded. Kornai has remarked that "Rising living standards in suction [excess demand] economy give less satisfaction to the consumer since there is continuous tension due to unfulfilled aspirations." (From Thornton, op. cit., p. 109.)

Irwin L. Collier, Jr., has estimated that the East Germans lose the equivalent of 13 percent of their consumer expenditures because they cannot find the items they wish to buy. See his "Effective Purchasing Power in the Quantity Constrained Economy: An Estimate for the German Democratic Republic," *The Review of Economics and Statistics,* Vol. 68 (February 1986), pp. 24–32.

[44] But chances are that future Stalins and Maos will find some·other enemies to struggle against. If necessary, they will invent them.

[45] If the reader is interested in some quick and simple contrasts between the American and Soviet economic systems, here are a few examples: American folklore abounds in anecdotes about salesmen, but neglects purchasing agents, while in the Soviet folklore it is the purchasing agent (the famous *tolkach* or pusher) who plays a major (and often a nefarious) role. A famous American play is called "The Death of a Salesman," not "The Death of a Purchasing Agent." Our business schools offer a variety of courses on marketing, but I have not seen any on purchasing. I doubt if courses on marketing are offered in the Soviet Union. Do they teach purchasing? (Bishop makes similar points in his manuscript, op. cit., Book II, Chapter 3, pp. 41–42.)

Economic growth and productivity

PART II

Economic growth and productivity

On the measurement of technological change

An historical play about growth models might consist of three acts: in the first, labour, supported by an invisible chorus of capital, land and technological progress, holds the stage; in the second, capital and labour exchange roles. Finally, in the third act now being performed, labour, capital (and sometimes land) and technological progress appear on the stage together, with the first two (or three) reading from the script while technological progress holds forth the rest of the time.[1] So treated, this newcomer has done remarkably well. According to several recent American studies, it has been responsible for some 80-90% of the growth of output per unit of labour, the remaining 10-20% being all that capital (and land) could claim. True enough, this large contribution has not been made by technological progress alone; a whole group of actors consisting of technological progress in the narrow sense, economies of scale, external economies, improved health, education and skill of the labour force, better management, changes in product mix and many others have been involved. For this reason, the names given to this group have ranged from "output per unit of input," "efficiency index,"[2] "total factor productivity," "change in productive efficiency,"[3] "technical

Reprinted by permission from *The Economic Journal,* Vol. LXXI, December 1961, pp. 709-29.

Without sharing my errors with them, I am grateful for many helpful comments to A. Bergson, S. Chakravarty, S. Clemhout, P. Dhrymes, R. Eckaus, E. Kuh, L. Lave, A. Ølgaard, J. Schmookler, R. Solow and H. Wan.

[1] A sample from the first act is a study by Everett E. Hagen and Nora B. Kirkpatrick, "The National Output at Full Employment in 1950," *The American Economic Review,* Vol. XXXIV, September 1944, pp. 472-500, while the second act features the so-called Harrod-Domar models with all their ancestors, relations and offspring united by the use of one or more, usually constant, capital coefficients.

What about an epilogue banishing labour and capital into the chorus and leaving technological progress in sole possession of the stage?

[2] Jacob Schmookler, "The Changing Efficiency of the American Economy: 1869-1938," *The Review of Economics and Statistics,* Vol. XXXIV, August 1952, pp. 214-31.

[3] John W. Kendrick, "Productivity Trends: Capital and Labor," *The Review of Economics and Statistics,* Vol. XXXVII, August 1956, pp. 248-57, reprinted as National Bureau of Economic Research, Occasional Paper 53 (New York, 1956), to which further references are made. I am grateful to Mr. Kendrick and the N.B.E.R. for giving me a

change,"[4] all the way to "measure of our ignorance."[5] To emphasise the nature of this concept and to avoid loaded words, let us call it the "Residual."[6]

So far I have seen essentially four methods of expressing the Residual: (1) it is defined as the difference between the values of outputs and inputs in constant prices by Hiram S. Davis;[7] (2) it is the ratio between arithmetic indexes of output and of input, in the works of Schmookler, Abramovitz and Kendrick, which I shall call the SAK method; (3) the Residual is the ratio between an aggregate arithmetic index of output and inputs embodied in a linear homogeneous production function – the work of Solow; (4) finally, the Residual, or more correctly, its relative percentage rate of growth, is the weighted arithmetic average of relative changes in input coefficients between two points of time, derived by Leontief from his input-output studies.[8] This is a very rough and not a chronological description of the several methods, which differ in many other respects as well.[9] When applied to large, slowly growing aggregates they are likely to yield similar results, with or without my suggestions. But in rapidly growing industries and sectors and in problems involving integration and aggregation of industries both the differences and the arguments about them may be more significant.

manuscript of his forthcoming book on *Productivity Trends in the United States.* [Published in 1961.]

[4] Robert M. Solow, "Technical Change and the Aggregate Production Function," *The Review of Economics and Statistics,* Vol. XXXIX, August 1957, pp. 312–20.

[5] Moses Abramovitz, "Resource and Output Trends in the United States since 1870," *American Economic Review, Papers and Proceedings,* Vol. XLVI, May 1956, pp. 5–23, reprinted as National Bureau of Economic Research, Occasional Paper 52 (New York, 1956).

[6] It is indeed estimated as a residual after the contribution of other inputs to the growth of output has been accounted for. Many a time it will be tempting, however, to call it "an index of technological change."

[7] Hiram S. Davis, *Productivity Accounting* (Philadelphia, 1955). He also uses the SAK method (see below).

[8] Wassily Leontief *et al., Studies in the Structure of the American Economy* (New York, 1953), pp. 27–35.

[9] Nor is it a complete list of the many works in the field. For a brief historical note see Kendrick *op. cit.,* pp. 2–3. The SAK method was recently used by W. B. Reddaway and A. D. Smith, "Progress in British Manufacturing Industries in the Period 1948–1954," *Economic Journal,* Vol. LXX, March 1960, pp. 17–37; the Solow method by Olavi Niitamo, "The Development of Productivity in Finnish Industry 1925–1952," *Productivity Measurement Review,* No. 15 (November 1958), pp. 30–41; Odd Aukrust, "Investment and Economic Growth," *Productivity Measurement Review,* No. 16, February 1959, pp. 35–53; and by Benton F. Massell, "Capital Formation and Technological Change in United States Manufacturing," *The Review of Economics and Statistics,* Vol. XLII, May 1960, pp. 182–8. Solow himself was anticipated by J. Tinbergen, "Zur Theorie der langfristigen Wirtschaftsentwicklung," *Weltwirtschaftliches Archiv,* Vol. LV, May 1942, pp. 511–49, translated as "On the Theory of Trend Movements," *Selected Papers* (Amsterdam 1959), pp. 182–221.

My original aim was to argue about all four methods. But space has admitted only two of them: the Solow and the Leontief, plus the geometric index on which both are based.

I.   The Solow method

List of symbols (in order of appearance)

Y index of output in physical units
A Residual (sometimes interpreted as an index of technological change in the broad sense)
t time
L index of labour input in physical units
K index of capital input in physical units
α ratio of the value of labour input to the value of output in the base period
β ratio of the value of capital input to the value of output in the base period
$\bar{Y}, \bar{A}, \bar{L}, \bar{K}$ relative (percentage) rates of change of the respective variables per unit of time

Assuming that technical change, "a shorthand expression for *any kind of shift* in the production function,"[10] is neutral, Solow starts with the production equation

$$Y = A(t) f(L, K) \tag{4.1}$$

and with two traditional assumptions: (1) that $f(L, K)$ is linear and homogeneous, and (2) that factor prices equal their respective marginal products, he obtains the simple, and valuable for us, result that

$$\bar{Y} = \bar{A} + \alpha \bar{L} + \beta \bar{K} \tag{4.2}$$

and hence that

$$\bar{A} = \bar{Y} - \alpha \bar{L} - \beta \bar{K} \tag{4.3}$$

with $\alpha + \beta = 1$.[11] Since $\bar{Y}, \bar{L}, \bar{K}, \alpha$ and β can be derived empirically, $\bar{A}$, the rate of growth of the Residual, can be estimated.

---

[10] Solow, *op. cit.,* p. 312.
[11] Differentiating (4.1) with respect to time, he obtains

$$\frac{dY}{dt} = A \left(\frac{\partial f}{\partial L} \frac{dL}{dt} + \frac{\partial f}{\partial K} \frac{dK}{dt} \right) + f \frac{dA}{dt} \tag{4.3a}$$

The division of both sides by $Y = A(t) f(L, K)$ and the substitution of

$$\alpha = A \frac{\partial f}{\partial L} \cdot \frac{L}{Y} \quad \text{and} \quad \beta = A \frac{\partial f}{\partial K} \cdot \frac{K}{Y}$$

gives (4.2).

So far the exact form of the production function has not been specified, but should it be of the Cobb–Douglas type,

$$Y = AL^\alpha K^\beta \tag{4.4}$$

with constant α and β, and $\alpha + \beta = 1$, (4.2) and (4.3) can be obtained more directly by taking logarithms of both sides of (4.4) and differentiating them with respect to time. For reasons explained below and because, a humble mathematician, I am more comfortable with a specific function, the Cobb–Douglas will be used here.

A simple numerical example will help to understand why the contribution of the Residual is so large relative to that of capital. Let us take $\bar{L} =$ 1·5% per year, $\bar{K} = 3\cdot0\%$, while α and β are 75 and 25% respectively, as suggested more or less by the aggregate American data. In the absence of the Residual, $\bar{Y}$ would be a weighted mean of $\bar{L}$ and $\bar{K}$, and since labour's weight is much larger than capital's, $\bar{Y}$ would be much closer to $\bar{L}$ than to $\bar{K}$, equalling in our example 1·9%. Actually $\bar{Y}$ has approximated 3·5%, and the difference between 3·5 and 1·9% yields an $\bar{A}$ of 1·6%. The rate of growth of output per unit of labour input being 2% (3·5−1·5), the ratio of $\bar{A}$ to the latter is 80%, a figure not far from Solow's 87%. With a weight of only 25% (more or less) there is not much that capital can do. Even if $\bar{K}$ should double, other variables remaining the same, $\bar{Y}$ would increase only from 3·5 to 4·2%, less than a modest reward for a major effort. A doubling of $\bar{A}$ (I almost said, "of the rate of technological progress") would help much more.

Before we order our economic developers to substitute technological progress for capital accumulation, two attributes of the model should be recalled: (1) by its very nature, A is a Residual. It absorbs, like a sponge, all increases in output not accounted for by the growth of explicitly recognised inputs. It is not the input into technological progress even in the broadest sense; we do not as yet know the nature and the magnitude of inputs which would result in a given increment in A. (2) The magnitude of A is completely divorced from investment and capital accumulation. Capital merely accumulates; it does not change its quality, form or composition; *it does not serve as the instrument for the introduction of technical change into the productive process.* It is this kind of capital accumulation (wooden ploughs piled up on the top of existing wooden ploughs) that contributes so little to economic growth.[12]

---

[12] Needless to add, such a complete isolation of capital formation from technological progress is empirically impossible, and to the extent that our deflation methods of capital formation do not fully account for quality changes, K may be understated and $\bar{A}$ overstated. The same may be true of labour as well. It should be recalled, however, that we deal here not with the absolute magnitudes of inputs but with their relative rates of growth. A constant relative bias in estimating K or L will not affect the results.

Let us now compare the present model with the so-called Harrod-Domar variety based on a constant K/Y ratio or $\bar{K} = \bar{Y}$.[13] With this condition, (4.3) is transformed into

$$\frac{\bar{A}}{\bar{Y} - \bar{L}} = \alpha \qquad (4.5)$$

Thus the fraction of the rate of growth per unit of labour accounted for by the Residual (the rest being claimed by capital) equals labour's relative share in the output. Since this share is supposed to be rather large – from two-thirds to three-quarters and even higher – and the aggregate average capital coefficient is thought not to increase too rapidly, if at all, the Residual is bound to be a large fraction of the rate of growth of output per unit of labour. A falling capital coefficient makes this fraction even larger than α. In Solow's study the implied capital coefficient fell from 3·3 in 1909 to 2·1 in 1949, while α hovered around 67%, resulting in an estimate of $\bar{A}/(\bar{Y} - \bar{L})$ of some 87%. The authors of constant capital coefficient models did assume *some* technological progress, but they hardly suspected how very specific their assumption could become. The ease with which their secret has been revealed takes my breath away, and now we can all expect that the estimate of $\bar{A}/(\bar{Y} - \bar{L})$ of some 75% will soon occupy at least as hallowed a place in our economic mythology as a stable coefficient in the vicinity of 3![14]

But to return to the Cobb–Douglas with constant $\alpha + \beta = 1$. Another look at $L^\alpha K^\beta$ identifies it as the good old weighted geometric mean, and if both L and K are index numbers with a common base, which they should properly be, then $L^\alpha K^\beta$ is a geometric index of inputs, each weighted by its share in output in the base period. If output consists of several products, then common sense and consistency in aggregation calls for making Y their weighted geometric index as well, and the Residual the ratio between two such indexes. But it would be a bit strange to compare a geometric index of inputs with an arithmetic index of outputs, such as gross or net national product or some part of it, as has been

---

It is not implied here that these characteristics of the Residual are news. On the contrary, Solow is well aware of them. See, for instance, his paper on "Investment and Technical Progress," *Mathematical Methods in the Social Sciences,* edited by Kenneth J. Arrow, Samuel Karlin and Patrick Suppes (Stanford, California, 1960), pp. 89–104. This paper also contains additional sources on the subject.

13 Since the Cobb–Douglas function allows substitution between labour and capital, a constant capital coefficient should be interpreted in an historical rather than a technical sense.

14 A numerical table of $\bar{A}/(\bar{Y} - \bar{L})$ for given values of the other variables can be easily constructed. Imagine the awe inspired by an economic adviser who, within an hour of his arrival in a country new to him, will be able to tell the local experts what the approximate magnitude of their $\bar{A}/(\bar{Y} - \bar{L})$ has been!

repeatedly done, even though the numerical error in the aggregate was not large.[15]

Since we do not need here the properties of $L^\alpha K^\beta$ as a production function (elasticities of substitution, for instance), we shall treat this expression as a geometric index of inputs and claim the freedom traditionally afforded index makers to cut hard knots (such as the choice of weights) with eyes half closed. Like any index number, ours should be tailored for a specific purpose: to help in the understanding of growth processes of industries, sectors and economies. We should be free to take the economy apart, to aggregate one industry with another, to integrate final products with their inputs, and to reassemble the economy once more and possibly over different time units without affecting the magnitude of the Residual. The latter's rate of growth should, therefore, be invariant to the degree of aggregation and integration and to the choice of the time unit, be it a year or a decade.

II.　　The geometric index method

List of additional symbols

R　index of raw material input in physical units

$\bar{R}$　relative (percentage) rate of change of R per unit of time

γ　ratio of the value of raw material input to the value of output in the base period

v　weight (explained in the text)

y, l, k, r　values of the respective variables in the base period

Y_{ij}　index of output of the ith industry used by the jth industry as an input

y_{ij}　value of Y_{ij} in the base period

---

[15] I do not mean to imply that because a Cobb–Douglas function is geometric no arithmetic index of outputs produced with such functions should be made. Only that some results will not be invariant to aggregation and integration of industries. This need not deprive the arithmetic index of other desirable properties. For one, arithmetic indexes are much easier to construct because economic data are gathered in an arithmetic and not a geometric form (the components being added up rather than multiplied). Secondly, if given resources can produce outputs X_1 and X_2 in varying proportions, the weighting of each X by some base period price p and the maximisation of the function $p_1 X_1 + p_2 X_2$ is intuitively sensible, as is the familiar result $dX_1/dX_2 = -p_2/p_1$. In a geometric index the absolute magnitudes are replaced by their logarithms, and the prices by some shares v_1 and v_2. The maximisation of $v_1 \log X_1 + v_2 \log X_2$, with a given transformation function between $\log X_1$ and $\log X_2$ gives $(dX_1/X_1)/(dX_2/X_2) = -v_2/v_1$, a meaningful expression, yet not as intuitively understandable as the other one.

On the consistency in aggregation, see two papers by Lawrence R. Klein: "Macroeconomics and the Theory of Rational Behavior," *Econometrica*, Vol. XIV, April 1946,

Several less frequently used symbols are explained when introduced.
A subscript indicates that the variable belongs to a particular industry
rather than to the whole sector.

A given industrial process with a single output and a number of inputs
is expressed by the production equation

$$Y = AL_1^{\alpha_1}L_2^{\alpha_2}\dots L_n^{\alpha_n}K_1^{\beta_1}K_2^{\beta_2}\dots K_m^{\beta_m}R_1^{\gamma_1}R_2^{\gamma_2}\dots R_s^{\gamma_s} \tag{4.6}$$

where by Rule I each exponent is the ratio of the value of the corresponding input to the value of the output in some base period, and the sum of
these constant exponents equals one. With prices and quantities not infrequently moving in opposite directions, the system of weights given by
this Rule may receive a passing mark, but its arbitrary nature, like that
of any index number system of weights, should not be forgotten.[16]

Ideally, the output and each input is an index of physical units, such
as tons, man-hours, machine-hours, kilowatt-hours, etc., with a common base period. No distinct inputs are merged unless they are always
proportional to each other (though sub-indexes can be made). Otherwise
even two machines, similar in all respects but of different vintage, are
kept apart, and so are different kinds of labour and of raw materials.
Since most available statistics, even if detailed, are arithmetic aggregates
(obtained by *adding* and not by *multiplying* their components), our ideal
requirements will be far from satisfied, and we are likely to end up with
a geometric mean of arithmetic indexes supported by the hope that, the
same procedure being used on the input and output sides (see Part III,
Section 4), the resulting errors will cancel out, at least to some extent.

Of the several kinds of input, raw materials look most tractable because they are usually purchased outside (of the firm) in ordinary physical units.[17] So is direct labour paid by the hour, except for overtime
(perhaps this should be treated as a separate kind of labour) and fringe
benefits. Managerial labour input is harder to measure (what do hours

pp. 93–108, and "Remarks on the Theory of Aggregation," *ibid.*, October 1946, pp. 303–
12, reprinted as Cowles Commission Papers, New Series, Nos. 14 and 19. Judging from
Solow's paper on "The Production Function and the Theory of Capital," *The Review of
Economic Studies*, Vol. XXIII, 1955–56, pp. 101–8, the aggregation problem has not
escaped him.

16 For additional implications of Rule I see Part III, Section 1. Once the physical series of
inputs and outputs have been obtained – the major part of the job – the remaining computations are sufficiently simple to allow experiments with different sets of weights and
with periodic changes in weights (a chain index).

17 Raw materials used in a single industrial process may be outputs of another process in
the same firm. If detailed data are not available it is still possible to estimate the Residual
for the whole firm by using the integration and aggregation procedures discussed below.

mean here?), and its compensation (which includes bonuses, stock options and the like) is complex. In non-incorporated business there is the perennial problem of the division of income between owner's wages and profits. The worst problems are created by capital input and its compensation. Ideally, each machine and building should be rented and paid for by the hour of actual use. In reality capital is usually owned, recorded in value terms and assigned not costs but profits (including interest), not necessarily tied to its use. So we may have to get along with value estimates of large sets of capital assets in some constant prices, with a possible adjustment for under-utilisation, while profits are somehow allocated among the different kinds of assets to set their respective weights.[18] But what about selling and advertising expenses, taxes and depreciation charges? The first two should probably be treated like any other inputs, unless the study is concerned with the production activities of the firm only.[19] Depreciation will be discussed below (see pp. 57–58, 64–65, 69), while for taxes no reasonable treatment is in sight because of the impossibility of identifying the input of government services into a given firm or industry. Perhaps corporate income taxes should be retained in gross profits while all other taxes are simply excluded from the value of output in the base period, though different procedures could be defended just as well.[20]

Assuming that all these qualifications (and yet more to come in Part III) do not destroy the reader's curiosity completely, we shall now consider the following problems: (1) the treatment of raw materials, and (2) of

[18] Whether capital, and also labour and other inputs, should be adjusted for under-utilisation depends on the meaning to be attached to the Residual. It can reflect the efficiency of the utilisation of all resources available or only those actually used. For a firm or an industry the second meaning makes more sense, but for the economy as a whole, and particularly for international comparisons, such as between the United States and the U.S.S.R., both meanings are of interest. The rate of growth of the Residual will not reflect the presence of unemployed resources, however, if their fraction of total resources remains unchanged.

This allocation of profit really refers to fixed capital, raw materials being treated as separate flow inputs. But it seems proper to assign a part of the profit to inventories of raw materials and finished goods as the necessary cost of holding them. In wholesale and retail trade this adjustment may be quite important. Needless to say, profits in the base period should be as "normal" as possible. See also note 24.

[19] I would hesitate to exclude these, or for that matter any other, expenses on the ground that their presence implies their necessity. On the other hand, there are no objections to deriving a Residual for any industrial process or a department of a firm.

[20] The exclusion of corporate taxes could be justified on the ground that ideally the share of capital should consist of rental payments only. But the magnitude of the latter depends on the interest rate used (and the longevity of capital), and that can be gross or net of taxes. (See also note 24.) Perhaps state and local taxes should be treated as payments for more identifiable services, while federal taxes are excluded because of the prevailing nature of federal activities, *i.e.,* defence. In some industries, such as road haulage, the treatment of government services – highways – can strongly affect the Residual.

depreciation; then (3) the more interesting questions of aggregation and integration among firms, industries and economic sectors.

1. *The treatment of raw materials*

It is common in studies of this kind to exclude raw materials from both sides of the production equation, presumably in order to avoid double counting. Then the full production equation (with one kind of labour, capital and raw material),

$$Y = AL^\alpha K^\beta R^\gamma \tag{4.7}$$

is replaced by

$$Y' = A'L^{\alpha'}K^{\beta'} \tag{4.8}$$

where Y' is an index of value added in real terms, and $\alpha' = \alpha/(1-\gamma)$, and $\beta' = \beta/(1-\gamma)$. Thus R is given a weight of zero, and its former weight is assigned to L and K in proportion to their former weights. It is obvious that in the general case $A' \neq A$, and it will be shown in Part IV that, subject to a proper definition of Y', $A' > A$.[21]

Thus the exclusion of raw materials from both sides of the production equation exaggerates the Residual, or more correctly, results in a Residual with a different meaning. At this stage my preference is for A: we are interested in the Residual (it would be convenient to say here "technological progress") involved in the production, say, of shoes made from leather by labour and machinery with the help of electric power. The output of such a firm or industry is clearly shoes, familiar physical objects, and not shoes lacking leather and made without power. Leather and power are inputs not less essential than, and not inherently different from, labour or machinery, and as far as the danger of double counting is concerned, ways will be found (see below) for dealing with it. But let us not prejudge the issue: a use for A' will yet be found in Part IV.

2. *The treatment of depreciation*

There are three questions here: whether gross or net terms are more appropriate for expressing: (1) the stock of capital; (2) the output of a single firm or industry; and (3) the capital formation of the economy.

(1) *The stock of capital:* In the ideal case the problem is absent because capital of each vintage is treated as a separate input. When the value of

---

[21] On the statistical aspects of this problem see Zvi Griliches, "Specification Bias in Estimates of Production Functions," *Journal of Farm Economics,* Vol. XXXIX, February 1957, pp. 8–20.

the capital stock in some constant prices is used instead it should be gross or net of depreciation, depending on the relation between the productive qualities of capital and its age. This may vary among different countries, industries and kinds of assets. In the absence of relevant information, some deduction from the value of the gross stock of capital should be made, though I suspect that, at least in the advanced countries, it should be below conventional depreciation, heavily weighted as the latter is with tax considerations.[22]

(2) *The output of a firm or industry:* A rental payment for the use of capital consists of depreciation and interest, or profit.[23] This also is its cost when it is owned by the firm, the form of ownership being irrelevant.[24] This cost is similar to that of raw materials, and its retention in the production equation is based on the same grounds (see above). Its exclusion will likewise overstate the Residual, or rather change its meaning. More about it will be said in Parts III and IV.

(3) *Capital formation:* But from that it does not follow that all fixed capital formation, essentially the output of construction and machine-building industries, should be treated as a final product. To this we shall also return in Parts III and IV.

3.   *Aggregation and integration*

The purpose of this section is to work out a method, to be called Rule II, making the Residual invariant to aggregation and integration of processes,

---

[22] The difficulties may be smaller than they look, because all we need are the rates of growth of the several kinds of capital, not their absolute magnitudes. In the so-called seasoned industries the ratio of net to gross capital stock is likely to be fairly stable; hence they grow at similar rates. Elsewhere, given the rate of growth of either gross or net stock, the other can frequently be deduced.

[23] Perhaps more correctly, of depreciation, interest and profit, but no distinction is made in this paper between interest and profit.

[24] If a firm has assets with different longevities the allocation of gross profit among them in proportion to their values may be a poor approximation to their respective costs, because for some assets depreciation charges can be relatively more important than for others. It seems better to allocate net profit first and then add to it the corresponding "correct" depreciation charge. But an industry consisting of a number of firms is likely to have a variety of net profit rates, and the use of our method implies that high profit rates mean relatively high capital costs, which need not be true. Perhaps a uniform profit, or more correctly, interest rate, should be used instead, as was done by Reddaway and Smith, *op. cit.* This, however, leads to a further complication that the sum of all costs may exceed or fall short of the value of output of specific firms, and besides, this uniform interest rate may depend on the level and manner of aggregation. Unfortunately, I do not see any general and simple way of separating the cost of using capital from profit.

firms, industries and sectors. The following relations may exist among industries (or processes, or firms) comprising a given sector:

(1) All industries produce final goods only, in the sense that all goods are disposed of outside the sector. The finality of a good depends on the definition of the sector. Thus leather is a final good for the leather industry, but not for manufacturing.

(2) The whole output of one industry is used as an input by another industry in the same sector.

(3) A part of an industry's output serves as an input for another industry in the same sector, but not vice versa.

(4) An industry uses a part of its own output as an input.

(5) Industries use parts of each other's outputs (including their own) as inputs – a mutual input–output relationship.

Case (1). Simple aggregation: final goods only: Let the sector consist of two completely integrated industries producing final goods only

$$Y_1 = A_1 L_1^{\alpha_1} K_1^{\beta_1} \quad \text{and} \quad Y_2 = A_2 L_2^{\alpha_2} K_2^{\beta_2} \tag{4.9}$$

To aggregate these industries we must decide on: (1) the nature of the weights, and (2) the manner of their use. The first choice is simple, because the three weights suggested by reason and/or convention – the value of each industry's output, the value of its final product and its value added – are identical here (in a given base period).[25] Hence *by our new Rule II* their weights are

$$v_1 = \frac{y_1}{y_1 + y_2} \quad \text{and} \quad v_2 = \frac{y_2}{y_1 + y_2} \tag{4.10}$$

where (as indicated in the List of Symbols) each y indicates the value of the corresponding Y in the base period. Applied to geometric indexes, these weights are used as exponents: both sides of each production equation are raised to the power of the corresponding weight and the two expressions are *multiplied* by each other.[26] It is then found that $\bar{A}$, the rate of growth of the Residual for the whole sector, is

$$\bar{A} = v_1 \bar{A}_1 + v_2 \bar{A}_2 \tag{4.11}$$

---

[25] Reason and/or convention may, of course, suggest other weights. Our criterion is invariance of the Residual to integration and aggregation, but the uniqueness of our set of weights has not been proved.

[26] Alternatively, each equation could be first expressed in terms of logarithms or relative rates of growth, multiplied by its weights and then added to the other. Obviously, the same procedure can be applied to any number of industries in a sector.

It is clear that arithmetic aggregation (addition) of the production equations would not give a consistent result. See above, note 15, and Klein, *op. cit.*

that is, the weighted arithmetic mean of the $\bar{A}$'s of its components, the relative shares of the value of output (or at this stage, of the value of final output, or of the value added) acting as weights.

Case (2). *Simple integration:* Let the sector consist of industry

$$Y_1 = A_1 L_1^{\alpha_1} K_1^{\beta_1} R_2^{\gamma_1} \tag{4.12}$$

producing final goods only, and a fully integrated raw-material industry

$$R_2 = A_2 L_2^{\alpha_2} K_2^{\beta_2} \tag{4.13}$$

By substituting (4.13) into (4.12) we form one fully integrated industry which comprises the whole sector, and by the usual process of taking logarithms and differentiating in respect to time we obtain

$$\bar{A} = \bar{A}_1 + \gamma_1 \bar{A}_2 \tag{4.14}$$

If R_2 used R_3 as a raw material, which in turn used R_4, and so on, all of which belonged to our sector, with corresponding weights of γ_2 and γ_3, etc., then

$$\bar{A} = \bar{A}_1 + \gamma_1 \bar{A}_2 + \gamma_1 \gamma_2 \bar{A}_3 + \gamma_1 \gamma_2 \gamma_3 \bar{A}_4 + \cdots \tag{4.15}$$

As

$$\gamma_1 = \frac{r_2}{y_1}, \ \gamma_1 \gamma_2 = \frac{r_3}{y_1}, \ \gamma_1 \gamma_2 \gamma_3 = \frac{r_4}{y_1}, \ \text{etc.}$$

$$\bar{A} = \bar{A}_1 + \frac{r_2}{y_1} \bar{A}_2 + \frac{r_3}{y_1} \bar{A}_3 + \frac{r_4}{y_1} \bar{A}_4 + \cdots \tag{4.16}$$

where each r is the value of the corresponding R in the base period.[27]

Suppose now that materials R_2 and R_3 still belong to our sector (cloth and yarn in manufacturing), but R_4 does not (cotton). Then we cannot integrate Y_1 beyond

$$Y_1 = A_1 A_2^{\gamma_1} A_3^{\gamma_1 \gamma_2} L_1^{\alpha_1} L_2^{\gamma_1 \alpha_2} L_3^{\gamma_1 \gamma_2 \alpha_3} K_1^{\beta_1} K_2^{\gamma_1 \beta_2} K_3^{\gamma_1 \gamma_2 \beta_3} R_4^{\gamma_1 \gamma_2 \gamma_3} \tag{4.17}$$

and the rate of growth of the Residual of the sector is only

$$\bar{A} = \bar{A}_1 + \frac{r_2}{y_1} \bar{A}_2 + \frac{r_3}{y_1} \bar{A}_3 \tag{4.18}$$

Now the value of the *final* output of the sector y_1 is different from the total value of its output $y_1 + r_2 + r_3$, and from its value added $y_1 - r_4$, while for each component the value of its output differs from that of its value added. So in order to obtain expression (4.18) without first integrating

---

[27] By definition, $\gamma_1 = r_2/y_1$, $\gamma_2 = r_3/r_2$. Hence $\gamma_1 \gamma_2 = r_3/y_1$, etc.

the components, and yet making the Residual invariant to the degree of integration, the following (still temporary) reformulation of Rule II is required: the rate of growth of the Residual for the whole sector equals the sum of the $\bar{A}$'s of the component industries, each $\bar{A}$ weighted by the *ratio of the value of the output of its industry to the value of the final product of the sector* (in the base period).

The sum of the weights of the $\bar{A}$'s $(1+r_2/y_1+r_3/y_1)$ is larger than one, this being the most unusual and important attribute of Rule II. It is intuitively reasonable, at least at this stage, that the $\bar{A}$ of the combined, say, garment–weaving–spinning industry, should be a weighted *sum* of the $\bar{A}$'s of the components, and not just their weighted *mean* (with weights adding up to one), particularly if, for a moment, we think of the Residual as an index of technological progress.

It can easily be shown that if the weights assigned to each industry consisted of the ratio of its value added to the total value added of the sector, or of the value of its output divided by the value of the total output of the sector, the aggregation of industries would not give a result consistent with that of (4.18).[28]

Case (3). Simple aggregation and integration: If one industry produces final products only, while the other final products and materials used by the first, the reader can easily ascertain that Rule II continues to hold.

Case (4). An industry using a part of its own output as an input: This may be a coal mine using some of its own coal as a fuel. Let us go back to Case (2) and assume that the raw materials become more and more similar to each other and to the final product, so that their production equations approach that of Y_1 as given by (4.12). Integrating them into Y_1 we will have a fully integrated industry with a production equation of

$$Y_1 = A_1^{1/(1-\gamma_1)} L_1^{\alpha_1/(1-\gamma_1)} K_1^{\beta_1/(1-\gamma_1)} \qquad (4.19)$$

---

[28] Going back to a sector consisting of one final-goods industry and one raw material as given in (4.12) and (4.13), value added weights would give us

$$\bar{A} = \frac{(y_1-r_2)}{y_1}\bar{A}_1 + \frac{r_2}{y_1}\bar{A}_2 \qquad (4.18a)$$

while value of output weights would result in

$$\bar{A} = \frac{y_1}{y_1+r_2}\bar{A}_1 + \frac{r_2}{y_1+r_2}\bar{A}_2. \qquad (4.18b)$$

Both are different from the correct result as given by (4.14). The value of output of a sector in the sense used here is rather meaningless because its magnitude depends on the number of the sector's subdivisions (a source of error in the Leontief method discussed in Part V). Value added weights give an inconsistent result here, but a valid one in Part IV, where they are applied to specially defined value added indexes.

while the rate of growth of the Residual (most conveniently obtained from (4.15)) becomes

$$\bar{A} = \bar{A}_1(1 + \gamma_1 + \gamma_1^2 + \gamma_1^3 \cdots) = \frac{\bar{A}}{1 - \gamma_1} \tag{4.20}$$

If our industry, coal-mining, is to be aggregated with another one, copper-mining, then by Rule II (which can be now applied) the weight assigned to the former is y_1, that is the output of its *final goods* in the base period, and not $y_1 + r_2 + r_3 + \cdots$, the value of its *total* output. This is important, and Rule II should be amended (for the last time) as follows:

The rate of growth of the Residual for the whole sector equals the sum of the $\bar{A}$'s of the component industries, each $\bar{A}$ weighted by the ratio of the value of its product *final to the industry* (that is, used outside of the industry) to the value of the product *final to the sector* (used outside of the sector) in the base period.

This formulation shows the logical symmetry of the Rule: both the numerator and the denominator of each weight are values of final products, except that the numerator is final from the point of view of the component, while the denominator is from that of the whole sector. As industries are aggregated into sectors (dairy and bakery products into food), the latter into larger sectors (manufacturing) and so on, the weights are adjusted accordingly.

Case (5). *Complex integration and aggregation: industries using parts of each other's outputs as inputs:* Let the sector consist of a coal mine

$$Y_1 = A_1 L_1^{\alpha_1} K_1^{\beta_1} Y_{21}^{\gamma_1} \tag{4.21}$$

and a power station

$$Y_2 = A_2 L_2^{\alpha_2} K_2^{\beta_2} Y_{12}^{\gamma_2} \tag{4.22}$$

where Y_{21} indicates power used by the coal mine, and Y_{12} coal used by the power station. The value of the output final to the mine in the base period is y_1; that of the power station is y_2; and the value of the output final to the sector is $y_1 - y_{12} + y_2 - y_{21}$. The direct application of Rule II (as modified in Case (4)) would give

$$\bar{A} = \frac{y_1 \bar{A}_1 + y_2 \bar{A}_2}{y_1 - y_{12} + y_2 - y_{21}} \tag{4.23}$$

To prove that Rule II continues to hold we must note that because our weights are constant in value terms, y_{21} is proportional to y_1, and therefore to y_2. Since the prices of Y_{21} and Y_2 are identical and both Y_{21} and Y_2 are index numbers with a common base period, Y_{21} is equal to Y_2. (In reality these conditions need not hold; hence this result, like all our results, will depend on the choice of the base period.) All that remains to do now is to substitute (4.22) into (4.21), and vice versa, obtain two industries using their own outputs as inputs and then apply the results of Case (4).

The order of aggregation: Strictly speaking, our aggregation tests of Rule II were for sectors consisting of only two industries. To show that Rule II holds for any number, we must establish: (1) that the Residual obtained by applying Rule II to the whole sector at once is identical with that derived from combining industries into sub-sectors, and sub-sectors into larger sectors, two at a time; and (2) that the Residual is not affected by the order of aggregation. Both proofs are not difficult and are omitted to save space.

III. Qualifications and afterthoughts

1. *The meaning of the weight system*

According to Rule I (see p. 55), the constant weight assigned to each input is its value input coefficient, *i.e.,* the ratio of the value of the input to the value of the corresponding output in the base period. Thus we have here an input–output system in *value* terms, as distinguished from Leontief's well-known input–output scheme with constant *quantity* input coefficients, and from the SAK method (see p. 50) with its fixed *prices*. To the extent that prices and quantities move in opposite directions, which is not uncommon, our method violates reality not more, and frequently less, than the other two, but even a friendly reality will seldom move prices and quantities exactly in the required fashion.[29] The defect of this assumption is revealed most frankly when an industry uses a part of its output as an input. The prices of both being identical, this implies a constant quantity input coefficient, so that no economies in the use of an industry's own input could arise.

If Rule I squeezes our data, so to speak, through a grill with vertical parallel bars (the columns in the input–output scheme), Rule II adds the crossbars. As noted in Case (5), since y_{21}/y_1 and y_1/y_2 are constant, y_{21}/y_2 is also constant. Thus the combination of Rules I and II implies that the value of output of a given industry, and (its prices to all users being identical) the quantity of its output, are allocated among its users in constant proportions. This applies to homogeneous labour and capital as well.

---

[29] It is assumed here that income or revenue elasticity is one. Perhaps other elasticities should be experimented with, as suggested to me by Edwin Kuh.

Makers of index numbers have been traditionally free to choose arbitrary weight systems, and my grill squeezes life out of time series probably no harder than other common economic instruments. Laments do not absolve a crime, but they may temper one's affection for any particular system of weights and encourage experimentation. Invariance to the degree of integration and aggregation, however desirable or necessary, is not the only important attribute of an index number.[30]

2.   Depreciation once more

It was argued in Part II that depreciation, being a partial cost of the use of capital, should be treated like the cost of raw materials, and that neither should be excluded from the production equation of a given firm or industry. Yet in a general aggregation of the whole economy raw materials used up in production are excluded from the final output (employed as the denominator of weights according to Rule II), while gross capital formation, a part of which is also used up in the productive process, would presumably be left in. And yet the distinction between raw materials and short-lived capital is arbitrary, and it can become troublesome

---

[30] Experimentation with a chain index changing its weights periodically, or with continuously varying weights, might be a solution. If the shares in the following production equation are functions of time (but $\alpha + \beta = 1$)

$$Y = AL^{\alpha}K^{\beta} \tag{4.23a}$$

then the usual procedure of taking logarithms and then differentiating in respect to time gives

$$\bar{A} = \bar{Y} - \alpha \bar{L} - \beta \bar{K} + \frac{d\alpha}{dt} \log \frac{K}{L} \tag{4.23b}$$

(with outputs and inputs being indexes with a common base). In practically all growing economies $\log(K/L) > 0$, because $\bar{K} > \bar{L}$. In the United States at least, $d\alpha/dt > 0$. Hence $\bar{A}$ from (4.23b) will be larger than the corresponding one with constant shares. In general, an increase in the weight of a slowly growing input (and hence a reduction in that of a rapidly growing one) increases $\bar{A}$.

When the number of inputs exceeds two, the effect of varying weights is somewhat more complex.

If we have two industries producing final products with subscripts 1 and 2 and with both the v's and shares being functions of time (but $v_1 + v_2 = 1$), the rate of growth of the Residual for the sector will be

$$v_1 \bar{A}_1 + v_2 \bar{A}_2 = v_1 \left(\bar{Y}_1 - \alpha_1 \bar{L}_1 - \beta_1 \bar{K}_1 + \frac{d\alpha_1}{dt} \log \frac{K_1}{L_1} \right)$$
$$+ v_2 \left(\bar{Y}_2 - \alpha_2 \bar{L}_2 - \beta_2 \bar{K}_2 + \frac{d\alpha_2}{dt} \log \frac{K_2}{L_2} \right) \tag{4.23c}$$

The main problem regarding the use of variable weights lies not in algebraic manipulations, but in the meaning and usefulness of such a system. Space does not permit its analysis here.

if the length of the time period is changed (from a year to a decade and vice versa, for instance).[31]

To solve this difficulty, it may be suggested that the output of capital-producing industries (essentially construction and machine-building) should be divided into two parts: (1) equal to capital used up in the economy (or a sector), to be treated as a raw material; (2) the remaining part, net capital formation, in one sense or another, to be included in the final output.[32] In effect, capital formation would be treated like inventories under the last-in-first-out method, as if a part of currently produced capital were used up in the productive process, while the existing stock lasted for ever. But as our capital, by assumption (see above, p. 52), merely accumulates without changing its form no new fantasies are involved.[33]

3.   *The treatment of increments in inventories as final products*

Suppose the base year situation of some material to be as follows:

	$	$
Beginning inventory	10	
Produced during the year	100	110
Utilised during the year		95
Final inventory		15
Increment in inventory		5

It would seem at first glance that $5 should be included in the value of the economy's (or sector's) final product without much ado. But it can be also argued that out of $95 worth of materials utilised during the year, $10 came out of the preceding year's output – a temporal import – so that the full $15 worth of final inventory – a temporal export – should be treated as a final product. If so, the total value of final products produced during the base year (the denominator of the weight system according

---

[31] Thus, automobile dies lasting about a year can be put into either category. If we accept a general, and not unreasonable, rule that assets lasting more than, say, a year should be treated as capital formation if our time period is a year, they should become raw materials if we deal in decades. Since short-term fluctuations in output can strongly affect the magnitude of the Residual, working with longer time periods may be quite helpful, and yet different $\bar{A}$'s can result.

[32] I am intentionally avoiding here the distinction between depreciation, retirement and replacement. Whatever comes closest to measuring the deterioration of capital is relevant here.

[33] This should be taken with a good dose of salt. And, of course, on the firm and industry level the vintage of capital must be recognised. One more remark on depreciation will be made in Part IV.

to Rule II) will be larger, and the aggregate Residual (*ceteris paribus*) smaller.

The first approach – the net inventory or last-in-first-out method – implies that an inventory is never, so to speak, used up. It is a permanent piece of capital (and should be so treated), to which further additions may be made, while decrements are subtracted from other final goods. This is the more traditional method, easier to handle, closer to the national product framework and it yields a Residual invariant to the length of the time unit.

The second – the gross or first-in-first-out inventory method – may be closer to the spirit of Rule II with its strict distinction between inputs and outputs, but it creates complications. For the concept of temporal imports and exports implies a temporal input–output relationship, so that a consolidation of time periods (from annual to biennial, for instance), like that of raw material and final product industries, will affect the annual rate of growth of the Residual and at times may make it larger than that of either year. This need not be wrong, but it may be inconvenient.[34]

This strict separation between inputs and outputs required by Rule II is not a happy attribute, but it applies only to the construction of the weight system in the base period. Once that has been done, inputs and outputs can be freely offset against each other.

4.   *Multiple counting?*

There are several methods of obtaining the Residual for the whole economy: (1) each industry is completely integrated, and the $\bar{A}$ for the whole economy is a weighted arithmetic mean of the $\bar{A}$'s of the component industries, the weights being values of final products = values of total outputs = values added in the base period. This laborious method requires that the economy be completely closed both in space and in time (if the gross inventory method is used).

(2) The second method computes the $\bar{A}$'s of the individual industries and aggregates them by Rule II. Even if suspect of multiple counting, this method gives the same result (under the same conditions) as its more respectable predecessor.

(3) The third method aggregates all industries by Rule II and emerges with aggregate indexes of output and of input, with the ratio of the former to the latter being the Residual. Both indexes are so gross as to be almost meaningless, but the cancellation of outputs used as inputs from

---

[34] For any given year the gross method, with its larger final product, yields a smaller Residual than the net one. Consolidation of time periods reduces this difference, and as the time unit expands the difference declines.

both sides restores normality and leaves on the output side the usual final goods, while labour, capital, land and spatial imports (with the net inventory method) remain on the input side. The sum of the weights of each reduced index being one, tradition is restored, but the aggregate Residual remains the same.

Though thus absolved of multiple counting, a system of weights based on the values of final products, which assigns such a heavy weight to retail trade, for instance, may still look suspicious. Yet the very fact that the ratio of value added to value of output in retail trade is small shows that materials purchased are resold with little change, thus making a large Residual rather unlikely. To weight this Residual with value added would penalise, as it were, retail trade twice. It is shown in the next section that when value added weights are chosen a different Residual must be used.

IV.   Geometric value added index

Value added weights are so deeply embedded in index-number construction that both duty and curiosity call for the derivation of the corresponding Residual and for a comparison of it with our A. As in Case (2) of Part II, let our sector consist of an industry

$$Y_1 = A_1 L_1^{\alpha_1} K_1^{\beta_1} R_2^{\gamma_1} \tag{4.24}$$

producing final goods only, and a fully integrated raw material industry

$$R_2 = A_2 L_2^{\alpha_2} K_2^{\beta_2} \tag{4.25}$$

The use of the value added method does not change (4.25), but (4.24) now becomes

$$Y_1' = A_1' L_1^{\alpha_1'} K_1^{\beta_1'} \tag{4.26}$$

where Y_1' is the index of value added in real terms obtained by some as yet unknown method, $\alpha_1' = \alpha_1/(1-\gamma_1)$, and $\beta_1' = \beta_1/(1-\gamma_1)$, and A' is the new Residual.

Since our sector is completely integrated, both methods should yield the same Residual for the sector as a whole. By Rule II,

$$\bar{A} = \bar{A}_1 + \gamma_1 \bar{A}_2 \tag{4.27}$$

Indicating the value added of the first industry in the base period by $y_1' = y_1 - r_2$, while r_2 remains that of the second, and weighting $\bar{A}_1'$ and $\bar{A}_2$ by $y_1'/(y_1'+r_2)$ and $r_2/(y_1'+r_2)$ respectively (which is a standard procedure), we find that

$$\bar{A}' = \bar{A}_1' \frac{y_1'}{y_1'+r_2} + \bar{A}_2 \frac{r_2}{y_1'+r_2} = (1-\gamma_1)\bar{A}_1' + \gamma_1 \bar{A}_2 \tag{4.28}$$

The equality of (4.27) and (4.28) results in

$$\bar{A}'_1 = \frac{\bar{A}_1}{1-\gamma_1} \tag{4.29}$$

It can be easily shown that the nature of the result does not depend on the number of raw materials involved, or on the number of integration steps (as when R_2 uses R_3 and so on).

Thus $\bar{A}'_1$ is a simple multiple of $\bar{A}_1$, and each can be readily computed from the other, provided of course that Y'_1 is correctly defined. The substitution of (4.29) into (4.26) defines

$$\bar{Y}'_1 = \frac{\bar{Y}_1 - \gamma_1 \bar{R}_2}{1-\gamma_1} \tag{4.30}$$

or

$$\log Y'_1 = \frac{\log Y_1 - \gamma_1 \log R_2}{1-\gamma_1} \tag{4.31}$$

At first glance, both expressions look strange. But if the logarithms are omitted for a moment we shall recognise in (4.31) the formula for the derivation of an arithmetic index of value added in base-year prices from the indexes of output and of raw material.[35] So Y' is an index of value added, but of a rather peculiar type. Its derivation is logical because the logarithm of a geometric mean is, after all, merely an arithmetic mean of the logarithms of its components. Yet I wonder whether an index of value added so defined has ever been used in problems of this type.

Derived from large aggregates, such as the American economy with relatively small spatial imports, A and A' will differ little, particularly if the net inventory method is used. But in smaller sectors, such as specific industries and firms where raw materials are important, the two measures can be far apart. Of the two, A seems to have a clearer meaning: it is derived from a production equation containing all identifiable outputs and inputs, without any arbitrary exclusions from either side. But this Residual is too absolute, so to speak; a small A may be simply caused by the "thinness" of the industry, that is by the small degree of transformation its raw materials undergo. The Residual A' is free from this defect, and

---

[35] Let X and M indicate the absolute magnitudes of a final product and a raw material, p and h their corresponding prices, subscripts 0 and 1 base and given year respectively, and X', the value added in real terms, be defined as $p_0 X'_1 = p_0 X_1 - h_0 M_1$. We are to prove that

$$\frac{X'_1}{X'_0} = \left(\frac{X_1}{X_0} - \gamma \frac{M_1}{M_0}\right) \Big/ (1-\gamma) \tag{4.31a}$$

The substitution of $\gamma = h_0 M_0 / p_0 X_0$ into (4.31a) gives the desired result after a few simple cancellations.

its use greatly simplifies aggregation and integration of industries, but the meaning of a Residual arising, say, from the production of shoes without leather is less easy to understand.[36] Perhaps it is best to think of A' as an A adjusted in a way for the "thickness" of the industry rather than as a Residual directly obtained from a peculiar value added index, though one's attitude may be merely a matter of convenience and habit.

Following the suggestion made in Part III, Section 2, regarding the treatment of depreciation as a currently produced input from the capital-producing to the capital-using industry, we can show by the method just applied to raw materials that the rate of growth of the Residual computed from "net of depreciation" data equals $\bar{A}/(1-\delta)$, where δ is the share of current depreciation in the value of the industry's output in the base period. Once again the logarithm of the index of the "net of depreciation" output of the industry is derived in the peculiar manner just described from the logarithms of the indexes of the gross output and of capital.

Perhaps I should add that the Residuals computed net of raw materials and/or of depreciation are based on the same assumptions as A is, and thus share both its sins and virtues.

V. Leontief's index of structural change

Leontief's method of measuring the structural change of an economy (or any part of it) suggested by him in 1953 was a natural by-product of his dynamic input–output scheme.[37] It consists of the following steps:

1. The absolute difference between the magnitudes of a particular input coefficient (in quantity terms) at two points of time (such as 1929 and 1939) is divided by the arithmetic mean of the magnitudes in order to obtain the *relative* change in the coefficient.
2. These relative changes in all input coefficients for a given industry or economy are aggregated, each change weighted by the ratio of the mean value of the corresponding input in the two periods to the sum of mean values of all inputs.[38]
3. Since most of the changes (at least the important ones) in the input coefficients are likely to be negative (showing a saving in

---

[36] The exclusion of leather might be justified by viewing the production process as "work" done on a given amount of raw materials. But electric power purchased outside is just as much a part of this "work" as labour is; yet the former is excluded and the latter is not from the usual definition of value added.

It should be noted that a large A or A' may be caused not by an industry's own efforts but by those of its suppliers.

[37] Wassily Leontief et al., *Studies in the Structure of the American Economy* (New York, 1953), pp. 27–35.

[38] Leontief's own formulation is as follows: "The total value (price times quantity) of the corresponding input items can appropriately serve as a measure of the relative importance

the use of inputs), it is convenient to place a negative sign before the index in order to make it positive.

Let the magnitudes of an input coefficient be q and q', and the values of the corresponding inputs x and x', in the beginning and in the end period respectively. Then the relative change in the coefficient is $[q'-q]/[(q'+q)/2]$, and the corresponding weight $[(x'+x)/2]/\sum_{i=1}^{n}[(x_i'+x_i)/2]$, n indicating the number of inputs in the industry or the economy.

In order to compare Leontief's index with our Residual, we shall replace his discrete terms with continuous ones. There are no restrictions on the selection of the base period in our method; hence Leontief's choice of averaging two periods, rather than selecting one, is fully acceptable. For convenience, I shall continue to use production equations of the same types as before, but Leontief's index does not depend on their particular form, except for the assumption that the sum of the values of all inputs (during the base period as defined) equals the value of the corresponding output.[39]

Case (1). *One industry producing final products:* Let its production equation be

$$Y = AL^\alpha K^\beta R^\gamma \qquad (4.32)$$

with input coefficients of L/Y, K/Y and R/Y, and $l/y = \alpha$, $k/y = \beta$ and $r/y = \gamma$ as the corresponding weights. Designating the relative rate of change of Leontief's index by $\bar{I}$, we have

$$\bar{I} = -\left[\frac{d(L/Y)/dt}{L/Y}\alpha + \frac{d(K/Y)/dt}{K/Y}\beta + \frac{d(R/Y)/dt}{R/Y}\gamma\right] \qquad (4.33)$$

as

$$\frac{d(L/Y)/dt}{L/Y} = \bar{L} - \bar{Y}, \quad \frac{d(K/Y)/dt}{K/Y} = \bar{K} - \bar{Y}, \quad \text{and} \quad \frac{d(R/Y)/dt}{R/Y} = \bar{R} - \bar{Y} \qquad (4.34)$$

$$\bar{I} = -[\alpha(\bar{L}-\bar{Y}) + \beta(\bar{K}-\bar{Y}) + \gamma(\bar{R}-\bar{Y})]$$
$$= \bar{Y} - \alpha\bar{L} - \beta\bar{K} - \gamma\bar{R} = \bar{A} \qquad (4.35)$$

Thus for one industry Leontief's index and our Residual are identical.

---

of the respective individual changes, if considered from the point of view of the system as a whole." He then adds that the weight is the mean value of the input, without specifically stating what the denominator of the weight is (p. 28). The interpretation given in the text seems to me to be fair; it was confirmed by a telephone conversation with the author.

[39] Leontief's index requires so few assumptions if it is interpreted in the same general sense as our Residual: to contain not only technological progress as such, but economies of scale, better management, etc.

Case (2). *Simple aggregation: two industries producing final products:* Let the sector consist of two industries

$$Y_1 = A_1 L_1^{\alpha_1} K_1^{\beta_1} R_1^{\gamma_1} \tag{4.36}$$

$$Y_2 = A_2 L_2^{\alpha_2} K_2^{\beta_2} R_2^{\gamma_2} \tag{4.37}$$

without any input–output relationship between them. By Leontief's rule the corresponding weights will be of the form $l_1/(y_1+y_2)$, $k_1/(y_1+y_2)$, etc., because the sum of the value of all inputs equals y_1+y_2. Following his rule and utilising the results of Case (1), we obtain

$$\bar{I} = -\left[\frac{\begin{array}{c}(\bar{L}_1-\bar{Y}_1)l_1+(\bar{K}_1-\bar{Y}_1)k_1+(\bar{R}_1-\bar{Y}_1)r_1\\ +(\bar{L}_2-\bar{Y}_2)l_2+(\bar{K}_2-\bar{Y}_2)k_2+(\bar{R}_2-\bar{Y}_2)r_2\end{array}}{y_1+y_2}\right] \tag{4.38}$$

Multiplying and dividing the first three parentheses by y_1, and the last three by y_2, we find

$$\bar{I} = \frac{y_1\bar{I}_1}{y_1+y_2} + \frac{y_2\bar{I}_2}{y_1+y_2} = \frac{y_1\bar{A}_1}{y_1+y_2} + \frac{y_2\bar{A}_2}{y_1+y_2} = \bar{A} \tag{4.39}$$

so that Leontief's index and our Residual are again identical.

Case (3). *Integration:* Let the first industry produce final products and the second raw materials used by the first:

$$Y_1 = A_1 L_1^{\alpha_1} K_1^{\beta_1} R_2^{\gamma_1} \tag{4.40}$$

$$R_2 = A_2 L_2^{\alpha_2} K_2^{\beta_2} \tag{4.41}$$

The integration of R_2 into Y_1 gives

$$Y_1 = A_1 A_2^{\gamma_1} L_1^{\alpha_1} L_2^{\gamma_1\alpha_2} K_1^{\beta_1} K_2^{\gamma_1\beta_2} \tag{4.42}$$

and the application of the results of Case (1) of this part and of Case (2) of Part II,

$$\bar{I} = \bar{Y} - \alpha_1\bar{L}_1 - \gamma_1\alpha_2\bar{L}_2 - \beta_1\bar{K}_1 - \gamma_1\beta_2\bar{K}_2$$

$$= \bar{A} = \bar{A}_1 + \frac{r_2}{y_1}\bar{A}_2 = \bar{I}_1 + \frac{r_2}{y_1}\bar{I}_2 \tag{4.43}$$

If, however, we do not integrate R_2 into Y_1, but aggregate (4.40) and (4.41) then, as given in Case (2), the result will be

$$\bar{I} = \frac{y_1\bar{I}_1 + r_2\bar{I}_2}{y_1+r_2} < \bar{I}_1 + \frac{r_2}{y_1}\bar{I}_2 \tag{4.44}$$

Thus Leontief's index is not invariant to the degree of integration. His method disregards the fact that an input–output relationship among industries produces a Residual, or an index of structural change, whose relative rate of growth is larger than the conventionally weighted sum of the $\bar{A}$'s or $\bar{I}$'s of the individual industries.[40]

This identity between the corrected Leontief's index and our Residual becomes particularly interesting when the diverse origins of the two concepts – an input–output matrix and a geometric index – are recalled. The latter method is less laborious, but at this stage at least, the changing input–output matrix is a more familiar and powerful analytical tool.

Any reader who has managed to get this far will undoubtedly sympathise with Schumpeter's reported remark that methodology is the last refuge of the scoundrel. My justification for the long journey into this swampy land lies in the conviction that further work on Residuals, defined in one way or another, will help in understanding the process of economic growth, and possibly not only that. As mentioned in Part I, the heavy weight usually assigned to the labour input in aggregate studies almost insures a close relationship between the rates of growth of the Residual and of ordinary labour productivity, and thus does not add much to our knowledge. But Residuals obtained from individual industries and sectors (and perhaps even from firms) and their comparisons in time and in space look more promising, however difficult the conceptual and statistical problems may turn out to be.

[40] Suppose a sector consists of shoes and leather, with equal $\bar{A}$'s (or $\bar{I}$'s) of 2% per year. Then Leontief's method would give a combined $\bar{I}$ also of 2%. Our Residual would be larger because the sector benefits from a Residual (may I say here "from technological change?") in the shoe *and* in the leather industries. But if leather was replaced by boots, both methods would give a combined $\bar{A}$ or $\bar{I}$ of 2%.

On total productivity and all that: a review article

John W. Kendrick's *Productivity Trends in the United States*[1] is a major addition to the long and honorable list of the National Bureau of Economic Research studies in American economic development, crowned (but let us hope, not terminated) by Simon Kuznets' recent *magnum opus*.[2] Like some of its weighty predecessors, Kendrick's is an impressive book: 630 pages long, with ten appendixes, 205 tables, and 25 charts. Some of its materials came from the Bureau's previous publications; others were derived by the author from a variety of sources. The result is a vast array of data for the American economy and for a number of industrial subdivisions over the 1899–1953 period that (like most of the Bureau works) will be used (and probably misused) by economists for many years to come. As required by tradition, I shall try to quarrel and to find fault with the author's work, but the total impact of all my comments will, I suspect, amount to little compared with the sheer accomplishments of this book. I can now understand how the puppy in an old Russian fable must have felt when barking at an elephant.

There are three subjects that a reviewer of such a volume might discuss: (1) the derivation of statistical data, (2) the methodological skeleton, and (3) the most significant findings. The first subject is beyond my knowledge and time; the third will be presented, like a dessert, at the end of what promises to be a rather tedious paper; and on the second I shall concentrate. The intricate and ingenious mosaic of the index numbers comprising the study is described in great detail. But what the book lacks, oddly enough, is a simple model showing the implications of the basic assumptions on which it rests. Even if obvious to the index-number specialists, they are worrisome to amateurs like myself. The airing of such

Reprinted by permission from *The Journal of Political Economy*, Vol. LXX, December 1962, pp. 597–608.

[1] A study by the National Bureau of Economic Research (Princeton, N.J., 1961). Unless otherwise indicated page numbers cited refer to this work. I am grateful for valuable comments to A. Ando, F. M. Fisher, N. M. Kaplan, L. Lefeber, and R. M. Solow, none of whom is responsible for the views expressed here.

[2] *Capital in the American Economy: Its Formation and Financing* (Princeton, N.J., 1961).

worries is usually a reviewer's golden opportunity, unfortunately marred in this case by the existence of another paper of mine.[3] While the latter deals with a geometric index and Kendrick's is an arithmetic one, there is a sufficient methodological overlap to make the writing of a paper, self-contained but not too repetitive, something of a task. If the reader is irritated by frequent reference to the other paper, he should at least be consoled by the relative brevity of this one.

I

"The story of productivity, the ratio of output to input," Kendrick starts his book, "is at heart the record of man's efforts to raise himself from poverty."[4] The productivity of labor has been the oldest and the most commonly studied variety, both because of the relative ease of deriving it and its welfare aspects.[5] The last two decades have seen a strong interest in capital productivity, or its reciprocal, the capital coefficient – the mainstay of certain growth models. There are also productivities of various materials, such as the quantity of energy obtained from a unit of fuel, or of metal from a unit of ore, or some aggregate measure of output divided by the material input. All these are partial productivities, in the sense that output is compared with only *one* input at a time, without an explicit recognition of the changes in other inputs. Thus a given rise in labor productivity may be caused by substitution of capital for labor, a rather familiar and hence less interesting case, or by the work of more mysterious and therefore more interesting "other forces," such as technological change broadly defined, economies of scale, better management, education, and so on. Kendrick's book is generous in providing conventional partial productivity data, but his main objective is to derive the productivity of labor, capital, and land (when relevant) combined. As the reader may already know from Kendrick's earlier publications, the result is striking: the growth of the combined inputs accounted for only about one-half of the rate of growth of national product from 1899 to 1957 and for even a smaller fraction during the latter part of the period.[6]

Similar results have been obtained by a number of other studies, different in their methods but usually not in basic assumptions. Some of them regress output on production functions that have become increasingly sophisticated. Others express input as a weighted mean or index of

---

[3] See Essay 4.
[4] P. 3.
[5] A rise in average productivity of labor will usually, but not necessarily always, be accompanied by a higher wage rate and standard of living.
[6] P. 62.

particular inputs (labor and capital) and compare it with output.[7] The latter is Kendrick's method and only it will be discussed here. But first we must define a few symbols.

List of symbols (more or less in order of appearance)

Y output of an industry in both physical and value terms (see below)

C arithmetic index of productivity (defined in the text)

w_0 real wage rate in the base period

i_0 real return to capital in the base period

L labor input in a given year (in physical units)

K capital input in a given year (in physical units)

α share of labor in the value of output in the base period

β share of capital in the value of output in the base period

A geometric index of productivity (defined in the text)

$\bar{Y}, \bar{L}, \bar{K}, \bar{A}$ relative annual rates of growth of the respective variables

R input of materials in a given year (in physical units)

h_0 real price of materials in the base year

C' value-added arithmetic index of productivity

C'' same, but more peculiar

The zero subscript indicates base year magnitudes. It is assumed that all prices have been divided by the price of output in the base year. Hence Y indicates both physical and value output in base year price.

Abstracting from the complex of the detailed index number problems which Kendrick had to face, we can express his production equation for a *fully integrated* industry with a single product as

$$Y = C(w_0 L + i_0 K), \tag{5.1}$$

with land (if any) being included in capital. The constant prices used as weights can be derived from any one period or can be an average of several. Kendrick uses quite a mixture, but for questions discussed here it is

---

[7] For a partial bibliography on this mushrooming subject see Essay 4. I do not know to whom the prize for the earliest attempt belongs, but Kendrick has certainly been one of the pioneers. His first paper, a part of his doctoral dissertation, on "National Productivity and Its Long-Term Projection," was presented to the 1951 Conference on Research in Income and Wealth and published in Vol. XVI of the National Bureau's *Studies in Income and Wealth.*

The most sophisticated paper that I have seen so far is that by K. J. Arrow, H. B. Chenery, B. S. Minhas, and R. M. Solow, on "Capital–Labor Substitution and Economic Efficiency," *Review of Economics and Statistics,* XLIII (August, 1961), 225–50. There is no danger of excessive simplicity in the future works in this field.

most convenient to use base (first) year weights.[8] If desired, all variables can be expressed as index numbers with a common base period, and weights expressed as factor shares:

$$\frac{Y}{Y_0} = C\left(\alpha \frac{L}{L_0} + \beta \frac{K}{K_0}\right). \tag{5.2}$$

The two expressions are equivalent, the choice being a matter of convenience. Kendrick prefers expression (5.2), but we will find (5.1) more useful because the basic assumption consists in freezing prices and not factor shares. The reader is aware that identical prices of each component in any two periods used as bases produce equal arithmetic indexes, while identical shares do not. Kendrick's index is defined as

$$C = \frac{Y}{w_0 L + i_0 K}, \tag{5.3}$$

or

$$C = \frac{Y/Y_0}{\alpha(L/L_0) + \beta(K/K_0)}. \tag{5.4}$$

Since the value of the whole product is absorbed by the inputs in the base year, C will start from unity and will usually increase with time; but retrogression is also possible.

Kendrick's index is then the average productivity of an arithmetic combination of labor and capital (the latter including land). But this is a clumsy and colorless name, and both Kendrick and others have been ingenious in avoiding it. Kendrick calls it "Total Factor Productivity," which is not the happiest choice.[9] The index has life and interest because the "other forces" have not been counted among the inputs. If some of them, such as investment in education and training, are included, C is likely to grow less fast. If we somehow manage to identify *all* the "other forces," C will never budge from unity and the index will be dead.[10]

On these grounds, and to emphasize that an index of this type absorbs everything left over by conventionally defined inputs, I have called it the "Residual" in Essay 4. But because this term has a different meaning in statistics, I am not very happy with it either, and shall call it here "Kendrick's index" or the "Index."

However tempting, it would be just as well not to treat the Index as a measure of efficiency, or even as an approximation to it, though Fabricant

---

[8] See pp. 10, 55, 284, and others. A few words about given years' weights will be said in the Appendix.

[9] For various names see Essay 4. The best name, "Measure of Our Ignorance," was coined by Moses Abramovitz.

[10] Economies of scale would presumably require a different production equation.

attempts to do so in his Preface,[11] while Kendrick tries to distinguish between "efficiency in the use of resources," which the Index is supposed to measure, and "economic efficiency," which it is not.[12] If efficiency is understood in the usual sense of a ratio of the actual to some potential output, or of the proximity to some optimum, clearly the Index measures neither, and no such comparisons (if they could be made at all) are attempted in the book. In the post-World War II period the Soviet Index has grown much faster than ours;[13] yet I am not quite ready to award the Soviets the efficiency prize. A fall in the rate of growth of the Index of a country or of an industry is not necessarily a sign of inefficiency: utilization of poorer lands or ores, or expansion of activities like services where the "other forces" have less room to play, may depress the Index and yet be economically justified. Nor is a rapidly growing Index in some industry a sufficient reason for congratulations: it may have been caused by a peculiar behavior of the industry's inputs or output. Thus the Index in electric power grew much faster than that in electric machinery presumably because of the better machinery produced by the latter and used by the former.[14] The high rate of growth of the Index in Other Transportation (trucking, airlines, and pipelines) may have been caused by the omission of government inputs (roads and airports) in the first two, and the increasing utilization of capacity of the pipelines.[15]

So long as the cost of the "other forces" is not accounted for, it is hard not to welcome a rapid growth of the Index like the fall of heavenly manna.

[11] See pp. xxxix–xlii. Discussing the productivity of labor alone, he says: "But if what is wanted is a measure of increase in efficiency alone - and it is efficiency on which we are concentrating here - the index of output per man-hour is deficient. A better measure, for our purpose, is one that compares output with the combined use of *all* resources" (p. xxxix). As stated above in the text, this scholarly triumph would almost obliterate the index.

[12] See pp. 17–18, 31, 34.

[13] Bergson's estimates for the 1950–58 period vary between 2.7 and 4.1 per cent per year depending on weights chosen. See his "Soviet National Income," in Abram Bergson and Simon Kuznets, *Economic Trends in the Soviet Union* (Cambridge, Mass., 1963), p. 6. For the same period, the American index for the private domestic economy, computed from Kendrick's Table A-XXII (p. 335) and its extension kindly supplied by him, grew at 1.6 per cent per year.

[14] The annual rates of growth over the 1899–1953 period were 5.5 and 2.2 per cent, respectively. See pp. 136–37.

[15] See p. 141. All this shows that the division of the honors between two or several industries with input–output relationships can be rather arbitrary. Kendrick confirms this by his expressed preference for the metallic content of ore rather than for the volume of ore dug out as a measure of output of mining (p. 42). He is also much worried about double-counting if quality improvements in capital are recognized (p. 35). Actually such improvements would increase the output of capital-making industries and the input of capital-using industries, thus increasing the growth of the Index in the former and reducing it in the latter. It is also likely that the growth of the aggregate Index would be reduced because of the faster growth to be expected in the stock of capital so defined.

But for the same reason we cannot yet compare the marginal productivities of a dollar spent on education and research and a dollar invested in physical capital, particularly if the quality of physical capital is by assumption unchanged. Similarly, it is premature to predict the future growth of national product by extrapolating the past rate of growth of the Index in the hope that no major changes in the "other forces" are in sight, as Kendrick does.[16] We simply do not as yet have a good understanding of the origin and nature of these forces.

II

The preceding comments apply not only to Kendrick's study but to the whole family of similar endeavors. Let us now consider the more specific aspects of Kendrick's method, such as his choice of the production equation, the variables, and their weights. Kendrick could easily justify his approach by an appeal to the tolerance with which index number standards, a mixture of arbitrariness and common sense, are usually treated. But he prefers to present the expressions (5.1) and (5.2) as production functions expressing a meaningful relationship between inputs and output (or outputs). This claim deserves an examination.

The constant prices chosen as input weights represent, or at least approximate, the respective marginal products. Little need be said about the implied assumption of purity of competition, not because it is true but because of the absence of a simple alternative. The implied assumption that the firm is in short-run equilibrium with respect to its use of labor can also be accepted, even if with some reservations. But for capital, the equality of its (value) marginal product with its price calls for a long-run equilibrium, a rather hazardous assumption in a study of economic growth. The treatment of capital will give us plenty of trouble later on. Suffice it to say now that Kendrick's price of capital is not a rental payment for the use of capital, nor the market rate of interest, but the average rate of return.[17] Since the average rate of return is apt to be high in expanding and low in stagnant industries, Kendrick's weighting of capital in each industry by its rate of return seems to be a step in the

[16] See p. 15. The same comment applies, though with less force, to Edward F. Denison's work on *Sources of Economic Growth in the United States and the Alternatives before Us* (Committee for Economic Development, Supplementary Paper No. 13, New York, Jan. 1962).

[17] See pp. 64–65, 91, 280. For government capital he uses the interest rate on government bonds (pp. 282–83). Since governments can hardly be said to maximize their profits (not to mention other complications), there is little ground for this assumption and it probably understates the marginal product of government capital.

right direction. At least I cannot suggest a reasonable alternative in the context of Kendrick's method.

That the arithmetic combination of inputs used in expressions (5.1) and (5.2) is not a good production function is of course well known. It assumes that the marginal products of the inputs are changed only by the "other forces" and always in the same proportion, so that their ratios remain constant and independent of the ratio of the quantities of the inputs, however fast capital may grow relative to labor. In fact, Kendrick found that the real income per unit of labor rose 3.7 *times* over the 1899–1957 period, while that of capital remained nearly constant (with only a 13 *per cent* increase).[18] To alleviate the defects of his production function, Kendrick changed his weights several times. The resulting chain Index suffers from the usual ambiguities of its family, but it differs surprisingly little from a constant weight one, presumably because constant weights produce effects in the aggregation of outputs similar to those produced in the aggregation of inputs.[19]

Kendrick might, however, have considered at least one alternative – the geometric index, where the weights are not prices but income shares. True enough, the labor share has increased from some 70 per cent in 1899 to 81 per cent in 1957, but the assumption of constant shares does not create as much trouble as that of constant relative prices.[20] Similarly, the negative correlation existing between the rate of growth of particular outputs and their prices should make the value shares of the several industries more stable than the ratio of their prices.[21] Yet the difference between the rate of growth of a geometric and an arithmetic index is quite small if the period is not long and the rates of growth of labor and of capital are not far apart.[22]

Over the long pull the arithmetic Index does give dubious results which the geometric does not (see the Appendix). The use of the latter may be

[18] P. 125. Real income per unit of capital reached a maximum of 124.8 in 1948 (with 1929 = 100) and then declined to 95.2 in 1957.

[19] P. 55.

[20] P. 121. See also Table A-10, p. 285.

[21] P. 54.

[22] With the annual rates of growth of output, labor, and capital being 3.5, 1.5, and 3.0 per cent, respectively, and a labor share of 80 per cent (capital's being 20 per cent), the geometric Index will grow at a constant relative rate of 1.7 per cent per year. The corresponding rate of growth of the arithmetic Index will *average* 1.68 per cent over ten years, and 1.66 per cent over twenty years. With given factor shares, the difference between the rates of growth of the two indexes is an increasing function of the rate of growth of the capital–labor ratio and of time.

I should add that because our data are gathered arithmetically (the components being added and not multiplied) a pure geometric Index cannot be computed unless the series are truly homogeneous.

justified on two additional grounds: (i) since our main interest seems to lie in the relative rate of growth of the Index, it may be just as well to use the rate concept all the way, that is, to combine both inputs and outputs geometrically; (ii) when derived from the expression

$$Y = AL^\alpha K^\beta, \tag{5.5}$$

the rate of growth of the geometric Index becomes

$$\bar{A} = \bar{Y} - \alpha \bar{L} - \beta \bar{K}, \tag{5.6}$$

a very simple expression, much easier to manipulate and experiment with than its clumsy arithmetic counterpart. For that matter, the relative similarity of the results of the two indexes (as qualified above) allows us to think in terms of expression (5.6) while actually working with (5.1) or (5.2).[23]

Putting this interindex rivalry aside, let us now turn to the content of Kendrick's formula. For the whole economy the output is expressed as net national, or rather domestic, product at factor cost.[24] Consistency apparently calls for expressing the output of individual industries in a similar manner, that is, as net value added. This leads Kendrick to the use of the stock of capital net of depreciation, and to exclusion of both the current depreciation and the cost of materials from both sides of the production equation. This is his *ideal* procedure. He does not always succeed and is forced by the lack of data to use an index of output gross of both materials and depreciation for a number of industries, but always in the hope that such an index will not greatly diverge from the desired one. When the divergence is thought to be important, the results are qualified. In any case, such an index of output is treated *as if it were net,* so that neither materials nor current depreciation appear on the input side.[25]

Like politics, empirical work is the art of the possible. Let us examine Kendrick's ideal method instead of complaining about his deviations from it.

The treatment of labor is relatively simple. Kendrick presents two estimates of aggregate labor input: an unweighted sum of man-hours worked, and a sum weighted by the wage rate in each industry.[26] He prefers the latter, as recognizing differences in labor quality, at least on the interindustrial level. This choice is supported by an interesting table showing considerable stability of wage-rate ranking of the several industries

---

[23] As Fabricant does on pp. xli–xlii, though without a proper explanation. For a more detailed discussion of the geometric index, see Essay 4.

[24] P. 28.

[25] See pp. l–li, 38, 114, 187.

[26] See pp. 34, 64–65, 252, 266.

over the whole period.[27] To the extent that interindustrial wage differences reflect characteristics not acquired by education and training, such as sex, physical prowess, and mental ability, Kendrick is clearly right; we may only suggest that in his next study intraindustrial differences be also considered. But some large, even if as yet unknown, part of wage differences arises from education and training. Their recognition implies the inclusion of *some* of the "other forces" among the inputs and thus changes the meaning of the Index.[28] Perhaps some day human capital will be treated as a regular input, but until this becomes possible Kendrick's procedure can be looked upon as a partial substitute. For connoisseurs of index purity, data on unweighted man-hours are provided. Over our whole period the unweighted index of labor productivity grew at 2.4 per cent per year, while the weighted one grew at 2.0 per cent, the difference being caused by the shift of labor to higher paying industries.[29]

The treatment of capital raises very nasty problems because (i) it is usually not hired but purchased, (ii) it lasts long, and (iii) its cost is ambiguous.

All these difficulties could be avoided if capital were rented by the hour or the month as labor is.[30] Presumably an old machine would command a lower rental than a similar new one. Hence Kendrick's use of net rather than gross stock of capital is a proper, even if only an approximate, adjustment. The rental will obviously include current depreciation and some interest or profit, depending on market conditions. Clearly, current depreciation is a part of the cost of using capital, as depreciation of human skill is undoubtedly an implicit element of the wage. Yet Kendrick's *ideal* excludes depreciation from both sides of the production equation.[31] When the Index is larger than one (its rate of growth being positive) the subtraction of an equal magnitude from both the numerator and denominator of C (see expression [5.3]) increases the fraction; the opposite is true when C is less than one. Thus in both cases the *absolute* rate of growth of the Index is exaggerated.[32] For that matter, a consistent application of Kendrick's method would exclude the whole rental payment, interest and all, as an input purchased from the capital-leasing industry. When

---

[27] Table 54, p. 197. The similarity in the ranking of wage rates by industries among several countries was pointed out by Stanley Lebergott in "Wage Structures," *Review of Economic Statistics,* XXIX (November, 1947), pp. 274–85.

[28] This is merely a matter of degree. In spite of all his efforts some quality changes must have crept into the measurement of capital and output.

[29] P. xxxix.

[30] It would be strange to rent inventories, but not being subject to depreciation they do not create so much trouble.

[31] See pp. 9, 24, 112, 114.

[32] This remains true even if the indexes of output gross and net of depreciation are identical.

aggregated, the capital-renting and capital-leasing industries will be consolidated without affecting the total Index, but in the capital-renting industry taken by itself, the exclusion of capital cost will produce a rather strange result discussed below.

With depreciation being some 10 per cent or less of the national product and even a smaller fraction of the value of output of many industries, the exaggeration of the Index will be, roughly speaking, of a similar magnitude and hence quite small. It may be also offset by Kendrick's possible overstatement of the *net* cost of capital.

The retention of depreciation in the production equations of particular industries need not prevent us from excluding it from a national aggregate by treating a part of the current output of capital-producing industries as materials absorbed by capital-using ones.[33]

Now let us consider the meaning of capital cost. Like most workers in the field, Kendrick identifies the cost of capital with profit (net of depreciation but gross of interest), a residual left over after the payment of wages (and materials costs).[34] This implies a *capital* theory of surplus value (which Marx would not like): profit is derived not from a combination of all factors of production, and not even from all of a firm's assets, but only from its physical capital, such as buildings, machinery, equipment, inventories and the like (including land).

A more satisfying method would express capital cost as the sum or some other combination of depreciation and interest rate. But this would leave a positive or negative balance for the mythical entrepreneur. How will his input be measured? Who shall decide on the correct interest rate? Should it vary from one firm and industry to another, depending on risk and other conditions, or be the same in all?[35] However much a theorist may complain about Kendrick's neglect of these fine points, he would, I am sure, complain even louder if Kendrick chose some *particular* interest rate or even a set of rates. So having bravely looked into the problem's face, we will quietly pass on to other things.

[33] See Essay 4.
[34] See pp. 64–65, 91, 280.
[35] A uniform interest rate (net of depreciation) was used by W. B. Reddaway and A. D. Smith in their study of "Progress in British Manufacturing Industries in the Period 1948–1954," *Economic Journal*, LXX (March, 1960), pp. 17–37.

To add to all the other difficulties, there is an ambiguity in the very concept of the value of the marginal product of capital. Is it the increment in the value of the output caused by the use of an extra machine-hour, or that caused by the expenditure of an extra dollar on capital goods? If the price of a capital good falls, the value of its marginal product is unchanged if defined in the first sense, but it rises if defined in the second. Kendrick evidently uses the concept as the return to a dollar of constant purchasing power invested in capital goods.

The computation of the Index for a particular industry or sector, which forms the most interesting part of Kendrick's study, raises the problem of material inputs. To allow for these we need a slightly more complex production equation for a non-integrated industry, such as

$$Y = C(w_0 L + i_0 K + h_0 R), \tag{5.7}$$

and therefore

$$C = \frac{Y}{w_0 L + i_0 K + h_0 R}. \tag{5.8}$$

By eliminating the cost of materials in constant prices from both sides of the production equation, Kendrick transforms these expressions into

$$Y = C'(w_0 L + i_0 K) + h_0 R, \tag{5.9}$$

and

$$C' = \frac{Y - h_0 R}{w_0 L + i_0 K}, \tag{5.10}$$

respectively, and thus implicitly assumes that while the marginal products of labor and capital are increased by the "other forces" (when $C > 1$) in the same proportion, the marginal product of materials remains constant.[36] Just as in the case of depreciation dealt with above, the subtraction of the cost of materials from both the numerator and denominator of (5.8) increases C when $C > 1$ and reduces it when $C < 1$, and thus increases the absolute rate of growth of the Index. All this need not be wrong, but it would be nice to have a better justification for this procedure than the fear of double counting. As shown in the Appendix this can be avoided without excluding materials, though the required weighting system is rather complicated.

On the national level the problem almost disappears because the consolidation of industries obviously eliminates their input–output relationships. Imports from other countries form the only exception, but for the United States their relative magnitude is small. For specific industries Kendrick's preference for C' over C can make a substantial difference. Unfortunately, we cannot decide on a priori grounds whether the marginal product (that is, the real price) of materials stayed constant or changed,

[36] See pp. 29, 38, 45–46, 94–95, 99. As mentioned in the text above, this is his ideal method, which is seldom followed. In most industries output is expressed as an index gross of materials. But no materials appear on the input side.

The study of the Index (or the Residual) for a group of industries with input–output relationships is most interesting because of the cumulative effect which the indexes of the particular industries exert on the Index of the whole group. For a lengthy discussion of this subject see Essay 4.

and, if the latter, in what direction. The answer will vary among industries, periods, and types of materials. After all, most materials are outputs of other industries (like leather, yarn, steel, and power). If their real price remained constant or fell, expression (5.10) would be more appropriate; if it increased significantly, expression (5.8) would be a better choice. Since the prices of the several material inputs into a single industry may have moved in different directions the choice of the proper expression is indeed awkward.

There is another complication. If the behavior of the real price of a particular input is used as a criterion for its inclusion or exclusion from the production function, an excellent case can be made for the exclusion of capital, since as noted above its real price has remained almost constant. If capital were excluded, we would have

$$Y = C'' w_0 L + i_0 K + h_0 R, \tag{5.11}$$

giving a Kendrick Index of

$$C'' = \frac{Y - i_0 K - h_0 R}{w_0 L}, \tag{5.12}$$

which is merely an index of the real wage rate, surely not the aim of this great study!

The best escape from all these difficulties, it seems to me, is to treat expressions (5.1)–(5.4) *not* as a meaningful production function but merely as a simple and arbitrary arithmetic index of inputs divided into that of output, and not to ask too many questions. On this interpretation I do not see any reason why material inputs should be treated differently from labor and capital inputs.

This, however, is no simple solution because the aggregation of industries with input–output relationships requires a great deal of data which do not now exist and are hard to produce. The omission of materials may be the only practicable method but its cost is high. For capital, left alone with labor and assigned a modest weight, plays a minor role, and the Index imitates the movements of labor productivity (ratio of value added to labor input), the rank correlation by industries between the two measures of productivity reaching 94 per cent.[37] Hence the derivation of the Index does not make as great a contribution to our existing knowledge as could be expected, in spite of the great efforts which capital estimates require.[38]

[37] P. 155.
[38] Of course the Index will be of greater interest in industries with a heavy capital weight.

III

Let us now bury the hatchet and savor some of Kendrick's products. The book abounds in interesting and provocative (sometimes too provocative) findings. Some of them have already been mentioned; since a summary is given in Fabricant's Preface we can be brief here.

1. There has been a marked acceleration of the rate of growth of all three productivities – the Index, labor, and capital – since World War I. Now labor productivity might have increased because of reduced immigration and pulled the Index along with it, but why did capital productivity also increase? Traditionally, it should have been reduced by the substitution of capital for labor. Did the relative shortage of labor make us so cost-conscious as to result in the saving of capital as well?

2. While the Index in the private domestic economy grew most rapidly in 1948–53 (at 2.7 per cent per year), its performance since has been disappointing.[39] From Kendrick's additional table, I obtained the corresponding rate of only 1.8 per cent during 1953–60. It is true that 1960 was not a full-employment year, but an increase of the 1960 output by 5 per cent *without any corresponding increase in inputs* (which is not plausible) would have raised this rate to only 2.5 per cent. This result is inconclusive, and we will have to wait for a full-employment year to find the potential rate of growth of the Index in recent years.

3. There was a positive correlation between the rate of growth of output and that of the Index, both by periods and by industries. This of course is not surprising: a rapid growth of the Index in any industry reduces the prices of its output (the correlation between the logarithms of the Index and of the unit value of output, 1953 relative to 1899, was −87 per cent) and thus stimulates sales; a rapidly growing output allows a fuller utilization of capacity, economies of scale, and the introduction of better methods. But it is interesting that there was also a positive correlation between the rate of growth of the Index and that of employment.[40]

4. Similarly, the Index grew much faster during the upswing phase of the business cycle than during the contraction. It is tempting to conclude as Kendrick does that the milder the fluctuations the faster will be our growth (even though Schumpeter might have dissented), and this may very well be true, but the cyclical behavior of the Index may have been strongly affected by differences in capacity utilization.[41]

[39] Pp. 136–37.
[40] See pp. 134, 184–85, 201–3, 209–10.
[41] See pp. 12, 67–68, 73.

5. There has been a remarkably small increase in productivity, this time of labor, in the construction industry – only 1.1 per cent per year over the period 1899–1953. Either our methods of deflating its output are strange or there is something strange about that industry.[42]

6. As already noted, there has been a persistent and sharp fall in the share of capital in national income – from 36 per cent in 1899–1909 to 21 per cent in 1948–53.[43] Perhaps a part of this fall could be explained by the treatment of depreciation and capital gains under our income tax laws, but surely not all. Fabricant suggests that since World War I there has been a substitution of intangible for physical capital. Even though, according to Kendrick, real educational outlays per capita were increasing at only 1.6 per cent per year (which he regards as an understatement), Fabricant's suggestion, if true, has far-reaching implications.[44] If land was the most important means of production before the Industrial Revolution, and physical capital in the subsequent period, will this intangible capital take their place? Will the scientist and the engineer inherit the political power of the capitalist, just as the capitalist had wrested it from the landowner? The fact that outlays on physical capital are financed by business, while those on intangible capital are financed mostly by government and philanthropy, lends additional significance to this question.

7. I have saved for the end the most interesting question: what are the causes of the growth of the Index? Kendrick makes some remarks about the beneficial effects of individual initiative, freedom, and the like.[45] This is very touching, but, as mentioned above, the Russians have managed to achieve quite a respectable rate of growth of the Index, much higher than ours in recent years, without possessing these virtues. So have the Germans and the Japanese, whose democracies are not supposed to be as perfect as ours.[46] The relation between social and political conditions and the growth of productivity is anything but simple.

One might expect a strong positive correlation between the rate of growth of the Index and that of capital, on the grounds that investment serves

---

[42] See pp. 152–53, and also an interesting paper by R. A. Gordon on "Differential Changes in the Prices of Consumers' and Capital Goods," *American Economic Review*, LI (December, 1961), 937–57.

[43] Table A-10, p. 285. Similar results were obtained by Irving B. Kravis for the period 1900–1909 to 1949–57, though between 1929–38 and 1949–57 the property share in national income remained constant or rose slightly (depending on the method used) (see his "Relative Income Shares in Fact and Theory," *American Economic Review*, XLIX [December, 1959], 917–49).

[44] See pp. xlvii–xlviii, 106.

[45] See p. 178.

[46] The rate of growth of the German and Japanese Indexes was estimated to have been 3.6 and 3.7 over the 1950–59 and 1951–59 periods, respectively (see Essay 6).

as a vehicle for the introduction of technological progress.[47] Kendrick tried, however, to exclude quality changes from his capital stock estimates, and the resulting correlation between the Index and capital input, 1953 relative to 1899, turned out to be positive but not strong (36 per cent). [48] Several attempts made by Nestor E. Terleckyj and cited by Kendrick correlated the rates of growth of the Index in manufacturing with (1) extent of competition, (2) rate of change of output, (3) amplitudes of cyclical fluctuations, and (4) ratios of research and development outlays to sales, or of research and development personnel to total man-hours worked. The extent of competition had no effect at all; the other three (or four) measures gave mildly positive results. The field is still wide open.[49]

These are just a few examples of Kendrick's results. There are many others. The book is a treasure chest of data and suggestions for future explorations.

Appendix on arithmetic measurements of productivity

Additional symbols

Symbols y, l, k, and r are the *values* of the respective variables in base year prices.

$z = l + k + r$ = total cost of inputs in base year prices.

v_1 and v_2 are weights.

Subscript 1 pertains to final goods industry; and subscript 2, to one producing materials; r_2 stands for the output of materials produced by the second industry and used by the first.

I   *The concept as a difference*

A simple absolute measure suggested by Hiram S. Davis[50] is defined by the expression

$$B = y - l - k - r. \tag{5.1a}$$

As any item can be moved from one side of the equation to the other with a change in sign, materials and/or depreciation or even the total

---

[47] On this see the interesting paper by Robert M. Solow, "Technical Progress, Capital Formation, and Economic Growth," *American Economic Review Papers and Proceedings*, LII (May, 1962), 76–86.

[48] See Chart 25, p. 215.

[49] Pp. 179–88. The most provocative study on the subject is that by Denison, *op. cit.* I am sure he will agree that, like many good books, it raises more questions than it answers.

[50] *Productivity Accounting* (Philadelphia, 1955).

cost of capital can be included or excluded without affecting the magnitude of B. No difficulties are created by aggregation and integration of industries. We should simply fish out all the B's from every nook and cranny of the sector of the economy and *add* them together. No weights are needed because B, an absolute number, already contains weights.

The concept B should be interpreted, I presume, as a social profit in base year prices derived by the society from the working of the "other forces." But for comparison among industries, countries or periods B will presumably have to be divided by something, such as the value of the final output, or the value added, resulting in a ratio of one kind or another, some of which are discussed below.

It will hardly make sense to compute the relative rate of growth of B because in the base period $B = 0$. This operation is more appropriate to an exponential rather than to a linear world, and in the former B will hardly feel at home: as a difference between two or several exponentials it will in time be dominated by the fastest growing one. In a linear world B will stay happily linear and its absolute rate of growth will be the difference between the absolute rates of growth of the values of output and of all inputs in base year prices. Since the passage of time will make the original base year prices obsolete, some chain index may be suggested.

II   *The index as a ratio of value of output to cost in base year prices*

As indicated previously, this Index is defined for a uniproduct industry as

$$C = \frac{y}{l+k+r} \tag{5.2a}$$

and is obviously not quite at home either in a linear or in an exponential world. If the values of output and of inputs are linear in time, C will gradually approach a constant. If they are exponential, the relative rate of growth of C will approach the difference (positive or negative) between the rates of growth of output and of the fastest growing input. If the latter happens to be capital growing at the same rate as output (the constant capital–output ratio), C will eventually become a constant, in sharp contrast to the behavior of the geometric Index in a similar case.[51] But with slowly growing variables, much time will pass before these peculiarities of C become pronounced. Also, when the numerator in (5.2a) contains several outputs combined arithmetically, the biases of the numerator and denominator are likely to offset each other, at least in part.

---

[51] The ratio of the rate of growth of the geometric Index to the rate of growth of output per unit of labor will equal labor's share in income (see Essay 4).

When two industries without an input–output relationship are aggregated, the C for the combined sector can be obtained either by dividing the total value of all outputs by that of all inputs (all in base year prices), or by computing the C of each industry separately and then combining them with the values of the respective inputs used as weights. These weights are not constant in time.

If one industry buys materials produced by another or if they have a mutual input–output relationship, their integration consists in cancelling out all interindustrial (that is, intrasectorial) transactions, and retaining in the numerator the value of the products final to the sector (sold outside of the sector), and in the denominator the value of inputs purchased from outside the sector. This merely repeats the traditional treatment given to a particular industry or a single firm.

It is also possible to compute the C's of each industry and then combine them into the C for the whole sector, but the presence of input–output relations complicates the weights. Thus if the first industry bought raw materials from a second which was completely integrated, the corresponding weights would be

$$v_1 = \frac{z_1}{z_1 + z_2 - r_2},$$ (5.3a)

$$v_2 = \frac{z_2[1 - (r_2/y_1)]}{z_1 + z_2 - r_2}.$$ (5.4a)

It is important to note that $v_1 + v_2 > 1$, that is, the "other forces" produce a cumulative effect.[52] If the second industry acquires raw materials from the third, and so on, the weights become more complex, but they are always based on the distinction between inputs and outputs acquired or sold inside and outside the sector.

All these weights are not constant in time, the only assumed constancy being that of *prices* of inputs and outputs. Of course constant weights may be introduced for special purposes, for example, for distinguishing between changes in the C of the whole sector produced by changes in the C's of individual industries and those produced by the changing importance of these industries.

III   *The value-added Index and other varieties*

As explained in the text, the value-added Index is defined as

$$C' = \frac{y - r}{l + k}.$$ (5.5a)

[52] For a more detailed discussion of this effect see Essay 4. I have not proved the uniqueness of this set of weights.

As noted previously (except for a completely integrated industry where the question does not arise), for $C > 1$, $C' > C$; also, for a given r/y, C'/C is an increasing function of C and is apt to increase with the passage of time. All this holds true if r stands for the current depreciation charge.

The elimination of the cost of materials from both sides of the production equation simplifies aggregation of industries (integration of them now becomes identical with aggregation). The weights are the sum of labor and capital costs of each industry in base year prices.

All these indexes could also be expressed in given (terminal) year prices. Then the C in the last year would be unity, and the C in the first year less than unity (with positive "other forces"). The subtraction of equal magnitudes from both the numerator and denominator of the C would make it smaller in the first year and thus increase its rate of growth toward unity. I have omitted this case both to save space and because I have nothing to add to the large literature on the subject.[53]

---

[53] For the best treatment see Abram Bergson, *The Real National Income of Soviet Russia since 1928* (Cambridge, Mass., 1961), chap. 3.

Economic growth and productivity in the United States, Canada, United Kingdom, Germany, and Japan in the post-war period

with Scott M. Eddie (United States), Bruce H. Herrick (Canada), Paul M. Hohenberg (Germany), Michael D. Intriligator (United Kingdom), and Ichizo Miyamoto (Japan)

I

This is a brief summary of a long report on the rates of growth of outputs, inputs, and factor productivities in the United States, Canada, United Kingdom, Germany, and Japan in the post-war period, for the countries as a whole and for major economic sectors. Like many empirical studies, this paper shows numerous scars from battling statistical data: frequent use of the "n.a." abbreviation, insufficient disaggregation (particularly for Germany), heavy reliance on ingenuity in bridging statistical gaps, and finally a rather weak conceptual framework chosen under duress. For all these reasons, the reader is urged to take our findings with a good dose of salt. Space does not permit us to discuss the numerous qualifications, sources, and statistical procedures.

Reprinted by permission from *The Review of Economics and Statistics,* Vol. XLVI, February 1964, pp. 33–40.

The original study was sponsored by the Organization for Economic Cooperation and Development, whose financial support is gratefully acknowledged. The study does not necessarily reflect the views of, or the approval by, the sponsor.

We are grateful to Professor John M. Kendrick and his assistant, Mrs. Maude Pech of the National Bureau of Economic Research, for their generous help; they are not, of course, responsible for our errors and conclusions.

Mr. Carl Riskin and Mrs. Marilyn Wright helped with computations; Miss Sharon Dewar deserves thanks for her aid in typing and computations, and Mrs. Juliet Raventos for preparing the final copy.

We are also grateful to the Center for Advanced Study in the Behavioral Sciences at Stanford, where the final version of this paper was written, for the use of its facilities and for many other things.

Since there exists a large literature on the methodology of such studies, we can be brief here.[1] On the whole, we have used the Kendrick method in obtaining what he calls the "Index of Total Factor Productivity" and what is called here the "Residual," as well as in measuring specific factor productivities, with the following major modifications: (1) the outputs (in their several variants) are expressed gross rather than net of depreciation; (2) labor input is aggregated without being weighted by the average wage of each industry, as Kendrick did; (3) imports (when present) are treated as inputs. Much as we wanted to deviate from Kendrick and to include materials among the inputs (in the several sectors), lack of data forced us to follow him in subtracting material inputs from both sides of the production equation and to express output as value added (in constant prices). This exclusion of material inputs is unfortunate: it reduces the usefulness of Kendrick's Index and of our Residual, the most novel feature of both studies, because labor endowed with a large weight dominates the input side (capital playing a rather minor role) and frequently pushes the Residual rather close to the conventional measure of labor productivity (see below).

One special qualification of our results should be mentioned. Neither Kendrick's nor our indexes of productivity have been corrected for the degree of utilization of inputs. During slack periods, even labor, although paid for, is not fully utilized, nor of course is capital. Hence both the rates of growth of the index of labor productivity and of the Residual will usually rise during the expansion phase of the economy or a sector and fall during a contraction. This can bias international and interindustrial comparisons and exaggerate the growth of all productivities in a rapidly growing country or industry as compared to slowly growing ones.[2]

It is very likely that the rates of growth of German and Japanese Residuals will exceed those of the United States, Canada, and the United Kingdom even after all adjustments for underutilization of capacity in the latter three countries are made, but not to the extent shown in our study.[3]

---

[1] The most important recent work on factor productivities belongs to John W. Kendrick, *Productivity Trends in the United States,* a study by the National Bureau of Economic Research (Princeton, 1961). See also essays 4 and 5.

[2] Kendrick's Table 5, *op. cit.,* p. 73, shows that during the expansion periods the annual rate of growth of the American Residual was as high as 2.8–2.9 per cent, while during contraction it was near zero or negative.

Of course, if we are interested in knowing what a country does with all its available resources of labor and capital, rather than with those actually used, no adjustment for underutilization of factors should be made.

[3] There was evidently some underutilization of capacity in the latter part of our period even in Germany, and some adjustment for this was made in Part III of our full Report.

In his aggregate study of the American economy, Solow assumed that the relative underutilization of capital was equal to the fraction of the labor force unemployed. See his

Over a longer period of time, comparisons can be limited to full employment (or rather full capacity utilization) years, but the shortness of our period – about ten years – allowed us no such luxury.

II

1. *The growth of output (value added) in constant prices*

This is presented in Table 6.1. Here, as in all our tables, the respective rates of growth were computed exponentially by comparing the first and last years, rather than by fitting a logarithmic regression. The arbitrary element so introduced is not likely to be very large compared with the defects of the data.[4] The pattern of disaggregation arose out of the data, time available, and our desire to obtain some degree of comparability among the several countries. We have been least successful with Germany, while for the United Kingdom more detailed estimates are available.

The purpose of Table 6.1 is not to reveal new data on the growth of output (these have appeared in several recent sources), but to show those rates of growth which were derived from our data and used in subsequent computations.[5] If the latter look strange, their peculiarities can be partially traced back to Table 6.1.

Table 6.1 confirms the well known facts that German and Japanese performance was excellent, American and Canadian fair, and British poor. The relatively high unemployment rates in the United States and Canada (particularly in the later half of the period) point to underutilization of capacity, at least as a partial cause. But this explanation is not applicable to the United Kingdom, unless of course hoarding of labor was widespread there.[6] Subsequent tables may suggest additional clues.

"Technical Change and the Aggregate Production Function," *Review of Economics and Statistics,* XXXIX (August 1957), 312–20. It should be noted that because of the relatively small weight usually assigned to capital in the computation of value-added Residuals, an adjustment of this kind will not make much difference.

[4] It is possible that this method may have allowed the slower rate of growth of output observed in most of the countries in the second half of the period to depress somewhat our rates of growth of output and of the Residual, as compared with the results of the regression method. This and many other defects can be corrected when we acquire greater faith in our data.

[5] See for instance Kendrick, *op. cit.*; United Nations, *World Economic Surveys* for 1959 and 1960; and "Economic Growth: the Last Hundred Years," *National Institute Economic Review,* No. 16 (July 1961), 24–49.

[6] The fraction of the labor force unemployed during the 1950–59 period (1951–59 for Japan) averaged 4.1 per cent in the United States, 4.2 per cent in Canada, 1.6 per cent in the United Kingdom, 4.5 per cent in Germany, and only 1.3 per cent in Japan. On the whole, unemployment in the United States and Canada rose considerably over the period, in the

Table 6.1. *Annual percentage rates of growth of output (gross value added) in constant prices*

	U.S. 1948–60 1954	Canada 1949–60 1949	U.K. 1949–59 1954	Germany 1950–59 1954	Japan 1951–59 1955
Base year:					
The economy					
Gross domestic product at constant market prices	3.4[a]	4.0	2.4	7.4	8.4
Gross domestic product at constant factor cost	3.3[a]	4.0	2.4	7.2	8.4
Gross domestic product at constant factor cost plus imports	3.4[a]	4.2	2.7	8.6	8.9
Private economy (at factor cost)	3.0	3.5	2.3	n.a.	8.3
Private non-farm economy (at factor cost)	3.2	3.8	2.5	n.a.	9.7
Gross value added by sectors					
Agriculture	.9	1.7	2.1	2.8	3.3
Forestry, fishing, trapping	n.a.	3.1			
Mining, quarrying, oil wells	n.a.	8.5	–.2		2.1
Manufacturing	4.0	3.7	3.3		10.7
Construction	3.8	3.8	2.1	8.8	11.6
Public utilities	3.6	9.9	5.1		
Transportation, communication		3.8[b]	1.8		9.0
Wholesale and retail trade	3.3	4.1	2.6	6.2[b]	6.4
Finance, insurance, real estate	4.2	4.9	1.7[b]		
Other services		3.8	.5	5.5	10.3
Government	n.a.				

[a] Gross National Product.   [b] Includes storage in this and subsequent tables.

2.   *The behavior of labor productivity (value added in constant prices divided by man-hours)*

Table 6.2 gives the rates of growth of labor input. This is simply the sum of unweighted man-hours. Like all such estimates, the figures are more reliable in manufacturing, public utilities, and similar industries, and least reliable in agriculture and services. It is interesting to note that in all countries labor input into agriculture fell; in Canada and Japan there was a rapid growth in services; in manufacturing only Japan had a rapid rise, while the German figures are unfortunately too aggregative to judge, and the American and Canadian figures are particularly low; in the public utilities and transportation and communication group the movements were diverse, with a negative rate in the United States, and a high positive in Canada. All countries seem to have had a reasonably high rate of growth of labor input in construction (though the German situation is obscured by aggregation), the Japanese figure of 7.6 per cent being particularly high.

The rates of growth of labor input in Germany and Japan, though higher than in the other three countries, were small when compared with the corresponding increases in output. As shown in Table 6.3, the rates of growth of aggregate labor productivity (value added per unit of labor input) were strikingly higher in the first two countries, being more than double those in the United States and Canada, and four times as large as in the United Kingdom. The poor performance of the latter is confirmed by subsequent tables.

Perhaps the most interesting feature of Table 6.3 is the rapid increase in labor productivity in agriculture in all five countries (however imperfect the measure of labor input is). No longer is agriculture to be thought of as a backward sector, at least in the advanced capitalist countries (in sharp contrast with its performance in the U.S.S.R.). Other characteristics of Table 6.3 are well known: reasonably rapid growth of labor productivity in manufacturing (but, except for Japan, below that of agriculture), and very rapid (subject to our aggregation difficulties) in public utilities. The striking difference between the fall of labor productivity in government in the United Kingdom and the sharp rise in Japan may be due to different methods of estimating government output. We cannot help remarking that, with all due qualifications, every item in the United

United Kingdom it increased slightly, and in Japan it remained steady, while in Germany it actually fell. Unfortunately, these figures are not quite comparable: in the United States and Canada they are obtained from a sample survey; in the United Kingdom and Germany from registration at employment exchanges; the Japanese figures arise from labor practices different from those of the other countries and too complex to be discussed here.

Table 6.2. *Annual percentage rates of growth of labor input (man-hours)*

	U.S. 1948-60	Canada 1949-60	U.K. 1949-59	Germany 1950-59	Japan 1951-59
The economy	.8	1.2	1.0	1.7	2.7
Private economy	.4	n.a.	.9	n.a.	2.7
Private non-farm economy	.9	n.a.	1.1	n.a.	4.7
Sectors					
Agriculture	−3.6	−3.7	−2.0[a]	−3.1[a]	−.7
Forestry, fishing, trapping	n.a.	1.1			2.2
Mining, quarrying, oil wells	n.a.	.5	−1.5	2.9	
Manufacturing	.6	.7	1.2		4.5
Construction	1.8	2.6	1.3		7.6
Public utilities	−.9	4.0	1.6	3.9	2.8
Transportation and communication		1.3	−.1		
Wholesale and retail trade	1.2	3.3	2.0		5.6
Finance, insurance, real estate	2.3	4.1	.4	2.4	6.5
Other services		4.4			
Government	n.a.		1.4		2.5

[a] Rate of change of employment (hours worked per week not available).

Table 6.3. *Annual percentage rates of growth of labor productivity (gross value added per man-hour)*

	U.S. 1948–60	Canada 1949–60	U.K. 1949–59	Germany 1950–59	Japan 1951–59
The economy	2.5	2.8	1.4	5.5	5.8
Private economy	2.6	n.a.	1.4	n.a.	5.7
Private non-farm economy	2.2	n.a.	1.4	n.a.	5.0
Sectors					
Agriculture	4.5	5.4	4.1 ⎱	5.9 ⎱	4.0 ⎱
Forestry, fishing, trapping	n.a.	1.9	1.3	⎰	–.1
Mining, quarrying, oil wells	n.a.	7.9	2.0	5.9 ⎱	6.2
Manufacturing	3.4	3.0	.8		4.0
Construction	2.0	1.3	3.6	⎰	4.0
Public utilities	4.5 ⎱	5.9	1.9	2.3 ⎱	6.3 ⎱
Transportation and communication	⎰	2.5		⎰	⎰
Wholesale and retail trade	2.2	.8	.6	3.1 ⎱	.9
Finance, insurance, real estate	1.9 ⎱	.8	1.4 ⎱		3.8 ⎱
Other services	⎰	–.5 ⎱	–.8		7.8
Government	n.a.	⎰		⎰	⎰

Kingdom column is smaller than the corresponding items in all other countries, Canadian services and Japanese mining being the only exceptions.

3.   *The behavior of capital productivity (value added in constant prices divided by the stock of capital)*

Rates of growth of capital stock (net of depreciation) contained in Table 6.4 are our weakest link, because of conceptual difficulties, the paucity of data and the consequent use of arbitrary assumptions. In the United States, for instance, only for a few industries could the relevant data be found, though it is highly likely that further work could find additional components, however roughly estimated.

While Germany and Japan retain their usual leadership in growth, it is worth noting that Japanese rates of growth of the capital stock were considerably above the German ones, that the Canadian aggregate rate was closer to the German than the preceding tables might suggest, and finally that British and American aggregate rates were very close. Evidently considerable differences in the behavior of capital productivity must have developed among the several countries, and this expectation is borne out by Table 6.5.

Here we find that only in Germany was the *aggregate* rate of growth of capital productivity positive; in the United Kingdom and Canada the rates were negative and large; in the United States, negative and small; and in Japan, the several aggregate measures give divergent results.[7] If rapid growth of labor productivity indicates economic progress (in the accepted sense), no such generalization can be made about capital productivity: our old notion that the latter falls with economic development has not been confirmed by recent findings, and either a slow or a rapid growth of an economy may be accompanied by a falling, constant or rising capital productivity.[8] Hence, the negative rates in the United States, Canada, and the United Kingdom, taken by themselves, are not indicative of the

---

[7] We were puzzled by this strange pattern of the Japanese rates and checked our calculations several times. No error was found. Such behavior of productivity rates happens from time to time because of the changing structure of the components of an economy.

[8] The behavior of capital productivity in the United States over a long period of time seems to depend not only on the specific period chosen but also on the investigator. According to Kendrick (*op. cit.*, Table 45, pp. 166–67) it was rising (in the private domestic economy) in every subperiod studied by him from 1899 to 1953. Kuznets, however, found it to be falling from 1869/79 to about 1919 or so (depending on which of his several variants is chosen), and (omitting the Great Depression) rising thereafter. (Simon Kuznets, *Capital in the American Economy: Its Formation and Financing*, a study by the National Bureau of Economic Research (Princeton, 1961), Table 6, pp. 80–81 and 216.) The two studies used different coverage and concepts.

Table 6.4. *Annual percentage rates of growth of capital input (capital stock in constant prices)*

| | U.S. 1948–60 | Canada 1949–60 | U.K. 1949–59 | Germany 1950–59 | Japan 1951–59 |
Base year:	1929	1949	1954	1954	1955
The economy	n.a.	5.5	3.5	6.8[d]	8.8
Private economy	3.6	n.a.	3.2	n.a.	8.1
Private non-farm economy	n.a.	n.a.	n.a.	n.a.	6.5
Sectors					
Agriculture	1.7[e]	3.7	4.0[a]	6.9	11.5
Forestry, fishing, trapping	n.a.	4.7	6.5		5.3
Mining, quarrying, oil wells	n.a.	11.5	4.6[a]	9.1	9.8
Manufacturing	2.9[f]	4.8	5.4[b]		20.3
Construction	n.a.	6.8	5.5[c]		
Public utilities	2.6	9.3	.2	5.8	10.7
Transportation and communication		4.7	7.4[b]		
Wholesale and retail trade	n.a.	7.2			6.5[d]
Finance, insurance, real estate	n.a.	4.4	2.3	6.0	5.7
Other services	n.a.	5.7			
Government	n.a.		7.7		6.2

[a] 1950–1959. [b] 1953–1959. [c] 1950–1958. [d] Including inventories. [e] Base year: 1948. [f] Base year: 1954.

Table 6.5. *Annual percentage rates of growth of capital productivity (gross value added per unit of capital stock)*

	U.S. 1948–60	Canada 1949–60	U.K. 1949–59	Germany 1950–59	Japan 1951–59
The economy	n.a.	−1.5	−1.1	.4	−.4
Private economy	−.5	n.a.	−.8	n.a.	.2
Private non-farm economy	n.a.	n.a.	n.a.	n.a.	3.2
Sectors					
Agriculture	−.8	−1.9	−1.9[a] ⎫	4.1 ⎫	−8.2 ⎫
Forestry, fishing, trapping	n.a.	−1.6	⎭	⎭	⎭
Mining, quarrying, oil wells	n.a.	−3.1	−6.7	n.a.	−3.2
Manufacturing	1.1	−1.2	−1.3[a]	−.3 ⎫	.8
Construction	n.a.	−3.0	−3.3[b]	⎭	−8.7
Public utilities	1.0 ⎫	.6	−.4[c]	.4 ⎫	−1.7 ⎫
Transportation and communication	⎭	−.9	1.5	⎭	⎭
Wholesale and retail trade	n.a. ⎫	−3.1	−4.8[b]	−.5 ⎫	4.7 ⎫
Finance, insurance, real estate	⎭	.5	−.5 ⎫	⎭	⎭
Other services	n.a.	−1.9 ⎫	⎭		⎭
Government	n.a.	⎭	−7.1	−.5	4.2

[a] 1950–1959. [b] 1953–1959. [c] 1950–1958.

presence or absence of economic progress. In Canada and the United States, the underutilization of productive capacity was the probable cause; one cannot help wondering whether this was also true of the United Kingdom, in spite of its small fraction of labor force registered as unemployed. Both in Canada and the United Kingdom not only the aggregate rates, but also most sectorial rates were negative.

Looking at the sectorial rates one notices that, except for Germany, agriculture had negative rates (particularly in Japan); construction (where data are available) was also negative; in manufacturing the picture is mixed, as it is in public utilities and the transportation and communication sector. On the whole negative rates predominate in Table 6.5: capital was increasing faster than output.

4.   *The behavior of the arithmetic (value-added) Residual*

An analysis of labor and/or of capital productivities, computed separately, gives an incomplete picture of economic progress of particular industries or countries. A sharp rise in, say, labor productivity can be merely the reverse side of the fall in capital productivity, without an indication whether the rise in one is more important, in some sense, than the fall in the other. The computation of the Residual remedies this defect to some extent and thus may provide additional information.[9] The Residual as computed here is simply the ratio of the index of value added (in constant prices and gross of depreciation) to the index of labor and capital inputs, each input weighted by its share in the corresponding value added of output in the base year.[10] The rates of growth of these Residuals are shown in Table 6.6.

On the whole they are not particularly striking and reinforce rather than contradict the tentative conclusions arrived so far from Table 6.3.[11] Again Germany and Japan are in the lead, far ahead of the others, and again the United Kingdom is deep in the cellar. But the rate of growth of the aggregate American Residual is slightly above or equal to the Canadian (unfortunately the two measures are not quite comparable), even though both total output and labor productivity advanced faster in Canada. It

---

[9] This should not give the impression that the Residual, particularly as computed here and by Kendrick, is a really good measure of economic progress or of economic efficiency, although it is of course better than the partial productivity of some one factor. On this see Essay 5.

[10] Our choice of the base year varied among the several countries depending on availability of data. The aggregate inputs consist of labor, capital, and imports.

[11] A contradiction would be much more dramatic and interesting. It is not likely to arise, however, because the relatively large weight assigned to labor in the computation of the value-added Residual makes the latter's behavior similar to that of labor productivity.

Table 6.6. Annual percentage rates of growth of value-added arithmetic Residual

	U.S. 1948–60	Canada 1949–60	U.K. 1949–59	Germany 1950–59	Japan 1951–59
The economy	n.a.	1.2	.6	3.6	3.7
Private economy	1.4	n.a.	.7	n.a.	3.8
Private non-farm economy	n.a.	n.a.	n.a.	n.a.	3.9
Sectors					
Agriculture	2.6	2.0	2.0^a }	4.3 }	1.2 }
Forestry, fishing, trapping	n.a.	.7			
Mining, quarrying, oil wells	n.a.	.9	.3	3.4 }	–.6
Manufacturing	2.6	1.4	.7^a	3.4	4.1
Construction	n.a.	.6	.2^b		2.2
Public utilities	3.4 }	2.0	1.9^c		4.5 }
Transportation and communication	3.4	1.5	1.8	1.5 }	4.5
Wholesale and retail trade	n.a.	–.6	–1.0^b		–.5
Finance, insurance, real estate	n.a. }	.6	.6	1.4 }	4.1 }
Other services	n.a.	.6 }			4.1
Government	n.a.	–.8	–2.8		6.7

^{a} 1950–1959. ^{b} 1953–1959. ^{c} 1950–1958.

is possible that the high rate of capital accumulation in Canada produced unutilized capacity rather than growth to a greater extent than in the United States. In every sector for which data are available (unfortunately for very few in the United States), the American Residuals (or their rates of growth, to be exact) are larger than the corresponding Canadian ones. Even the rates of growth of the British Residuals, low as they are, are not far from the Canadian, and in one sector – transportation and communication – slightly higher. If capital input had been adjusted for underutilization, both American and Canadian Residuals would have looked somewhat better, but so might have the British as well.[12]

The examination of the sectorial rates of growth of the Residuals by countries shows that in Canada and the United Kingdom agriculture and public utilities had the highest rates; in Germany, agriculture; in Japan and in the United States, public utilities and transportation and communication. Manufacturing did relatively well in the United States, in Japan, and probably in Germany; poorly in Canada; and very poorly in the United Kingdom. Of course, with data and methods as rough as ours, too much significance should not be attached to a difference of a few decimal points, particularly over a span of time as short as a decade. It is also obvious that further and more uniform disaggregation is needed before the causes of the more significant differences in the several countries can be usefully analyzed.

How important is the growth of the Residual as compared with the growth of output? The percentage ratios of the rates of growth of the Residuals to the corresponding rates of growth of output (value added) are given in Table 6.7. For the United States, Germany, and Japan this ratio is about 40–50 per cent, with the American ratio being of the same order of magnitude as the other two. But in Canada and the United Kingdom the ratio is only 25–30 per cent. It is very likely that if the American economy had been working at capacity, its ratio would have exceeded those of Germany and Japan. It is tempting to speculate that technological progress (in the broadest sense) played a *relatively* more important role in the American economy than elsewhere, and that an increase in the rate of capital accumulation in that country might have led not to diminishing returns but to faster growth of output, provided sufficient demand had been present. In Canada, on the other hand, the rate of growth of

---

[12] Our aggregate American Residual does not look particularly well even in comparison with Kendrick's which also was not adjusted for capital underutilization. The rate of growth of his Residual in the private domestic economy for the whole period 1899–53 is 1.7 per cent, but for a more recent period of 1948–53 it is 2.3. His labor input is weighted by relative wages in each industry. An unweighted labor input would give a somewhat higher Residual. See Kendrick, *op. cit.*, pp. 136–37.

Table 6.7. *Ratios between annual rates of growth of Residual and output in percentages*

	U.S. 1948–60	Canada 1949–60	U.K. 1949–59	Germany 1950–59	Japan 1951–59
The economy	n.a.	30	25	50	44
Private economy	47	n.a.	30	n.a.	46
Private non-farm economy	n.a.	n.a.	n.a.	n.a.	40
Sectors					
Agriculture	289	118	⎱ 95[a]	⎱ 154	⎱ 36
Fishing, forestry, trapping	n.a.	23	⎰	⎰	⎰
Mining, quarrying, oil wells	n.a.	11	*	⎱	−29
Manufacturing	65	38	21[a]	39	38
Construction	n.a.	16	10[b]	⎰	19
Public utilities	⎱ 94	20	37[c]	⎱ 24	⎱ 50
Transportation and communication	⎰	39	100	⎰	⎰
Wholesale and retail trade	n.a.	−15	−38[b]	24	−8
Finance, insurance, real estate	⎱ n.a.	12	⎱ 35	⎱ 25	⎱ 40
Other services	n.a.	⎱ −21	35	25	40
Government	n.a.	−21	−560	25	65

*Negative rate of growth of output.   [a] 1950–1959.   [b] 1953–1959.   [c] 1950–1958.

capital was quite high (5.5 per cent as contrasted with some 3.6 for the United States, though the two rates are not entirely comparable), but without any spectacular results. There was either an underutilization of capacity even greater than in the United States (which is quite probable), or diminishing returns to capital, or heavy investment for future use (as in mining and oil wells), or some degree of technological stagnation, or finally some combination of these factors and others familiar to those with more intimate knowledge of the various sectors of the Canadian economy. All these factors might have operated in the United Kingdom as well, except that its stock of capital increased more slowly (at some 3.2–3.5 per cent), and the degree of underutilization of capacity, if reflected by official unemployment statistics, was presumably lower. Hence the probability of technological stagnation (not in every sector, though) in the United Kingdom seems to be higher than in the other countries. The German and Japanese ratios were not particularly high; this might suggest that the rapid rate of growth of output in these countries was to a considerable extent caused by the growth of inputs, and particularly by that of capital (which grew there at some 7–8 per cent). The high rate of investment implied by this growth of capital might have been partly responsible for the rapid growth of the Residual.

However enticing these and other speculations may be, it may be wiser, with our flimsy empirical foundation, not to spin too many now lest they boomerang and embarrass the authors. The derivation of a reasonably reliable and meaningful Residual requires input–output data covering some period of time.[13] With the strong interest now shown in input–output work in a number of countries, we may look forward to better data and better Residuals, and of course to more speculations.

The rest of Table 6.7 is self-explanatory. The performance of agriculture in all countries except Japan should, however, be noted again. If our calculations are correct, agriculture in the four countries went through a technological revolution. This is particularly true of the United States.

In the remaining part of the paper we would like to report briefly on several very rough attempts to examine the correlation between the rates of growth of the Residuals and of other variables. The coefficient of correlation between the former and the rates of growth of labor productivity turned out to be 83 per cent, rather uncomfortably high.[14] Obviously, the

---

[13] Although many laborious computations usually involved in input–output work can be omitted. On this see Essay 4.

[14] This is a very rough calculation in which the countries' aggregate and sectorial rates were all thrown in. It is quite possible that a more careful procedure might even increase this coefficient. Kendrick obtained a coefficient of correlation between these two variables of 94 per cent (*op. cit.*, p. 155), but that was of rank correlation.

higher this coefficient is, the less useful is the Residual: ordinary labor productivity is much easier to compute. If material inputs were not excluded from both sides of the production equation, labor would have a smaller relative weight and the Residual so computed would be more significant. But this attempt was out of our reach.

We also made regression diagrams of the rates of growth of the Residuals (aggregate and sectorial) plotted against (1) rates of growth of the corresponding output, and (2) those of the capital stock. The first correlation looked positive, but not strong. It is tempting to conclude that the growth of the Residual, as a rough measure of technological progress, and growth of output are positively and mutually interrelated: rapidly growing industries are apt to enjoy faster technological progress; conversely, technological progress (as expressed by the Residual) is a major cause of their growth. But before the luxury of further theorizing is allowed, our figures should be adjusted for underutilization of capacity; otherwise, rapidly growing industries may enjoy a higher Residual simply because they utilize their capacities more fully. But the hypothesis is interesting and deserves further exploration.

Our second regression tried to test the hypothesis that gross investment may be an important vehicle for the introduction of technological progress and thus be positively correlated with the Residual.[15] We had no data for gross investment (in the several sectors) and used the rate of growth of the (net) stock of capital instead. Not surprisingly, the results were rather disappointing. If there was a positive relation at all, our data made it very slight (and the United Kingdom and Canadian figures suggested a negative relationship). For that matter, the correlation between the rates of growth of labor productivity and of the capital stock did not look very impressive either.

So much for our attempt to scratch the surface of this most important and interesting subject. We hope that this study will stimulate further explorations.

---

[15] There may be a mutual relationship: rapid technological progress in particular industries may call forth large investment.

An index-number tournament

For the Colonel's Lady and Judy
O'Grady
Are sisters under their skins!
Kipling: *The Ladies*

Use every man after his desert, and
who should 'scape whipping?
Hamlet, Act II

This essay tries to answer three simple questions:

1. Is a Soviet-type index of industrial production as bad as it looks?
2. Is a Federal Reserve-type index as good as it is reputed to be?
3. Is the latter index clearly superior to the former?

I. Introduction

The indictment of the Soviet official index of industrial production, as drawn by our experts, usually runs as follows:

Reprinted by permission from *The Quarterly Journal of Economics,* Vol. LXXXI, May 1967, pp. 169–88.

The original draft of this paper was written at the Center for Advanced Study in the Behavioral Sciences at Stanford (The Academic Paradise) in 1962–63. My gratitude to the administration, the staff and the fellows at the Center is immense. Among other things, the fellows contributed the two epigraphs after an intense interdisciplinary search. The final part of the work was financed by Grant GS-95 of the National Science Foundation, whose assistance is gratefully acknowledged.

I have had several excellent assistants: Simone Clemhaut Wan, Wallace E. Oates, Michael E. Alferieff, Michael Manove and Myra H. Strober, who helped with the survey of literature and with computations; my daughter Erica also lent a hand. Abram Bergson and Richard Moorsteen read the earlier draft and made valuable comments.

I owe a great debt to Anne P. Carter of the Harvard Economic Research Project for providing unpublished data for Part II of Table 7.4 and for carrying out a number of computations on my behalf; also to Clayton Gehman, Cornelia Motheral and their associates at the Board of Governors of the Federal Reserve System for unpublished materials for Table 7.5 and for other help.

Needless to say, the responsibility for possible errors, for the use and misuse of the data, and for all conclusions is solely mine.

1. the use of the 1926–27 weight base long since obsolete;
2. the introduction of new products into the index at inflated prices;
3. the use of value-of-output (or of price) weights instead of the more respectable value-added weights;
4. miscellaneous offenses, such as the exclusion of small-scale industry in early years, unreliable reporting of original data, arbitrary prices, use of multiple prices since 1952, if not earlier, and many others.

Of all these indictments, I will deal here with only the third – the use of value-of-output, or of prices, as weights, all others having been thoroughly discussed elsewhere.[1] My concern with this particular item stems not from its numerical importance – if anything, our experts tend to minimize its effects as compared with those of the other transgressions and are even a bit uncertain about its sign – but from plain curiosity about an aggregate index of industrial production with such obviously wrong weights, a curiosity which has remained unsatisfied because of the scarcity of analytical literature on the subject. Most authors (see Section III) usually condemn an index of this type, presumably in comparison with its more respectable rivals with value-added weights, for being infected with "double-counting," that is, for being sensitive to changes in the aggregation of data, and hence arbitrary.

At the risk of elaborating the obvious, let me say that changes in *horizontal* aggregation can be dismissed as irrelevant. Whether boots and shoes are reported separately or consolidated into footwear should make no difference in an otherwise correctly computed index. It is only when the two or several industries have *input–output relationships,* such as leather and shoes, that their treatment matters.[2] From now on, the words "aggregation" and "disaggregation" will be used in the vertical sense only.[3]

---

[1] A. Gerschenkron, "Reliability of Soviet Industrial and National Income Statistics," *American Statistician,* VII (April–May 1953), 18–21; "The Soviet Indices of Industrial Production," *Review of Economics and Statistics,* XXIX (Aug. 1947), 217–26; D. R. Hodgman, "A New Production Index for Soviet Industry," *Review of Economics and Statistics,* XXXII (Nov. 1950), 329–38; *Soviet Industrial Production, 1928–1951* (Cambridge, Mass., 1954); N. Jasny, "Intricacies of Russian National-Income Indexes," *Journal of Political Economy,* LV (Feb.–Dec. 1947), 299–322; N. M. Kaplan and R. H. Moorsteen, "An Index of Soviet Industrial Output," *American Economic Review,* L (June 1960), 295–318; R. Moorsteen, *Prices and Production of Machinery in the Soviet Union* (Cambridge, Mass., 1962); G. W. Nutter, *The Growth of Industrial Production in the Soviet Union* (Princeton, 1962); F. Seton, "The Tempo of Soviet Industrial Expansion," *Bulletin of the Oxford University Institute of Statistics,* XX (Feb. 1958), 1–28.

[2] I am sure that all authorities cited above are aware of this, though they do not always make a clear distinction.

[3] I would have preferred to use the word "aggregation" in the horizontal sense, and "integration" in the vertical; "disaggregation" has the required meaning, but unfortunately "disintegration" does not. Hence the choice made in the text.

Two separate aggregation problems may arise here:

1. the index is derived from data consistently classified into the *same* number and character of industries;
2. such consistency is absent, the series of the base and given year arising from different industrial classifications. The resulting index may be so arbitrary as to require little comment. It is possible to show a great increase in the value of total output in a given year over the base year (in constant prices) by sufficient disaggregation of the data in the given year. The excellence of the economic performance so measured will be limited only by the time and diligence of the index-makers, and of course by their desire to show future achievements.

Whether the Russians have engaged in this practice, with or without intention, or not at all, is not investigated in this paper. Instead, I shall construct a "pure" Soviet-type index of industrial production based on a consistent classification scheme and value-of-output (or price) weights and compare it with several more respectable ones. The required theoretical framework will be made as simple as possible. Only base-year weights will be used. The output and the inputs of each industry and the corresponding values will be regarded as unambiguously defined and free from numerous complications which beset the practical work in this field.

Section II deals with this "pure" Soviet-type index just described. In Section III the Federal Reserve-type index with value-added weights is put on the rack. Some empirical results and a few concluding remarks are made in Section IV.

List of symbols (more or less in order of appearance)

y_{ij} $(1 \leq i, j \leq m, i \neq j)$ the value of output of industry i used by industry j

y_{iF} $(1 \leq i \leq m)$ the value of final output of industry i

y_i $(1 \leq i \leq m)$ the total value of output of industry i

y_{nj} $(1 \leq j \leq m)$ the value of imports absorbed by industry j

y_n total value of imports

y_i' $(1 \leq i \leq m)$ value added by industry i

Every y and y' belong to the base year.

m number of domestic industries

n number of all industries (including imports)

X index or relative rate of growth of quantity

X' index or relative rate of growth of value added

The subscripts of every X and X' have the same meaning as those of the corresponding y and y'.

S "pure" Soviet-type index defined in (7.1)
V "pure" value-added index defined in (7.2)
F index of final products defined in (7.3)
M index of intermediate products or material inputs defined in (7.8)
M^* index of intermediate products or material inputs, excluding imports, defined in (7.7)
H "hybrid" index of output with value-added weights defined in (7.9)
$B\ =\ H - V$
$u_i\ =\ y_i/(\Sigma_1^m y_i) - y_i'/(\Sigma_1^m y_i')$
a material input coefficient (with the same subscripts as above)
Z physical quantity (with the same subscripts as above)
t time
$X^*\ =\ (\Sigma_1^m X_i)/m$
$w_i'\ =\ y_i'/(\Sigma_1^m y_i)$
$Q_i\ =\ X_i - X_i'$
$Q^*\ =\ (\Sigma_1^m Q_i)/m$

II.   The "pure" soviet-type index

Two incomplete input–output tables (without labor and capital rows) are required.[4] Table 7.1 shows the distribution of values (quantities times prices) in the base period. The components of Table 7.2 can be interpreted either as indexes of quantities (ratios between the given and the base year), or as their relative rates of growth. This versatility allows us to work simultaneously with both arithmetic and geometric indexes (their weight systems being identical in the present context), except for one instance in Section III where they differ. With this understanding, the X's will be referred to as index numbers. While the formulas given below are expressed in summation form to save space, I'll share with the nonmathematical reader the secret that they were all derived from 3×3 input–output tables and then checked to ascertain their generality. With the exception of a few lines pertaining to Section III (on changes in input coefficients) no mathematics above simple algebra is involved; and all of it has been tucked away into the appendix.

---

[4] Both input–output tables are expressed net of each industry's output used by it as an input. It seems to me that the inclusion of that quantity (or value) would make the tables highly arbitrary: its magnitude could vary greatly depending on the number of productive processes recognized. We do not normally include in the output of, say, a yarn mill the goods-in-process arising from the several transformations of raw cotton or wool into yarn; hence consistency requires that the same method be applied to the output of an industry. Otherwise, consolidation of industries would have little meaning. See, however, footnote 9.

Table 7.1. *Values of inputs and outputs in the base year*

Industries	1	2	...	m	Value of final output	Value of total output
1	0	y_{12}	...	y_{1m}	y_{1F}	y_1
2	y_{21}	0	...	y_{2m}	y_{2F}	y_2
...	...	...	...	...	...	...
m	y_{m1}	y_{m2}	...	0	y_{mF}	y_m
n (imports)	y_{n1}	y_{n2}	...	y_{nm}	0	y_n

Table 7.2. *Indexes or relative rates of growth of inputs and outputs between the base and given years*

Industries	1	2	...	m	Final output	Total output
1	0	X_{12}	...	X_{1m}	X_{1F}	X_1
2	X_{21}	0	...	X_{2m}	X_{2F}	X_2
...	...	...	...	...	...	...
m	X_{m1}	X_{m2}	...	0	X_{mF}	X_m
n (imports)	X_{n1}	X_{n2}	...	X_{nm}	0	X_n

The "pure" Soviet-type index is defined as

$$S = \frac{\sum_1^m y_i X_i}{\sum_1^m y_i}. \tag{7.1}$$

My first inclination was to compare it with a Federal Reserve-type index (the H index of Section III) directly. But since the latter is also under suspicion, it will be better to use as standards of comparison two other indexes, neither of them a stranger to the reader. The first is a "pure" value-added index defined as

$$V = \frac{\sum_1^m y_i' X_i'}{\sum_1^m y_i'}, \tag{7.2}$$

which Fabricant, and Kaplan and Moorsteen *wanted* to use but could not because of lack of data, no obstacle in this essay.[5] Our second "ideal" is

[5] S. Fabricant, *The Output of Manufacturing Industries, 1899–1937* (New York: National Bureau of Economic Research, 1940), Chap. 2; "Problems in the Measurement of the Physical Volume of Output, by Industries," *Journal of the American Statistical Association,* XXXIII (Sept. 1938), 564–70; Kaplan and Moorsteen, *op. cit.*

the index of final goods produced by the sector weighted by their values
(or prices) and expressed as

$$F = \frac{\sum_1^m y_{iF} X_{iF}}{\sum_1^m y_{iF}}. \tag{7.3}$$

Such an index was suggested by Frickey in 1936.[6] It was used by Gerschenkron and Moorsteen for Soviet machinery output, by Kuznets for
commodity flow in the United States, and undoubtedly by many others.[7]
To avoid confusion, it should be noted that "material inputs" include
services as well, that changes in inventories are disregarded, and that a
"final" good is defined here as any output produced by the given sector and sold outside. It may or may not be final in the national product
sense.

Both V and F are invariant to changes in aggregation, and their qualifications are too well known to warrant a lengthy defense of their appointment. Obviously, they serve different purposes and require no competitive ranking. In a closed system (without imports) they happen to be
identical because the value of final products (in a given period) equals the
value added by the sector. In an open system the sector's value added
equals the value of final products less the value of imports. Hence V is
the weighted *difference* between F and the index of imports X_n, that is

$$V = \frac{(\sum_1^m y_{iF})F - y_n X_n}{\sum_1^m y_{iF} - y_n} = \frac{(\sum_1^m y_{iF})F - y_n X_n}{\sum_1^m y_i'}. \tag{7.4}$$

The relations between S on the one hand, and F and V on the other,
can take several forms, the most convenient ones (see the appendix) being

$$S = \frac{(\sum_1^m y_{iF})F + (\sum_1^m \sum_1^m y_{ij})M^*}{\sum_1^m y_i}, \tag{7.5}$$

and

$$S = \frac{(\sum_1^m y_i')V + (\sum_1^n \sum_1^m y_{ij})M}{\sum_1^m y_i}, \tag{7.6}$$

where M^*, the index of *domestic* material inputs (intermediate products)
is defined as

[6] E. Frickey, "Some Aspects of the Problem of Measuring Historical Changes in the Physical Volume of Production," *Explorations in Economics: Notes and Essays Contributed
in Honor of F. W. Taussig* (New York, 1936), pp. 477–86. I do not know how original this
suggestion was with Frickey.

[7] A. Gerschenkron, *A Dollar Index of Soviet Machinery Output, 1927–28 to 1937*, The
RAND Corporation, Report R-197 (Santa Monica, California, 1951); Moorsteen, *op. cit.*,
S. Kuznets, *Commodity Flow and Capital Formation* (New York: National Bureau of
Economic Research, 1938).

$$M^* = \frac{\Sigma_1^m \Sigma_1^m y_{ij} X_{ij}}{\Sigma_1^m \Sigma_1^m y_{ij}}, \tag{7.7}$$

and M, which includes imports as well, is

$$M = \frac{\Sigma_1^n \Sigma_1^m y_{ij} X_{ij}}{\Sigma_1^n \Sigma_1^m y_{ij}}, \tag{7.8}$$

the summations being 1 to n for the rows (to include imports), and 1 to m for the columns (because X_n is not included in total output).[8]

Expressions (7.5) and (7.6) confirm our worst suspicions about S. It contains a bias which will disappear only in special cases when $M^* = F$ or when $M = V$ respectively. In fact, S is a weighted mean of F or V, which is good, and of M^* or M, which is bad, each of its components being weighted by its respective value. The magnitudes of M^* and M are obviously affected by aggregation changes.[9] Moreover, the greater the degree of disaggregation, the greater are the weights attached to M^* and M, while those of F and V remain fixed, and therefore the less sense is contained in S, though disaggregation does not *necessarily* increase the bias in S. At first glance, S suffers from two maladies: both the magnitudes of M and of M^* and their weights are arbitrary. Actually, there is only one (if this be a consolation): a given system of classification (an input–output matrix) will automatically yield the magnitudes of M and M^* and their weights. But this is bad enough.

It would be a shame to end this section without a word of advice to those who wish to maximize their S: disaggregate those industries where material inputs increase most rapidly and aggregate those where they show less vigor. Some experimentation will naturally be necessary to find the most promising classification, but I am sure that such problems will delight rather than embarrass a determined statistician and that he will in time find the optimum solution yielding the highest S.

III.   The output index with value-added weights

This index, expressed as

$$H = \frac{\Sigma_1^m y_i' X_i}{\Sigma_1^m y_i'}, \tag{7.9}$$

[8] As explained in the List of Symbols and in footnote 4, $i \neq j$ in all these summations, because $y_{ij} = 0$, $X_{ij} = 0$ when $i = j$.

[9] Provided the input-output tables are net in the sense of footnote 4. If they are gross, changes in aggregation do not affect the magnitude of M, and therefore of S, because no true consolidation of industries takes place. As was argued in footnote 4, the quantity and the value of an industry's own output used by it as an input are too arbitrary to be made use of.

is a hybrid between the V index which provides the correct weights, and the S index which supplies the wrong quantities. Lack of data usually brings additional impurities into (7.9), but they need not concern us here.[10]

If the S index, even in its "pure" form, comes to us with the guilty look of a culprit, the H index radiates an aura of innocence, its mixed parentage notwithstanding. Among many of our Soviet experts its superiority to S is taken almost for granted.[11] This attitude is shared by most other economists who have bothered to compare the two indexes at all.[12] The majority of the writers on index numbers either disregard the problem created by the presence of input–output relations entirely, or direct the reader to construct the H index without much ado, and without warning him that the H index is merely *some* approximation to V chosen because of lack of value-added data.[13] But there are a few notable exceptions,

---

[10] Most indexes of industrial production use price, or value-of-output, weights for aggregation *within* industries, where no significant input–output relations are expected, and value-added weights for aggregation *among* industries, to the extent that value-added figures are available and make sense. The best description of the Federal Reserve index is given in the following two publications of the Board: *Industrial Production: 1959 Revision* (Washington, D.C., 1960) and *Industrial Production Measurement in the United States: Concepts, Uses, and Compilation Practices* (Washington, D.C., Feb. 1964).

Hodgman, both in his article and book, *op. cit.,* used payroll weights for his index of Soviet industrial production to avoid an arbitrary assignment of returns to capital and land; Nutter, *op. cit.,* used value-added weights and a rather complex scheme of substitutes.

[11] According to Hodgman, "The new index [with payroll weights] is thus free of that double counting of output, varying with the degree of industrial integration, which is inescapable in a gross value index" (article, *op cit.,* p. 338). I could not find such forceful statements in Nutter's book, *op. cit.,* and in the Kaplan and Moorsteen article, *op. cit.,* but I think it is fair to conclude from the methods they used that they clearly preferred H to S. Kaplan and Moorsteen were, however, aware of the limitations of the former. See footnote 14.

As usual, Jasny, *op. cit.,* p. 313, forms an exception. He felt that while the League of Nations certainly [?] had good reasons for preferring value-added to gross-value weights in its index of industrial production, the use of this method in the Soviet case would have brought about even more questionable results than obtained by the other method.

[12] For instance, A. F. Burns in "The Measurement of the Physical Volume of Production," *Quarterly Journal of Economics,* XLIV (Feb. 1930), 242–62. The U.S. Bureau of the Census and the Federal Reserve Board justified their use of the H index in 1947 in the following typical, though abbreviated, manner: the S index is obviously affected by duplication; therefore V should be used; unfortunately, it cannot be constructed because of lack of data on value added; hence, the H index should be employed as an approximation to V. See U.S. Bureau of the Census and Board of Governors of the Federal Reserve System, *Census of Manufactures: 1947. Indexes of Production* (Washington, D.C., 1952), pp. 2–3.

[13] It is quite understandable if Irving Fisher (*The Making of Index Numbers* (3d ed.; Cambridge, Mass., 1927)) and Warren M. Persons (*The Construction of Index Numbers* (Cambridge, Mass., 1928)) did not worry about this problem: they lived in pre-input-output days and were more concerned with price than with quantity indexes. It is less

headed by Fabricant, Geary and Siegel.[14] And Gehman's recent work at the Federal Reserve Board has been most useful.[15]

Since the H index is used as an approximation to V and not to F, let us compare it with V only. Their most convenient relation is expressed as

$$H = V + \frac{\sum_1^n \sum_1^m y_{ij}(X_{ij} - X_j)}{\sum_1^m y_i'}. \qquad (7.10)$$

It seems then that H, like S, also contains a bias; it is of sufficient interest to be given a name B defined as

$$B = H - V = \frac{\sum_1^n \sum_1^m y_{ij}(X_{ij} - X_j)}{\sum_1^m y_i'}. \qquad (7.11)$$

Now X_{ij} is the index (or the rate of growth) of a material input; X_j is that of the corresponding output. Obviously, $B = 0$ if every $X_{ij} = X_j$, that is, if every input coefficient remains constant. This, however, is a sufficient but not a necessary condition; $B = 0$ if the changes in input coefficients offset each other exactly, as specified by (7.11), a point sometimes missed in the literature.[16]

If we interpret the X's in the geometric sense (as relative rates of growth) and take another look at B, we'll recognize in it a modified version of that

easy to understand the absence of any discussion in seven or eight recent statistical textbooks which we have examined, and particularly in three recent books on index numbers: B. D. Mudgett, *Index Numbers* (New York, 1951); C. F. Carter, W. B. Reddaway and R. Stone, *The Measurement of Production Movements* (Cambridge, 1948); and W. R. Crowe, *Index Numbers – Theory and Applications* (London, 1965).

[14] Fabricant, article and book, *op. cit.*; R. C. Geary, "The Concept of Net Volume of Output, with Special Reference to Irish Data," *Journal of the Royal Statistical Society,* CVII, Parts III and IV (new series, 1944), 251–59; I. H. Siegel, "Concepts and Measurement of Production and Productivity," Working Paper of the National Conference on Productivity, mimeo (Washington, D.C.: U.S. Bureau of Labor Statistics, 1952). Unfortunately (for me) I did not know of this most important contribution until my own derivations had been finished.

Several other contributions should also be mentioned: United Nations Statistical Office, *Studies in Methods: Index Numbers of Industrial Production* (New York: Sept. 15, 1950), which was evidently inspired by Geary's article; F. C. Mills, *Statistical Methods* (3d ed.; New York, 1955), pp. 491–93, who refers to Fabricant; Kaplan and Moorsteen, *op. cit.*; Board of Governors of the Federal Reserve System, *op. cit.*; and Robin Marris, *Economic Arithmetic* (London, 1958), pp. 332–43.

In defense of our Soviet scholars it should be said that having recoiled from the highly "impure" Soviet official index they were not in a mood to deal with its "pure" variety either; also that they must have wished to obtain results comparable with American production indexes which are usually of the H type.

[15] Board of Governors of the Federal Reserve System, *Industrial Production Measurement in the United States: Concepts, Uses, and Compilation Practices* (Washington, D.C.: Feb. 1964).

[16] By Kaplan and Moorsteen, *op. cit.*, p. 299, and by Fabricant in his book, *op. cit.*, pp. 31–32, but not in his article, *op. cit.*, p. 567.

part of Leontief's Index of Structural Change which arises from the saving (if $B < 0$) on material inputs (the rest of the Index consisting of saving on labor and capital).[17] Leontief's Index is close to what I have elsewhere called the Residual, and both are cousins of Kendrick's Index of Total Factor Productivity, derived arithmetically and based on somewhat different assumptions. All three are designed to measure technological change in its broadest meaning, and all three, arithmetic or geometric, usually give similar results.[18]

The use of H as an index of output implies an asymmetric treatment of changes in input coefficients: those of labor and of capital are duly recognized, but the change in material coefficients is obliterated. Let our sector consist of two industries – fuel and power – with all fuel consumed by power, and all power sold outside the sector, and let each industry's output in the base period equal 100 units. If a reduction in labor or in capital requirements takes place in either or both industries, the rate of growth of the sector's output as measured by the H index will be correct, and so will be the rates of growth of the Residual and of other productivity measures. But suppose that the power industry becomes more efficient in its use of fuel, so that the production of 100 units of power in the given year requires only 80 units of fuel. The F and V indexes for the given year will remain at 100, but the H index will fall to some weighted mean of 80 and 100. No significant growth in the Residual or in labor or capital productivities is likely to be recorded (the actual outcome depending on the specific numbers involved), even though a technological change of this type should not, in the present context, differ in its results from direct saving of labor or of capital. If, however, both industries should have been consolidated into one fuel-power industry prior to the technological change, the H index would correctly stand at 100. That the S index would not have behaved any better in this example is hardly much of a consolation.

Thus H is hardly a good index for measuring the rate of growth of the Residual (of one variety or another), or of productivity in general, unless, of course, the various changes in material requirements luckily offset each other, and $B = 0$. Even if the rate of growth of B should be small in relation to that of H or V, it will be about twice as large when compared with the rate of growth of the Residual, the latter being (in this country) some one-half of the rate of growth of output.[19]

---

[17] W. W. Leontief, *Studies in the Structure of the American Economy* (New York, 1953), Chap. 2. The numerator of B in (7.11) is identical with Leontief's, but in the denominator he used $\sum_1^n \sum_1^m y_{ij}$ instead of the correct (for his purposes) $\sum_1^m y_{iF}$. On this see Essay 4.

[18] J. W. Kendrick, *Productivity Trends in the United States* (Princeton, 1961). See also Essay 5.

[19] See Kendrick, *op. cit.*

That the H index is not invariant to changes in aggregation can be seen by examining expression (7.11). The denominator of B is the total value added by the sector in the base period and is obviously invariant to aggregation. But the numerator has no such immunity and can vary depending on the system of classification used. Although one may get the impression that the absolute magnitude of the numerator of B (its denominator being fixed) will increase with a greater degree of disaggregation, this need not be so. The changes produced by disaggregation among material input coefficients in successive stages of fabrication are not entirely arbitrary;[20] also, the increments in the several components of the numerator may have different signs and thus offset one another. We cannot tell on a priori grounds whether disaggregation by itself will increase or diminish the absolute magnitude of B.[21] But we should be able, as we were in Section II, to tell those who wish to maximize their H index how to do it: disaggregate industries with rising material input coefficients and aggregate those with falling ones. While this operation will probably require more effort and finesse than the inflation of the S index (one has to compute the input coefficients to begin with and then watch for nasty little tricks they sometimes play during disaggregation), I am sure here, as I was in Section II, that the required skill can be acquired with time, and that the peculiarities of the H index are no match for a diligent statistician bent on maximizing it.

All this sounds remarkably similar to the last paragraph of Section II.

The practical question, however, is not whether S and H are sisters under their skins, which they seem to be, but finding the conditions under which the bias in one can be confidently expected to be larger or smaller than in the other. Here I have had very little success. On the whole, if material inputs increase less rapidly than outputs, $B < 0$, $M < V$ (or $M^* < F$) and both S and H are understated in the given year. If material inputs increase more rapidly then both are overstated, but which is more off the mark? It is shown in the appendix that $S - H$ equals the covariance between X_i and u_i, defined as

$$u_i = \frac{y_i}{\sum_1^m y_i} - \frac{y_i'}{\sum_1^m y_i'}.$$

(A similar but less meaningful relation is also obtained there for $H - V$.) Combining this result with $B = H - V$ (by definition), we can derive the relationships between S, H and V given in Table 7.3.

---

[20] As the reader can ascertain for himself by setting up an algebraic or numerical example. This does not invalidate the conclusion reached in the text regarding the arbitrary nature of B.

[21] Hence, I do not understand why the U.N. Statistical Office, *op. cit.*, p. 22, recommended that the data be disaggregated as much as possible.

Table 7.3. *The relationships between the indexes S, H, and V expressed in terms of B and the covariance between u_i and X_i*

	$B<0$	$B=0$	$B>0$
Covariance <0	(1.1) $S<H<V$	(1.2) $S<H=V$	(1.3) $H>V$ $H>S$
Covariance $=0$	(2.1) $S=H<V$	(2.2) $S=H=V$	(2.3) $S=H>V$
Covariance >0	(3.1) $H<V$ $H<S$	(3.2) $S>H=V$	(3.3) $S>H>V$

This table shows that H is superior to S in squares 1.1, 1.2, 3.2, and 3.3, while S beats H in 1.3 and in 3.1 if $S-V$ has the same sign as $H-V$ (which happened in all empirical tests given in Section IV), or if the $S-H$ difference is not large. But if instead of using B as a criterion we employed $M \lessgtr V$ (which is just as legitimate), the scores of S and H would be reversed. Anyhow, the counting of the number of squares has no meaning unless we know the probability to be attached to each. This we cannot do because of our insufficient knowledge about the behavior of the relevant time series. In actual computations, Table 7.3 is also of little help: it is just as easy to compute the indexes directly as to infer their behavior from that of B, the above covariance, or $M-V$.

IV.   Empirical experiments

Frustrated by my algebra, I turned to empirical data in order to test the relative virtues of the S and H indexes, as approximations to F, and particularly to V. Obviously, no number of numerical tests, however thoroughly conducted, will by itself establish the superiority of a particular index – there is always the surprise hidden in another test – but such an exercise may give us at least a feeling about the probable nature of the outcome and about the magnitudes involved. Three such tests were made.

The first was based on three consistent input–output tables for 1919, 1929, and 1939, in 1939 prices computed by Leontief.[22] Unfortunately, their consistency was achieved at the expense of detail: the tables have

[22] Sources given in Table 7.4.

only thirteen industries (excluding households and imports) and are highly aggregated. The results, for what they may be worth, are reported in Part I of Table 7.4. Here is a summary:

1. Rather surprisingly, the H index came closer to F, which it is not supposed to approximate, than to V, which it is supposed to.

2. The S index was a better approximation to F than H was to V. This held true in every line, and particularly in 1929/1939.

3. In 1919/1939 all four indexes were close to each other, the greatest differences appearing in comparison with V (columns 7 and 8). In 1929/1939, S, H and F were again huddled together, while V stood rather far apart, so much so that in lines 5 and 7 the direction of the movement was reversed. In that year, none of the other three indexes, not excluding H, was a good approximation to V.

4. In the crucial test of whether $|S-V|$ was larger than $|H-V|$, S lost in every line in 1929/1939, but beat H in two out of four lines in 1919/1939, the fourth line being a draw. But all margins of victory and defeat were very small.

5. The exclusion of agriculture, transportation and electric utilities in one calculation, and the consolidation of all metal industries in another, not shown in the table, failed to produce any special results.

6. It may be interesting to note that all values of $B = H - V$ in column 8 were positive. Had the indexes been computed on a 1919 base, B would have probably been negative. This implies that some saving on material inputs in 1919/1939 and in 1929/1939 might have taken place (see below).[23]

The second experiment was based on two input–output tables for 1947 and 1958 in 1958 prices. The 1947 table was deflated and both tables made approximately comparable by Anne P. Carter of the Harvard Economic Research Project.[24] The resulting indexes are given in Part II of Table 7.4. Only the manufacturing sector was used this time, its data being more reliable than those of the other sectors.

These two input–output tables were much richer in content than the three just reported upon, but the results (with one exception) were remarkably similar. Again S, H and F were close together and far apart from V. Once more the H index was an excellent approximation for F, and a poor one for V. As for the comparison between $|S-V|$ and $|H-V|$, S won in line 9 and was beaten in line 10, but both times by small margins. The only difference between Parts I and II of the table lies in the

---

[23] These and other findings about the behavior of B should be treated with caution. In a 1929/1919 calculation for all industries (not given in Table 7.4) B was positive. Leontief, *op. cit.*, p. 31, had obtained positive B's for 1919–29 and for 1929–39 from the same data. Though he used a different denominator, this should not have changed the sign of B.

[24] Sources given in Table 7.4.

Table 7.4. A comparison of index numbers

	(1) S	(2) H	(3) F	(4) V	(5) S−F	(6) H−F	(7) S−V	(8) H−V	(9) $\|S−V\|−\|H−V\|$
I									
1939 Prices and weights									
1919/1939									
(1) All industries	71.6	71.8	68.9	68.3	2.7	2.9	3.3	3.5	−.2
(2) Excluding agriculture	76.8	77.3	76.7	75.6	.1	.6	1.2	1.7	−.5
(3) Excluding transportation	67.1	67.0	65.8	63.2	1.3	1.2	3.9	3.8	.1
(4) Excluding agriculture and transportation	71.0	71.0	71.6	69.2	−.6	−.6	1.8	1.8	0
1929/1939									
(5) All industries	107.3	106.6	105.4	99.3	1.9	1.2	8.0	7.3	.7
(6) Excluding agriculture	120.6	120.1	120.1	113.1	.5	0	7.5	7.0	.5
(7) Excluding transportation	104.2	103.2	103.4	95.9	.8	−.2	8.3	7.3	1.0
(8) Excluding agriculture and transportation	117.3	116.5	117.5	109.5	−.2	−1.0	7.8	7.0	.8

II

1958 Prices and weights

(9) Manufacturing 1947/1958	73.7	73.6	83.0	.1	0	−9.3	−9.4	−.1

1958 Prices and 1947 Weights

(10) Manufacturing 1958/1947	135.7	134.2	135.9	120.5	−.2	−1.7	15.2	13.7	1.5

Note: I have not checked Leontief's calculations, except as noted below, and I have tried to tamper with his data as little as possible. The following adjustments were made: (1) The value of total output had been given in the tables net of imports. I assumed that the total of all columns in a given row gave the value of total output gross of imports, and that the difference between this magnitude and the original one in each row was the correct value of imports. (2) This procedure revealed that the rows of metal fabricating in 1919 and of automobiles in 1929 contained errors. I assumed that the correct value of imports in metal fabricating in 1919 was one-half of 1 per cent (suggested by comparison with other years) of the "total output less imports"; also, that the "total output less imports" in automobiles was correct, that the "all other" was wrong, and that there were no imports of automobiles in 1929.

These corrections received Leontief's blessing via a long-distance telephone call. His help does not make him responsible for the consequences.

Sources: Part I: W. W. Leontief, *Studies in the Structure of the American Economy* (New York, 1953), Chap. 2.

Part II: Unpublished materials provided by Anne P. Carter of the Harvard Economic Research Project and based on the 1947 input-output table described in W. D. Evans and M. Hoffenberg, "The Interindustry Relations Study for 1947," *Review of Economics and Statistics*, XXXIV (May 1952), 97–142, and on the 1958 study published by H. R. Goldman, M. L. Marimont and B. N. Vaccara as "The Interindustry Structure of the United States: A Report on the 1958 Input-Output Study," *Survey of Current Business*, XLIV (Nov. 1964), 10–29. Mrs. Carter's methods used in adjusting the two tables are described in her "Changes in the Structure of the American Economy, 1947 to 1958 and 1962," *Review of Economics and Statistics*, XLIX (May 1967), 209–24. Further work on the reconciliation of the two tables is being carried on by B. N. Vaccara at the Office of Business Economics.

Table 7.5. *A further comparison of index numbers*

Manufacturing sector	(1) 1957/1947	(2) 1962/1953	(3) 1962/1947
S_1. *FRB gross value weights*			
(1) 1947 weights	149.2		
(2) 1958 weights		126.5	
(3) Linked weights			170.0
H_1. *FRB value-added weights*			
(4) 1947 weights	158.6		
(5) 1957 weights		128.0	
(6) Linked weights			178.8
H_2. *FRB index with OBE coverage*			
(7) 1954 weights	147.6	123.8	174.3
V_1. *OBE gross product in manufacturing*			
(8) 1954 prices and weights	141.8	119.8	161.4
(9) $S_1 - V_1$	7.4	6.7	8.6
(10) $H_1 - V_1$	16.8	8.2	17.4
(11) $H_2 - V_1$	5.8	4.0	12.9

Sources: Lines (1)–(7) – Board of Governors of the Federal Reserve System, *Industrial Production Measurement in the United States: Concepts, Uses, and Compilation Practices* (Washington, D.C., Feb. 1964), Table 2, and unpublished Federal Reserve materials. The corrected weights in lines (2) and (5) were given to me by Cornelia Motheral of the FRB. Line (8) – M. L. Marimont, "GNP by Major Industries: Comparative Patterns of Postwar Growth," *Survey of Current Business*, XLII (Oct. 1962), 6–18; *Survey of Current Business*, XLIII (Sept. 1963), 9–10.

behavior of *B* (line 10, column 8). This time *B* was positive (in line 10), indicating a greater use of material inputs (including services), though only in manufacturing.

Table 7.5 presents the third index-number comparison. The indexes were computed at the Federal Reserve Board (FRB) and at the Office of Business Economics (OBE) of the U.S. Department of Commerce, my own role being limited to a few simple calculations.[25] Coming almost ready-made, the indexes vary in base years, coverage and concepts; on the other hand, they were computed by professionals from a large array of data, and are probably better than any of mine. The first index, S_1, with gross-value weights, approximates our old *S*; the next two, H_1 and H_2, with value-added weights, are more or less similar to our *H*; the last one, V_1, is related to our *V*. Here are the conclusions:

[25] Sources given in Table 7.5.

1. The V_1 index was again isolated from the others, particularly in 1962/1947. It showed a consistently lower rate of growth than that of any other index, thus confirming the finding of Part II of Table 7.4 regarding an increasing use of material inputs in manufacturing since 1947. Whether this has actually happened or not is an interesting question but outside of the scope of this paper.[26]

2. The S_1 index was below H_1 in every period. According to Gehman, this was caused by the heavier weights given the slowly growing food manufactures (and the smaller weights of rapidly-growing machinery and aircraft) in the S_1 index.[27] If this phenomenon turns out to be widespread, and hence the H-type index more flattering to national pride than the S-type, we may live to see the Soviets change to H, unless the other attributes of their index (which is certainly not the "pure" S-type, see Section I) more than compensate for this effect.[28]

3. But what really came as a surprise, was the closer proximity to V_1 of S_1 than of H_1 in every period, and even of H_2 in 1962/1947. An explanation of this curious phenomenon cannot be given without a detailed study of the structure of the several indexes, which cannot be made here.[29] I would guess that this victory of S_1 over H_1 was caused by some fortuitous combination of ingredients. Of course, the word "victory" implies that V_1 is the correct index, which may or may not be true. Finally, one may question the usefulness of comparing indexes with different base years and coverages. The adjustment for base and coverage of the published FRB index certainly moved it closer to V_1. It is too bad that a similar adjustment was not made for S_1.

But it would be unfair not to admit that the S index has done much better both in the theoretical and empirical comparisons than I had ever

---

[26] The Federal Reserve Board regularly publishes indexes of output of final products and of materials. Though these do not correspond to the series discussed in the text, it is interesting to note that in each of the periods 1947–57, 1953–62 and 1947–62, the index of materials grew more slowly than that of final products. See Board of Governors of the Federal Reserve System, *Industrial Production – 1957–59 Base* (Washington, D.C., 1962), p. 8, and *Industrial Production Indexes, 1961–63* (Washington, D.C., 1964), p. 3. The behavior of purchased services may be of importance here.

[27] Board of Governors of the Federal Reserve System, *Industrial Production Measurement in the United States: Concepts, Uses and Compilation Practices* (Washington, D.C., Feb. 1964), p. 8 and Table 1.

[28] Maurice Ernst in his computation of a Polish index of industrial production also found that the H-type index increased faster than the S-type. "Overstatement of Industrial Growth in Poland," *Quarterly Journal of Economics,* LXXIX (Nov. 1965), 623–41. It seems that the Soviets may already be moving toward using an H-type index, at least in the light industries. See T. Shabad's dispatch "New Index Adopted to Measure Output in the Soviet Union," *New York Times,* CXIV (Feb. 15, 1965), 39, 43.

[29] On this see Clayton Gehman, "Alternative Measures of Economic Activity," and the discussion, American Statistical Association, *1964 Proceedings of the Business and Economic Section,* pp. 103–13.

anticipated: I had expected it to be thoroughly beaten by H. As it was not, I believe it is fair to answer the third question raised at the beginning of the essay (the answers to the other two now being obvious) in the negative, and to call our index-number tournament a draw. But since S entered it as an underdog, and H as a popular favorite, the proponents of S (if there are any) may justly claim a moral victory – for the moment. A draw should give the S index a practical edge because it is easier to construct. But let us not overdo our welcome to S, lest its luck should turn in the next contest.

Mathematical appendix

The purpose of this Appendix is not to develop any new formulations but merely to facilitate the understanding of the formulas given in the text.

To Section II

Since to most of us operations with index numbers are something of a rarity, it is useful to recall that to add several indexes we first multiply each by its weight and divide the resulting sum by the sum of their weights. Similarly, to find the difference between two index numbers, we take their weighted difference and divide it by the *difference* between their weights. In this manner, the index of final products X_{iF} is obtained as

$$X_{iF} = \frac{y_i X_i - \sum_{j=1}^{m} y_{ij} X_{ij}}{y_i - \sum_{j=1}^{m} y_{ij}} = \frac{y_i X_i - \sum_{j=1}^{m} y_{ij} X_{ij}}{y_{iF}}. \tag{7.1a}$$

Substituting (7.1a) into the formula for F given by (7.3) in the text, we find

$$F = \frac{\sum_1^m y_i X_i - \sum_1^m \sum_1^m y_{ij} X_{ij}}{\sum_1^m y_{iF}}. \tag{7.2a}$$

Dividing and multiplying the first item in the numerator by $\sum_1^m y_i$, and the second by $\sum_1^m \sum_1^m y_{ij}$, we obtain

$$F = \frac{(\sum_1^m y_i)S - (\sum_1^m \sum_1^m y_{ij})M^*}{\sum_1^m y_{iF}}. \tag{7.3a}$$

From (7.3a) the expression (7.5) for S given in the text readily follows. Expression (7.6) in the text is obtained in a similar manner from (7.4) and (7.5).

To Section III

Expression (7.10) in the text is derived by subtracting (7.9) from (7.2), by cancellation of some terms and the rearrangement of the remaining ones.

To understand the meaning of $X_{ij} - X_j$ let us first interpret the X's as relative rates of growth and define the material input coefficient $a_{ij} = Z_{ij}/Z_j$, where the Z's are physical *quantities*. By taking the derivative of a_{ij} in respect to time and dividing it by a_{ij} we readily find that $(da_{ij}/dt)/a_{ij} = X_{ij} - X_j$.

If the X's are interpreted as indexes (and not as rates of growth), it can be readily established that $X_{ij} - X_j = [(a_{ij}^1 - a_{ij}^0)/a_{ij}^0]X_j$, where the superscripts 0 and 1 indicate the base and given year respectively.

By definition of u_i (see the List of Symbols)

$$S - H = \sum_1^m u_i X_i. \tag{7.4a}$$

The covariance between X_i and u_i is then

$$\sum_1^m (X_i - X^*)u_i = \sum_1^m X_i u_i = S - H. \tag{7.5a}$$

By definition of w_i' and Q_i

$$H - V = \sum_1^m w_i' Q_i. \tag{7.6a}$$

The covariance between Q_i and w_i' is

$$\sum_1^m (Q_i - Q^*)\left(w_i' - \frac{1}{m}\right) = \sum_1^m Q_i w_i' - Q^*. \tag{7.7a}$$

Thus $H - V$ equals the covariance between Q_i and w_i' only when $Q^* = 0$. Since Q^*, the unweighted mean of the difference between X_i and X_i', is quite arbitrary, I do not see any special reason why it should equal zero.

On the measurement of comparative efficiency

This essay began as an ordinary comment on Professor Bergson's paper. If by now it has become rather long and involved and has strayed into other, let us hope not unrelated, subjects, the fault is his and not mine: his paper was simply too interesting and too stimulating to be left in peace. On my first reading of Bergson's paper I jotted down even more comments than are reported here, only to find that Bergson, with his usual conscientiousness, had disposed of most of them in the next paragraph or on the next page. Obviously, it is impossible to comment on every aspect of his paper; utilizing my comparative advantage, I shall say very little about his statistical data (except at the very end) and shall concentrate instead on his general methods and on the meaning and significance of his results.

1. The theory

The theoretical part of the paper continues the discussion of intertemporal and interspatial comparisons of index numbers of inputs and of outputs began by Bergson and Moorsteen some years past.[1] There is no doubt that everyone who constructs index numbers transgresses against honesty, and that every user thereof is an accomplice in the act: it is impossible to reduce a vector of quantities or of prices to a single number in an honest way. But what Bergson and Moorsteen have done is to make clear and explicit the assumptions on which the construction of these index numbers rests, and the rationale involved in preferring one set of

Reprinted by permission from *Comparison of Economic Systems: Theoretical and Methodological Approaches,* edited by Alexander Eckstein, University of California Press, Berkeley, 1971, pp. 219–33.

Bergson's paper discussed in this essay is "Comparative Productivity and Efficiency in the USA and the USSR," published in the same volume. Unless otherwise indicated, the references are to that paper.

[1] Abram Bergson, *The Real National Income of Soviet Russia since 1928,* Cambridge, Mass., 1961, particularly Ch. III; Richard H. Moorsteen, "On Measuring Productive Potential and Relative Efficiency," *The Quarterly Journal of Economics,* LXXV:3 (1961) 451–467.

weights to another, even if no true set of weights exists. I have learned much from Chapter III of Bergson's *magnum opus* and so have my graduate students.

And yet, after all these illuminating explanations, we still have to construct index numbers of inputs and of outputs in a more or less traditional way. Having constructed them, we usually obtain the Index of Total Factor Productivity (to use Kendrick's term), or what I have called elsewhere the Residual, and of their interspatial equivalents, either by fitting to them a simple production function like the Cobb–Douglas, or by assigning to the inputs and the outputs a certain set of weights, like income shares, the two methods yielding very similar results.[2] Because the results are so similar, I would suggest either the use of less restrictive and more interesting production functions, with constant elasticity of substitution, for instance, as Weitzman has recently done, or the use of unpretentious index numbers with assigned weights, as Bergson has done through most of his paper.[3] In the latter case, I think, the emphasis should be placed on logical consistency and on simplicity, so that the reader could see exactly what the investigator is doing.

In a sense, Bergson's comparative index is a hybrid: it has two outputs – consumer and investment goods – which are aggregated arithmetically, and two inputs – labor and capital (the latter including land) – aggregated geometrically. (The Cobb–Douglas formula with assigned weights adding to one is merely a weighted geometric index.) Although I prefer the geometric index for comparisons of this kind (for reasons explained elsewhere), I must admit that a pure geometric index is too laborious to be constructed in practice, and that every geometric index hides arithmetic sub-aggregation.[4] The recognition of a large number of separate components makes each of them more homogeneous and minimizes the aggregation problem within each component, thus resulting in a purer geometric index, but neither I nor any other consumer of Bergson's products can fairly ask him to spend additional time and effort on a more refined aggregation. I doubt that Bergson's general results, which have so large a margin to spare, would be much affected if he used a pure geometric or a pure arithmetic index. For algebraic manipulations, however, his hybrid

---

[2] John W. Kendrick, *Productivity Trends in the United States,* National Bureau of Economic Research, Princeton, N.J., 1961; see also essays 4 and 5.

[3] Martin L. Weitzman, "Soviet Postwar Economic Growth and Capital Labor Substitution," Cowles Foundation Discussion Paper No. 256, Yale University, New Haven, Conn., October 30, 1968, since published in *The American Economic Review,* LX:4 (1970), 676–692.

Bergson did consider the effects of different magnitudes of the elasticity of substitution between labor and capital on his results.

[4] See essays 4 and 5.

is rather clumsy and hard to handle. For this reason, I shall discuss here only the two pure varieties, the arithmetic and the geometric, without worrying about the practical difficulties of computing the latter kind.

List of symbols

A	arithmetic index
E	average factor productivity
G	geometric index
L	labor input
K	capital input
T	Residual or Index of Total Factor Productivity
Y	real output of one or of several sectors
i	rate of return on capital stock
p	price of output
w	wage rate
λ	share of labor
$\mu = 1 - \lambda$	share of capital
$\rho = (1 - \sigma)/\sigma$	
σ	elasticity of substitution

Subscripts

A	US
R	USSR
L	labor
K	capital

In summation formulas the variables of summation have been omitted to avoid an excessive number of subscripts.

1.1.   The arithmetic index

In Soviet prices, this index A_R is defined as

$$A_R = \frac{\Sigma Y_R p_R}{\Sigma Y_A p_R} \left/ \frac{\Sigma L_R w_R + \Sigma K_R i_R}{\Sigma L_A w_R + \Sigma K_A i_R} \right. . \tag{8.1}$$

After a few simple manipulations A_R[5] can be expressed as

---

[5] The expression (8.1) in the text can be rewritten as

$$A_R = \frac{\Sigma Y_R p_R}{\Sigma L_R w_R + \Sigma K_R i_R} \left/ \frac{\Sigma Y_A p_R}{\Sigma L_A w_R + \Sigma K_A i_R} \right. . \tag{8.1n}$$

Its numerator is one by definition. Therefore

$$A_R = \lambda_R \frac{E_{LR}}{E_{LA}} + \mu_R \frac{E_{KR}}{E_{KA}}, \tag{8.2}$$

which is a weighted arithmetic mean of the ratios of the labor and capital productivities (Soviet divided by US), each weighted by its corresponding Soviet income share.

In US prices the index A_A is similarly defined, and after a few manipulations[6] it can be expressed as

$$A_A = 1 \Big/ \left(\frac{\lambda_A}{E_{LR}/E_{LA}} + \frac{\mu_A}{E_{KR}/E_{KA}} \right). \tag{8.3}$$

Thus the A_A index is a weighted harmonic mean of the ratios of labor and capital productivities (Soviet divided by US), this time weighted by US income shares.

Since for any unequal positive numbers an arithmetic index is larger than a harmonic one, it follows that A_R should be larger than A_A, provided

$$A_R = \frac{\Sigma L_A w_R}{\Sigma Y_A p_R} + \frac{\Sigma K_A i_R}{\Sigma Y_A p_R}. \tag{8.2n}$$

Multiply each numerator and denominator by the same magnitude and reassemble the terms:

$$A_R = \frac{\Sigma L_A w_R}{\Sigma Y_A p_R \, \Sigma w_R} \cdot \frac{\Sigma Y_R p_R \, \Sigma w_R}{\Sigma L_R w_R} \cdot \frac{\Sigma L_R w_R}{\Sigma Y_R p_R}$$

$$+ \frac{\Sigma K_A i_R}{\Sigma Y_A p_R \, \Sigma i_R} \cdot \frac{\Sigma Y_R p_R \, \Sigma i_R}{\Sigma K_R i_R} \cdot \frac{\Sigma K_R i_R}{\Sigma Y_R p_R}. \tag{8.3n}$$

Now the expression $\Sigma Y_A p_R / (\Sigma L_A w_R / \Sigma w_R)$ is the average productivity of US labor, with Soviet prices and Soviet wages used as weights to be indicated by E_{LA}. The next term is the average productivity of Soviet labor also with Soviet prices and wages, while $\Sigma L_R w_R / \Sigma Y_R p_R$ is the share of Soviet labor in the value of the Soviet output. The same reasoning applies to the capital items. Thus we obtain

$$A_R = \lambda_R \frac{E_{LR}}{E_{LA}} + \mu_R \frac{E_{KR}}{E_{KA}}. \tag{8.4n}$$

[6] A_A is defined as

$$A_A = \frac{\Sigma Y_R p_A}{\Sigma Y_A p_A} \Big/ \frac{\Sigma L_R w_A + \Sigma K_R i_A}{\Sigma L_A w_A + \Sigma K_A i_A} = \frac{\Sigma Y_R p_A}{\Sigma L_R w_A + \Sigma K_R i_A}, \tag{8.5n}$$

because American outputs and inputs cancel out by definition (as the Soviet ones did when Soviet prices were used). Performing the same manipulations as we did with A_R we'll have

$$A_A = \left[\frac{\Sigma L_R w_A}{\Sigma Y_R p_A \, \Sigma w_A} \cdot \frac{\Sigma Y_A p_A \, \Sigma w_A}{\Sigma L_A w_A} \cdot \frac{\Sigma L_A w_A}{\Sigma Y_A p_A} \right.$$

$$\left. + \frac{\Sigma K_R i_A}{\Sigma Y_R p_A \, \Sigma i_A} \cdot \frac{\Sigma Y_A p_A \, \Sigma i_A}{\Sigma K_A i_A} \cdot \frac{\Sigma K_A i_A}{\Sigma Y_A p_A} \right]^{-1}$$

$$= 1 \Big/ \left(\lambda_A \frac{E_{LA}}{E_{LR}} + \mu_A \frac{E_{KA}}{E_{KR}} \right) = 1 \Big/ \left(\frac{\lambda_A}{E_{LR}/E_{LA}} + \frac{\mu_A}{E_{KR}/E_{KA}} \right). \tag{8.6n}$$

the two indexes are composed of the same productivity ratios and use the same weights. But the Soviet income shares (or the shares of other countries less developed than the United States) favor capital more than US shares do; a larger capital share should work to the Soviet advantage because capital productivities of the two countries are much closer to each other than their labor productivities are; finally, in the A_A index the ratio of capital productivities, being close to unity, plays a much smaller role than that of labor productivities (note that it is US to Soviet, and not the other way around in this case), which is a rather large number (about 3 in this case).[7] For all these reasons, if the ratios of respective productivities in Soviet and in US prices were the same, the A_R index should be larger than the A_A one. And yet in every international comparison that I have seen, each country does better in foreign prices than in its own.[8]

This contradiction between my theoretical expectations and empirical results is caused by the inequality of the ratios of factor productivities in Soviet and in US prices; the relative factor productivity of each country is favored by the use of the other country's prices. This phenomenon is well known and it is usually called the "Gerschenkron Effect."

While constructing indexes of Soviet machinery output, Professor Gerschenkron found that early-year weights impart an upward bias to an output index as compared with one based on later-year weights, because the rates of growth of specific outputs and of their prices are negatively correlated.[9] Evidently, the same situation holds true in international comparisons, that is, a negative correlation must exist between ratios of outputs and ratios of the corresponding prices. Thus Bergson found that the ratio of Soviet output to US is 49.7 per cent in US prices, and only 31.5 per cent in Soviet prices.[10]

The A_R and A_A indexes, however, are not merely ratios of outputs, but ratios of outputs divided by the corresponding ratios of inputs. Does the Gerschenkron Effect exist in input ratios as well? The Soviet capital stock is 52.2 per cent of the US in US prices, and 41.7 per cent in Soviet prices.[11]

---

[7] To see this point, express (8.3) as

$$A_A = 1 \bigg/ \left(\lambda_A \frac{E_{LA}}{E_{LR}} + \mu_A \frac{E_{KA}}{E_{KR}} \right). \tag{8.7n}$$

[8] See Table 1 below, and Edward F. Denison, *Why Growth Rates Differ*, Brookings Institution, Washington, D.C., 1967.

[9] Alexander Gerschenkron, *A Dollar Index of Soviet Machinery Output, 1927-28 to 1937*, The RAND Corporation, Santa Monica, Calif., 1952. For a mathematical treatment of the Gerschenkron Effect see Edward Ames and John A. Carolson, "Production Index Bias as a Measure of Economic Development," *Oxford Economic Papers*, XX:1 (1968) 12–24.

[10] Table 4, pp. 180–181.

[11] *Ibid.*

So the Gerschenkron Effect is certainly present here, though in a weaker form than in the output comparisons above. I wonder why this is so. Perhaps the Soviet capital industry, presumably the most advanced sector of the Soviet economy, is closer to its US counterpart in the structure of its output and of its prices than the rest of the Soviet economy; or perhaps the Gerschenkron Effect is weaker in any particular sector, as compared with the economy as a whole, because of the given sector's greater homogeneity of output.

It would be interesting to discover whether the Gerschenkron Effect exists in the aggregation of labor as well, that is, whether US wage rates used as weights give a higher ratio of Soviet to US labor input than Soviet wage rates do. Is there a negative correlation between the ratios of labor inputs by occupation in the two countries and the ratios of the corresponding wage rates? Perhaps it does exist; both countries have many workers in poorly paid occupations: in Soviet agriculture and in US services (though services were excluded from Bergson's comparisons). Unfortunately, labor is usually aggregated by adding unweighted man-hours (or man-days, or man-years), or man-hours adjusted by sex and by educational level. This is not a satisfactory method because these characteristics need not correspond closely to wage rates by occupations and hence, hopefully, to the corresponding values of the marginal product of labor.[12] In the spirit of aggregation used for output and for capital input, each labor series should be weighted by its wage rate, first Soviet, then US. This task is laborious but also rewarding: If a substantial Gerschenkron Effect is found in the ratios of labor inputs as well, it will counteract this Effect in the output ratios and thus bring Bergson's two estimates (in Soviet and in US prices) closer together – a most welcome outcome.

1.2. *The geometric index*

Whether Soviet or US weights are used, the expressions are formally identical, because the geometric index is reversible. As mentioned above, I assume that both inputs and outputs were properly aggregated by summing up the weighted logarithms of the individual series and use the symbol Y as the total output in this sense. The geometric index is defined as

$$G = \frac{Y_R/Y_A}{(L_R/L_A)^\lambda \cdot (K_R/K_A)^\mu} \tag{8.4}$$

and can be transformed into a more convenient expression

---

[12] In one of his variants, Kendrick, *op. cit.,* (note 2), did weight the labor input in each industry by the corresponding wage rate.

$$G=\left(\frac{E_{LR}}{E_{LA}}\right)^{\lambda}\cdot\left(\frac{E_{KR}}{E_{KA}}\right)^{\mu}.\qquad(8.5)$$

Thus, the G index is a geometric mean of the ratios of labor and capital productivities, each weighted by its income share (Soviet or US).[13]

The construction of the comparative geometric index is based on the assumption that it is one country's *income shares* (both in inputs and in outputs), and not prices, which exist in the other country as well. Since Soviet capital productivity is fairly close to that of the US, while the labor productivities are far apart, and since the Soviet capital share is usually assumed or found to be larger than that of the US (see below), the use of Soviet rather than of US weights should favor the USSR unless a strong Gerschenkron Effect is present in the geometric index as well. I do not know whether in a given country a negative correlation exists between the rates of growth of specific quantities (outputs or inputs) and of their income shares; or whether in international comparisons such a correlation is to be found between the respective ratios of quantities and of their shares. It is quite possible that this correlation does not exist, or even that it is positive. In the latter case, the Gerschenkron Effect would work in reverse, reinforcing the favorable impact of Soviet weights on Soviet performance.

Thus it does not necessarily follow that each country is favored by the other country's weights. The outcome depends on the particular index chosen and on the system of aggregation used. I think this subject deserves further study.

2.   Several small points

Let me leave the main subject of my discussion for a moment and make several minor digressions.

---

[13] From expression (8.4) in the text, we derive

$$G=\frac{Y_R L_A^{\lambda} K_A^{\mu}}{Y_A L_R^{\lambda} K_R^{\mu}}=\left(\frac{Y_R}{L_R}\right)^{\lambda}\cdot\left(\frac{Y_R}{K_R}\right)^{\mu}\cdot\left(\frac{L_A}{Y_A}\right)^{\lambda}\cdot\left(\frac{K_A}{Y_R}\right)^{\mu},\qquad(8.8n)$$

from which (8.5) readily follows.

The Residual, or the Total Factor Productivity, obtained from the constant-elasticity-of-substitution function, indicated here by T, can also be expressed in terms of factor productivities. Let

$$Y=T(\lambda L^{-\rho}+\mu K^{-\rho})^{-1/\rho},\quad\text{with }\lambda+\mu=1.\qquad(8.9n)$$

Then

$$T=\frac{Y}{(\lambda L^{-\rho}+\mu K^{-\rho})^{-1/\rho}}=1\Big/\left[\lambda\left(\frac{L}{Y}\right)^{-\rho}+\mu\left(\frac{K}{Y}\right)^{-\rho}\right]^{-1/\rho};\qquad(8.10n)$$

$$T=\left[\lambda\left(\frac{Y}{L}\right)^{\rho}+\mu\left(\frac{Y}{K}\right)^{\rho}\right]^{1/\rho}=(\lambda E_L^{\rho}+\mu E_K^{\rho})^{1/\rho}.\qquad(8.11n)$$

2.1. *Rates of return on capital*

The Soviet rates of return on the capital stock – 12 and 16 per cent – assumed by Bergson are much higher than his US rate of 9.5 per cent. I have often wondered why it is taken for granted that the Soviet rate of return – and by assumption the marginal productivity of capital – must be so high. No doubt, a good American or German capitalist, if given the opportunity, could make more than the 12 or 16 per cent on *his* investment in the Soviet Union, but do the Russians themselves use their capital so efficiently? Their own complaints on this score are well known; they have been investing a very high fraction of their national product; the average productivity of their capital has been falling, and in the sectors examined by Bergson it was below that of the US in 1960. And yet Weitzman has found that the income share of Soviet capital in that year was 59 per cent gross of depreciation.[14] Allowing some 6 percentage points for depreciation, yields the net income share of capital as 53 per cent. With an average net capital (and land) coefficient of 2.0–2.3[15] this implies a net rate of return on capital of 23–26 per cent, a figure even higher than Bergson's. It seems that my doubts should be put aside, at least for the time being. But if Weitzman's (and my) calculations are correct, the weight of Soviet capital assigned by Bergson should be increased; this adjustment would favor the USSR when their weights were used.

2.2. *Depreciation*

Quite correctly Bergson includes the depreciation charge in the share of capital: depreciation, together with interest (or profit) is the true cost of capital, just as the wage, which also includes an element of depreciation, is that of labor.

When it comes to the capital stock, he takes neither the gross stock nor the net but the mean of the two. Since an old piece of capital commands a lower rental than a new, the net stock of capital should be used in estimating the rental value rather than the gross. But Bergson may feel that existing methods of capital write-off, particularly in the US, though

---

[14] Weitzman, *op. cit.,* (note 3), p. 11. The capital share of 58.7 per cent was obtained from calculations based on Western sources; Soviet sources yielded an even higher share – 69.9 per cent.

Weitzman has excluded not only services (like Bergson) but agriculture as well. It is hard to tell what effect this exclusion had on the share of capital because both agricultural prices in the Soviet Union and Western estimates of Soviet agricultural rent are rather arbitrary. Combining Weitzman's capital share with Bergson's estimates of depreciation and of capital-output ratio in the same economic sectors (that is, excluding farms) gives a rate of return, net of depreciation, of 27 per cent.

[15] From Bergson's Appendix, Table 6.

hardly in the USSR, may exaggerate actual depreciation; hence, the net-gross mean may be a better approximation to the true value of capital than either component alone. One cannot argue about this procedure without a thorough examination of depreciation methods in the two countries. Let me just mention in passing that in the US the net-gross mean is some 29 per cent larger than the net stock, while in the USSR it is 12 per cent above the net.[16] So Bergson may be giving the USSR the benefit of the doubt, which is not inappropriate in view of my comments on the Soviet capital share above and of his treatment of unemployment.

2.3.   *Exclusion of unemployed workers*

Bergson's labor input in the US excludes the 5.6 per cent of unemployed workers in 1960. If he aims at the comparison of what each country does with its employed resources, his procedure is correct, though a similar adjustment should perhaps be made to the stock of capital as well. But if he tries to compare the relative efficiency of the two systems, then the elimination of what is probably the greatest single cause of US inefficiency is questionable. In his defense it can be said that Soviet discussions about the presence of labor reserves, particularly in smaller cities and towns, undoubtedly point to the existence of some unemployment. But no unemployment statistics are published in the Soviet Union, because officially unemployment does not exist. So if US unemployed were included in the labor input, the Soviet jobless would have to be treated likewise, a rather difficult statistical task.

2.4.   *Exclusion of services*

Bergson has good reasons for this decision, because productivity in many service sectors (education, public health, the military, and general government, for instance) is difficult to conceptualize, let alone to measure. But because the US service sector is relatively larger than the USSR's, and because productivity (essentially of labor) in the services is thought to be lower than elsewhere, this exclusion may favor the United States.

2.5.   *Turnover, sales and excise taxes*

Bergson's exclusion of Soviet turnover taxes from output totals is accepted by most investigators, because these taxes fall almost exclusively on consumer goods, and their retention would distort relative output shares. But why should the same procedure not be followed in respect to

---

[16] From Bergson's Appendix, Table 5.

US sales and excise taxes? They also fall mostly on consumer goods and amount to some 7 per cent of consumer expenditures.

The total impact of these five points which act in different directions would be very small, even if all were accepted by Bergson. His general conclusion – that both in US and in Soviet prices, Soviet inputs are much less productive in generating outputs, as they are usually defined and measured – would not be affected, even if his indexes were to advance or to fall by a few percentage points. The interesting question lies not in the exact magnitudes of his indexes but in their meaning and significance.

3.   The meaning of the results

The word "efficiency" used in the title of Bergson's paper is one of the most difficult economic concepts to define, let alone to measure. In physics it usually means the fraction of the maximum potential which a given machine can produce. Perfectly efficient machines do not exist; the efficiency of existing ones could frequently be increased to some extent, but at a cost. Hence, of two machines the one with a higher physical efficiency may or may not be more efficient from an economic point of view.

The application of some efficiency criteria to a country's performance over time or to a comparison of a pair of countries raises even more difficult problems. For instance, the Soviet Union and the United States could each increase its own efficiency by reorganizing its agriculture; yet both refuse to do so for ideological (when the Russians are obstinate) or political (when we are) grounds. Obviously, the social welfare function of each country, as seen by its government, or by its "ruling circles," to use a Russian phrase, is not composed of economic variables alone. Since these noneconomic objectives – and even some economic ones, like income distribution – never become sufficiently explicit to be assigned proper weights, we usually find ourselves in an uncomfortable position between two extremes: on the one hand, justifying much foolishness by reference to noneconomic objectives, and on the other, denouncing any departure from narrow economic goals as inefficient. In other words, we do not know where the influence of noneconomic factors ends and true inefficiency begins. It seems that governments or ruling circles of all countries enjoy their own political systems well enough to be willing to pay high economic prices for maintaining them.

But even if we knew the proper social welfare function of each country, the pursuit of efficiency would result in the fulfillment of certain conditions *on the margin*. In general, it would not take the form of the maximization of the average productivity of some factor, such as labor, nor of that

Table 8.1. *Real national income per unit of factor inputs, selected countries, 1960 (USA = 100 per cent)*

	With employment unadjusted		With employment adjusted for labor quality	
	Based on foreign national price weights (1)	Based on US price weights (2)	Based on foreign national price weights (3)	Based on US price weights (4)
United States	100	100	100	100
Northwest Europe	50	63	53	67
France	49	62	53	66
Germany	52	63	56	69
United Kingdom	50	63	52	66
Italy	28	45	32	52
USSR	28	45	34	56

Source: Abram Bergson, *Planning and Productivity under Soviet Socialism*, New York, 1968, Tables 1 and 2, pp. 22 and 26.

of some particular combination of factors. Thus the cultivation of marginal lands in the Soviet Union will depress the Bergson Index (this term referring to all comparative indexes in his and in my papers), unless the quality of land were very carefully measured, and yet that cultivation may be economically justified. If the Soviet authorities dismissed all but the best of their workers, or shipped to Africa (a few years ago I said "to China") all their obsolete capital, the Index would register an improvement (again unless the quality of labor and of capital were properly allowed for), even if the Soviet people had less to eat and less to wear.

But let me not overdo my criticism of the Bergson Index. A firm's profit need not necessarily be raised by an improvement in labor productivity, but frequently it will be. Similarly, a country's "true" relative efficiency need not be positively related to the Index, but usually such a relationship will exist. Hence, if the Index shows that the average factor productivity in one country is markedly inferior to another, greater efficiency of the latter is not an unreasonable hypothesis. But there may be other explanations as well.

Table 8.1 contains several such comparative indexes for a number of countries computed by Bergson himself. We find that the Soviet Union and Italy are very close to each other, with the former doing a bit better in Columns 3 and 4. It comes as a surprise that West Germany – our symbol of efficiency – is so close to the ailing United Kingdom, and that the latter is slightly superior to France in Columns 1 and 2. And all these countries are way behind the United States.

It seems to me that Bergson's calculations testify not so much to Soviet inefficiency, however great it may indeed be, but to an earlier stage of economic development, as confirmed by the presence of 38.5 per cent of Soviet labor force in agriculture.[17] Historical studies of particular countries, such as the United States, that have been conducted in a manner very similar to Bergson's interspatial comparisons, suggest that around 1925, in terms of the Index of Total Factor Productivity, this country was, roughly speaking, at the same stage as the Soviet Union in 1960.[18] Now, in what sense was the US economy inefficient in 1925? Of course, the US technology of 1960 was unavailable in 1925, but at that time this country need not have made any poorer use of its then available resources than it did in 1960. What these historical studies show is that the growth rate of a particular country's output cannot be completely explained in terms of growth of inputs of labor, capital, and land, as they are traditionally defined.[19] The same evidently holds true in international comparisons as well, although with one important qualification: If modern US technology was not available in this country in 1925, much of it was certainly available to the Soviet Union in 1960. Yet studies of economic development show that borrowing foreign technology is not an easy and simple process.

The two hypotheses suggested here to explain the relatively poor Soviet performance in terms of the Bergson Index – low efficiency of a socialist economy to which Bergson is inclined, and an early stage of development (as compared with the US) which I would favor – need not be mutually exclusive. Each can provide a part of the explanation. Usually problems of this type can be solved, or at least investigated, by means of a multiple regression, in this case of the Bergson Index for a number of countries regressed against the relative stage of each country's development and the presence or absence of socialism. Unfortunately, this procedure will not work here, because just about every index of economic development, such as per capita income, labor productivity, or the fraction of the labor

[17] Bergson, *op. cit.*, p. 162.

[18] I assume that the US Residual was growing at some 2 per cent a year as found by Kendrick, *op. cit.*, and that in 1960 the Bergson Index amounted to 50 per cent. An annual rate of growth of 2 per cent implies doubling every 35 years.

[19] The growth of output can be almost completely explained if inputs and outputs are properly redefined. On this see D. W. Jorgenson and Z. Griliches, "The Explanation of Productivity Change," *The Review of Economic Studies,* XXXIV:3 (1967) 249–283.

force in nonfarm occupations, depends to a considerable extent on the efficiency of the economy; in addition, the large weight usually assigned to labor in the calculation of the Bergson Index assures a high correlation between labor productivity, or per capita income, and the Index.

But it may be possible to stabilize the data for the stage of development by taking pairs of countries which were at the same stage, more or less, before one of them went socialist, and compare their performance on the Bergson scale at a later date. Such pairs may consist of East and West Germany (probably the ideal pair), Czechoslovakia and Austria, Yugoslavia and Greece, or either of these Balkan countries may be compared with Bulgaria or Rumania (to judge the performance of the Yugoslav as compared with the Soviet-type socialism). It is too bad that two other good pairs – North and South Korea, and North and South Vietnam – have been devastated by wars, but perhaps Burma (if that country can be regarded as socialist) and Thailand may make a pair, as may Cuba and some other Latin-American country.

Even if the socialist member of such a pair has fallen from the original state of parity with its capitalist partner on the Bergson scale, this fact by itself is not sufficient to establish the inferiority of socialism as an economic system. Suppose, for instance, that the socialist partner invested a much larger fraction of its national product and thus grew more rapidly than the capitalist one, but because of diminishing returns to capital, or because of poorer allocation of resources in general, it performed worse on the Bergson scale. How are we to tell which path of development, the socialist or the capitalist, was better or more efficient? Is it more important to be efficient in the micro-sense and score well on the Bergson scale, or is macro-efficiency which is only partly registered on that scale more desirable? What about other economic criteria, such as income and wealth distribution or security of employment? All this brings us back to the homely truth that weighty questions, such as these, cannot be resolved on the basis of the behavior of one simple index.

So far (and rather wisely), I have not questioned the methods used by Bergson and by other western scholars in estimating Soviet output. Yet any reader of the *Economic Newspaper* (*Ekonomicheskaia Gazeta*), of the *Krokodil*, or of the delightful little book by Antonov[20] cannot help wondering about the methods by which Soviet production procedures, methods of pay, market organization, and the quality of products are recorded in statistics of output. In comparing Soviet performance over

---

[20] O. N. Antonov, *Dlia Vsekh i Dlia Sebia*, [For everyone and for oneself] Moscow, 1965. This is an excellent and an amusing description of defects of Soviet planning. It includes remedies, some of which are equally amusing: the author is an engineer.

time, these troublesome questions are usually disregarded on the assumption that the defects of statistical recording, whatever they are, have persisted for some time and hence are not likely to affect the relative rate of growth of output and similar figures, even though the enlarged production of consumer durables may have intensified these problems in recent years. In international comparisons, on the other hand, these defects, if they are large, cannot be dismissed. I do not refer particularly to simple quality differences of supposedly identical products, such as the smaller number of threads per square inch of men's shirts counted by Nutter,[21] or the reportedly short longevity of Soviet tires. These can be duly taken into account by adjusting corresponding prices, however laborious this job would be.

Suppose for instance that workers in a Soviet truck plant stand idle for want of parts. If national product is measured as output (as it should be), the correct number of trucks produced will be properly recorded. On the income side, no problem arises if the workers are paid by the piece. If they are paid by the hour, their idleness should be reflected in lower profit of the enterprise; but Soviet profits are not a reliable statistic, and in our estimates of Soviet national income it is customary to replace profits by some more or less arbitrarily assigned rate of return on the capital stock. Now suppose that this production delay takes place on a construction site, a very common occurrence. If the workers are paid by the piece, no statistical harm is done, but hourly payments are likely to inflate the cost of construction; and construction expenditures are very difficult to deflate properly (in any country) because of the absence of a reliable unit of output. Hence, the output of the construction industry, and of the national product, may be exaggerated.

If a Soviet citizen buys a refrigerator, its production and sale are duly recorded. But if at a later date the refrigerator stands idle because of lack of repairmen or of parts, no method of social accounting known to me would record this fact. Nor would it be recorded that a portable ice box (to mention a report in the *Krokodil*), again duly included in the national product, turns out to be absolutely useless because its purchaser cannot buy any ice, or that airconditioning apparatus manufactured and installed, and thus again duly recorded, does not condition any air.

Let me not exaggerate this problem. Many deficiencies of Soviet organization and of the type and quality of Soviet products are reflected in statistics of lower output, of lower labor productivity, and so forth, particularly when the production of intermediate products is involved.

---

[21] G. Warren Nutter, *The Growth of Industrial Production in the Soviet Union,* National Bureau of Economic Research, Princeton, N.J., 1962.

With capital goods the situation is more complex: at the time of its production a defective machine will be recorded in the output of capital goods without any allowance for its quality and usefulness, but these will be reflected at some later date in the lower output of the machine. To record the low quality of housing and of consumer goods in general, an extremely careful deflation of Soviet national product is required, and even such a deflation is not likely to catch the frustration and anger felt by buyers of poor consumer services and owners of useless consumer products.

PART III

Soviet economics

Special features of industrialization in planned economies: a comparison between the Soviet Union and the United States

I

My original assignment stated in the first half of the title implied some comparison between a number of planned and nonplanned economies. The limitation of my knowledge and time and of the reader's (estimated) patience has restricted my set of countries to the Soviet Union and the United States, who appear sufficiently different to make the comparison worthwhile and yet similar enough in many essential features to make it meaningful. A broader coverage would, of course, be preferable, but it should be done by someone better versed in the economic history of a number of countries than I am.

If I had a free choice of variables to be compared, I would try to relate the economic performance of each country to the training given to, and the use made of, the 5 or 10 percent most able persons of its labor force. Some American information on the use of ability exists, but I have never seen any Soviet data.[1] Hence, I had to turn to the more conventional, if

Reprinted by permission from the proceedings of *The Second International Conference of Economic History*, held in Aix-en-Provence in August–September 1962. Published by Mouton & Co., Paris, 1965, pp. 529–60.

I am very grateful to Abram Bergson, Norman M. Kaplan, and Nancy Nimitz for repeatedly explaining to me the intricacies of their own works, for permission to use their unpublished materials, and for many helpful comments; to Leon Trilling for his help in dealing with the distribution of engineers given in Table 9.9; to Robert S. Lande of Stanford University for correcting the errors in my tables and for general research assistance; to H. Pack of M.I.T. for preliminary spade work; to the RAND Corporation (and particularly to Burton H. Klein and Oleg Hoeffding) and to the Center for Advanced Study in the Behavioral Sciences at Stanford for giving me access to their excellent facilities. None of them is responsible for my misuse of data and for the conclusions, even for the correct ones.

I am also grateful to the Harvard University Press, National Bureau of Economic Research, the RAND Corporation, and *The American Economic Review* for their generous permission to reproduce materials from their publications.

[1] For instance, Dael Wolfle, *America's Resources of Specialized Talent* (New York, 1954). There is a good deal of information about training given to Soviet students in various fields and about the distribution of trained personnel by economic sectors, but none, to my knowledge, regarding the performance of the several groups on ability tests, if such

less interesting, variables, such as capital formation, price movements, labor productivity, and the like, in the hope that this well-worked mine had not been completely exhausted. Not aiming at the specialist in Soviet economics, I have thought it useful to present a number of tables containing some basic facts about both economies over several periods. But such materials, in their impartial purity, are just as boring to read as they are to assemble from known sources.[2] Therefore my selection of data was motivated to some extent by the desire to examine the following two propositions, which will be given the imposing titles of First and Second hypotheses:

1. Soviet efforts to achieve economic growth have been greater than American efforts.
2. Economic progress in the United States has advanced on a broad front without a significant difference between consumer and capital goods industries, while in the Soviet Union progress has been highly uneven, with capital goods industries forming the spearhead of the advance.

Since neither "effort" nor "economic progress" can be measured directly, substitutes or approximations must be designed. Thus "effort" will be expressed here as the fraction of gross or net national product invested. This undoubtedly constitutes a good part of the "effort," but certainly not all of it; its other aspects, such as education, research and development activities, and others, will be omitted here.[3]

Similarly, a sector of an economy will be said to "progress" faster than the others if *at least* one of the following conditions holds over a reasonably long period of time:

are given at all. See Nicholas DeWitt, *Education and Professional Employment in the U.S.S.R.,* National Science Foundation (Washington, D.C., 1961), and *Vysshee obrazovanie v SSSR* [Higher education in the USSR] (Moscow, 1961). Among the tables distributed by me at the Conference, there was one on the "Structure of Graduating Classes in the USSR and the U.S." taken from DeWitt's book (Table IV-51, p. 341). The table showed that some 57 percent of Soviet graduating students majored in technical fields, including medicine, as compared with only 24 percent in the United States. The table was omitted from the final draft of the essay to save space.

The statement in the text is based on the implicit assumption that ability can be reliably measured, which is not at all certain.

2 The reader will soon discover that in spite of the large "value of output" of this essay, as measured by the number of pages and tables, the "value added" by me is quite modest. The essay is based on a number of important, and for the most part highly competent, studies of the Soviet economy made by American scholars. Official Soviet data in the raw are very difficult to use, and only a sprinkling of them are given here.

3 A comprehensive study of the Soviet research and development effort is being done by Alexander Korol at M.I.T. under the sponsorship of the National Science Foundation. [Since published as *Soviet Research & Development: Its Organization, Personnel and Funds,* Cambridge, Mass., 1965.]

a. The prices of the output of the given sector fall relative to the general price level.
b. Its labor productivity grows faster than in the rest of the economy.
c. Its index of total factor productivity, that is, the productivity of labor, capital, and land (when relevant) combined in some reasonable manner, behaves in a similar fashion.[4]

Of these three indicators, the index of total factor productivity (c) is a better approximation to what we intuitively mean by economic progress than are the other two; labor productivity by itself may increase merely because of substitution of capital for labor, while the prices of an industry's output are affected not only by its internal developments, but also by its pricing policies (particularly in the Soviet Union), prices of its inputs, and the demand for its output. Usually the three indicators point in the same direction (for instance, prices declining and both productivities increasing);[5] they are all listed here because the relative difficulty of obtaining them increases from the weakest (a) to the stronger (b) and to (c). Much as we would like to work with (c), lack of data will frequently force us to be content with (b) or even (a).

It is impossible to divide the economy into capital and consumer goods industries with any degree of precision because many industries serve both sectors. Hence, capital goods are usually represented by machinery (or producer durables) and construction (the "final" capital goods). Productivity estimates in construction are usually so unreliable that we shall limit the capital goods sector to machinery only;[6] even this industry will be defined inexactly, and (depending on availability of data) will sometimes appear in our tables as "machinery and allied products," "civilian machinery," and even "metals and metal products." To make matters worse, little is known about the output of machinery used in the Soviet Union for military purposes. However these munitions are treated, the reliability of the estimates of labor (and of total factor) productivity in this industry suffers. Their inclusion spoils the numerator in the ratio of output to labor, while their exclusion impairs the denominator because we

---

[4] There exist many computations of the index of total factor productivity, defined in one manner or another. The most comprehensive work is by John W. Kendrick, *Productivity Trends in the United States* (Princeton, N.J., 1961). See also Essay 5.

[5] As found by Kendrick, op. cit., pp. 155 and 202.

[6] It is very difficult to construct a proper deflator for the value of construction because of the absence of a standard unit of output. For this reason, the index of prices of construction materials and of wages is frequently used instead. This substitution implies that productivity in the industry remains almost constant. See R. A. Gordon, "Differential Changes in the Prices of Consumers' and Capital Goods," *The American Economic Review,* Vol. LI (December 1961), pp. 937–57.

do not know how much labor to exclude.[7] Since the productivity of the machinery industry is a most vital variable in this essay, the situation is most unfortunate.

This difficulty is only one of many. In an earlier draft, I tried to list a number of them, only to find that hardly a tenth could be described in the six pages I wrote. Sixty pages of qualifications, warnings, and complaints are certainly more than anyone can stand. I have therefore dismissed the subject altogether, except for the preceding remarks, a few brief comments directly related to each table, and the notes given in the tables. The relevant qualifications can be found in great detail in most of the sources used. I have managed to avoid some trouble, however, by limiting my comparisons to *relative* magnitudes expressed as ratios to other variables of the *same* country. But enough difficulties have remained to suggest to the reader not to take this essay too seriously, and to treat it as merely an *experiment* in comparative economic studies.

To spare the reader any future disappointments, I should say now that, of my two hypotheses, the First, dealing with the relative magnitudes of capital formation in the two countries, has been so well supported by empirical data as to make its testing rather trivial. It will be handled here briefly. The Second, about differential rates of economic progress, is more interesting, both as an historical phenomenon and as an analytical problem, but my several attempts to test it have met with a most modest degree of success. The two hypotheses look interdependent, and they are certainly so treated in Soviet economic literature. If capital formation is the key (or at least *an* important key) to economic growth, one would expect the machine-building industry to form the spearhead of economic advance.[8] But things are not that simple; we will return to this question in Part III.

II

The first four tables present the aggregate picture of economic development in the two countries. Table 9.1 shows the relative magnitudes of

[7] Because of these difficulties, Soviet munitions were completely excluded from our most comprehensive study of Soviet machinery by Richard Moorsteen, *Prices and Production of Machinery in the Soviet Union, 1928–1958* (Cambridge, Mass., 1962), and from the Kaplan–Moorsteen index of Soviet industrial production given in Table 9.10.

[8] The importance of capital goods industries in economic development was emphasized by the Soviet economist (or engineer) G. A. Fel'dman in a series of articles published in the Soviet journal *Planovoe khoziaistvo* [Planned economy] in 1928–29, which was my point of departure in thinking about this essay. I discussed his work in my "A Soviet Model of Growth," *Essays in the Theory of Economic Growth* (New York, 1957), pp. 223–61.

capital formation as a ratio to national product. Column 1 requires no comment except to point out the existence of a mild upward trend in the Soviet Union and its absence in the United States. Soviet data in column 2 have been adjusted by removal of turnover taxes – the main source of government revenue – both from the numerator and the denominator, because these taxes fall almost exclusively on consumer, but not on capital, goods. Compared with column 1, every figure in column 2 has been increased by several percentage points, the upward trend has become steeper, and the advantage over the United States sharper. But column 2 may exaggerate the difference because American indirect taxes also imposed mainly on consumer goods have not been eliminated.[9]

The deflation of the Soviet data in column 2 and American data in column 1 by the respective price indexes has accentuated the difference between the two countries: the upward trend in the Soviet figures has become much steeper, though most of the rise took place between 1928 and 1937; but in the United States we now find a downward trend. We shall return to this point in a moment.

Column 5 gives the corresponding ratios net of depreciation. For the Soviet Union the drop from the gross to the net ratios is small, about a quarter if not less, but for the United States, particularly in the last several decades, the drop is striking. It is caused by the relatively slower rate of capital formation in this country.[10]

[9] Subsidies have also been eliminated from the Soviet data. It is not easy to find the exact turnover tax rates on specific commodities; in 1937, for instance, they were 0.5 percent on coal and steel, 1.0 percent on most machinery, from 17 to 35 percent on leather shoes, and on many types of cotton textiles, for at least a part of the year, 44 percent and even higher. Abram Bergson, *The Real National Income of Soviet Russia Since 1928* (Cambridge, Mass., 1961), p. 106.

A very good case can indeed be made for eliminating American indirect taxes as well. On the other hand, in the Soviet Union profit rates on consumer goods are much higher than on means of production. In 1959 they were 29.7 and 18.4 percent, respectively (*Narodnoe khoziaistvo SSSR v 1960 godu* [The people's economy of the USSR in 1960], p. 144), though it is not clear whether these rates are gross or net of turnover taxes. I do not know the relative distribution of profit rates in the United States. It is usually assumed that competitive forces prevent wide and long-lasting disparities among industries, which may or may not be true. Actually, the problem is more complex. It is not the profits on sales that are supposed to tend toward equality but profits on invested capital and even on net worth. Even in equilibrium they may, however, vary, depending on the risk involved, and thus leave us no clear criterion for judging when a significant deviation from the "normal" rate takes place. To make matters worse, yields from turnover taxes in the Soviet Union fell from 58.7 percent of all government revenues in 1940 to 40.7 percent in 1960, and those from profits rose from 12.1 percent to 24.2 percent. As this trend continues, some rethinking of the whole question of the proper adjustment of Soviet prices will become necessary.

[10] For the effect of the rate of growth of gross investment on the ratio of depreciation to gross investment, see my "Depreciation, Replacement and Growth," op. cit., pp. 154–94.

Table 9.1. *Relative magnitudes of capital formation, USSR and U.S.*

Year	USSR 1928–58 Ratio of Gross Capital Formation to Gross National Product				(5) Ratio of Net Capital Formation to Net National Product 1937 factor cost (%)
	(1) Current rubles (%)	(2) Adjusted current rubles[a] (%)	(3) Ruble factor cost of 1937 (%)	(4) Ratio of implicit deflators[b] Col. (2) ÷ Col. (3)	
1928	22.7	25.0	12.5	200	9.3
1937	21.2	25.9	25.9	100	21.9
1940	15.6	19.2	19.1	101	14.6
1950	22.8	27.9	26.9	105	21.1
1953	23.6	28.2	27.0	104	
1955	24.1	27.9	28.1	99	21.6
1958	27.6	31.6			

U.S. 1869/78–1946/55

	(1) Current prices (%)	(2)	(3) 1929 prices (%)	(4) Col. (1) ÷ Col. (3)^c	(5) NCF ÷ NNP 1929 prices (%)
1869–78	19.8		22.9	86	15.1
1879–88	19.8		22.2	89	14.0
1889–98	22.0		25.1	88	15.2
1899–1908	21.4		23.0	93	13.8
1909–18	20.5		22.1	93	11.9
1919–28	20.6		20.6	100	10.4
1929–38	14.5		13.4	108	1.9
1939–48	17.5		16.0	109	5.4
1946–55	20.2		17.3	117	4.8

[a] Column 2 is column 1 expressed in current ruble factor cost. The effects of turnover taxes and subsidies have been eliminated.

[b] Column 4 is the ratio of the implicit deflator of capital formation to that of national product obtained by dividing column 2 by column 3.

[c] Column 4 is the ratio of the implicit deflator of capital formation to that of national product obtained by dividing column 1 by column 3.

Sources: First part (USSR), columns 1–3, and 5: Abram Bergson, *The Real National Income of Soviet Russia Since 1928* (Cambridge, Mass.., 1961), Tables 3, 22, 62, 82, pp. 46, 128, 237, 300. Abram Bergson, "Soviet National Income," prepared for the Conference on Economics of Soviet Industrialization, Princeton, N.J., May 1961, p. 49. Nancy Nimitz, *Soviet National Income and Product, 1956–1958*, The RAND Corp. RM-3112-PR (Santa Monica, Calif., June 1962), Tables 3 and 6, pp. 11, 17.

Second part (U.S.), columns 1, 3, and 5: Simon Kuznets, *Capital in the American Economy: Its Formation and Financing* (Princeton, N.J., 1961), Tables 8 and 9, pp. 92–3, 95–6. The Commerce Department concepts are used.

Thus the data in columns 3 and 5 (and even column 1, for that matter) show a greater Soviet "effort" as it is defined here. The reader's choice between column 3 and column 5 will depend on his attitude to capital formation: if the latter is essentially an increment in the stock of capital, he will take column 5; if it is an instrument for the introduction of new techniques into industry, he will prefer column 3. I would pick a compromise, but slanted toward column 3.[11]

In the Soviet Union the magnitude of capital formation (or at least its major part) is presumably determined by the planners, according to their own lights, and limited by the existing capacity of the capital goods industry (unless supplemented by imports). This restriction seldom operates in the United States; here capital formation is bound either by the population's propensity to save, or by business' willingness to invest, or by both. According to Kuznets, the first restriction seemed to be effective before World War I, but not since. I may venture a guess that the low rate of American capital formation in recent decades has been caused by (1) a capital-saving technological progress that has reduced capital requirements per unit of output, and (2) by widespread underutilization of capacity, which makes investment unprofitable from the firm's point of view.[12]

But the most interesting part of Table 9.1 is not, I believe, in columns 3 or 5, but in column 4. It shows that in the Soviet Union the prices of capital goods took a sharp drop from 1928 to 1937 and remained more or less stable thereafter *compared with* the general price level, while in the United States there was a continuous rise, particularly recently. Table 9.2 supplies additional details. In both countries, construction prices rose rapidly (after 1937 in the Soviet Union), but in the Soviet Union their rise was offset by the fall in machinery prices (all in relation to the general

---

[11] For that matter, if "effort" is understood in the sense of "sacrifice," a comparison in current prices (column 1) may be more meaningful. If we mean by "effort" an input into growth, then columns 3 or 5 are more relevant. This is just one interpretation; the reader may have his own.

The relation between capital formation and technological progress, always a fascinating subject, has become very popular among economists recently. See a paper by Robert M. Solow on "Technical Progress, Capital Formation, and Economic Growth," *The American Economic Review Papers and Proceedings,* Vol. LII (May 1962), pp. 76–92.

[12] Simon Kuznets, *Capital in the American Economy: Its Formation and Financing* (Princeton, N.J., 1961), pp. 114–17; Daniel Creamer, *Capital Expansion and Capacity in Postwar Manufacturing,* National Industrial Conference Board Studies in Business Economics No. 72 (New York, 1961).

Compared with other countries, Soviet ratios of gross capital formation to gross national product are high, but not unique. In the 1950–59 period the ratio of gross domestic capital formation to gross domestic product was 28.4 percent in Australia, 28.5 percent in Japan, and 29.7 percent in Norway. See *United Nations World Economic Survey, 1960,* Table 1.1, p. 16.

Table 9.2. *Price movements of components of gross national product, USSR and U.S.*

	(1)	(2)	(3)	(4)
		USSR, 1937 = 100[a]		
Period	GNP	Gross investment	Domestic civilian machinery[b]	Construction
1928	22	44	70	56
1937	100	100	100	100
1940	132	132	106	156
1944	142	154	110	196
1950	215	223	191	271
1955	210	208	153	254
		U.S., 1929 = 100		
	GNP	Gross fixed investment[c]	Producers' durables	Construction
Kuznets' concept				
1869–78	68	54	75	48
1879–88	55	47	53	45
1889–98	47	41	44	41
1899–1908	52	48	50	48
1909–18	70	64	73	60
1919–28	103	101	103	100
1929–38	84	93	91	94
1939–48	113	128	124	135
1944–53	145	172	154	201
Commerce concept				
1929	100	100	100	100
1939	84	95	94	94
1949	154	189	166	202
1959	196	262	231	281

[a] The USSR prices can be more accurately defined as index numbers of 1937 ruble factor cost per unit of output for various components of GNP.

[b] Excludes imported machinery, important in 1928 and 1944.

[c] Includes government construction but excludes net changes in inventories and foreign investment.

Sources: First part (USSR), columns 1–4: Abram Bergson, *The Real National Income of Soviet Russia Since 1928* (Cambridge, Mass., 1961), Tables 63, E-3, F-1, F-4, pp. 238, 367, 381, 388.

Second part (U.S.), columns 1–4: R. A. Gordon, "Differential Changes in the Prices of Consumers' and Capital Goods," *The American Economic Review*, Vol. LI (December 1961), Tables 1, 4, pp. 938, 946.

price level); in the United States, machinery prices did not fall (and even rose between 1929 and 1959). Hence the prices of all capital goods rose faster than other prices.[13]

Leaving construction alone (for reasons already explained), we can note with a mild degree of satisfaction that the behavior of machinery prices in the two countries lends some support to the Second hypothesis regarding the *relatively* faster economic progress in Soviet machine-building as compared with the rest of that economy. Unfortunately, it confirms the hypothesis in its weakest form (a).

Table 9.3 is designed not to test any hypotheses but to provide general information. Even here we notice the relatively even character of American development and the sharp contrasts in the Soviet. The growth rates of Soviet national product and of industrial production are certainly impressive, either by themselves or in comparison with the American experience. An annual rate of growth of national product of 5.2 percent over the 1928–55 "effective years" and an 8.0 percent growth of industrial production have seldom been equaled or exceeded by any country, and it would be quite reasonable to deduct not four years from the 1928–55 period to account for World War II but as many as eight (since prewar production was not reached until the late 1940s and early 1950s), which would raise these rates still higher.[14] In contrast, agriculture performed poorly until 1950, and its record over the whole 1928–58 period was anything but inspiring. Not much pride can be taken in household per capita consumption either, to put it mildly. We can now see the price paid for rapid capital formation.

If the rates of growth of national product per capita are still impressive, those per employed worker are much less so. Here the Soviet advantage over the American performance is not large (and will almost disappear in the next table), and all of it was created after 1950. It seems that the rapid growth of Soviet industrial output prior to World War II was achieved not so much by "economic progress" as by a large increase in inputs. This impression will be strengthened by the data in Table 9.4.

---

[13] The *relative* rise of capital-goods prices has been a frequent phenomenon, observed in Canada in 1870–1953, Sweden in 1873–1938, Denmark between 1890–99 and 1947–52, and the United Kingdom in the period 1890–99 to 1946–52. In the 1953–59 period it took place in Belgium, Germany, The Netherlands, Norway, Canada, and the United States. The opposite situation was observed in Austria, Denmark, France, Italy, and Sweden. See R. A. Gordon, op. cit. It is a subject worth further study.

[14] The Soviet rates of growth were approximated by Germany in 1950–59 and by Japan in 1951–59. Gross domestic product in constant factor cost grew in Germany at 7.2 percent (in 1954 prices) and at 8.4 percent in Japan (in 1955 prices). Industrial production (mining, manufacturing, construction, and public utilities) grew at 8.8 percent in Germany and at some 10–11 percent in Japan. See Essay 6, Table 6.1.

Here we find that the growth of national product per worker adjusted for nonfarm hours was lower in the Soviet Union than in the United States before 1950, and that the respectable average rate of 2.4 percent for the 1928–58 "effective years" was all created by the rapid growth after 1950. Even the excellent Soviet performance in 1950–58, greatly superior to the American, is of the same order of magnitude as the German and the Japanese.[15]

The behavior of Soviet capital productivity (the reciprocal of the capital-output ratio) shown in the second line of Table 9.4 is markedly different from the American: in every period except for 1940–50 (which hardly need be considered) the former was falling, even during the Soviet "golden age" of 1950–58. The American pattern depends, to some extent, on the sources used. Kendrick has found a rise in capital productivity (in private domestic economy) in every subperiod studied by him from 1899 to 1953. According to Kuznets, it was falling from 1869–79 to about 1919 or so (again depending on which of his several variants is chosen), and (omitting the great underutilization of capital during the depressed 1930s) rising thereafter. Here is his explanation of this phenomenon:

> ...High capital–output [the reciprocal of capital productivity] ratios are likely to be found among industries in the early stages of growth, when extensive expansion is at a high rate and building is in advance of current needs. It is in these industries that the relative increase in output is also likely to be at a high rate, and it is in these industries, all other conditions being equal, that the capital–output ratio is likely to decline most precipitously.[16]

[15] All these conclusions, whether favorable or unfavorable to the Soviet Union, depend to a considerable extent on the methods of measurement and on the choice of the base year. Bergson, whose care and conscientiousness are unique in the profession, has experimented with a number of alternative assumptions and usually presented several estimates of most of his results. Among them, I have chosen those based on the 1937 weights, because that year was in the middle of the period considered here and was likely to give more reasonable results than a very early year such as 1928 (when Soviet industrialization was just beginning) or a very late year such as 1955. Even with 1937 weights Bergson frequently presents several alternative calculations. I have usually tried to steer a middle course and to choose those based on the most reasonable assumptions. But it should be noted that, had I taken 1928 as a base, Soviet performance would have looked much better. But so would the American if an early year of American industrialization had been used as a base.

For the classical example of the importance of alternative sets of weights in index number construction, or for what has become known as the "Gerschenkron Effect," the reader is referred to his study on *Dollar Index of Soviet Machinery Output, 1927–28 to 1937,* The RAND Corporation, Report R-197 (Santa Monica, Calif., April 6, 1951).

[16] Kendrick, op. cit., Table 45, pp. 166–67; Kuznets, op. cit., Table 6, pp. 80–81 and 216. The behavior of American capital productivity is quite sensitive to coverage and concepts used (such as the whole economy, private economy, certain sectors of the latter, net or gross of depreciation, etc.), not to mention the degree of utilization of the capital stock. Hence the description given in the text should be taken with caution.

Table 9.3. *Average annual percentage rates of growth of principal economic indicators for the USSR and U.S.*[a]

	(1)	(2)	(3)	(4)	(5)	(6)	(7)	(8)
USSR	1928-37	1937-40	1928-40	1940-50	1950-55	1950-58	1928-55	1928-55 effective years[b]
U.S.	1869/78-1879/88 (1929 dollars)	1879/88-1889/98 (1929 dollars)	1889/98-1899/1908 (1929 dollars)	1869/78-1899/1908 (1929 dollars)	1899/1908-1929 (1929 dollars)	1929-1948 (1954 dollars)	1948-1957 (1954 dollars)	1929-1957 (1954 dollars)
Gross national product								
Bergson, 1937 ruble factor cost	5.5	3.4	5.0	2.1	7.6		4.4	5.2
Gross national product, per capita	4.5	1.0	3.6	2.9	5.8		3.8	4.4
Gross national product, per employed worker[d,e]	1.7	0.8	1.5	1.8	6.1		2.4	2.9
Household consumption per capita	-0.3	-1.5	-0.6	1.9	6.7		1.7	2.0
Industrial production								
Nutter, moving weights	12.1	3.7	9.9	2.1	9.6		6.9	8.1
Industrial production								
Kaplan and Moorsteen, 1950=100	10.4	1.9	8.2	3.5	9.6	9.2	6.7	8.0
Gross agricultural production								
Johnson	1.0[c]	-1.3[c]	0.4[c]	-0.3	5.0	6.5		
Gross national product	6.6	3.3	4.6	4.8	3.4	2.5	3.7	2.9
Gross national product, per capita	4.1	1.2	2.6	2.6	1.7	1.5	1.9	1.7
Gross national product, per employed worker[e]				1.9	1.6	1.6	1.7	1.6
Household consumption, per capita	4.0	0.8	2.9	2.6	1.9	1.4	1.7	1.5

	(1) 1870–80	(2) 1880–90	(3) 1890–1910	(4) 1870–1910	(5) 1900–28	(6) 1928–50	(7) 1950–55	(8) 1950–58
Industrial production Nutter, moving weights	5.1	5.6	4.5	5.0	4.4	3.5	5.3	2.7[f]

[a] Average annual growth rates are calculated by the compound interest formula.

[b] Counting 23 rather than 27 years.

[c] Territory of 1939.

[d] With output in 1937 ruble factor cost.

[e] Figures on output per worker do not consider variations in working hours. Such adjusted figures tend to lower the USSR rates while moderately increasing the U.S. figures. See Bergson, Table 75, p. 273.

[f] Federal Reserve Index.

Sources: First part (USSR), columns 1–8: Abram Bergson, *The Real National Income of Soviet Russia Since 1928* (Cambridge, Mass., 1961), Tables 71, 72, 74, 78, pp. 261, 264, 271, 284. G. Warren Nutter, *The Growth of Industrial Production in the Soviet Union* (Princeton, N.J., 1962), Tables 30, 35, pp. 150, 163. Norman M. Kaplan and Richard H. Moorsteen, *Indexes of Soviet Industrial Output*, The RAND Corp. RM-2495 (Santa Monica, Calif., May 1960), Vol. II, Tables 22 and 31, pp. 235, 248. D. Gale Johnson, "Soviet Agriculture," prepared for the Conference on Economics of Soviet Industrialization at Princeton, N.J., May 1961, Table 3, p. 26.

Second part (U.S.), columns 1–8: Bergson, op. cit., Tables 71, 72, 74, 78, pp. 261, 264, 271, 284. Nutter, op. cit., Tables 61, 62, pp. 227, 229. *Statistical Abstract of the United States, 1961*, Table 1086, p. 778.

Table 9.4. *Average annual percentage rates of growth of principal productivity indexes*[a]

	USSR				
	(1)	(2)	(3)	(4)	(5)
1937 ruble factor cost	1928-40	1940-50	1950-58	1928-58	1928-58 effective years[b]
Net national product per worker adjusted for nonfarm hours	0.5	1.1	5.6	2.1	2.4
Net national product per unit of reproducible capital	−5.1	1.3	−3.9	−2.7	−3.1
Net national product per unit of selected inputs[d]	0.1	1.3	2.7	1.2	1.4
	U.S. 1948-60	Canada 1949-60	U.K. 1949-59	Germany 1950-59	
Labor productivity (gross value added per man-hour)	2.5	2.8	1.4	5.5	
Capital productivity (gross value added per unit of capital stock)	−0.5[e]	−1.5	−1.1	0.4	
Productivity of labor and capital combined	1.4[e]	1.2	0.6	3.6	

[a] The average annual rates of growth are calculated by the compound interest formula in the first part and exponentially in the second, by comparing the first and last years.
[b] Counting 26 rather than 30 years.
[c] Negligible.
[d] Unit of selected inputs is a weighted sum of labor, reproducible fixed capital, farm land, and livestock herds.

The Soviet experience may very well be in accord with Kuznets' explanation, but it is a bit surprising that, instead of beginning to rise, capital productivity has fallen even after 1950. Perhaps the heavy rate of capital formation has led to perceptively diminishing returns from capital, though there is nothing wrong with diminishing returns (the most beloved law in traditional economics), at least to a point. It seems that the average capital productivity in the two countries has been of the same order of magnitude in recent years. The Soviet Union must have started then with a high productivity and has gradually reduced it more or less to the present American level.[17] It will be most instructive to watch future developments.

[17] See Norman M. Kaplan, "The Stock of Soviet Capital on January 1, 1960," prepared for the Conference on Economics of Soviet Industrialization, Princeton, N.J., May 1961,

U.S.				
(6) 1869/78– 1899/1908 (1929 dollars)	(7) 1899/1908– 1929 (1929 dollars)	(8) 1929– 1948 (1954 dollars)	(9) 1929– 1957 (1954 dollars)	(10) 1948– 1957 (1954 dollars)
1.7	2.2	2.2	2.1	2.0
−0.5	0.1	2.3	1.5	– ^{c}
1.5	1.8	2.2	2.0	1.7
Japan 1951–59				
5.8				
−0.4				
3.7				

^{e} For private economy only.

Sources: First part, columns 1–10: Abram Bergson, "Soviet National Income," prepared for the Conference on Economics of Soviet Industrialization, Princeton, N.J., May 1961, Table 2, p. 7.

Second part, columns 2–6: Essay 6, Tables 6.4, 6.6, 6.7.

Of the several components of Soviet capital formation and of the capital stock, the behavior of inventories is rather perplexing. One usually imagines that the Soviet economy, always bursting at its seams, is perpetually short of inventories. Yet the fraction of inventories in capital formation in 1955 (in 1937 prices) was 13.2 percent, much higher than the corresponding American figure (in 1929 prices) of 7.0 percent in 1946–55, though it is true that in earlier periods the American fraction had been higher.[18]

The RAND Corporation P-2248 (Santa Monica, Calif., March 15, 1961), pp. 65–67; Bergson, op. cit., p. 142.

[18] Bergson, op. cit., Tables 83 and G-1, pp. 301 and 392. Kuznets, op. cit., Table 14, pp. 146–47. The exact behavior of the American ratios (and probably of the Soviet as well) depends on the use of current or constant prices, but expressed either way American ratios have been falling.

More significant is the ratio of the stock of inventories to gross national product. In 1958 the Soviet ratio was some 40 percent as compared with some 30 percent for the United States.[19] Strangely enough, the Soviet Union is relatively rich in inventories. In trade these ratios are even more surprising. In wholesale trade, they were about equal in the two countries in 1960. But in retail trade the Soviet Union had some 85 days of sales embodied in inventories, while the Americans managed to get along with about 36 (assuming a 26-day month). Moreover, the Soviet ratio had risen from 40 days in 1937, though there was a slight fall from the 92 days in 1959.[20] Since Soviet trade is one of the most neglected sectors of the economy, one cannot help being puzzled at this inventory generosity. A few additional comments on this will be made shortly.

The last line in Table 9.4 shows the rate of growth of the total factor productivity (the ratio of output to a certain combination of the several factors of production), our closest approximation to "economic progress."[21] It is striking that with the exception of the 1950–58 period, every Soviet rate is below every American one, irrespective of the period chosen. The 1950–58 Soviet rate of 2.7 percent is quite good and higher than any American rate, but even it falls short of the corresponding German and Japanese rates given at the bottom of the table. Our earlier impression that Soviet economic growth, particularly before World War II, depended less on "progress" and more on inputs is now reinforced.[22]

The distribution of the labor force in the two countries by economic sectors, a standard item in most economic menus, is found in Table 9.5. Its significance (at least for our purposes) is moderate because a large concentration of labor in a particular sector may testify either to its importance (and even to its efficiency if it participates in international trade) or to the low productivity of labor in it. The American fraction of the labor force engaged in industry (mining and manufacturing) in 1960 is somewhat higher than the Soviet 1959 figure of 20.9 percent, but the latter

[19] These are very rough calculations, which may not be quite comparable. The data on which they are based were taken from the following sources: *Narodnoe khoziaistvo SSSR v 1960 godu* [The people's economy of the USSR in 1960], pp. 92–3; Nancy Nimitz, *Soviet National Income and Product, 1956–1958*, The RAND Corporation, RM-3112-PR (Santa Monica, Calif., June 1962), Table 3, p. 11; *Statistical Abstract of the United States, 1961*, Tables 412 and 443, pp. 302 and 324.

Similar conclusions were reached by Robert W. Campbell, "A Comparison of Soviet and American Inventory–Output Ratios," *The American Economic Review*, Vol. XLIII (September 1958), pp. 549–65.

[20] Sources: *Narodnoe khoziaistvo SSSR v 1960 godu* [The people's economy of the USSR in 1960], pp. 698, 709; *Statistical Abstract of the United States, 1961*, Table 657, p. 494; *Economic Indicators*, July 1962, p. 19. The Soviet data exclude collective peasant markets.

[21] See note 4, p. 145.

[22] See, however, note 15, p. 153.

was rising rapidly, and the difference would look smaller if the relatively larger American agricultural inputs produced by industry were taken into account.

Perhaps the most striking feature of this table is the extremely large concentration of labor in Soviet agriculture – 46.3 percent as compared with only 6.7 percent for the United States. For reasons just stated, these two figures (like most of ours) are not strictly comparable; also Soviet farmers spend some of their time on nonagricultural activities (see the notes in the table), but even a most generous correction would still leave the Soviet Union with a swollen agricultural labor force, out of harmony with the general level of the development of that country. The contrast between the two countries will become even sharper if we reflect on Soviet food shortages and American surpluses.

The other striking difference between the two countries lies in the fraction of labor force engaged in trade and public dining: in the Soviet Union a tiny 4.6 percent, and in the United States 22.4 percent if finance, real estate, and insurance are included, and 18.2 percent if they are not. Similarly, payrolls constituted only 2.2 percent of total sales in the Soviet retail trade in 1960, as compared with about 13 percent in the United States.[23] Combined with the preceding discussion of inventories in the retail trade of the two countries, this comparison leads to the unexpected conclusion that the highly developed American trade is relatively labor-intensive and capital-saving, while the inverse holds true for the other country, a situation forming just the opposite of what an economic theorist would expect. Perhaps the riddle can be partially explained by the Soviet unwillingness to allocate *fixed capital* – stores – to retail trade. But why then such large inventories? It is hard not to see in all this simply a poor organization of the Soviet distributive system.[24]

So much about labor. The distribution of capital is given in Table 9.6. This would be one of our most interesting tables if its data were not marred by lack of comparability. The Soviet data are gross of depreciation, the American are net. The former were obtained by a census taken in 1959–60

---

[23] The Soviet fraction is understated because high turnover taxes and profits in consumer goods industries are included in the denominator. But even doubling or tripling the fraction would still leave it far short of the American figure. The latter consists of two components: actual payrolls – 10.9 percent plus 2.6 percent for implicit wages of proprietors, estimated on the assumption that their average wage equaled that of employees in retail trade, which need not be true. Therefore the resulting sum of 13.5 percent is inexact, but the error could not be large. Sources: *Narodnoe khoziaistvo SSSR v 1960 godu* [The people's economy of the USSR in 1960], p. 710; *Statistical Abstract of the United States, 1961,* Table 1159, p. 833.

[24] Cf. Marshall I. Goldman, "The Cost and Efficiency of Distribution in the Soviet Union," *The Quarterly Journal of Economics,* Vol. LXXVI (August 1962), pp. 437–53.

Table 9.5. *Percentage distribution of employed persons by economic sectors in USSR and U.S.*

| | USSR 1937–1959 | | | | | |
	(1) 1937	(2) 1940	(3) 1950	(4) 1959	(5) 1959 official data	(6)
Total civilian employment (excl. domestics, day laborers, etc.)	100.0	100.0	100.0	100.0	100.0	
I. Nonagricultural branches	37.5	39.8	45.9	53.7		
A. Workers and employees	33.9	35.3	43.4	52.1		
1. Industry	14.3	13.7	17.5	20.9	38.3	
2. Construction	2.2	2.0	3.2	5.0		
3. Transportation and communications	4.3	4.9	5.7	6.9	32.8	
4. Trade and public dining	3.6	4.2	4.2	4.6	5.4	
5. Public health and education	4.9	5.6	7.2	9.1	10.3	
6. Other	4.5	5.0	5.6	5.6	4.9	
B. Members of producers' cooperatives	2.7	3.1	2.0	1.5		
1. Industry	1.9	2.2	1.5	1.2		
2. Services	0.8	0.9	0.5	0.2		
C. Independent artisans	1.0	1.3	0.6	0.2		
II. Agriculture[a]	62.5	60.2	54.1	46.3	40.2	

U.S. 1870–1960

	(1) 1870	(2) 1900	(3) 1920	(4) 1940[b,c]	(5) 1940[c]	(6) 1960
Total civilian employment	100.0	100.0	100.0	100.0	100.0	100.0
Agriculture, forestry, and fisheries	50.2	37.5	27.4	17.1	18.9	6.7
Mining and manufacturing	19.0	24.4	29.1	24.5	25.7	28.1
Construction	5.8	5.7	5.2	6.6	4.6	5.9
Transportation and other utilities	5.0	7.2	10.0	7.8	6.7	7.2
Trade, eating and dining places, finance, real estate, insurance[d]	6.4	9.5	11.7	16.4	19.9	22.4
Educational services	1.5	2.2	2.8	3.2	3.5	5.2
Other services	10.3	11.0	10.6	15.1	15.5	15.7
Government not elsewhere classified	0.8	1.0	2.2	3.2	3.1	5.0
Not allocated	1.1	1.3	0.9	6.2	1.6	4.0

[a] Agricultural employment includes some nonagricultural activities. In 1959 these activities were estimated (as percentage of all employment in the country) as follows: machine tractor and repair stations, 0.5 percent; forestry, 0.4 percent; education, culture, and public health, 1.3 percent; industry and construction, 1.7 percent; hunting and fishing, 0.5 percent; with a total thus obtained of nonagricultural activities of 4.4 percent; to this should be added an unknown percentage of trade activities. Perhaps the inclusion of all these activities in agriculture accounts for most of the difference between data in column 4 and the official statistics in column 5.

[b] The data for 1870–1940 as reported in *Historical Statistics of the U.S., Colonial Times to 1957* are obtained from a number of sources and are not strictly comparable.

[c] A comparison of the two columns for 1940 shows lack of complete comparability between the two sets of data.

[d] For the first four columns there is no specific entry for eating and dining places. Perhaps they were included in the Not Allocated sector. In columns 5 and 6, eating and dining places accounted for 2.5 and 2.8 percent, respectively, of total civilian employment.

Sources: First part (USSR), columns 1–4: Murray S. Weitzman and Andrew Elias, *The Magnitude and Distribution of Civilian Employment in the U.S.S.R.: 1928–1959,* U.S. Bureau of the Census, International Population Reports Series P-95, No. 58 (Washington, D.C., April 1961), Table 2, p. 58; column 5: *Narodnoe khoziaistvo SSSR v 1960 godu* [The people's economy of the USSR in 1960], p. 26.

Second part (U.S.), columns 1–4: *Historical Statistics of the U.S., Colonial Times to 1957* (Washington, D.C., 1960), U.S. Bureau of the Census, Series D 57-71, p. 74; columns 5–6: *U.S. Census of Population: 1960. General Social and Economic Characteristics, U.S. Summary,* U.S. Bureau of the Census, Final Report PC (I)-1C (Washington, D.C., 1962), Table 92, p. 1–223.

Table 9.6. *Distribution of the stock of fixed capital in USSR and U.S. (percent of total)*

	(1) Soviet capital, gross of depreciation[a] Jan. 1, 1960	(2) American capital, net of depreciation, at 1929 prices	(3)	(4)	(5)
		June 1, 1880	June 1, 1900	Dec. 31, 1922	Dec. 31, 1948
Total capital	100.0	100.0	100.0	100.0	100.0
1. Industry	28.3	6.3	10.2	17.4	19.6
a. Mining and manufacturing	24.9	6.3	9.5	15.2	15.5
b. Electric power production	3.4	0.0	0.7	2.2	4.1
2. Agriculture[b]	9.9	18.4	9.5	8.5	7.2
3. Transport and communications	13.7	33.0	22.2	17.7	14.4
4. Housing	33.3	29.2	38.8	32.5	32.0
5. Other[c]	14.7	13.1	19.3	24.0	26.8

[a] Capital is valued at July 1, 1955 replacement costs.
[b] Excludes livestock.
[c] Consists primarily of trade and services.

Source: Norman M. Kaplan, "The Stock of Soviet Capital on January 1, 1960," prepared for the Conference on Economics of Soviet Industrialization, Princeton, N.J., May 1961, The RAND Corp. P-2248 (Santa Monica, Calif., March 15, 1961), Table 5.5, p. 48.

Table 9.7. *Percentage distribution of gross fixed investment in USSR and U.S., 1950–59[a]*

	USSR (1) 1955 rubles	U.S.[b] (2) 1955 dollars
Total	100.0	100.0
Industry	40.4	29.2
Agriculture	17.0[c]	7.8[d]
Transport and communications	8.1	12.7
Housing	22.0	25.2
Other	12.5	25.0

[a] Excludes inventories.

[b] Excludes government purchases of equipment for military facilities, for government production facilities, for government independent agencies, for administrative use, and for transport.

[c] Excludes farm housing.

[d] Includes farm housing.

Sources: Columns 1–2: Central Intelligence Agency, *A Comparison of Capital Investment in the U.S. and the USSR 1950–59* (Washington, D.C., February 1961), Tables 4, 10, pp. 33, 41.

and based on 1955 prices. The job was done with care, and the results are probably more dependable than the American figures based on different and less reliable methods, too complex to be described here.[25] Disregarding these (and all other) difficulties, we note that the Soviet Union had a larger fraction of capital invested in industry – 28.3 percent as against 19.6 percent in the United States in 1948, certainly not a surprise. Nor is there anything strange about the American excess in the "other" sector (mostly trade and services). But the nearly equal fractions of capital invested in housing in the two countries do come as a surprise. Norman Kaplan, the author of this comparison, tried a number of adjustments, of which the most important was the use of the 1948 rather than the 1929 prices, and finally raised the American figure to some 40 percent because of the relative increase in construction costs.[26] On the other hand, the distribution of fixed gross investment in the two countries in 1950–59 in 1955 prices given in Table 9.7 shows only a slightly higher American

[25] The methods are described in detail in the several sources used by Kaplan and cited in his paper, op. cit.

[26] Ibid., pp. 51–55. Kaplan also included farm housing originally excluded from American housing. It is very likely that if evaluated in present-day prices, American housing would be a still higher fraction of the total.

fraction allocated to housing. Perhaps our surprise is easily explained: being strongly impressed with the inadequacy of Soviet housing, we simply forget that that whole economy is still relatively poor in capital.

The relative magnitudes of agricultural capital in the two countries are not very different, but they differ tremendously if expressed in relation to the distribution of the labor forces, as will be done in Table 9.8.

Estimates of the flow of recent investment are less involved and more dependable than those of the stocks of capital, though they serve different purposes. A short comparison of this kind is given in Table 9.7. It confirms the general results of Table 9.6: in the Soviet Union, the major share of investment went to industry (40.4 percent), followed by housing (22.0 percent) and agriculture (17.0 percent); in the United States, industry was closely followed by housing and the "other" sector.

So much for the general background. Let us return to our Second hypothesis. Tables 9.8 and 9.9 are related to it in a rather oblique manner: they are based on the *presumption* (with which the reader may or may not agree) that if a particular Soviet industry is *relatively* better endowed with capital (Table 9.8) or engineers (Table 9.9) than its American counterpart, then that Soviet industry will experience a *relatively* more rapid progress. Thus columns 3 and 6 in Table 9.8 show the ratio of the fraction of capital invested in a given sector (columns 1 and 4) to the fraction of the labor force employed in it (columns 2 and 5), or, what is of greater interest to us, the ratio of capital per worker in a given sector divided by the ratio of capital per worker in the whole economy.[27] If the result is unity, workers in a given sector have the *average* endowment of capital per worker for the whole economy; if it is larger than unity, they are endowed better than the national average; of course, no direct comparison is made here between the absolute amount of capital per worker in any given industry in the two countries.

Two pairs of figures stand out in the upper part of the table. First, the average industrial worker in the Soviet Union has a larger capital endowment in relation to the average worker in the whole Soviet economy than does his American colleague. It is to be fully expected that Soviet planners attach greater importance to their industry than the American market mechanism does. Second, the relative endowment of an average agricultural worker in the Soviet Union is poor indeed, being only 0.32, or not much more than a third of the corresponding American ratio. Much has been written about institutional obstacles to high labor productivity in Soviet agriculture, and much of it is true; but the capital poverty of Soviet agriculture has received less attention.

[27] Let K and L stand for capital and employment in the whole economy respectively, while K_i and L_i indicate these variables in a specific industry. Then we have $(K_i/K)/(L_i/L) = (K_i/L_i)/(K/L)$.

It is rather pleasant to find a higher Soviet ratio in metals and metal products than the American one, 1.0 as compared with 0.72. This is the presumption in favor of the Second hypothesis I was looking for. But wait until we get to Table 9.9.[28]

Before leaving Table 9.8, we note the distinct positive, though not very strong, correlation between the respective ratios in columns 3 and 6 in the lower half of the table. This suggests that the relative ratio of capital to labor is determined, at least to some extent, by the nature of each industry. Against this background, the difference between any two members of a pair of ratios becomes more significant. But we have explored the data in the table so little that it is better not to press the point.

The structure of Table 9.9 is similar to that of Table 9.8, except that capital is replaced by the employment of engineers.[29] Unfortunately, research and development activities in the two countries are organized differently: in the Soviet Union they are usually conducted in special organizations outside of individual enterprises, while in the United States a good part of them is done within the firms. In the absence of sufficient information about the industrial distribution of Soviet engineers so employed, I had to exclude privately employed American engineers engaged in research and development from my data, an adjustment that deprived the table of most of its meaning. To add to my troubles, engineers in the two countries even when employed by enterprises frequently perform dissimilar nonengineering functions (for instance, administration in the Soviet Union, sales and customer services in the United States). Under the circumstances it might have been better to save space and omit Table 9.9 altogether, and I would have done so if the results of the table had not been *contrary* to my hopes: the relative ratio of engineers to total employment in machine-building and metalworking in the United States turned out to be *higher* than in the Soviet Union. Perhaps this was caused by the intensive use of engineers in American aircraft industry; I do not know whether this industry is included in Soviet machine-building and metalworking. But just as I did not press the positive results of Table 9.8, so I hope the reader will not press the negative findings of Table 9.9. Let us wait for Korol's study.[30]

---

[28] Even before we get to Table 9.9, we should note that we have not attempted to analyze the structure of the metals and metal products industry in the two countries. They may have a different product mix, which may explain away or increase the difference in the ratios. Here is a good place to remind the reader about my original request not to take this essay too seriously.

[29] Nestor E. Terleckyj has found a mild positive correlation between the rate of growth of the index of total factor productivity and the ratios of research and development outlays to sales, or of research and development personnel to total man-hours worked. Kendrick, op. cit., pp. 179–88. This was my reason for constructing Table 9.9, but, as the text will presently show, with unsatisfactory results.

[30] See note 3, p. 144.

Table 9.8. *Relative distribution of capital and labor, USSR and U.S.*

	(1) USSR	(2)	(3)	(4) U.S.	(5)	(6)
	Distribution of nonresidential capital, Jan. 1, 1960 in 1955 prices[a,b] (%)	Distribution of civilian employment 1959 (%)	Ratio of col. (1) to col. (2)	Distribution of nonresidential capital, 1948 in 1929 prices[a,c] (%)	Distribution of civilian employment 1948[f] (%)	Ratio of col. (4) to col. (5)
Total	100.0	100.0	1.0	100.0	100.0	1.0
Industry	42.4	20.9	2.0	28.8	29.0	0.99
Agriculture	14.9[a]	46.3	0.32	10.6[a,d]	11.9	0.89
Transport and communications	20.5	6.9	3.0	21.2	6.4	3.3
Other	22.1	25.9	0.85	39.5	52.7	0.75

	Employment 1956[e] (%)		Capital stock 1953 at 1929 prices[c,d]		Civilian employment 1953[f]	
Manufacturing and mining	100.0	100.0	1.0	100.0	100.0	1.0
Fuels	19.3	8.0	2.4	24.6	5.0	4.9
Chemicals; stone, clay, and glass	12.3	9.4	1.3	14.3	8.1	1.8
Metals and metal products	38.7	37.4	1.0	32.3	45.1	0.72
Forest products; paper, pulp and products	6.7	14.6	0.46	7.0	9.3	0.75
Light and food industries	15.4	26.3	0.59	13.3	24.7	0.54
Textiles and products	(4.2)	(17.2)	0.24	(4.7)	(15.5)	0.30
Food, beverages and tobacco	(10.3)	(9.1)	1.1	(8.3)	(9.2)	0.90
Other	7.6	4.3	1.8	8.5	7.8	1.1

[a] Excludes livestock.
[b] Gross of depreciation.
[c] Net of depreciation.
[d] Includes farm housing.
[e] Excludes electric power.
[f] Man-year of full-time equivalent, excluding unpaid family workers.

Sources: First part, columns 1, 4: Norman M. Kaplan, "The Stock of Soviet Capital on January 1, 1960," prepared for the Conference on Economics of Soviet Industrialization, Princeton, N.J., May 1961, The RAND Corp. P-2248 (Santa Monica, Calif., March 15, 1961), Table 5.5, p. 48; column 2: Murray S. Weitzman and Andrew Elias, *The Magnitude and Distribution of Civilian Employment in the U.S.S.R.: 1928-1959*, U.S. Bureau of the Census, International Population Reports Series P-95, No. 58 (Washington, D.C., April 1961), Table 2, p. 58; column 5: U.S. Department of Commerce, *National Income 1954 Edition* (Washington, D.C., 1954), Table 28, pp. 202-03.

Second part, columns 1, 4: Kaplan, op. cit., Table 5.6, p. 57; column 2: Weitzman and Elias, op. cit., Table 7, pp. 71-72; column 5: U.S. Department of Commerce, op. cit., Table 28, pp. 202-03.

Table 9.9. *Relative distribution of engineers in industry, USSR and U.S.*[a]

	USSR			U.S.			
	(1) Distribution of engineers 1960[b,c] (%)	(2) Distribution of employment 1956[c] (%)	(3) Ratio of col. (1) to col. (2)	(4) Distribution of engineers 1960[d] (%)	(5) Distribution of employment 1960 (%)	(6) Ratio of col. (4) to col. (5)	
Ferrous metals	7.3	3.4	2.1	8.5	7.1	1.2	Primary metal industries
Nonferrous metals	3.8	2.1	1.8				
Coal mining	5.4	6.5[e]	0.83				
Oil extraction	1.2	0.58[f]	2.1	9.1	2.8	3.3	Petroleum products and extraction
Oil refining	1.1	0.42	2.6				
Machine building and metalworking	48.7	31.9	1.5	49.7	29.0	1.7	Fabricated metal products, machinery, electr. equipment, aircraft, and parts
Chemicals	6.4	3.2	2.0	10.7	5.3	2.0	Chemicals and allied products
Forest, lumber, and paper products	4.9	14.6	0.34	2.0	3.4	0.59	Paper and allied products
Building materials	4.0	6.2	0.65	2.1	3.2	0.66	Stone, clay, and glass products
Textiles, apparel, leather, furs, and shoes	5.3	17.2	0.31	1.1	13.0	0.08	Textiles and apparel

Food processing	6.7	9.1	0.74	1.3	8.9	0.15	Food and kindred products
Other manufacturing	5.2	4.9	1.1	15.4[g]	27.3[g]	0.56	Other manufacturing
Total	100.00	100.00	1.0	100.0	100.0	1.0	Total

[a] The classifications used in this table are very rough. Not only are the classifications in the two countries different, but even the distribution of engineers and of total employment in each country may not be entirely consistent.

[b] Includes only engineers employed in Soviet industry (*v promyshlennykh predpriiatiiakh*).

[c] Excludes electrical and thermal energy industries.

[d] Excludes American engineers engaged in research and development.

[e] Includes peat.

[f] Includes shale and natural gas.

[g] Includes professional and scientific industries.

Sources: Column 1: *Vysshee obrazovanie v SSSR* [Higher education in the USSR], 1960, Table 15, p. 56; column 2: Murray S. Weitzman and Andrew Elias, *The Magnitude and Distribution of Civilian Employment in the USSR: 1928–1959*, U.S. Bureau of the Census, International Population Reports Series P-95, No. 58 (Washington, D.C., April 1961), Table 7, pp. 71–72; column 4: National Science Foundation, *Scientific and Technical Personnel in Industry, 1960*, NSF 61-75 (Washington, D.C., 1962), Tables A-1, A-10, pp. 20, 28; column 5: *Statistical Abstract of the United States, 1961*, Table 279, pp. 209–10.

We may note in passing that columns 3 and 6 in this table also show some positive correlation (as they did in Table 9.8); so the relative employment of engineers in the two countries depends to some extent on the characteristics of each industry.

Even if the data in Tables 9.8 and 9.9 were completely reliable (if such data ever exist) and pointed clearly in the right (for my hypothesis) direction, they would merely tell us that certain industries have a particularly good or particularly poor relative supply of specific inputs (capital or engineers), without indicating how these inputs are used, that is, without showing the ratio, or some other relationship, between output and the given input. We cannot yet estimate the index of total factor productivity for the several Soviet industries – the strongest of our three approximations to economic progress – and have to use the productivity of labor alone. This substitution is not a great loss because the two productivities usually move together, and all would be bearable if our estimates of Soviet labor productivities were reasonably good.[31] Sadly enough, this is far from certain for many reasons, all of which, with the exception of the munitions problem, we agreed not to discuss.

If the reader, after all these warnings, is still willing to take a look at Table 9.10, he will find in its upper part that, in the USSR, productivity per person engaged in machinery and allied products (as well as in civilian machinery and equipment) grew faster than that in any other industry over the 1928–55 period taken as a whole. This would be most encouraging if a closer examination of the data did not reveal several disturbing features. Machinery had its heyday in 1928–40, a period whose data because of sharp structural changes in the economy are particularly hard to interpret and use. Omitting the 1940–50 interval because of the war, we do not find any spectacular progress in Soviet machine building in the remaining 1950–55 period. On the contrary, productivity in this industry grew more slowly than in almost all others, even slower than in food and textiles, though the negative rate (-2.0 percent) in civilian machinery looks rather strange. So the data are with us or against us, depending on the period chosen, hardly a consoling thought. The official Soviet index is more helpful: here the productivity in machinery stands out both in 1940–60 and in 1950–60, and this help would be welcomed if not for its uncertain nature (compare the official index with the Kaplan–Moorsteen in columns 3 and 4). If the reader is now discouraged, this being the last table, at least he had been warned.

---

[31] Kendrick found the rank coefficient of correlation between total factor productivity and that of labor (ratio of value added to labor input) over the 1899–1953 period to be 0.94. Ibid., p. 155.

If our quantitative test of the Second hypothesis has not been spectacularly successful, we can derive some consolation from nonquantitative conclusions reached by Richard Moorsteen, our ablest student of the Soviet machinery industry. He states:

... Machinery has been consistently among the most favored sectors of Soviet industry with respect to the funds, materials, and personnel placed at its disposal. Its record must be among the best that the Soviet economy has to offer.

A similar opinion is expressed by Nutter.[32] The general tone of Soviet discussions supports this view. Let us hope that they all are correct.

I have not presented similar data for the United States because Kendrick's excellent work covering the 1899–1953 period is readily available and requires little comment. His findings on productivity (both labor and total factor) clearly show not an even but, nevertheless, a broad general advance in which

... The relative positions, or ranks, of the various groups have fluctuated over the subperiods....

Further analysis suggests that there has been a tendency for the groups with low average ranks to improve their position over the subperiods while the high-ranking groups have tended to slip in the scale.[33]

The pattern is quite different from the Soviet. Although Nutter has found the rank correlation between the rates of growth of output by industry between the two countries (1913–55 in the Soviet Union and 1909–53 in the United States) to be as high as 0.7, the corresponding correlation between the rates of growth of labor productivities was only 0.2 (not significant even on a 10 percent level).[34] The progress achieved in American machinery industry (as measured by either productivity index) has been neither spectacular nor poor.

With this information about the United States and on the grounds that our Second hypothesis was stated in comparative terms, we might beg a generous examiner to award it a passing grade, but obviously without honors, at least at this stage of our knowledge.

III

Irrespective of our success or failure in testing the Second hypothesis, let us now inquire whether the policy implied in it, which *for convenience*

---

[32] Moorsteen, op. cit., p. 4. G. Warren Nutter, *The Growth of Industrial Production in the Soviet Union* (Princeton, N.J., 1962), pp. 54, 82.

[33] Kendrick, op. cit., p. 146.

[34] Nutter, op. cit., p. 242.

Table 9.10. *Average annual percentage rates of growth of labor productivity in the USSR 1928–1960 (productivity per person engaged, Nutter, moving weights[a])*

Output per person engaged	(1) 1928–40	(2) 1940–55	(3) 1950–55	(4) 1928–55
All products	2.0	1.9	5.4	1.9
Ferrous and nonferrous metals	6.5	1.9	8.8	3.9
Fuel and electricity	7.7	1.7	5.4	4.3
Fuel	5.5	1.5	4.9	3.2
Electricity	5.3	3.2	7.7	4.4
Chemicals	0.6	3.4	−0.5	2.2
Construction materials	−1.7	1.6	4.0	0.1
Wood materials	−2.4	2.7	4.0	0.4
Mineral materials	1.3	0.8	3.1	1.0
Machinery and allied products[b]	9.1	1.0	3.5	4.5
Civilian machinery and equipment	8.4	2.2	−2.0	4.9
Food and allied products	−0.3	2.5	7.2	1.2
Textile and textile products	0.7	1.7	3.7	1.2

	Soviet official index of productivity per person engaged[c]		Productivity per man-hour Kaplan and Moorsteen[a] 1950 = 100	
	1940–60	1950–60	1927/28–1956	1937–56
Producer goods other than machinery			2.0	0.0
Ferrous metals and ores	4.9	6.3	4.4	1.8
Fuels			1.8	0.34
Coal	1.8	3.7	3.4	0.89
Oil extraction	4.6	11.0		
Electric power			4.3	2.6
Chemicals (incl. chemical mining, rubber, and asbestos)	7.6	8.5		1.8
Lumber, wood products, and paper	2.8–4.5	6.1–7.3		−0.12
Building materials	6.4	10.0		−2.7
Machinery	8.0	10.4		
Consumers' goods	3.8[d]	5.5[d]		0.93
Foods	3.2	6.3		−.10
Nonfoods				1.7
Agriculture – collective farms	3.1	6.2		
state farms	2.2	5.2		

[a] Average annual growth rates calculated by the compound interest formula.
[b] Includes consumer durables and military products.
[c] Average annual growth rates are calculated exponentially by comparing the first and last years.

we will call the Soviet method, is more conducive to economic growth than the broad general advance observed in the United States.

Static economic theory, strongly attached to the proposition that an optimal allocation of resources requires the equalization of the value of the marginal product of each factor in all its uses, would look with suspicion on the Soviet method and favor the American. Our productivity data, however, are neither in value terms nor are they at the margin. The first defect could be easily corrected (value productivity is more readily obtainable than is physical), but there is no apparent remedy for the second. Average productivities of a given factor in its several uses can differ greatly and can grow at different rates while the marginal do or do not tend toward equality. So even from this, admittedly inadequate, point of view of static theory, no clear preference for one method or another emerges.

On an intuitive level, however risky such notions are, I would venture to say that a continuous stress on the progress of one industry and the neglect of another are not likely to lead to an optimal allocation of resources, again from a static point of view. Even if the neglected industry is not deemed important for its own sake (I am not arguing here about Soviet economic goals), a time must surely come when even a relatively small application of capital (and, if static considerations allow, of technological progress as well) to this industry will release labor to be shifted to the favored industry, thus possibly increasing total output faster than if the same amount of capital were applied to that industry directly. But on the basis of data presented in this essay, we cannot say whether this point has been reached in the Soviet Union.

Once dynamic considerations enter the picture, intuitive notions become even less reliable, but the problem gains in interest. A new and better machine surely acts as an important instrument for the introduction of technological progress into an economy.[35] Hence it would seem that the Soviet policy of lavishing physical and human resources on machine building and related products (if such it indeed has been) could be well defended.

[35] See Solow's paper in note 11, p. 150.

Notes to Table 9.10 (cont.)
[d] Light industry.
Sources: First part, columns 1–4: G. Warren Nutter, *The Growth of Industrial Production in the Soviet Union* (Princeton, N.J., 1962), Table 41, p. 175.

Second part, columns 1, 2: *Narodnoe khoziaistvo SSSR v 1960 godu* [The people's economy of the USSR in 1960], pp. 162, 231–33; columns 3, 4: Norman M. Kaplan and Richard H. Moorsteen, *Indexes of Soviet Industrial Output,* The RAND Corp. RM-2495 (Santa Monica, Calif., May 1960), Vol. II, Table 46, p. 269.

So it could, if it were not for another complication. Economic progress in machine building can take two more or less distinct forms: (1) a better organization of the machine-building process, and (2) the invention and production of better machines, with frequent changes of models. To some extent, these are competing activities. For, to improve the efficiency of machine building as such, it will pay to avoid the retooling, reorganization of productive techniques, etc., that a change in output requires, and to concentrate on the production of known types and run them for long periods of time on a large scale. Under such conditions it is likely that economic progress in machine building, *as measured by all three approximations,* will be rapid, at least until the economies of the learning process are exhausted. But the growth of productivity in machine-using industries need not be impressive at all.

Under the second form when the production of machines is frequently disturbed by the introduction of new types, economies of scale are more limited, and the productivity in machine building will not increase as fast, but the machine-using industries will prosper.

The two policies can manifest themselves in other, though related, ways. Thus, under the first, relatively simple and universal machines are produced on a large scale. Under the second, machines are more specialized, even custom made for specific uses. Obviously, productivity in machine building, as it is usually measured, will thrive under the first policy; that in machine using, under the second.

This distinction should not be carried too far because, after all, machines are produced by means of other machines, and a complete freezing of types will eventually stop productivity advance even in machine building. Neither method has been used in any country in its pure form – under realistic conditions the difference between them is only a matter of degree – but one gets an impression (however unreliable impressions are) that the Soviet Union has leaned toward the first method and the United States toward the second. Of course, the Soviet Union now produces many types of machines practically unknown in that country in the past, but extensive use of standardization and the production of unchanged models over long periods of time are reported by Nutter and Moorsteen to be quite common.[36] Perhaps here lies at least part of the explanation of the relatively more rapid growth of productivity in Soviet machine building, at least in the early period (if that was the case).

[36] Nutter, op. cit., pp. 76–80; Moorsteen, op. cit., p. 51. During the discussion following the presentation of this essay at the Conference, Professor Postan remarked that it has been the Soviet policy to concentrate on large-scale production of relatively simple universal machines and to import more complex and specialized ones.

But, we ask again, which method, or what combination of methods, promotes faster growth of the economy as a whole? This is a most exciting analytical problem not yet completely solved, but a few preliminary notions may be suggested by economic theory.[37] It seems reasonable to expect that the optimal frequency of model changes and the introduction of new types of machinery will vary directly with the scale of the market for the machines and the wages of machine-using workers, and will vary inversely with the rate of interest (or some other measure of capital scarcity) and the compensation of engineering and technical personnel. If so, an underdeveloped country where both capital and technical personnel are scarce, if it builds any machines at all, should follow the first method at the beginning and then gradually mix with it larger doses of the second. In the early period we may witness a relatively more rapid economic progress in machine building than in the rest of the country's economy, while in the later period the difference will gradually diminish, though there is no reason to expect a uniform rate of progress in all industries at any stage of a country's development. Our examination of the upper part of Table 9.10 has revealed such a pattern in the Soviet Union: labor productivity rose faster than elsewhere in the 1928-40 period, and fell to the average, or even below the average, rate in 1950-55. For the United States the second method has been obviously better suited, as borne out by Kendrick's productivity data. Thus each country appears to have been pursuing the correct, though different from the other, course. But of all the numerous tentative conclusions reached in this paper, this last one, stemming from as yet an unfinished analytical problem and based on a shaky empirical foundation, is the most tentative.

[37] This problem is not new in economic analysis, and various aspects of it have been discussed in the literature. See, for instance, George Terborgh, *Dynamic Equipment Policy* (New York, 1949), concerned with the optimal replacement policy for a machine-using firm. A somewhat similar approach was taken by Vernon L. Smith, "The Theory of Investment and Production," *The Quarterly Journal of Economics,* Vol. LXXIII (February 1959), pp. 61-87. The optimal frequency of model changes for a machine-building firm was discussed in a promising paper by William H. Brown, Jr., "Innovation in the Machine Tool Industry," *The Quarterly Journal of Economics,* Vol. LXXI (August 1957), pp. 406-25. I have not yet seen a treatment of the problem from the point of view of the maximization of the rate of growth of an economy, but I would not be surprised if such a study existed.

The Soviet collective farm as a
producer cooperative

Imagine that most of the obstacles facing Soviet kolkhozes (collective farms) today, such as output and delivery quotas, administrative interference, shortage of strategic inputs (materials, spare parts, fertilizer), depressed prices of outputs, etc., suddenly vanish, and the kolkhozes find themselves in a Lange–Lerner type of a competitive world where everything can be bought and sold at a market price, and where peasants are free to run their own affairs *provided the essential structure of the kolkhoz is retained.* How would Soviet agriculture, or for that matter any economic sector so organized, fare in such a wonderland?[1]

Freed from existing restrictions and abuses, the kolkhoz would presumably revert to its prototype – a producer cooperative which utilizes the labor of its members, purchases other inputs, sells its outputs, pays a rent and/or taxes, and divides all or a part of its net proceeds among its members. The presumed democratic nature of such a co-op and its freedom from capitalist exploitation has made it highly attractive to socialists and social reformers for ages. But its popularity has not prompted its proponents to analyze it with the same loving curiosity that the "bourgeois" economists have shown toward the capitalist firm. And yet it must have been obvious, at least to some of these proponents, that co-op members

Reprinted by permission from *The American Economic Review,* Vol. LVI, September 1966, pp. 734–57.

I am very grateful to Abram Bergson, Michael R. Dohan, John G. Gurley, Michael D. Intriligator, Nancy Nimitz, David McGarvey, and Egon Neuberger for their generous assistance and helpful comments. Questions raised by Mr. Neuberger made me rewrite the whole essay. David Conklin acted as my research assistant, and Martin Weitzman went over the mathematics. I had intended to include in the essay a brief survey of relevant recent Soviet literature, and James R. Millar of Cornell University kindly lent me three chapters of his dissertation [8]. This project was abandoned because of lack of space; besides, Mr. Millar's survey is more comprehensive and thorough than mine could have been. I am also grateful to the RAND Corporation for its facilities, encouragement and support. Some of the research was supported by the National Science Foundation as well. None of these persons or organizations is of course responsible for my conclusions or for any errors which may still be lurking around.

[1] The question is not as academic as it sounds. Recent changes in Soviet agricultural policies represent another step toward that wonderland, though there is still a long way to go [16] [17] [18] [20] [21] [22] [23] [24].

are likely to be ordinary human beings bent on maximizing the benefits from their participation in the co-op.[2] The first and only attempt to construct a model of a co-op that I have seen belongs to Benjamin Ward in a path-breaking paper published in 1958 [12].[3] But like many a pioneering work, it has not attracted much attention.[4]

The present study consists of three parts: in the first, Ward's creation, called here the "Pure Model" of a co-op, is reworked with a generalized production function. The tenor of Ward's findings (based on a single-output, one-or-two-input function) is confirmed, but some of the results are made more definite, and one is reversed. In the second part, the co-op is faced with a supply schedule of labor; this makes the model much more realistic and reverses the paradoxical results of the "Pure Model." Finally, a summary and a few conclusions are presented in the third part.

List of symbols (in order of appearance)

R a fixed rent paid by the co-op $(R > 0)$

v $(-\pi/x_n)$ – dividend rate or dividend per labor unit $(v > 0)$

x_n labor input $(x_n < 0)$

n number of outputs and inputs

π profit of the co-op gross of dividend payments $(\pi > 0)$

p_i price of x_i $(i = 1, ..., n-1)$

x_i an output when $x_i > 0$, an input when $x_i < 0$ $(i = 1, ..., n-1)$

p_n wage rate paid by the "capitalist twin"; originally $p_n = v$

λ Lagrange's multiplier

$E_{x_i p_j} = (\partial x_i / \partial p_j) \cdot (p_j / x_i)$ elasticity of demand for, or supply of, x_i in response to change in p_j $(i, j = 1, ..., n)$

$u_i = p_i x_i$ value of an output when $x_i > 0$, or of an input when $x_i < 0$.

A few other symbols are defined when introduced.

An asterisk indicates that the expression pertains to the "capitalist twin."

---

[2] I do not discuss here producer co-ops organized for essentially noneconomic reasons, such as by religious orders, Israeli pioneers, etc.

[3] There have of course been a number of analyses of firms which do not maximize total profit in the usual way. See for example Scitovsky [10]; F. and V. Lutz [7]; Baumol [5]; Averch and Johnson [4]; and Westfield [13]. A very interesting book on cooperatives was published by Tugan–Baranovsky [11a] in 1921. His conclusions were very similar to mine given in Sec. III of this essay. I owe this reference to Steven Rosefielde.

[4] In my sample of some forty or fifty reputable economists about a third of whom work in the Soviet and related fields, Ward's article had been read by three or four persons at most. Perhaps the paper's title gave the wrong impression that it pertained to Yugoslavia only. Or – who knows – this might have been the normal fate of an excellent paper.

I.   The "Pure Model" of a co-op

Assumptions

1. All nonlabor inputs are bought and all outputs are sold by the co-op at given (parametric) prices.
2. The production function of the co-op, if possessed by a profit-maximizing firm, would have all necessary and sufficient properties for a stable equilibrium under perfect competition [2] [3].
3. The co-op pays a fixed rent $R > 0$ per year.[5]
4. Instead of paying wages, the co-op divides all (or a constant fraction) of its income net of all other costs and rent equally among its members or among homogeneous labor units in the form of a dividend.[6]

[5] Soviet kolkhozes do not pay rent as such, but the system of compulsory deliveries and differentiated zonal prices is directed against the richer farms and regions and allows the government to extract some rent. Until 1966, the farms paid a 12.5 per cent tax imposed on income net of nonlabor cost (excluding 80 per cent of income from animal products), but gross of dividend payments. The rate could be modified by regional authorities in favor of poorer and against richer farms [11].

Beginning with 1966, the tax rate is set at 12 per cent, and the taxable income seems to exclude two items: (1) profit equal to 15 per cent of nonlabor costs, and (2) dividend payments not exceeding a certain average per member, to be set by the government [17]. If the post-tax dividend rate is indicated by v_t, it follows that

$$v_t = v(1-t) + \frac{Cet}{L} + wt,$$

where t is the tax rate (12 per cent), e is the 15 per cent exclusion, w is the exemption per member, C is the nonlabor costs

$$\left(C = - \sum_{k}^{n-1} p_i x_i, \text{ and } k \text{ is the first input} \right),$$

and $L = -x_n$ (to avoid negative numbers). Now, t, e, and w are constants, but C/L is not. Hence the imposition of the tax in its new form will affect economic decisions in the kolkhoz. I am not sure, however, that my interpretation of this tax reform is correct (the official statement being rather confusing). For this reason and to save space, I will disregard the complexities of the tax law both before and after 1966, and mean by the word "tax" a simple proportional levy on profits before dividend payments. But a further investigation of the effects of this new tax may be worthwhile.

[6] Actually it is the Soviet practice to transform most of the labor of kolkhoz members into a homogeneous sum by a system of weights depending on the required skill and the nature of work. The weights vary from one kolkhoz to another, but the range seems to be around $2\frac{1}{2} : \frac{1}{2}$. If the relative weights correspond to the ratios of the values of the marginal products of the several kinds of labor this is a reasonable procedure. It would not matter if the co-op first paid uniform wages per labor unit (as Ward assumed) and then used the balance of income for dividends.

It should be also noted that a substantial fraction of the income of the kolkhoz is retained by it (the so-called "Indivisible Fund") for reinvestment and improvements, and that this fraction varies from one farm to another and from one year to the next, depending on economic conditions and on administrative decisions.

5. The objective of the co-op is the maximization of the dividend per unit of labor or of the dividend rate $v > 0$. There is complete certainty.[7]

6. The co-op is *actually able* to employ the optimal number of labor units maximizing the dividend rate. This assumption (used by Ward) distinguishes this model from those presented in Part II.

7. Finally, there exists a profit-maximizing firm, the "capitalist twin," with the same production function and prices as the co-op, and with a wage rate initially equal to the co-op's dividend rate.

We are concerned in this model with a rent rather than with a tax because a glance at expression (10.1) below will show that neither an income tax (imposed on net income before dividends), nor a poll tax (per unit of labor) would affect the co-op's decisions in the context of this model: the optimal allocation of resources yielding the maximum dividend before the tax remains unchanged by the tax.[8]

The rent is assumed to be positive because an $R < 0$ (a subsidy) would induce the co-op to maximize the dividend rate v by reducing labor input to zero. Even an $R = 0$ can produce this effect if v declines from the very beginning and has no maximum point. We shall assume that R is large enough to give us a meaningful problem but not to eliminate the co-op's net income or to convert it into a loss.

Note that in the generalized production function given in (10.2), it is customary to express outputs in positive units, and inputs, including labor (x_n), in negative. Hence many derivations in the Mathematical Appendix have seemingly perverse signs, and a minus sign is attached to expression (10.1).

Our basic problem consists of maximizing the dividend rate

$$v = - \frac{\pi}{x_n} = - \frac{\sum_1^{n-1} p_i x_i - R}{x_n}, \tag{10.1}$$

subject to the production function

$$f(x_1, \ldots, x_n) = 0. \tag{10.2}$$

The solution of equations (10.1) and (10.2), while not difficult, is somewhat involved, and can be safely relegated to the Appendix. It is shown there that the equilibrium position of the co-op is identical in every respect to that of its capitalist twin defined in assumption 7. On reflection, this is to be expected: for any given labor input the co-op simply maximizes

---

[7] No dynamic elements are considered either. Even though some comments about investment decisions will be made, the model essentially refers to the short run.

[8] In models presented in Part II an income tax does affect economic decisions. A gross receipt tax would have the same effects as a proportional reduction in the price of every output. See note 5.

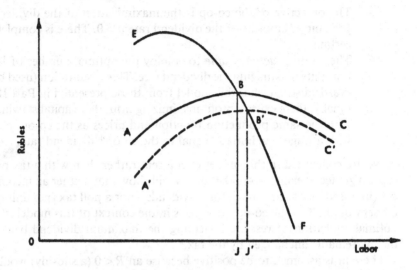

Figure 10.1. The effect of an increase in rent.

total profit like the twin, and hence chooses the same outputs and non-labor inputs. When it comes to labor, the attitudes of the two organizations differ: the twin hires labor until the value of the marginal product equals the wage; the co-op uses labor to the point where the value of the marginal product equals the dividend paid (a unit of labor contributing less than the going dividend rate will not be used).[9] But since the two schedules of the value of the marginal product of labor are identical and the wage paid by the twin initially equals the dividend paid by the co-op (by assumption 7), the labor inputs used by both organizations are identical as well.

The *reactions* of the two enterprises to changes in rent or in prices, however, are altogether different. An increase in R has no (short-run) effects on the twin because it changes neither the value of the marginal product of labor nor the wage rate. But it reduces the dividend rate paid by the co-op and therefore moves the point of intersection between the dividend rate ABC (on Figure 10.1) and the value of the marginal product of labor EBF further to the right, from B to B' because of the assumed negative slope of EBF. So, as Ward has shown, more labor will be used (OJ' instead of OJ) and (in the absence of Hicks's "regression" [6]) output

[9] The schedules of the dividend rate and of the value of the marginal product of labor, as used here, are based on the assumption that equilibrium conditions are satisfied for all outputs and all nonlabor inputs all along the schedules. See, however, note 18.

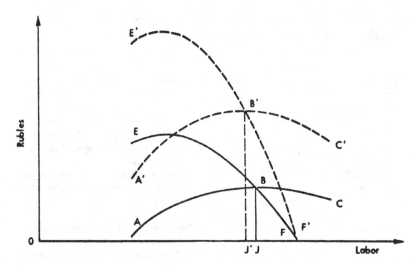

Figure 10.2. The effect of a rise in price of output.

will increase as well.[10] But before the reader concludes that the best way to increase peasant participation in Soviet kolkhozes is by imposing (or increasing) rents, he should take a look at Part II.

The effect of a price change on the co-op is more complex because both the dividend rate and the value of the marginal product of labor are affected.[11] If there is only one output (x_1) and labor is the only input, the outcome is certain: a doubling of p_1 will double the value of the marginal product of labor, while the dividend rate, as shown by expression (10.1) rewritten for this occasion as

$$v = -\frac{p_1 x_1 - R}{x_n},^{12} \tag{10.3}$$

will *more* than double. The intersection point of the curves *EBF* and *ABC* will now move to the left, from *B* to *B'* on Figure 10.2, and both the labor input and hence the output will contract, as proved by Ward.

---

[10] See the Appendix, Sec. 3.

[11] The values of the marginal products of other inputs will also be affected.

[12] The relative increase in v is greater than in p_1 because R is subtracted from $p_1 x_1$ in the numerator. However, x_1 and x_n also change. It is shown in the last section of the Appendix that

$$\frac{dv}{dp_1} \cdot \frac{p_1}{v} = \frac{p_1 x_1}{p_1 x_1 - R} > 1$$

if the production function consists of x_1 and x_n only. See also Sec. 3(a) of the Appendix.

Table 10.1. *A summary of the effects of an increase in p_1 on the magnitudes of outputs and inputs (in absolute terms)*

Effect on	Usual capitalist reaction	Probable co-op reaction
If x_1 is an output:		
x_1	Positive	Positive, unless x_1 is a very important user of labor (or the only output)
$|x_n|$	Positive	Negative (except in a special case in the Appendix)
x_2 as all other outputs	Positive, if x_2 is complementary to x_1	Negative if input proportions remain unchanged; otherwise, indeterminate
	Negative, if x_2 is competitive with x_1	Negative
$|x_2|$ as an input	Positive	Negative with high complementarity between x_2 and x_n
		Indeterminate with partial complementarity
		Positive if x_2 and x_n are substitutes
If x_1 is an input:		
$|x_1|$	Negative	Negative, except for constant proportions between x_1 and x_n when the effect is zero
$|x_n|$	Negative if x_1 and x_n are complementary	Positive, except for a zero effect if x_1 and x_n are used in constant proportions
	Positive if they are substitutes	
x_2 as an output (or all output)	Negative	Indeterminate
$|x_2|$ as an input	Negative if x_1 and x_2 are complementary	Indeterminate
	Positive if they are substitutes	

With one output and several inputs the situation becomes clouded, but a plausible assumption (that the isoquants of the production function are radially parallel to each other) saves the day and preserves the restrictive conclusion just reached.[13] The solution of the general case of several outputs and inputs is given in the Appendix;[14] the results are summarized in Table 10.1.

On the whole, the co-op's reactions to an increase in p_1 are rather peculiar. When x_1 is an output, there is a general tendency to restrict operations; when x_1 is an input, to expand them. Even when the co-op moves

[13] Appendix, Sec. 3(b).
[14] Appendix, Secs. 3(c) and 3(d).

in the same direction as a capitalist firm, its response is usually more slug-gish. For market stability, the picture is not particularly reassuring.

True enough, if x_1 is one of several outputs, a rise in its price is likely to *increase* its production; its own market can therefore be stable, con-trary to Ward's expectations based on the one-output production func-tion. But the input of labor is very likely to decrease and hence lead to a contraction of other outputs. Since many agricultural products are rea-sonably good substitutes for each other, the conditions which have led to a rise in the price of, say, wheat may very well raise the prices of rye and corn as well. The simultaneous rise in several prices, being similar to the rise in the price of some *important* single user of labor (see the first line of Table 10.1), can cause a general restriction of output. Although a negatively sloping supply curve is not a sufficient condition for market instability, it is too close to it for comfort.

Of course the undesirable negative effect of the rise in p_1 can be coun-teracted by an appropriate increase in rent. But such manipulations of rent in response to changing prices would require more knowledge and skill than are likely to be possessed by the Soviet or, for that matter, by most other governments. And besides, the whole idea of rent implies a sum fixed in advance for a reasonably long period of time. It would not help to replace it with a tax on net income because (as mentioned above) such a tax does not affect the co-op's decisions. Some other tax might, but it is hardly worth investigating in the light of Part II to come.

The model augurs little good for the allocation of resources among the co-ops. As Ward has observed, the labor market will be rigid. Indeed, if a rich and a poor co-op should each be in its respective equilibrium, no movement of labor from the poor co-op to the rich is possible (except through a merger) because any movement would reduce the dividend rates in both co-ops. Since the dividend rate in equilibrium equals the net value of the marginal product of labor, there is a definite misallocation of la-bor, and of course of other resources as well, among the co-ops. The hir-ing of the members of the poor co-op by the rich is the obvious solution, but it is not permitted in the present model.

The best measure both on equity and resource allocation grounds to be taken here is an increase in the rent paid by the rich co-op (or a relief for the poor one, if it pays any). Equity alone could be satisfied by a system of differential prices both for outputs and for inputs discriminating against the rich co-op,[15] but the equalization of the dividend rate so achieved would obviously not equate the social value of the marginal product of labor (and of other inputs) in the two co-ops.

---

[15] A standard remedy in Soviet literature and practice.

All these equalizing measures can backfire if the wealth of the rich co-op is due not to its better natural conditions and location, but to greater effort and interest of its members not accounted for in the conventional measures of labor input. But these considerations are outside of the scope of this model and even of this paper.

In making investment decisions, each co-op will behave like its own capitalist twin paying a wage rate equal to the co-op's dividend rate. For the rich co-op labor is expensive, for the poor it is cheap. Hence the former will prefer ready-made labor-saving machinery, while the latter will look for labor-using projects and be inclined, for instance, to use its own labor in construction. To the extent that the poor co-op is poor because of shortage of capital, it will be more inclined to invest than the rich. Whether it will have the means to do so is less likely.

II.   The model with a supply schedule of labor

The "Pure Model," for all its interesting and amusing (I hope) paradoxes, has one slight defect: it is unreal. It assumes that labor can be varied with changing prices and rent in order to maximize the dividend rate (assumption 6), a highly unlikely situation once the co-op has been organized. Surely the co-op, by its very nature, cannot admit and expel members at will. Hours of labor contributed by each member can of course be varied, but it is rather improbable that the members' welfare functions should call for a maximum dividend either per hour or per year irrespective of the number of hours worked.

Two possibilities will be considered here. First, the number of members is given (at least in the short run), and so is the number of hours contributed (according to some custom) by them. Then labor input is fixed, and the co-op simply maximizes total profit. Second, the co-op members may have other opportunities for employment and for leisure. In Soviet kolkhozes, they may cultivate their own plots, work in town, on a neighboring state farm, or even "lie on the stove" and do nothing according to the age-old Russian custom. In other words, the co-op is faced with a supply schedule of labor, which will be assumed here to have the usual positive slope. The equilibrium position of the co-op is found in two steps: first the co-op maximizes total profit for every given labor input, and obtains the familiar dividend rate curve ABC on Figure 10.3. The latter now serves as the demand schedule for labor as well, and its intersection with the labor-supply curve determines the labor input contributed by members *acting as such*. It need not correspond to the highest point B on the ABC curve, where it is intersected by the marginal curve EBF.

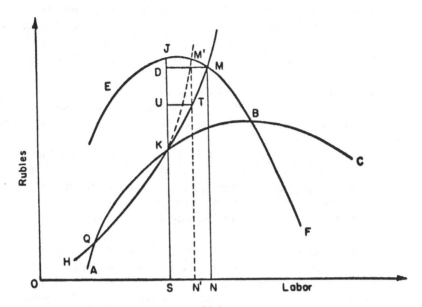

Figure 10.3. The supply curve of labor.

The appearance of this innocent-looking supply curve of labor produces a drastic difference in the reactions of the co-op to changes in prices and in rent as compared with the "Pure Model." Also, an income tax imposed on the co-op's income gross of dividend payments, ineffective previously, becomes relevant here.[16] Depending on the position of the labor-supply curve in relation to *ABC*, three variations of the present model will be discussed.

Case 1. Moderate labor shortage

The supply curve of labor *HKM* in Figure 10.3 intersects the dividend-rate curve *ABC* at *K*, to the left of the maximum point *B*. If, to preserve the purity of the co-op, no discrimination among its members is permitted, the co-op has to reconcile itself to the situation and simply stay at point *K*.[17] But its paradoxical behavior disappears. Any improvement

---

[16] For practical reasons, we need not bother with a poll tax. In any case, its effects are similar (but not identical) to those of the income tax. Income or poll taxes *imposed on the members* (rather than on the co-op) are not considered here. See note 5.

[17] Provided it gets to point *K* in the first place. Point *K* is stable in both directions, but *Q* is not. An upward movement from *Q* will bring the co-op to *K*, but unfortunately even a slight downward movement from *Q* can destroy the co-op altogether.

in the dividend rate, be it from lower rent or taxes, or from better prices, lifts the *ABC* curve, increases the employment of labor, and presumably raises output. In the light of this model, which is much closer to Soviet reality than the "Pure" one, price reforms promulgated by Khrushchev and his successors are justified.

It is not clear what labor cost will be used in making economic decisions. The correct cost should be *SJ* – the net value of the marginal productivity of labor – but since no one is actually paid this rate, the management may not know what it is.

If it is possible to discriminate among members and to hire those with particularly attractive outside opportunities (or the laziest ones) between *K* and *M*, new possibilities open up. In treating its hired members, the co-op will behave *more or less* like a capitalist employer, depending on the standing of these members in the co-op and other circumstances. Three subcases will be considered:

(a) If the hired members have different skills (or if the co-op management is very adroit), the co-op may act as a discriminating monopsonist and pay each of them the wage indicated by the supply curve. The area *KJM* represents the profit so obtained; presumably it will be added to the dividend paid to the regular members.

(b) The hired members may persuade or force the co-op to hire all of them at the highest wage *NM*. A smaller profit equal to the area *DJM* is now made.

(c) As a compromise between these two extremes, the co-op may operate like an ordinary monopsonist, draw the dotted curve *KM'*, representing the marginal labor cost, to its intersection with the value of the marginal product curve *EBF*, employ altogether *ON'* units of labor, pay a wage of *N'T*, and make a profit from hiring of *UJM'T*.[18]

In all these cases, the total employment of labor exceeds *OS*, output expands, and dividend rate rises over the original level of *SK*.[19] Everyone is better off provided the ordinary members are not consumed with envy. They need not be if the hired members do possess special skills. But if they are common members who refuse to work for the co-op more than

[18] There is some incongruity among the several curves in Figure 10.3. Schedules *ABC* and *EBF* are drawn on the assumption that the co-op is in equilibrium position in respect to all outputs and all nonlabor inputs for every given labor input, or that with every change in the labor input everything else is adjusted accordingly. The supply curve of labor *HKM* and the marginal cost of labor curve *KM'* indicate labor cost only, without allowing for these adjustments. I can take refuge in the approximate nature of Figure 10.3 used here for illustration only. A similar qualification applies to Figure 10.4 as well.

[19] It will be above *SK* but somewhat below the corresponding point on the *ABC* curve because the latter implies that no members are paid a wage in excess of the dividend.

the minimum required to retain their membership, the social situation can be rather difficult.[20]

The reactions of the co-op to changes in rent, income tax and prices now take still another turn and become more similar to those of a capitalist firm. An increase in rent lowers the average ABC curve but leaves the marginal EBF schedule intact. Hence, in cases (a) and (b) no reduction in labor input takes place, except that some members who were previously satisfied with dividends will now demand a wage. But output remains undisturbed. In case (c), however, the fall in the ABC curve has a special effect: now that hiring begins earlier (that is, to the left of point K) the curve KM' moves leftward and intersects EBF to the left of the old point M'. Hence, total employment of labor falls and so does output.

An increase in the income tax rate lowers both the average and the marginal curves (because it falls on profit *gross* of dividends) and thus reduces the employment of labor, while better prices raise both curves and have a positive effect on labor and on output.

Without the income tax, the wage rate paid to the marginal hired worker (or to all of them) in cases (a) and (b) equals the net value of the marginal product of labor. In case (c) there is the usual disparity created by monopsony. But the presence of the income tax creates a special gap between the social and private (as seen by the co-op) values of labor's marginal product in all three cases, and distorts allocation of resources.

So far only the hiring of its own members by the co-op has been considered. If the co-op can hire outsiders as well, as for instance a rich co-op hiring workers from a poor one, the allocation of labor may be further improved. The hiring co-op will simply behave like a profit-maximizing firm. We'll return to the hiring-out co-op in Case 3.[21]

---

[20] Strictly speaking, we assume either that the labor force is homogeneous, or that more skilled labor is transformed into ordinary labor according to some fixed weights, as it is done in Soviet kolkhozes (see note 6). So a refusal of a carpenter to work for the kolkhoz means his unwillingness to accept a multiple of the dividend rate paid to common workers.

In the text, all members working for the co-op receive *either* the dividend *or* a wage. In reality, some combinations of the two are sometimes encountered (see note 21). But this paper is already too long to analyze such a situation.

[21] In the actual operation of Soviet kolkhozes, some discrimination and hiring are permitted. The more skilled members are paid dividends at a higher rate (see note 6). In Abramov's delightful story about a kolkhoz [1] carpenters are paid one ruble a day in addition to the dividend rate. In a *Krokodil* story, two neighboring kolkhozes hire *each other's* carpenters (presumably the carpenters have refused to work for dividends on either farm and demanded market wages). Finally, kolkhozes hire agricultural specialists and other experts and skilled workers. It seems that the richer farms even hire ordinary workers in busy times.

The Soviet government has been recommending that kolkhozes pay their members a wage in money equal to some 80 per cent of the expected dividend (for the given type of

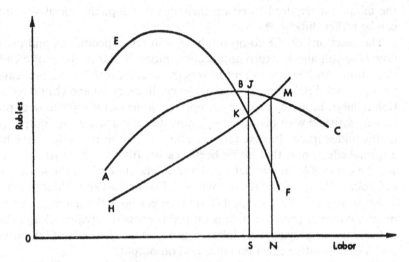

Figure 10.4. The excess supply of labor.

Case 2. Severe labor shortage

When the supply curve of labor *HM* lies completely to the left of the *ABC* dividend curve, the co-op as such cannot function at all. And yet it *may* be possible to hire every member at the wage demanded by him and still pay a rent! The members may be divided into groups (by skill, for instance) and each group paid a wage demanded by its marginal member. Freedom in hiring certainly increases the flexibility of the organization. Perhaps this is one of the reasons why Soviet state farms who hire all their labor are doing better than the kolkhozes, and why some weak kolkhozes have been transformed into state farms[22] [19, p. 19].

Case 3. An excess supply of labor

The supply curve of labor *HKM* intersects the *ABC* curve at *M* to the right of the optimum point *B* in Figure 10.4. The co-op may be either

work). But this was an advance payment of a dividend rather than a true wage. It seems that some of the kolkhozes who have tried to follow this recommendation ran out of funds [14]. New measures for alleviating the seasonal shortage of funds in the kolkhozes were announced on January 5, 1966 [23].

[22] It seems that the definite wage paid by the state farms has a better incentive effect than the promise of an uncertain dividend. An official promise to investigate the possibility of "guaranteed compensation of labor in all kolkhozes" was recently made [21]. But there are many other reasons for the relative success of state farms, such as the payment of higher wages, and – most important – access to the government budget. For that matter, not all state farms have been successful.

very rich or located far from other employment opportunities. The situation is analytically similar to Case 1. If it is impossible to get rid of some members or to reduce labor input by rationing, the co-op will simply stay at *M*. Any improvement in conditions, such as lower rent and taxes, or better prices, will raise the *ABC* curve and increase the quantity of labor used, as in Case 1. But if each member between *K* and *M* can indeed take an outside job and earn a wage at least equal to the corresponding point of the supply curve, it will be better for all concerned to *hire out* the members in *KM*, and, in fairness to them, collect their earnings and pay them the regular dividend. The members who are to the right of point *M* will prefer to remain on their own. In the absence of an income tax, the net value of the marginal product of labor will equal its supply price at *K*, which is good, but since the dividend rate paid to the members will be approximately equal to *SJ* rather than *SK*, there is a danger of over-evaluation of labor cost by the management.[23] The presence of an income tax creates the same distortions as in Case 1. When the hiring out of labor is permitted, changes in rent, income tax rates, and prices in Case 3 will have the same effects on the total employment of labor by the co-op as in Cases 1(a) and 1(b).

The (positive or negative) hiring of members improves the allocation of resources within each co-op, but so long as it is confined to its own members (as assumed here) the distribution of labor among the co-ops remains unchanged.[24] In contrast to the "Pure Model" where the inequality of dividend rates among the co-ops indicated misallocation of labor (and of other resources) and where the transfer of labor from the poor to the rich units was clearly in the social interest, the present situation is ambiguous because the value of the marginal product of labor in each co-op no longer equals (except accidentally) the dividend rate: in Figure 10.3 it is above the dividend rate, in Figure 10.4 below it. In the improbable (at least among Soviet kolkhozes) case when Figure 10.3 depicts a rich unit, and Figure 10.4 – a poor one, the transfer of labor from the poor to the rich co-op will be welcomed by all parties. But in the more realistic case when the poor co-op is to the left of the point *B* (as in Figure 10.3) and the rich to its right (as in Figure 10.4), both co-ops will object to this transfer because the poor co-op seeks more labor (so as to

---

[23] It will be somewhat higher than *SJ* because the *ABC* curve disregards the higher wages earned outside. See note 19.

Perhaps a Soviet kolkhoz can act as a monopolist in hiring out labor. An analysis of this case is similar to that given in Cases 1(b) and 1(c) above.

It should be noted that Figure 10.4 suffers from the same incongruity as Figure 10.3. See note 18.

[24] Except when the hired-out members of one co-op are hired by another.

Table 10.2. *The effects of changes in rent, tax rates, and prices on the employment of labor by the co-op*

		The model with a supply curve of labor	
Nature of change	"The Pure Model"	Without hiring	With hiring
Increase in rent	Positive	Negative	Neutral, except in Case 1(c)
Increase in income tax rate	Neutral	Negative	Negative
Improvement in prices	Negative	Positive	Positive

reach point *B*), and the rich less labor, while social desirability remains obscured by the differences (in opposite directions) between the value of the marginal product of labor and the dividend rate in each co-op.

III.   Concluding remarks

The results of all our models are summarized in Table 10.2. I now turn to those aspects of Soviet agricultural policy to which this paper may be relevant. I think they can be fairly listed as follows:

1. To increase labor participation in the kolkhozes.
2. To improve resource allocation on the farms.
3. To improve allocation of labor among the farms.
4. To bring about greater equality of income per member (or per labor unit) among the farms.
5. To siphon off the excess purchasing power which will be acquired by some peasants if agricultural prices are moved closer to their marginal costs.

All these (and other) aspects have been discussed in Soviet literature in recent years, with point (4) – the high degree of inequality among peasant incomes – receiving particular attention. I have not found a comprehensive distribution of peasant incomes, but it is fair to conclude from various sources that ratios of four to one, six to one, and even higher between rich and poor farms are not uncommon.[25] This inequality is attacked on equity grounds – unequal pay for equal work, the suggested remedy consisting of price manipulations in favor of the poor and against the rich farms. That both the existing inequality and the remedy for it are linked

[25] According to V. N. Starovsky, Director of the USSR Central Statistical Administration, "...in 1961 payments per man-day on about 30 per cent of the USSR's collective farms came to only one-fourth to one-fifth as much as on the 20 per cent of the farms where the

with allocation of resources is hardly ever mentioned. Perhaps the discussion of these finer points in Soviet literature is premature, plagued as their agriculture still is with crude central planning, administrative interference and other problems.

In making the list of my recommendations based on Table 10.2, however, I shall retain our initial, though still unrealistic under Soviet conditions, assumptions that the peasants will be free to run the kolkhozes as they see fit (short of disbanding the kolkhoz system altogether) – there have been definite moves in that direction lately – and that relative price ratios will reflect real scarcities. Now a difficult (for an economic theorist) choice must be made between being original, if unrealistic, and being conventional and practical. For what could be more original and striking than recommendations derived from the "Pure Model," namely that rent should be increased (or imposed) and terms of trade turned against the peasants in order to make them work longer and harder for the kolkhoz? This would indeed vindicate Stalin's agricultural policies, even though he had arrived at them without building any models.

Dismissing the "Pure Model," we come to the following list of recommendations:

1.   To allow the prices of material inputs and of agricultural outputs to move to their equilibrium levels as determined by demand-supply conditions, even at the expense of a sharp rise in peasant gross incomes.

pay was the highest" [15]. It is not clear whether Starovsky referred to total or to money incomes only.

In the last few years many changes in Soviet agriculture have taken place, but it is hard to judge whether income inequality among the peasants has gone up or down. The following compilation of the official average kolkhoz money income per household among 66 provinces (*oblasti*) of the Russian Republic in 1960 and 1963 indicates little change [25]:

	1960	1963
Ratio between the fourth and first quartiles of the distribution of the provinces	2.0	1.8
Ratio between the means of the highest and lowest 25 per cent of the provinces	3.1	3.2
Ratio between the highest and the lowest single provinces	8.4	8.6

Among the several republics comprising the Soviet Union, the richest one (in the above terms) – Turkmenia – had almost four times as large an income in 1963 as the poorest one – Georgia [26]. A number of scattered sources indicate that ratios of 2 to 1, 3 to 1, and even higher *within* a republic or a province are quite usual. If so, income disparities between the richer and poorer farms become large indeed, and considerably larger than the ratios stated in the text above. On the other hand, a comparison of money income alone can exaggerate the advantage enjoyed by a cotton-producing area like Turkmenia, or by the seemingly rich Far-Eastern provinces where the price level is likely to be higher than in the more central parts of the country. But it is important to note that these inequalities persist in spite of price differentials against the richer regions.

2. To abolish the income tax paid by the kolkhozes.
3. To impose a rent on each farm related to its location, soil fertility, and other natural conditions.[26]

If this list is so conventional as to create an anticlimax, I apologize. Now and then conventional economic theory does give the right answers, even when applied to a Soviet kolkhoz. And – I almost forgot to make explicit a rather essential recommendation – the kolkhoz should be permitted to engage in as much positive or negative hiring of labor as it can and wants. If this freedom brings it suspiciously close to a profit-maximizing capitalist firm, the similarity could be declared to be purely coincidental.

Two *caveats* are in order: (1) These conclusions have been derived from a model which proved to be highly sensitive to seemingly innocent changes in assumptions. If I think that my final creation is fairly realistic, so must Ward have thought about his.

(2) Judged by strictly economic criteria, the co-op has not come out well. But even on these grounds, it is quite possible that a co-op may be more efficient than a capitalist or a state-owned firm in societies where membership in the co-op, as contrasted with hiring out for a job, has a strong positive effect on workers' incentives (though hardly the case in Soviet kolkhozes). And so may the co-op's capitalist cousin – a firm with a profit-sharing scheme.

Mathematical appendix to the "Pure Model"

1.   *Equilibrium conditions for the co-op*

Maximize (10.1a) subject to (10.2a)

$$v = -\frac{\pi}{x_n} = -\frac{\sum_1^{n-1} p_i x_i - R}{x_n},\qquad(10.1a)$$

$$f(x_1, \ldots, x_n) = 0,\qquad(10.2a)$$

and form with a Lagrange's multiplier

$$z = -\frac{\pi - \lambda f(x_1, \ldots, x_n)}{x_n}.\qquad(10.3a)$$

---

[26] I do not mean to imply that these three measures are all that is required to create a healthy agriculture in the Soviet Union. Others, such as increased investment, may be as, or even more, important, but they are not relevant to this paper. Recent agricultural reforms [16] [17] [18] [21] [22] [23] [24] have raised prices on agricultural products, reduced prices on machinery and vehicles, cut taxes, promised more investment financed by the state, short- and long-term credit, and greater freedom to peasants in decision-making (see note 5). But there was no mention of the imposition of rent as such. Since the Soviet constitution assures the kolkhozes of the free use of their land, the imposition of a formal rent would require a major change which would encounter ideological difficulties.

Equating $\partial z/\partial x_i = 0$ $(i = 1, \ldots, n)$ we obtain

$$\lambda f_i = p_i \quad (i = 1, \ldots, n-1), \tag{10.4a}$$

$$\lambda f_n x_n = -\pi. \tag{10.5a}$$

To derive second-order conditions, take

$$dz = -\frac{x_n d\pi - \pi dx_n}{x_n^2}, \tag{10.6a}$$

$$d^2z = -\frac{-\pi x_n d^2 x_n - 2x_n d\pi dx_n + 2\pi dx_n^2}{x_n^3}, \tag{10.7a}$$

on the assumption that x_n is the only dependent variable, so that

$$d^2\pi = \sum_1^{n-1} p_i d^2 x_i = 0.$$

From (10.2a) and (10.7a),

$$d^2z = -\frac{\pi x_n \sum_1^n \sum_1^n f_{ij} dx_i dx_j - 2f_n x_n d\pi dx_n + 2f_n \pi dx_n^2}{f_n x_n^3}. \tag{10.8a}$$

From (10.1a) and (10.4a),

$$d\pi = \lambda \sum_1^{n-1} f_i dx_i. \tag{10.9a}$$

Substituting (10.5a) and (10.9a) into (10.8a), we obtain

$$d^2z = \frac{\lambda}{x_n^2}\left(x_n \sum_1^n \sum_1^n f_{ij} dx_i dx_j + 2dx_n \sum_1^{n-1} f_i dx_i + 2f_n dx_n^2\right); \tag{10.10a}$$

$$d^2z = \frac{\lambda}{x_n}\left(\sum_1^n \sum_1^n f_{ij} dx_i dx_j + 2\frac{dx_n}{x_n} \sum_1^n f_i dx_i\right), \tag{10.11a}$$

which can be expressed as

$$\begin{aligned}
d^2z = \frac{\lambda}{x_n}\bigg[& f_{11}dx_1^2 + f_{12}dx_1 dx_2 + \cdots + \left(f_{1n} + \frac{f_1}{x_n}\right)dx_1 dx_n \\
& + f_{12}dx_1 dx_2 + f_{22}dx_2^2 + \cdots + \left(f_{2n} + \frac{f_2}{x_n}\right)dx_2 dx_n \\
& + \cdots \\
& + \left(f_{1n} + \frac{f_1}{x_n}\right)dx_1 dx_n + \left(f_{2n} + \frac{f_1}{x_n}\right)dx_2 dx_n \\
& + \cdots + \left(f_{nn} + \frac{2f_n}{x_n}\right)dx_n^2\bigg],
\end{aligned} \tag{10.12a}$$

subject to

$$\sum_{1}^{n} f_i dx_i = 0. \tag{10.13a}$$

Since $\lambda/x_n < 0$ (because $x_n < 0$), second-order conditions for a maximum of d^2z require that the determinant

$$D = \begin{vmatrix} 0 & f_1 & f_2 & \cdots & f_n \\ f_1 & f_{11} & f_{12} & \cdots & f_{1n}+f_1/x_n \\ f_2 & f_{12} & f_{22} & \cdots & f_{2n}+f_2/x_n \\ \cdots\cdots\cdots\cdots\cdots\cdots\cdots\cdots\cdots\cdots\cdots\cdots\cdots\cdots\cdots \\ f_n & f_{1n}+f_1/x_n & f_{2n}+f_1/x_n & \cdots & f_{nn}+2f_n/x_n \end{vmatrix} < 0. \tag{10.14a}$$

Multiplying the first row by $1/x_n$ and subtracting it from the last, and performing the same operation on the first and the last columns as well, we reduce D to the well known "bordered" determinant F.

$$F = \begin{vmatrix} 0 & f_1 & f_2 & \cdots & f_n \\ f_1 & f_{11} & f_{12} & \cdots & f_{1n} \\ f_2 & f_{12} & f_{22} & \cdots & f_{2n} \\ \cdots\cdots\cdots\cdots\cdots\cdots\cdots \\ f_n & f_{1n} & f_{2n} & \cdots & f_{nn} \end{vmatrix} < 0. \tag{10.15a}$$

Thus the second-order conditions for the equilibrium of the co-op and of the capitalist firm are the same.

In order to find the reactions of the co-op to changes in rent and prices, equations (10.2a), (10.4a), and (10.5a) are differentiated in the usual manner. The solutions of the resulting system of equations prove to be functions of the determinant F and of its co-factors. So, of course, are the reactions of a capitalist firm to a change in price. Hence it is possible to express the reactions of the co-op in terms of the corresponding reactions of the twin, marked here with asterisks. As stated in the List of Symbols,

$$E^*_{x_i p_j} = \left(\frac{\partial x_i}{\partial p_j}\right)^* \cdot \frac{p_j}{x_i} \quad (i, j = 1, \ldots, n),$$

all indicating capitalist reactions. No asterisk is required for x_i because the twin and co-op are originally in the same equilibrium position.

2.   The effects of a change in R

The differentiation of (10.2a), (10.4a), and (10.5a) in respect to R gives the system of equations

$$\sum_1^n f_i \frac{\partial x_i}{\partial R} = 0$$

$$f_1\left(\frac{1}{\lambda}\frac{\partial \lambda}{\partial R}\right) + \sum_1^n f_{1i}\frac{\partial x_i}{\partial R} = 0$$

$$f_2\left(\frac{1}{\lambda}\frac{\partial \lambda}{\partial R}\right) + \sum_1^n f_{2i}\frac{\partial x_i}{\partial R} = 0$$

$$\vdots$$

$$f_n\left(\frac{1}{\lambda}\frac{\partial \lambda}{\partial R}\right) + \sum_1^n \left(f_{in} + \frac{f_i}{x_n}\right)\frac{\partial x_i}{\partial R} = \frac{1}{\lambda x_n}. \tag{10.16a}$$

Multiplying the first equation by $1/x_n$ and subtracting it from the last we reduce the latter to

$$f_n\left(\frac{1}{\lambda}\frac{\partial \lambda}{\partial R}\right) + \sum_1^n f_{in}\frac{\partial x_i}{\partial R} = \frac{1}{\lambda x_n}. \tag{10.17a}$$

Now the system of equations (10.16a) and (10.17a) is based on the matrix given in (10.15a). We can immediately derive

$$\frac{\partial x_n}{\partial R} = \frac{1}{x_n}\cdot\frac{F_{nn}}{\lambda F} = \frac{1}{x_n}\left(\frac{\partial x_n}{\partial p_n}\right)^*, \tag{10.18a}$$

where F_{ij} is the co-factor of f_{ij} in F, and

$$\frac{\partial x_i}{\partial R} = \frac{1}{x_n}\cdot\frac{F_{in}}{\lambda F} = \frac{1}{x_n}\left(\frac{\partial x_i}{\partial p_n}\right)^* \quad (i \neq n). \tag{10.19a}$$

Since

$$\left(\frac{\partial x_n}{\partial p_n}\right)^* > 0 \quad \text{and} \quad x_n < 0, \quad \frac{\partial x_n}{\partial R} < 0, \quad \text{and} \quad \left(-\frac{\partial x_n}{\partial R}\right) > 0.$$

If x_i is an output and

$$\left(\frac{\partial x_i}{\partial p_n}\right)^* < 0, \quad \frac{\partial x_i}{\partial R} > 0.$$

If x_i is a nonlabor input, the sign of $\partial x_i/\partial R$ depends on whether x_i is complementary to or substitutable for x_n.

3.   *The effects of a change in* p_1

Differentiate (10.2a), (10.4a), and (10.5a) in respect to p_1, and using the same methods as in the preceding section obtain the system of equations

$$\sum_1^n f_i \frac{\partial x_i}{\partial p_1} = 0$$

$$f_1\left(\frac{1}{\lambda}\frac{\partial \lambda}{\partial p_1}\right) + \sum_1^n f_{1i} \frac{\partial x_i}{\partial p_1} = \frac{1}{\lambda}$$

$$f_2\left(\frac{1}{\lambda}\frac{\partial \lambda}{\partial p_1}\right) + \sum_1^n f_{2i} \frac{\partial x_i}{\partial p_1} = 0$$

$$\vdots$$

$$f_n\left(\frac{1}{\lambda}\frac{\partial \lambda}{\partial p_1}\right) + \sum_1^n f_{in} \frac{\partial x_i}{\partial p_1} = -\frac{x_1}{\lambda x_n}, \tag{10.20a}$$

again based on the matrix given in (10.15a). Hence,

$$\frac{\partial x_1}{\partial p_1} = \frac{F_{11}}{\lambda F} - \frac{x_1}{x_n}\cdot\frac{F_{1n}}{\lambda F} = \left(\frac{\partial x_1}{\partial p_1}\right)^* - \frac{x_1}{x_n}\left(\frac{\partial x_n}{\partial p_1}\right)^*, \tag{10.21a}$$

$$\frac{\partial x_n}{\partial p_1} = \frac{F_{1n}}{\lambda F} - \frac{x_1}{x_n}\cdot\frac{F_{nn}}{\lambda F} = \left(\frac{\partial x_1}{\partial p_n}\right)^* - \frac{x_1}{x_n}\left(\frac{\partial x_n}{\partial p_n}\right)^*, \tag{10.22a}$$

$$\frac{\partial x_2}{\partial p_1} = \frac{F_{12}}{\lambda F} - \frac{x_1}{x_n}\cdot\frac{F_{2n}}{\lambda F} = \left(\frac{\partial x_1}{\partial p_2}\right)^* - \frac{x_1}{x_n}\left(\frac{\partial x_n}{\partial p_2}\right)^*. \tag{10.23a}$$

By multiplying both sides of expressions (10.21a)–(10.23a) by the proper variables, they can be expressed in a more convenient form:

$$E_{x_1 p_1} = E_{x_1 p_1}^* - E_{x_n p_1}^*, \tag{10.24a}$$

$$E_{x_n p_1} = \frac{u_1}{u_n}(E_{x_1 p_n}^* - E_{x_n p_n}^*), \tag{10.25a}$$

$$E_{x_2 p_1} = \frac{u_1}{u_2}(E_{x_1 p_2}^* - E_{x_n p_2}^*). \tag{10.26a}$$

It is important to note that $u_i = p_i x_i < 0$ when x_i is an input.

Two assumptions are made here: (1) a given relative increase (or decrease) in all inputs in the twin results in a smaller relative increase (or decrease) in outputs taken as a whole, either because the production function has this attribute throughout the relevant range, or because the firm makes a profit (with $R > 0$) and hence operates to the right of the maximum average product point; (2) the absence of Hicks's "regression," so that $E_{x_i p_j}^* < 0$ if x_i is an output, x_j an input, and $E_{x_i p_j}^* > 0$ if x_i is an input, x_j an output.

Actually, the presence of regression would weaken some results while strengthening others. It does not seem to me that the problem in hand is sufficiently important to warrant additional explorations of cases arising

from the great variety of relationships among inputs and outputs possible
in a generalized production function (even subject to the constraint given
in (10.15a)). Only the more probable cases are considered here.

(a) One output, labor the only input: In (10.24a), $E^*_{x_1 p_1} < E^*_{x_n p_1}$ because
of diminishing returns; therefore, $E_{x_1 p_1} < 0$ and output contracts. So does
the labor input.

(b) One output, several inputs: The general case is indeterminate. We
can establish the sign of $E_{x_1 p_1}$ in (10.24a) by making the plausible assumption that the isoquants are radially parallel to each other, so that a change
in price (p_1) of the output leaves input ratios unchanged, or that $E^*_{x_i p_1} =
E^*_{x_j p_1}$ $(i, j = 2, ..., n)$. From (10.2a),

$$\sum_1^n p_i \left(\frac{\partial x_i}{\partial p_1} \right)^* = 0. \tag{10.27a}$$

$$p_i \left(\frac{\partial x_i}{\partial p_1} \right)^* = p_i \left(\frac{\partial x_i}{\partial p_1} \right)^* \cdot \frac{p_1 x_i}{p_1 x_i} = \frac{u_i E^*_{x_i p_1}}{p_1}. \tag{10.28a}$$

$$\sum_1^n u_i E^*_{x_i p_1} = 0. \tag{10.29a}$$

If now

$$E^*_{x_i p_1} = E^*_{x_j p_1} = E^*_{x_n p_1} \quad (i, j = 2, ..., n),$$

$$u_1 E^*_{x_1 p_1} + E^*_{x_n p_1} \cdot \sum_2^n u_i = 0, \tag{10.30a}$$

$$E^*_{x_n p_1} = - \frac{u_1 E^*_{x_1 p_1}}{\sum_2^n u_i}. \tag{10.31a}$$

The substitution of (10.31a) into (10.24a) gives

$$E_{x_1 p_1} = \frac{\sum_1^n u_i}{\sum_2^n u_i} \cdot E^*_{x_1 p_1}. \tag{10.32a}$$

Now,

$$\sum_1^n u_i > 0, \quad E^*_{x_1 p_1} > 0, \quad \text{and} \quad \sum_2^n u_i < 0$$

because $x_i < 0$ $(i = 2, ..., n)$. Therefore $E_{x_1 p_1} < 0$.

In (10.25a) both $E^*_{x_1 p_n} < 0$ and $E^*_{x_n p_n} < 0$, but because of the presence of
other inputs (and diminishing returns) $|E^*_{x_1 p_n}| < |E^*_{x_n p_n}|$. It follows that
$E_{x_n p_1} < 0$ (because $u_n < 0$).

For the sign of $E_{x_2 p_1}$ in (10.26a) see section (c–iv) below.

(c) Several outputs and inputs; x_1 is an output:

(i)   *The sign of $E_{x_1 p_1}$ in (10.24a):* If x_1 is a very important user of labor, diminishing returns may make $E^*_{x_1 p_1} < E^*_{x_n p_1}$ (though this also depends on the behavior of other inputs and outputs), and $E_{x_1 p_1} < 0$, similar to the two preceding cases. But if x_1, being one of the several outputs, uses only a moderate part of total labor, then $E^*_{x_1 p_1} > E^*_{x_n p_1}$ and $E_{x_1 p_1} > 0$.

(ii) *The sign of $E_{x_n p_1}$ in (10.25a):* $E^*_{x_n p_n} < 0$ and, by assumption, $E^*_{x_1 p_n} < 0$. In the presence of other inputs (and diminishing returns), we can expect $|E^*_{x_1 p_n}| < |E^*_{x_n p_n}|$ and $E_{x_n p_1} < 0$. But if wages constitute the major part of the cost of x_1 and if the value of the marginal product in the production of x_1 declines more slowly than in other uses of labor, it is possible that the sign of $E_{x_n p_1}$ may be reversed.

(iii) *The sign of $E_{x_2 p_1}$ in (10.26a), x_2 being an output:* Let x_2 be at first all other outputs, or the only other output. Assume $E^*_{x_n p_2} > 0$. If x_1 and x_2 are produced in constant proportions, the result is the same as if x_1 were the only output given in (b) above. If there is some, but not perfect, complementarity between x_1 and x_2 the result is indeterminate unless we assume that all ratios among inputs in the twin remain constant in spite of a change in p_2, in which case diminishing returns will give $E^*_{x_2 p_2} < E^*_{x_n p_2}$. Since $0 < E^*_{x_1 p_2} < E^*_{x_2 p_2}$, $E_{x_2 p_1} < 0$. If x_1 and x_2 are competing outputs, $E^*_{x_1 p_2} < 0$ and $E_{x_2 p_1} < 0$.

In general, a rise in p_1 is likely to increase the output of x_1 and reduce the input of labor as shown above. Hence a reduction in other outputs taken as a whole is highly probable.

If x_2 is one of several outputs and is competitive with x_1, $E_{x_2 p_1} < 0$. Otherwise, the result is indeterminate.

(iv) *The sign of $E_{x_2 p_1}$ in (10.26a), x_2 being an input:* Assume $E^*_{x_1 p_2} < 0$. If x_2 is highly complementary with x_n, it is likely (but not certain) that $|E^*_{x_1 p_2}| < |E^*_{x_n p_2}|$ and $E_{x_2 p_1} < 0$. If the complementarity is slight, the result is indeterminate. If x_2 and x_n are substitutes, $E^*_{x_n p_2} > 0$ and $E_{x_2 p_1} > 0$.

(d) Several outputs and inputs; x_1 is an input:

(i)   *The sign of $E_{x_1 p_1}$ in (10.24a):* Here $E^*_{x_1 p_1} < 0$. If there is some complementarity between x_1 and x_n, $|E^*_{x_1 p_1}| > |E^*_{x_n p_1}|$ and $E^*_{x_1 p_1} < 0$, unless they are used in constant proportions, in which case $E_{x_1 p_1} = 0$. If x_1 and x_n are substitutes, $E^*_{x_n p_1} > 0$ and $E_{x_1 p_1} < 0$.

(ii) *The sign of* $E_{x_n p_1}$ *in (10.25a):* Here $E^*_{x_1 p_1} < 0$. With some complementarity between x_1 and x_n, $|E^*_{x_1 p_n}| < |E^*_{x_n p_n}|$ and $E_{x_n p_1} > 0$. If they are substitutes, $E^*_{x_1 p_n} > 0$ and again $E_{x_n p_1} > 0$. Only when x_1 and x_n are used in constant proportions $E_{x_n p_1} = 0$. So the increase in the price of any nonlabor input, even when complementary with labor, increases the use of labor (except for constant proportions).

(iii) *The sign of* $E_{x_2 p_1}$ *in (10.26a),* x_2 *being an output or an input:* Unless specific assumptions are made about the interrelationships among the variables involved, the result is indeterminate.

A comment on the effects of the magnitude of R on $E_{x_1 p_1}$ and $E_{x_n p_1}$ in (10.24a) and (10.25a). Since $p_n = v$, we obtain from (10.1a)

$$p_n x_n = -\left(\sum_1^{n-1} p_i x_i - R\right).$$
(10.33a)

Differentiating both sides of this expression in respect to p_1 and taking advantage of

$$\sum_1^n p_i \cdot \frac{\partial x_i}{\partial p_1} = 0$$

in equilibrium [3, p. 615], we find that

$$\frac{\partial p_n}{\partial p_1} = -\frac{x_1}{x_n},$$
(10.34a)

and therefore

$$\frac{\partial p_n}{\partial p_1} \cdot \frac{p_1}{p_n} = \frac{p_1 x_1}{\sum_1^{n-1} p_i x_i - R}.$$
(10.35a)

Thus a larger R makes p_n more sensitive to a rise in p_1 and hence causes a greater reduction in labor input in response to a given rise in p_1. So $|E_{x_n p_1}|$ is increased. But on $E_{x_1 p_1}$ in (10.24a) R does not have a clear effect, because a large R implies a small payroll for the twin and a reduction in the importance of labor cost. It is possible that the magnitude of R has no effect on $E_{x_1 p_1}$ at all, and this is indeed the case with a Cobb–Douglas production function consisting of one output and of several inputs, and subject to decreasing returns to scale.

References

1. F. Abramov, "Vokrug da okolo," *Neva*, No. 1, 1963, 109–37. Translated into English under the title of *One Day in the "New Life,"* New York, 1963.

2. R. G. D. Allen, *Mathematical Analysis for Economists,* New York, 1939, pp. 350–83, 461–65, 495–520.
3. ———, *Mathematical Economics,* London, 1956, pp. 472–79, 613–17.
4. H. Averch and L. Johnson, "The Firm under Regulatory Constraint," *Am. Econ. Rev.,* Dec. 1962, *52,* 1052–69.
5. W. J. Baumol, *Business Behavior, Value and Growth,* New York, 1959.
6. J. R. Hicks, *Value and Capital,* 2nd ed., Oxford, 1946, pp. 96–98.
7. F. Lutz and V. Lutz, *The Theory of Investment of the Firm,* Princeton, 1951.
8. J. R. Millar, *Income and Price Formation in the Soviet Collective Farm Sector Since 1953.* Unpublished doctoral dissertation, Cornell Univ., 1965.
9. B. P. Rozhin, *Nekotorye voprosy pod"ema ekonomiki slabykh kolkhozov* [Certain questions regarding the uplifting of weak kolkhozes], Moscow, 1961.
10. T. Scitovsky, "A Note on Profit Maximization and Its Implications," *Rev. Econ. Stud.,* Winter 1943, *11,* 57–60; reprinted in *The Readings in Price Theory,* Am. Econ. Assoc., Homewood, Ill., 1952, pp. 352–60.
11. M. K. Shermeneva, *Financy i kreditovanie sel'skokhoziaistvennykh predpriiatii* [Finances and the supply of credit for agricultural enterprises], Moscow, 1963, pp. 172–79.
11a. M. I. Tugan-Baranovsky, *Sotsial'nyia osnovy kooperatisii* [The social foundations of cooperation], Berlin, 1921, pp. 237–56.
12. B. Ward, "The Firm in Illyria: Market Syndicalism," *Am. Econ. Rev.,* Sept. 1958, *48,* 566–89.
13. F. M. Westfield, "Regulation and Conspiracy," *Am. Econ. Rev.,* June 1965, *55,* 424–43.
14. Akademiia Nauk SSSR, Institut Ekonomiki, *Material'noe stimulirovanie razvitiia kolkhoznogo proizvodstva* [The Academy of Sciences of the USSR, Institute of Economics, Material stimulation of the development of the kolkhoz production], Moscow, 1963, pp. 54–56.
15. "The Calculation of Collective Farm Production Costs," *Kommunist,* Sept. 1962, No. 13, 46–59, as reported in *The Current Digest of the Soviet Press,* Oct. 10, 1962, *14,* 3–11.
16. *Izvestiia,* March 27, 1965, pp. 1–3.
17. ———, April 11, 1965, p. 1.
18. ———, April 13, 1965, pp. 1–2.
19. Nauchno-Issledovatel'skii Finansovyi Institut, *Denezhnye dokhody kolkhozov i differensial'naia renta* [Financial Research Institute, Money incomes of kolkhozes and the differential rent], Moscow, 1963.
20. *The New York Times,* March 28, 1965, *114,* pp. 1 and 6.
21. *Pravda,* Nov. 7, 1965, p. 2.
22. ———, Dec. 26, 1965, pp. 1–2.
23. ———, Jan. 5, 1966, p. 2.
24. ———, Feb. 20, 1966, p. 3.
25. Tsentral'noe Statisticheskoe Upravlenie pri Sovete Ministrov RSFSR, *Narodnoe khoziaistvo RSFSR v 1963 godu, Statisticheskii ezhegodnik* [Central Statistical Office at the Council of Ministers of the RSFSR, The people's economy of the RSFSR in 1963, Statistical yearbook], pp. 316–18.

26. Tsentral'noe Statisticheskoe Upravlenie pri Sovete Ministrov SSSR, *Narodnoe khoziaistvo SSSR v 1963 godu, Statisticheskii ezhegodnik* [Central Statistical Office at the Council of Ministers of the USSR, The people's economy of the USSR in 1963, Statistical yearbook], p. 347.

ESSAY 11

On the optimal compensation of a
socialist manager

I. The problem

The idea for this essay was suggested, unwittingly to be sure, by the Soviet
Premier Alexei Kosygin in his famous speech of September 27, 1965, inaugurating the Soviet Economic Reforms. Of the several changes in directives to enterprises, which he announced, two are relevant here: (1) the
greater emphasis to be placed on profits, and (2) the replacement of the
output target by sales.[1]

Taking advantage of the theorist's inherent right of simplification, I
would say that the enterprise manager (or director, as he is usually called)
was instructed to maximize an unspecified function of profits and sales,
subject to certain planning directives and several constraints that, though

Reprinted by permission from *The Quarterly Journal of Economics,* Vol. LXXXVIII, February 1974, pp. 1–18.

A number of persons have contributed to the development of this essay. My M.I.T. students and listeners elsewhere have allowed me to try these ideas on them for a number of
years. L. Dwight Israelsen helped with the research; John Broome and my colleague Professor Martin L. Weitzman improved the mathematics; Professors Michael Manove and
Abram Bergson made many helpful comments. Professor Karl G. Jungenfelt of the Stockholm School of Economics raised a number of questions that made me rework the whole
paper and develop Section III. He also suggested an alternative method of setting the managerial bonus that he may wish to develop on his own. My expression of gratitude to all
these persons does not of course make them accomplices in my mistakes.

I am also grateful to the Stockholm School of Economics for the use of its facilities during the Spring 1972 term and to the National Science Foundation (Grant NSF-GS-2627), to
the American Council of Learned Societies, and to the International Research and Exchanges Board for their financial support.

[1] Mr. Kosygin's speech was originally published in *Pravda* and *Izvestiia* on Sept. 28, 1965.
English translations can be found in *The Current Digest of Soviet Press,* XVII, No. 38
(Oct. 13, 1965), 3–12; in *Problems of Economics,* VIII (Oct. 1965), 3–28; and in Morris Bornstein and Daniel R. Fusfeld, eds., *The Soviet Economy: A Book of Readings,*
third edition (Homewood, Illinois, 1970), pp. 387–96. The last is a somewhat abbreviated
version.

Many comments and analyses of his speech have been published. See, for instance,
Gertrude E. Schroeder, "Soviet Economic 'Reform': A Study in Contradictions," *Soviet
Studies,* XX (July 1968), 1–21. For the discussions preceding the reforms, see Jere L.
Felker, *Soviet Economic Controversies* (Cambridge, Mass., 1966).

important in themselves, need not be considered here.[2] I will argue in Section II that the maximization of a weighted sum of profits and sales makes excellent sense when the enterprise is allowed to set the prices of its outputs. It is not needed, however, if prices are set by the State, as indeed they are in the Soviet Union. Under these conditions, why was the Manager not given freedom of decision and instructed to maximize profits only, in accordance with good old economic theory, and without the additional directives and constraints?

I suspect that Mr. Kosygin's solution was not based on fine theoretical considerations.[3] Even if he sympathized with them (for which there is little, if any, evidence), he would certainly be reluctant to abolish the planning mechanism and give complete freedom to Soviet enterprise managers. There was no telling in what kind of wild ventures these managers, unused to the freedom of the market, might get involved, and through how many perturbations the economy would have to pass until some reasonable equilibrium was achieved. Besides, Mr. Kosygin, like everyone else, must have known that Soviet prices, based on a markup system and usually unchanged for a number of years, do not equate demand and supply.[4] When such prices are combined with excess demand, still common

---

[2] The most important constraints were the "major assortment" of sales and a maximum payroll limitation that was expected to remain in force until a more adequate supply of consumer goods was achieved. Direct orders from the authorities to the managers have never ceased and have become more frequent in recent years. There has been a return to centralization.

An investigation of the actual objective function of a Soviet enterprise would require a separate essay and probably more than one. To put it briefly, much emphasis has been placed in recent years on the Material Incentive Fund from which bonuses are paid not only to the Manager but also to his staff, workers, and employees. The Fund is calculated by multiplying the wage fund of the enterprise by a ratio obtained from a formula containing a number of variables, such as increase in sales, rate of profit on capital, planned production of new products as a fraction of total production, improvement in labor productivity, and so on. It seems that when the authorities decide to correct some particular deficiency, such as low labor productivity, they make a corresponding change in the Incentive Fund formula. The formula also differs among industries and enterprises. See Michael Ellman, *Soviet Planning Today: Proposals for an Optimally Functioning Economic System* (Cambridge, 1971), pp. 131–62; Bertrand N. Horwitz, *Accounting Controls and the Soviet Economic Reforms of 1966* (American Accounting Association, 1970); S. I. Shkurko, *Material'noe stimulirovanie v novykh usloviiakh khoziaistvovaniia* [Material stimulation under new conditions of management] (Moscow, 1970).

[3] It is quite possible that his decision was simply a compromise, so common in governmental circles, between the advocates of managerial freedom via profits and the proponents of central control via sales.

[4] It seems that Mr. Kosygin did not wish prices to clear the market. Instead "Prices... must cover production and turnover outlays and secure the profits of each functioning enterprise." Bornstein and Fusfeld, *op. cit.*, p. 395. Note that President Nixon's Price Control Board also followed this doctrine. Perhaps a governmental body is incapable of regulating prices in any other way.

in the Soviet economy, the maximization of profits by enterprises can lead to all sorts of strange results.

The defects of the Soviet price system, like those of practically any system of controlled prices, are too well-known to require a long discussion here. Let me merely mention two: (1) unless all dimensions of a commodity, or of a service, are specified explicitly – a costly and laborious process – its numerous characteristics cannot be controlled by the single dimension of price; its quality will deteriorate. (2) The infrequency of Soviet price revisions discourages the introduction of new products and new models. A price set for a new commodity normally covers the average cost of production (when large-scale output begins) plus a modest markup. With time the cost of production declines, due to the learning process and similar reasons – there is little wage inflation in the Soviet Union. The old product becomes highly profitable. The manager has no incentive to replace it with a new one, subject to that modest profit margin.[5] More frequent price revisions are of course costly. In spite of the present trend toward recentralization, a day will come when Soviet planners will have to delegate at least some price-setting rights to the producers.[6] Hungary has already made some progress in this direction.

But price setting by producers involves at least two dangers: inflation and monopoly. On inflation I have little to say here, except to suggest that it can be avoided if the planners achieve a reasonable macro balance and retain some control over wages. It is not that I underestimate the difficulties of controlling inflation: this paper simply deals with a different subject. It is concerned with the second hazard – monopoly power. The high concentration of control over industry in Eastern Europe, the strong affection for large-scale enterprises by socialist planners, and the small size of European socialist countries, with the single exception of the Soviet Union, would allow the producers and their organizations to exercise monopoly powers beyond the fondest dream of any Wall Street operator.[7] Of

---

[5] Note that wage inflation, that is, wage rates rising faster than labor productivity, would produce an opposite result: the enterprise would be delighted to produce a "new" product to get a new price higher than the original one – the usual effect of price control during inflation. In the capitalist world, firms are anxious to produce something that is or looks new in order to enjoy temporary monopoly gains from higher prices until their competitors catch up.

As was stated in note 2, the proportion of output represented by new products is explicitly included in some of the Incentive Fund formulas.

[6] Whether the planners relinquish any of their price-setting rights will depend upon their desire to maximize consumer satisfaction by encouraging competition in prices, qualities, and services among producers.

[7] See Frederic L. Pryor, "Barriers to Market Socialism in Eastern Europe in the Mid-1960's," *Studies in Comparative Communism*, III (April 1970), 31–64.

course, the control over industry could be reorganized; perhaps even anti-trust departments could be set up in the respective ministries of justice – it takes some imagination to visualize that – and imports could be used to break monopoly power. But this last weapon, perhaps the most effective of them all, requires ample supplies of foreign exchange. Even then, would socialist managers and workers welcome foreign competition any more enthusiastically than do their capitalist colleagues?

I think it is safe to conclude that if socialist managers are given freedom of decision and are encouraged to maximize profits under a market system of prices set by themselves, monopolistic and oligopolistic practices will abound. But perhaps Mr. Kosygin's suggestion can be utilized to express their instructions in some other, still reasonably practical way to make the managers behave in a more socially desired manner.

II. The bonus as a function of profit and sales

We shall first consider an enterprise producing only one output and then proceed to the general case with any number of inputs and outputs. We shall assume that the Manager has the ability and all the necessary information about demand and cost schedules to maximize total profit within his time horizon if that is his objective. That is, for every planned range of output he will choose the lowest cost technology and input combination, and then proceed to the intersection of the marginal cost and marginal revenue curves, as shown by the solid lines on the three diagrams that we all learned in our first course in economics. (The schedules are represented by straight lines in Figures 11.1 and 11.2 only because straight lines are easier to draw.) How he gets this information, whether he takes the mode or the mean or some other moment of a probability distribution, how he protects himself against uncertainty in general, and how he deals with the complexities of oligopolistic strategy is none of our concern, though we shall have to return to oligopoly briefly in Section IV. The important point is that the change in his instructions to be suggested presently will not call for any additional information or any extra ability on his part.

Now, the Planner, as we shall call the official who determines the rules and who desires an optimal allocation of resources, wants the Manager to set his output price at point A where marginal cost equals price.[8] The

---

[8] In assuming that the Planner does want the Manager to be at the socially optimal point A, I am merely following the tradition. But the Planner may have his own motivations and incentives that may or may not be socially desirable. Perhaps this question deserves greater attention than it has received in the literature so far.

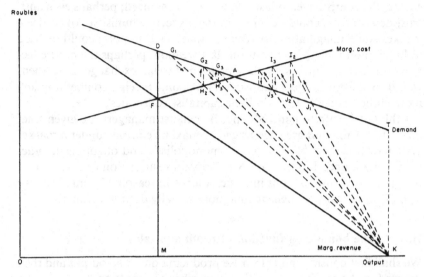

Figure 11.1. The movement toward the optimum with declining elasticity of demand and rising marginal cost.

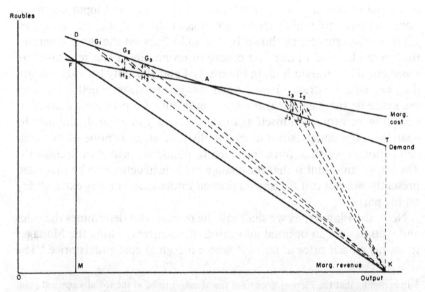

Figure 11.2. The movement toward the optimum with declining elasticity of demand and falling marginal cost.

trouble is that the Planner does not know the position of A. (Even if he did, he would still have to find some method, hopefully other than a direct order, to induce the Manager to move there.) The Planner does know, however, that if the Manager was maximizing total profit he would be at some point D, to the left of A. He also knows that if the Manager was instructed to maximize total sales he would move to the right of A.[9] Thus, *and this is the central point of this essay,* profits in the objective function move the Manager to the left and sales move him to the right of A along the demand curve. Surely, there must exist some combination of profit and sales that would induce the Manager to operate *at* point A. But first, a list of mathematical symbols (in order of appearance):

B The Manager's bonus
u, v parameters
N net profit (before the bonus)
R revenue or sales
p price
x output
C total cost
E elasticity, usually of demand
n number of outputs, or of inputs and outputs
E_s elasticity of supply
$z = (u+v)/u$
N^* adjusted net profit (with shadow prices)
q corporate income tax rate
t time (in adjustment units)
$*$ means optimal.

The symbols $'$ and $''$ indicate first and second derivatives in respect to x.

Let us assume that the Planner offers the Manager a bonus that the Manager *is absolutely determined to maximize* (both for the sake of income and as a success indicator). Let this bonus consist of a weighted sum of profits and of sales:[10]

---

[9] In Figures 11.1 and 11.2, where demand elasticity declines to the right, maximization of sales would be achieved at point T because there demand elasticity equals -1 and the marginal revenue is zero. In Figure 11.3, the rising demand elasticity provides no maximum point for sales.

[10] Several years ago Professor Edward Ames (*Soviet Economic Processes,* Homewood, Illinois, 1965, pp. 52–66) analyzed a similar bonus scheme, but *with parametric prices.* He of course found that sales were inimical to the optimal resource allocation.

$$B = uN + vR = u(px - C) + vpx = (u + v)px - uC. \tag{11.1}$$

To maximize it, differentiate B in respect to x and equate the derivative to zero:

$$\frac{dB}{dx} = (u + v)\left(p + x\frac{dp}{dx}\right) - uC' = 0, \tag{11.2}$$

which yields

$$p = C'\bigg/\left(\frac{u+v}{u}\right)\cdot\left(1 + \frac{1}{E}\right), \tag{11.3}$$

where $E = (dx/dp)\cdot(p/x)$ is of course the elasticity of demand.[11] But the Planner wants the price to equal marginal cost:

$$p = C'. \tag{11.4}$$

Hence u and v should be chosen in such a way that

$$C'\bigg/\left(\frac{u+v}{u}\right)\cdot\left(1 + \frac{1}{E}\right) = C', \tag{11.5}$$

which, after a few simple manipulations, reduces to

$$\frac{u}{v} = -(E + 1), \tag{11.6}$$

the E indicating here the demand elasticity at the optimal point A, the location of which is still unknown.

If the enterprise produces several outputs $x_1, x_2, \ldots, x_n$ and sets the corresponding prices of $p_1, p_2, \ldots, p_n$, the bonus should be expressed as

$$B = uN + \sum_{1}^{n} v_i x_i p_i. \tag{11.7}$$

By taking partial derivatives in respect to x_i and equating them to zero, we again obtain the result that

$$\frac{u}{v_i} = -(E_i + 1), \tag{11.8}$$

but with the very important qualification that *the cross elasticities of demand are sufficiently small to be disregarded.* Otherwise, the C_i' refuse to cancel out, and the mathematical solution is too complex for practical use. This means that the parameters v_i cannot be set separately for each product, but must be applied to the total output of each *department* of the enterprise, the departments being arranged in such a way as to make

---

[11] The second-order conditions are given in the Mathematical Appendix.

the interdepartmental cross elasticities of demand negligible. From an administrative point of view this may even be an advantage: the Planner would undoubtedly prefer not to have to compute demand elasticities for each model of, say, General Motors cars, to give an American example. But it might be difficult to divide General Motors into proper departments because of the continuous characteristics, so to speak, of its outputs. It is unlikely that Chevrolets compete with Cadillacs directly. But Chevrolets compete with Pontiacs, Pontiacs with Buicks, and Buicks with Cadillacs. Where are we to draw the line? It may be necessary to put all General Motors cars into one department, while trucks, Diesel engines, refrigerators, etc., each comprise a separate one. As a result, the ratios u/v_i will correspond not to the actual demand elasticities for specific commodities but to their weighted average. Hence, products whose elasticities are higher than the average for the department will be overproduced, and the others produced below the optimum. It is highly unlikely, however, that demand elasticities can be estimated with much precision even under the best of circumstances. Therefore, all we can expect from our bonus scheme is a movement to some approximation of the optimal output.[12]

Expressions (11.6) and (11.8) give only the relative magnitudes of u and v: they do not of course determine the absolute size of the bonus that the Planner will presumably set according to other considerations.

The whole scheme will make no sense if $|E| \leq 1$. Direct price regulation (perhaps similar to that practiced in our public utilities) would be required. Actually, many demand elasticities need not be particularly low because they pertain not to the demand for the whole industry but only to that for the individual enterprise.

To obtain some idea about the composition of the bonus, let us take a demand elasticity as high as -4. Set $v = 1$ percent, and $u = 3$ percent (as given by expression (11.6)) and assume sales of 1,000 and a net profit of 100 (a 10 percent profit margin seems reasonable). Then the bonus will equal 3 percent $\times$ 100 + 1 percent $\times$ 1000 = 3 + 10 = 13. Note that more than three quarters of this bonus (77 percent) is derived from sales. Even with $E = -6$, two thirds of the bonus still comes from that source. And these are high elasticities. If the profit margin was only 5 percent, the corresponding shares would be even higher – 87 and 80 percent. Mr. Kosygin certainly had a point.

Monopsony can be handled in exactly the same manner, except that in expression (11.1) the parameter v is applied not to sales, but, say, to the payroll, if labor is the factor subject to monopsonistic exploitation. But

---

12 In case of a discriminating monopoly the u/v ratios will have to be differentiated among the several markets. This point was made by Lars Jonung of the University of Lund.

because payroll is an expenditure rather than a receipt, the ratio u/v takes the form of

$$\frac{u}{v} = E_s + 1, \tag{11.9}$$

again on the condition that the cross elasticities, this time of the supplies of inputs, can be neglected. A solution for any number of inputs and outputs with a generalized production function is given in the Mathematical Appendix, but because of the close analogy between the cases of monopoly and monopsony, the latter will be omitted from the subsequent discussion.

III.   The iterative process

It now remains to find the correct elasticity of demand. If this elasticity is constant, at least in the relevant range, let us hope that it can be estimated. But it need not be constant. It is the elasticity at (or near) point A that the Planner needs. Yet all available empirical data will pertain to the region around point D if sales were not previously included in the bonus function, or around some other point on the demand curve if the bonus was set incorrectly, or if the demand or the cost curves shifted since the bonus had been arranged. How can the Planner discover that the bonus, as it is presently composed, is wrong and ascertain in what direction it should be changed? How can he induce the Manager to operate at point A when he does not know where this point is?

Two cases will be considered, depending on whether the (absolute magnitude of the) elasticity of demand declines or rises with increasing output.

1.   *Declining elasticity of demand*

Assume that the bonus scheme has been in operation for some time and that the Manager is now at some point G_1 on the demand curve, as shown in Figures 11.1 and 11.2. The Planner knows x_1 and p_1 at G_1 and the current bonus ratio arranged previously, which we shall call u/v_0. By assumption, he can estimate E_1 as well. Comparing u/v_0 with the u/v_1, which would correspond to E_1, he finds $u/v_0 > u/v_1$. This tells him that point G_1 is to the left of A, a piece of information which, while not absolutely necessary, is convenient to have.[13] He now sets a new $u/v_1 = -(E_1 + 1)$.

---

[13] Another way of ascertaining that the Manager is to the left of point A is by finding the p/C' ratio from expression (11.3). But if this ratio, or more exactly C' at G_1, can be calculated, why does not the Planner simply order the Manager to set the price and output

It will now be convenient to introduce a new parameter $z = (u+v)/u$. By definition, at any point on the demand curve,

$$z = \frac{1}{1+1/E} = \frac{1}{1+(dp/dx)\cdot(x/p)} = \frac{p}{p+x(dp/dx)} = \frac{p}{R'}. \tag{11.10}$$

Thus

$$z_1 R' = p_1, \tag{11.11}$$

i.e., $z_1 R'$ passes through point G_1.

The maximizing equation (11.2) can be rewritten as

$$zR' = C'. \tag{11.12}$$

This expression shows that our bonus scheme is simply a device for inducing the Manager, in his quest for the largest reward, to maximize an adjusted profit $N^* = zpx - C$, which determines his bonus. Mathematically speaking, this is a better scheme because it uses only one parameter z instead of our two - u and v (see the Mathematical Appendix). I think, however, that practical people (capitalist or socialist) will be more at home with a bonus expressed in terms of conventional profits and sales than with one based on a price adjustment. In either case, the Manager will work with adjusted marginal revenue curves zR' and equate them to C'. A family of such curves for particular values of z is represented by the dotted lines GHK and IJK in Figures 11.1 and 11.2. They all meet the original R' curve (corresponding to $z = 1$) at K where $R' = 0$.

It can be shown that point G_2 will lie between G_1 and A, that is, that the method of setting the bonus described here will result in a nonoscillatory movement converging on A. In the linear case represented in Figures 11.1 and 11.2, this is obvious. A general proof is given in the Mathematical Appendix.

After the Manager moved to point G_2, the Planner, having collected sufficient information about E_2 at G_2 and finding that it does not correspond to z_1, will calculate a new z_2 and change the bonus accordingly. The Manager will now move to point G_3 between G_2 and A, and so on. Only when the Planner ascertains that a newly calculated E corresponds to a previously set z does he know that the Manager has indeed reached the optimal point A where $zR' = p = C'$.

If the Manager's original position was at J_1 to the right of A, the same method of successive bonus adjustments would move him leftward toward A.

accordingly without bothering about a particular bonus scheme? First, C' at G_1 is not the marginal cost that the Planner needs. To get from G_1 to A a number of iterations would be needed that may prove to be oscillatory (in Figure 11.1 for instance). Second, such a direct order would merely follow the present Soviet practice of price and quantity controls with all its defects.

The negative slope of the marginal cost curve in Figure 11.2 creates no problems in this respect, so long as the stability conditions are satisfied, but it may call for one more decision: either the enterprise will have to be subsidized or the price will have to be set at some multiple of marginal cost by changing equation (11.4) accordingly – a subject amply discussed in welfare economics.

Thus our method, which may be called the "Simple Rule," does result in convergence without oscillations. But the speed of convergence remains unknown. An experienced Planner may improve on it by making stronger adjustments (in either direction), and thus sending the Manager to point A with fewer iterations. These must be disturbing to the Manager and particularly to his customers. But the Planner should take care not to overshoot. His reputation may be at stake.

2.   Increasing elasticity of demand

R. G. D. Allen regards this as an "abnormal" case, at least by implication.[14] I hope that it is most uncommon in practice.

A demand curve with an increasing (in absolute magnitude) E is presented in Figure 11.3. We again start at point G_1 and try to apply the Simple Rule. Unfortunately, as shown in Figure 11.3 and in the Mathematical Appendix, this Rule results in oscillations around A.[15] In Figure 11.3 the process converges (and rather rapidly at that), but this need not always be true. Even if it is, a practical Planner will be reluctant to use the Simple Rule because of the oscillations. To avoid them, he will have to dilute the Rule. Suppose that the original z_0 was set at 1.10, while the z_1 corresponding to E_1 at point G_1 is 1.18. The Planner sets the new z at 1.13 or even at 1.12 and watches the Manager's moves before making another change. I have not been able to devise a simple general method for dealing with this unusual case and I doubt that further effort is worthwhile. Let us hope that the Planner learns from experience.[16]

IV.   A practical look

The practical application of our method merely calls for periodic, perhaps annual, checks to see whether the u/v ratio (or the z) as it appears in the bonus corresponds to the E of the Manager's present position, and

[14] R. G. D. Allen, *Mathematical Analysis for Economists* (New York, 1939), pp. 257–58.
[15] The zR' may not even intersect the C' curve at all. See the stability conditions in the Mathematical Appendix.
[16] I have not presented a diagram showing a combination of increasing $|E|$ with a declining marginal cost. This combination has a good chance of being unstable.

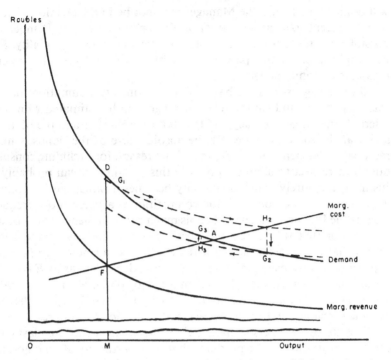

Figure 11.3. The movement toward the optimum with increasing elasticity of demand and rising marginal cost.

for an adjustment of this ratio when a significant discrepancy is found. More frequent changes would be irritating both to the Manager and to his customers. On the other hand, if the u/v ratio is changed infrequently, it may pay a group of managers to engage in fictitious sales with one another.[17] Hence some check of the sales record of the enterprise and of its profit-sales ratio may be required.

It is important to assure the Manager that the absolute size of his bonus is little affected by changes in the u/v ratio. Otherwise, the Manager, whose knowledge and intelligence need not be inferior to the Planner's, and who can readily figure out the Planner's rules, will be tempted to pursue a game strategy against the Planner. It may pay the Manager not to maximize his bonus at a given moment either in the hope that a change in the u/v ratio will increase his bonus or in the fear that such a change

---

[17] I was once told in Bogota, Colombia, about a pair of businessmen, one in Colombia and the other in Peru, who kept sending hides to each other in order to profit from special foreign exchange rates. Of course the hides never left either country; only papers were sent back and forth.

will diminish it. Hence the Manager may not be in the position dictated by the current u/v ratio, a situation that may mislead the Planner and possibly lead to wrong adjustments.[18] It may even cause instability. Further exploration of this potentially exciting process I leave to the connoisseurs of game theory.

All these suggestions are based on the optimistic assumption that the elasticity of demand (in the relevant range) can be estimated with some tolerable degree of accuracy and that both the Planner and the Manager arrive at the same estimate. (If the absolute size of the bonus is made reasonably independent of u/v, there is no reason for excluding consultations.) In respect to simple monopoly this assumption can probably be justified, but surely demand elasticity becomes a rather elusive concept under conditions of oligopolistic competition – a much more frequent case. Is the Planner to assume that his managers act independently of one another, or that they enter into possibly secret, collusive agreements? Even if he can estimate the E for the industry as a whole, can he really approximate it for each individual enterprise, dependent as its E is on the actions of its competitors? If problems of static oligopolistic price setting are very complex (and I have no desire to discuss them here), do they not become unmanageable in the presence of technological progress?

There are two answers to these objections: first, the needed elasticities pertain not to the specific products, but to departments of an enterprise (see Section II). Demand for their outputs in the aggregate should be more stable than that for individual products. Second, and more important, do we have better alternatives?

The defects of profit maximization as an instrument for achieving an optimal allocation of resources are well-known. Nevertheless, it seems to me that Soviet experience clearly shows that this very imperfect method is still the best available, at least for the normal operations of an ordinary enterprise. (Large investment decisions are a different matter.)[19] If an effective policy of price control without the usual difficulties (see Section I) could be devised, the Manager should be instructed to maximize profit without much ado. But for most goods and services a satisfactory policy of this kind has not yet been invented. It seems better then to let the Manager (except in special sectors) set his own prices. But if sales are not included in his instructions or in his bonus function, this is tantamount to

---

[18] Much will depend on the Planner's ability to estimate E and on his faith in his own estimates. The scheme will miscarry if the Manager's estimates of E are different from those of the Planner (see below). But if the Manager does not maximize the bonus at all, our whole scheme should be abandoned.

[19] It goes without saying that many enterprises, particularly in such fields as education, public health, cultural activities, and perhaps urban transportation, need not make any profits. Qualifications arising from external effects are too well-known to require comment.

the assumption of an infinite elasticity of demand. Surely more realistic assumptions can be made.

Perhaps the skeptical Planner may be persuaded, at the beginning, to set the u/v ratio in each industry in such a manner that the profit component in managerial bonuses approximately equals that of sales. With the profit-sales ratio of 10 percent, which we used previously (it varies among industries and enterprises), this amounts to the assumption that $E = -11$; with a 5 percent markup, $E = -21$, surely generous overestimates. Perhaps the profit component should be made equal to half of that of sales. This would still imply high elasticities: -6 and -11, respectively. In time, differentiated ratios adjusted to the characteristics of the various industries and firms could be worked out, even if the Planner did not follow each step of the fascinating process described in Section III.

But even if the Planner still rejects the bonus idea as being impractical, not everything is lost. He should at least make the Manager understand that his performance is evaluated by the Planner on the basis not only of profit but also of sales. So if a report of rising sales brings about a broad smile on the Planner's face, the Manager, a professional person interested in promoting his own career, may well behave as if sales were indeed included in his bonus formula. But the Planner, only a human being, may not always show the right breadth of a smile, and the Manager, another human being, may not always know how to quantify it.

The inclusion of sales in the bonus need not be limited to a socialist manager. It can be applied to the compensation of any decision maker who has monopolistic (or monopsonistic) powers, as for instance to that of a head of a department of a vertically integrated capitalist corporation.[20] The principle can also be used as a general antimonopoly measure by taxing profits at the rate q and subsidizing sales (or certain purchases) at the rate v, the $(1-q)/v$ ratio being determined by the elasticity of demand (or supply). But even if such a flexible tax subsidy policy could be used in a country like France, I doubt that the American legal system would tolerate it. For that matter, strange as it may seem, we may not need it. For if Professor Galbraith and others are right in asserting that

---

[20] That marginal costs, particularly in the absence of market prices, should be the basis of transfer prices is well recognized in the literature. See for instance Jack Hirshleifer, "On the Economics of Transfer Pricing," *Journal of Business*, XXIX (July 1956), 172–84; and his "Economics of the Divisionalized Firm," same *Journal*, XXX (April 1957), 96–108. It would be interesting to find out what specific incentives, if any, are offered to managers of departments to make them adhere to this policy.

In general, the instructions given to managers of branches or departments of capitalist firms, the evaluation of the managers' performance, the nature of their compensation, the delegation of powers to them, and similar subjects, should be of great interest to researchers on socialist countries.

sales are included in the objective functions of large corporations, the problem of monopolistic pricing may have already been solved, or at least seriously mitigated. In our new industrial state wonders never cease.[21]

Mathematical appendix

Assumptions: (1) Demand and cost functions are monotonic and twice differentiable in the relevant range. (2) $p'_i < 0$ if x_i is an output, $p'_i > 0$ if x_i is an input. (3) p intersects C' in a single point A in the region where $|E| > 1$. Hence it follows from the simple-monopoly-maximizing equation $p + xp' = C'$ that $p > C'$ at point D and between D and A and $p < C'$ to the right of A.

To Section II

Second-order conditions for profit maximization under ordinary monopoly are $R'' < C''$. The differentiation of equation (11.2) in the text expresses these conditions as $zR'' < C''$. Hence, if $R'' < 0$, stability is reinforced. But if $R'' > 0$ (which may happen with increasing $|E|$), a previously stable situation may become unstable.

In the general case,

$$N = \sum_1^n p_i x_i \quad (i = 1, \ldots, n), \tag{11.1a}$$

and

$$B = \sum_1^n (u + v_i) p_i x_i, \tag{11.2a}$$

subject to the production function

$$f(x_1, \ldots, x_n) = 0. \tag{11.3a}$$

Using Lagrangean multiplier λ, form

$$Y = \sum_1^n (u + v_i) p_i x_i - \lambda f(x_1, \ldots, x_n). \tag{11.4a}$$

Differentiate (11.4a) in respect to x_i and equate to zero:

$$p_i(u + v_i) \cdot \left(1 + \frac{x_i}{p_i} \cdot \frac{\partial p_i}{\partial x_i}\right) = \lambda f_i, \tag{11.5a}$$

provided of course that $\partial p_i / \partial x_j = 0$ for $i \neq j$.

---

[21] John Kenneth Galbraith, *The New Industrial State* (Boston, 1967, 1971), pp. 171-77. See also William J. Baumol, *Business Behavior, Value and Growth*, revised edition (New York, 1967), pp. 45-63, 68-77, 96-103.

$$p_i = \frac{\lambda f_i}{(u+v_i)(1+1/E_i)}. \tag{11.6a}$$

It is desired that prices should be proportional to the respective rates of transformation in production:

$$\frac{p_i}{p_j} = \frac{f_i}{f_j} \quad \text{for all } i \text{ and } j. \tag{11.7a}$$

Substituting (11.7a) into (11.6a) yields

$$(u+v_i)\left(1+\frac{1}{E_i}\right) = (u+v_j)\left(1+\frac{1}{E_j}\right) \quad \text{for all } i \text{ and } j. \tag{11.8a}$$

The solution given by expression (11.8) in the text is

$$\frac{u}{v_i} = -(E_i+1). \tag{11.9a}$$

It can easily be ascertained that (11.9a) satisfies equation (11.8a) because (11.9a) implies for all i and j:

$$(u+v_i)\left(1+\frac{1}{E_i}\right) = u = (u+v_j)\left(1+\frac{1}{E_j}\right). \tag{11.10a}$$

The condition (11.9a) is not the only solution that satisfies (11.8a). The latter expression says that the manager will produce (or buy) the proper amounts (and charge or pay the proper prices) provided that the $(u+v_i)$ are inversely proportional to the respective $(1+1/E_i)$. As was already mentioned in the text regarding expression (11.12), $(u+v_i)$ can be regarded as price-adjusting weights transforming our bonus scheme into an ordinary profit maximization with shadow prices defined as

$$\frac{p_i}{1+1/E_i}.$$

Note that if x_i is an output, $v_i \geq 0$, provided that $|E_i| > 1$. If x_i is an input, $v_i \leq 0$ because inputs have negative signs.

To Section III

1. *Declining* $|E|$:[22] The Simple Rule implies the following sequence of bonus ratios and outputs:

$$z_0 \rightarrow x_1 \rightarrow z_1 \rightarrow x_2 \cdots z_{t-1} \rightarrow x_t \rightarrow z_t \rightarrow x_{t+1} \cdots. \tag{11.11a}$$

A larger z means a greater relative weight given to sales. Hence if

---

[22] This is a modified version of a proof suggested by my colleague Professor Martin L. Weitzman. It is clearer and more rigorous than the one contained in an earlier draft of this essay.

$$z_t > z_{t-1}, \quad x_{t+1} > x_t,$$

and because of the declining $|E|$ if

$$x_{t+1} > x_t, \quad z_{t+1} > z_t.$$

By definition of z given in (11.10),

$$z_t = \frac{p_t}{R_t'}. \tag{11.12a}$$

Since z_t determines x_{t+1}, the maximizing equation (11.12) can be expressed as

$$z_t = \frac{C_{t+1}'}{R_{t+1}'}, \tag{11.13a}$$

and

$$z_{t-1} = \frac{C_t'}{R_t'}. \tag{11.14a}$$

As explained in the text, the Planner, starting from $x_1 < x^*$, activates the adjustment process by setting $z_1 > z_0$. Therefore $x_2 > x_1$, $z_2 > z_1$ and in general $z_t > z_{t-1}$. From (11.12a) and (11.14a),

$$\frac{p_t}{C_t'} = \frac{z_t}{z_{t-1}} > 1. \tag{11.15a}$$

Thus $p_t > C_t'$, and no overshooting takes place. Conversely, so long as $p_t > C_t'$, $z_t > z_{t-1}$; the process continues until $p_t = C_t'$ at A. This means convergence without oscillations.

A similar process, but in reverse, takes place when at the start $x_1 > x^*$.

2. *Increasing* $|E|$: The application of the Simple Rule still gives $x_{t+1} > x_t$ if $z_t > z_{t-1}$, but unfortunately $z_{t+1} < z_t$ if $x_{t+1} > x_t$ because of increasing $|E|$. Therefore, if $x_t < x^*$, $z_t > z_{t-1}$, and $x_{t+1} > x_t$, but from (11.12a) and (11.14a),

$$\frac{p_{t+1}}{C_{t+1}'} = \frac{z_{t+1}}{z_t} < 1, \tag{11.16a}$$

and oscillations around A are inevitable. Convergence is not assured.

Special appendix: The effect of a proportional subsidy or a tax on the quality and quantity of output[23]

I investigate here whether the bonus suggested in this essay (a linear function of profit and sales) is likely to induce a socialist manager to change,

[23] This Appendix was prompted by a question raised by one of my graduate students in the Seminar on Economic Development at La Trobe University in Melbourne (June–August,

and particularly to lower, the quality of his product: the latter effect would be most unwelcome in socialist countries. But because, as was shown earlier, this bonus is equivalent to a subsidy proportional to price, this investigation can be broadened to include the effects of such a subsidy, not restricted to its optimal value, on the quality and also on the quantity of the product.[24] And finally, since the subsidy can be less than unity, it can be interpreted as a proportional tax as well. It will be shown that this subsidy (or tax) can indeed affect both quality and quantity (and of course the price) of output, and sometimes in a rather unexpected manner.

List of symbols (in order of appearance)

p price of output
x quantity of output
k index of quality of output
C total cost
H profit (including the subsidy or the tax) $= zR - C$
R revenue (without the subsidy or the tax) $= px$
z subsidy (if $z > 1$) or tax (if $z < 1$)

$$H_x = \frac{\partial H}{\partial x}; \quad H_{xx} = \frac{\partial^2 H}{\partial x^2}; \quad H_{xk} = \frac{\partial^2 H}{\partial x \, \partial k}.$$

Similar notation is used for other derivatives.

$E_{R_x}^k = $ elasticity of R_x in respect to k.

Similar notation is used for other elasticities.

We assume that both the price and the cost of output are functions of quantity and of quality:

$$p = p(x, k), \qquad C = C(x, k), \tag{11.17a}$$

where k is some quality index. It can stand for some easily quantifiable characteristic, such as the strength of a material or the longevity of a machine, or for something more elusive, like the variety of dresses or the taste of wine. Quality is, of course, multidimensional, but no attempt at dealing with the general complex case will be made here.

1974) on whether my bonus scheme might not lower the quality of output. Unfortunately, I do not remember which student should be thanked for that.

    I am very grateful to my colleague Professor Peter A. Diamond for his gentle guidance through some labyrinths of welfare economics. He is not to be held responsible, however, for any of my remaining mistakes.

    I am also grateful to the National Science Foundation (Grant NSF-GS-2627) for its financial support.

[24] That optimal value of z was the one that induced the Manager to move to the point where marginal cost equaled price. See pp. 208, 214–15.

The firm (or the Manager) will maximize

$$H = zR - C \tag{11.18a}$$

in respect to x and to k:

$$H_x = zR_x - C_x = 0, \tag{11.19a}$$

$$H_k = zR_k - C_k = 0. \tag{11.20a}$$

The second-order conditions are:

$$H_{xx} = zR_{xx} - C_{xx} < 0, \tag{11.21a}$$

$$H_{kk} = zR_{kk} - C_{kk} < 0, \tag{11.22a}$$

and

$$H_{xk}^2 = (zR_{xk} - C_{xk})^2 < (zR_{xx} - C_{xx})(zR_{kk} - C_{kk}). \tag{11.23a}$$

We now want to find the signs of dx/dz and dk/dz. Differentiating (11.19a) and (11.20a) gives the following system of equations:

$$H_{xx}\frac{dx}{dz} + H_{xk}\frac{dk}{dz} = -R_x, \tag{11.24a}$$

$$H_{xk}\frac{dx}{dz} + H_{kk}\frac{dk}{dz} = -R_k, \tag{11.25a}$$

with the determinant

$$D = \begin{vmatrix} H_{xx} & H_{xk} \\ H_{xk} & H_{kk} \end{vmatrix} = H_{xx}H_{kk} - H_{xk}^2 > 0 \tag{11.26a}$$

by second-order conditions (11.23a).

$$\frac{dx}{dz} = \frac{-R_x H_{kk} + R_k H_{xk}}{D}, \tag{11.27a}$$

$$\frac{dk}{dz} = \frac{-R_k H_{xx} + R_x H_{xk}}{D}. \tag{11.28a}$$

Since we can readily assume that the firm operates in the region where $R_x > 0$, $R_k > 0$, while $H_{xx} < 0$, $H_{kk} < 0$ by (11.21a) and (11.22a), $dx/dz > 0$, $dk/dz > 0$ if $H_{xk} \geq 0$. Thus it only remains to explore the case when $H_{xk} < 0$. A change in the signs in (11.24a) and (11.25a) gives us two equations with all positive coefficients. We can immediately conclude that:

$$\text{if } \frac{dx}{dz} > 0, \quad \frac{dk}{dz} \gtrless 0; \tag{11.29a}$$

$$\text{if } \frac{dx}{dz} = 0, \quad \frac{dk}{dz} > 0; \tag{11.30a}$$

if $\dfrac{dx}{dz} < 0, \quad \dfrac{dk}{dz} > 0,$ \hfill (11.31a)

and by symmetry the same relations hold for dx/dz as a function of dk/dz. For either $dx/dz < 0$ or $dk/dz < 0$, the other derivative must be positive and *large*.

Propositions (11.29a)–(11.31a) can also be established by examining the second-order conditions. This method would give us more restricted results, but on the whole it would hardly justify the effort and the space. It may be worthwhile to examine in detail just two cases, say when $dx/dz < 0$, or when $dk/dz < 0$, though the results will be expressed in such unfamiliar elasticities that, I suspect, they will add little to our understanding of the problem.

If $dx/dz < 0$, then from (11.27a),

$$\frac{H_{xk}}{R_x} < \frac{H_{kk}}{R_k}.$$ \hfill (11.32a)

From (11.32a), (11.22a) and (11.23a),

$$\frac{zR_{xk}}{R_x} - \frac{C_{xk}}{R_x} < \frac{zR_{kk}}{R_k} - \frac{C_{kk}}{R_k}.$$ \hfill (11.33a)

From (11.33a), (11.19a) and (11.20a),

$$\frac{R_{xk}}{R_x} - \frac{C_{xk}}{C_x} < \frac{R_{kk}}{R_k} - \frac{C_{kk}}{C_k}.$$ \hfill (11.34a)

Introducing the elasticity of R_x in respect to k,

$$E_{R_x}^k = \frac{\partial(R_x)}{\partial k} \cdot \frac{k}{R_x} = \frac{kR_{xk}}{R_x},$$ \hfill (11.35a)

and using similar definitions for the other elasticities, we can express (11.34a) as

$$E_{R_x}^k - E_{C_x}^k < E_{R_k}^k - E_{C_k}^k$$ \hfill (11.36a)

or as

$$E_{R_x}^k - E_{R_k}^k < E_{C_x}^k - E_{C_k}^k,$$ \hfill (11.37a)

if $dx/dz < 0$.

Following the same procedure, we find that

$$E_{R_k}^x - E_{R_x}^x < E_{C_k}^x - E_{C_x}^x,$$ \hfill (11.38a)

if $dk/dz < 0$.

Although it is probable that $E_{C_x}^k > 0$ (because an improvement in quality should raise the marginal cost), $E_{C_k}^k > 0$ (because further quality improvements should be more expensive), and $E_{R_x}^x < 0$ (if demand elasticity declines to the right), I would not venture to predict on a priori grounds the signs of the other elasticities and particularly of the differences between them.

If we recollect that a $H_{xk} \geq 0$ always yields $dx/dz > 0$, $dk/dz > 0$, and that only a large negative H_{xk} (subject to the second-order restrictions) can give us $dx/dz < 0$ or $dk/dz < 0$, a negative effect of the subsidy either on quantity or on quality seems unlikely. But since we do not know the probabilities of each configuration, it is best to leave the question open. It is possible that a subsidy can improve the quality to such an extent as to reduce the quantity, and vice versa (while exactly the opposite would be true of a tax). All this can happen, but I wonder if it has ever happened in reality?[25]

It is also possible that a subsidy may have an unexpected effect on price. For

$$\frac{dp}{dz} = p_x \frac{dx}{dz} + p_k \frac{dk}{dz}. \tag{11.39a}$$

Assuming, as usual, that $p_x < 0$ and that $p_k > 0$, we find that only if $dx/dz > 0$, $dk/dz \leq 0$ (one of the "less probable" cases) will dp/dz be definitely negative. If $dx/dz < 0$, $dk/dz > 0$, then $dp/dz > 0$, while in the supposedly most "common" case when $dx/dz > 0$, $dk/dz > 0$, the result is uncertain.

The introduction of quality as a decision variable may also cast some doubts on the welfare effects of our bonus scheme. No longer can we assert (abstracting from the complex general equilibrium considerations) that the bonus, even if set correctly, will increase social welfare by inducing the Manager to move from the usual monopolistic position, point D on Fig. 11.1 or Fig. 11.2, to point A (of the same demand curve) where marginal cost equals price. All we can now claim is that, if quality changes, the manager will move from point D on the demand curve for products of one quality to point A on the demand curve for products of another quality. It is plausible that social welfare will increase, but it is not certain.[26]

[25] In the last few years there have appeared a number of articles on the effects of monopolization on the quality of output, most of them dealing with the durability of capital goods. For a bibliography see Richard W. Parks, "The Demand and Supply of Durable Goods and Durability," The American Economic Review, LXIV (March 1974), 37–55. It seems that the results of that discussion have been rather inconclusive. See also an unpublished paper by Michael Spence, "Product Selection, Fixed Costs and Monopolistic Competition" (1974).

[26] I have not proved yet that changes in quality will not affect the convergence of the iterative process (the "Simple Rule") described in the Mathematical Appendix.

PART IV

Slavery and serfdom

The causes of slavery or serfdom:
a hypothesis

I

The purpose of this essay is to present, or more correctly, to revive, a hypothesis regarding the causes of agricultural serfdom or slavery (used here interchangeably). The hypothesis was suggested by Kliuchevskii's description of the Russian experience in the sixteenth and seventeenth centuries, but it aims at a wider applicability.[1]

According to Kliuchevskii, from about the second half of the fifteenth century Russia was engaged in long and hard wars against her western and southern neighbors. The wars required large forces that the state found impossible to support from tax revenue alone. Hence the government began to assign lands (*pomest'ia*) to the servitors, who were expected to use peasant labor (directly and/or via payments in kind and/or money) for their maintenance and weapons. In exchange, the servitor gave the peasants a loan and permitted them, free men as yet, to work all or part of his land on their own. The system worked rather badly, however, because of shortage of labor. Severe competition among landowners developed, the servitors being bested by lay and clerical magnates. Things became particularly difficult for the servitors after the middle of

Reprinted by permission from *The Journal of Economic History,* Vol. XXX, March 1970, pp. 18–32.

For many helpful comments on an earlier draft, I am grateful to the following persons: Abraham Becker, Oleg Hoeffding, Clayton La Force, Edward Mitchell, William Parker, George Rosen, Matthew Edel, Peter Temin, Helen Turin and Charles Wolf, Jr. Alexander Gerschenkron's earlier suggestions were also very helpful. Thanks are also due Ann Peet for her excellent research assistance.

I am also grateful to the RAND Corporation for its support of an earlier version of this study (20 October 1966), and to the National Science Foundation for its assistance (Grant No. NSF-GS-2627) in revising and extending the first draft. Neither these two organizations, nor the persons listed above, are responsible for the views expressed here.

[1] V. Kliuchevskii, *Kurs russkoi istorii* [A course of Russian history] (Moscow: Gosudarst-vennoe sotsial'no-ekonomicheskoe izdatel'stvo, 1937). The original work was published in 1906. All my references apply to the 1937 edition. An English translation by C. J. Hogarth, *A History of Russia,* was published in New York by Russell and Russell in 1960. For specific references, see Part II.

the sixteenth century when the central areas of the state became depopulated because of peasant migration into the newly conquered areas in the east and southeast. Under the pressure of the serving class and for certain other reasons, the government gradually restricted the freedom of peasants, already hopelessly in debt to their landlords, to move. They became enserfed by the middle of the seventeenth century, though the process itself continued for many decades to come.

This is a very rough summary of Kliuchevskii's story which hardly does him justice but which will serve my purposes until Part II. Like many a historian, he assembled and described the relevant facts (and in beautiful Russian at that) and stopped just short of an analytical explanation.

The economist would recast Kliuchevskii's account as follows: The servitors tried to live off rents (in one form or another) to be collected from their estates. But the estates could not yield a significant amount of rent for the simple reason that land in Russia was not sufficiently scarce relative to labor, and ironically, was made even less scarce by Russian conquests. The scarce factor of production was not land but labor. Hence it was the ownership of peasants and not of land that could yield an income to the servitors or to any non-working landowning class.

A simple economic model may sharpen the argument (if any sharpening is needed) and help to develop it further. Assume that labor and land are the only factors of production (no capital or management), and that land of uniform quality and location is ubiquitous. No diminishing returns in the application of labor to land appear; both the average and the marginal productivities of labor are constant and equal, and if competition among employers raises wages to that level (as would be expected), no rent from land can arise, as Ricardo demonstrated some time past. In the absence of specific governmental action to the contrary (see below), the country will consist of family-size farms because hired labor, in any form, will be either unavailable or unprofitable: the wage of a hired man or the income of a tenant will have to be at least equal to what he can make on his own farm; if he receives that much, no surplus (rent) will be left for his employer. A non-working class of servitors or others could be supported by the government out of taxes levied (directly or indirectly) on the peasants, but it could not support itself from land rents.

As a step toward reality, let us relax the assumption of the ubiquity of uniform land, and let capital (clearing costs, food, seeds, livestock, structures and implements) and management be included among the factors of production. Owners of capital, of superior skill and of better-than-average land will now be able to pay a hired man his due (or to use a tenant) and still obtain a surplus. But so long as agricultural skills can be easily acquired, the amount of capital for starting a farm is small, and the per capita income is relatively high (because of the ample supply of land), a good worker should be able to save or borrow and start on his own in time. Most of the farms will still be more or less family-size, with an estate using hired labor (or tenants) here and there in areas of unusually good (in fertility and/or in location) land, or specializing in activities requiring higher-than-average capital intensity, or skillful management. But until land becomes rather scarce, and/or the amount of capital required to start a farm relatively large, it is unlikely that a large class of landowners, such as required by the Muscovite government, could be supported by economic forces alone. The American North in the Colonial period and in the nineteenth century would be a good example of an agricultural structure of this type.

So far the institutional structure has been shaped by economic forces alone without direct interference by the government.[2] Suppose now that the government decides to create, or at least to facilitate the creation of, a non-working class of agricultural owners. As a first step, it gives the members of this class the sole right of ownership of land. The peasants will now have to work for the landowners, but so long as the workers are free to move, competition among the employers will drive the wage up to the value of the marginal product of labor, and since the latter is still fairly close to the value of the average product (because of the abundance of land) little surplus will remain. The Russian situation prior to the peasants' enserfment corresponds to this case.

The next and final step to be taken by the government still pursuing its objective is the abolition of the peasants' right to move. With labor tied to land or to the owner, competition among employers ceases. Now the employer can derive a rent, not from his land, but from his peasants by appropriating all or most of their income above some subsistence level.[3] That Russian serfs could stay alive, and even to multiply, while working for themselves half-time and less suggests that the productivity of their labor (with poor technique, little capital, but abundant land) must have been quite high.

To recapitulate, the strong version of this hypothesis (without capital, management, etc.) asserts that of the three elements of an agricultural structure relevant here – free land, free peasants, and non-working landowners – any two elements but *never all three can exist simultaneously*. The combination to be found in reality will depend on the behavior of

---

[2] I mean by the "government" any organization capable of maintaining some measure of law and order and particularly of using non-economic compulsion. It can be a king, an assembly of landowners, a magnate, etc.

[3] He may be restrained by custom and by the fear that his serfs will run away – a common occurrence in Russia.

political factors – governmental measures – treated here as an exogenous variable.

The presence of this exogenous political variable seriously weakens the effectiveness of my model: it makes the presence of free land by itself neither a necessary nor a sufficient condition for the existence of serfdom. It is not a necessary condition because so long as marginal productivity of labor is high, serfdom may continue to exist even if free land is no longer present; it may even be imposed at this stage, as it was in the Russian Ukraine in the eighteenth century. Free land is not a sufficient condition because, as I stated above, without proper governmental action free land will give rise to free farmers rather than to serfs.

For the same reasons the model cannot predict the net effect of a change in the land/labor ratio on the position of the peasants. Suppose that with constant land, technology, and per capita stock of capital, population increases. The economic position of the peasants will worsen (even serfs can be exploited more), but the landowners will be less inclined to interfere with the peasants' freedom. Let population decline instead. The peasants will be better off provided they do not become less free. Thus a change in the land/labor ratio can set in motion economic and political forces acting in opposite directions.

The strength and usefulness of the model could be increased by making the political variable endogenous. But this I cannot do without help from historians and political scientists.

These difficulties notwithstanding, I would still expect to find a positive statistical correlation between free land and serfdom (or slavery). Such a correlation was indeed found by H. J. Nieboer of whom you'll hear more in Part III.

What about the end of serfdom (or slavery)? Traditionally it was assumed that it would or did disappear because of the inherent superiority of free labor. This superiority, arising from the higher motivation of the free man, was supposed to increase with greater use of capital and with technological progress. Let us disregard the possibly greater reliability of the slave and the longer hours he may be forced to work (particularly in traditional societies where leisure is highly valued), and let us assume that the economy has reached the position where the net average productivity of the free worker (P_f) is considerably larger than that of a slave (P_s). The abolition of slavery is clearly in the national interest (unless the immediate military considerations, such as of the Muscovite government, overwhelm the economic ones), but not necessarily in the interest of an individual slave owner motivated by his profit and not by patriotic sentiment. He will calculate the difference between the wage of a free worker (W_f) and the cost of subsistence of a slave (W_s) and will refuse to free his slaves unless $P_f - P_s > W_f - W_s$, all this on the assumption that either kind of labor *can* be used in a given field.[4]

As the economy continues to develop, the difference $P_f - P_s$ can be expected to widen. Unfortunately, the same forces – technological progress and capital accumulation – responsible for this effect are apt to increase W_f as well, while W_s need not change. We cannot tell on a priori grounds whether $P_f - P_s$ will increase more or less than $W_f - W_s$. Therefore we cannot be sure that technological progress and greater use of capital *necessarily* reduce the profitability of slave as compared with free labor. Much will depend on the nature of technological progress. Thus Eli Whitney's gin greatly increased the profitability of slavery, while a transition from raising crops to breeding sheep in medieval England might have acted in the opposite direction by creating a surplus of workers. (See Part II.) American planters must have used better agricultural techniques and more capital than their Latin-American and particularly Russian colleagues, but the Americans defended slavery with much greater zeal.

In a traditional society without technological progress and capital accumulation, the end of slavery is, paradoxically, more certain. As population continues to increase and the society eventually becomes Malthusian, the marginal product of labor descends to the subsistence level. Now the free man costs little more to employ than the slave, while, hopefully, being less bothersome and more productive. The ownership of human

---

[4] Actually, it is not easy to compare the relative profitability of free and slave labor. Since the free worker is paid more or less concurrently with his work, while a slave must be either reared or purchased, and may have children, etc., the streams of receipts and expenditures from the two kinds of labor must be properly discounted. It is assumed in the text that all indirect costs of using slaves, such as medical expense, extra supervision, etc., are included in W_s.

In a well-organized slave market, the price of a slave will approximate the present value of his discounted net lifetime marginal product. A buyer who pays this price will discover that he earns not much more than the going rate of interest; he will complain about the high cost of slaves and express doubt regarding the profitability of slavery in general, because at the margin he will be fairly indifferent between employing free or slave labor. But so long as the supply of food and of similar items for the maintenance of slaves is elastic (which it is likely to be), the slave-breeder should do very well. He benefits from the perpetual disequilibrium in the slave market created by the abundance of land and by the limited human capacity to procreate (assuming no importation of slaves). But if the slave-breeder computes his rate of return on the current value of his slaves and land, he may not record much more than the market rate of interest either. In other words, the market mechanism transforms the profit from slaves into capital gains.

On this see Lewis Cecil Gray, *History of Agriculture in the Southern United States to 1860*, published in 1933 and reproduced in part in Harold D. Woodman, *Slavery and the Southern Economy: Sources and Readings* (New York: Harcourt, Brace & World, Inc., 1966), pp. 106–09, and Alfred H. Conrad and John R. Meyer, *The Economics of Slavery and Other Studies in Econometric History* (Chicago: Aldine Publishing Company, 1964), pp. 43–92.

beings becomes pointless because of the great multiplication of slaves, and they become free provided they stay poor.[5] It is land that becomes valuable, and rents collected from estates worked by free laborers or tenants without any noneconomic compulsion are sufficient to support an army of servitors or idlers. If the Muscovite government could have only waited a few hundred years!

II

Where I come from, an economic model without empirical testing is equated with a detective story without an end. My attempts to test the present model, however, merely taught me that the job is not for the amateur. I shall report to you the results of my skin-deep investigation in the hope that my mistakes will stimulate the specialists. I concentrate on the Russian case, with short excursions into the histories of Poland-Lithuania, Western Europe and the United States.

1.   *Russia*

The phenomenon to be explained here is not only the development of serfdom but its particular timing: before 1550 Russian peasants were free men; a hundred years later they were serfs. The relevant variables are: (1) the number of servitors required by the military needs of the Moscow state, and (2) the population density.

According to Kliuchevskii, prior to the middle of the fifteenth century, Moscow, still a Tatar vassal surrounded by other Russian lands, fought very few foreign wars; its population became dense because Moscow was the safest spot in the area with few outlets for emigration.[6] We may conclude that there was no need as yet for a large class of servitors, and that the landowners could derive rents from their estates (patrimonies, to be exact) without enserfing the peasants. It is true that Russia, from the Kievan

---

[5] It is possible that even in a Malthusian society slavery (or serfdom) may linger on. Slaves may be kept for reasons of social prestige (a relic from the times when slavery was profitable), or simply because a slave is more reliable than a hired man. On the other hand, the use of a tenant (with a limited lease) or of a hired man allows the landowner to choose the best among several applicants with much greater ease than among slaves or serfs protected by custom.

[6] Kliuchevskii, Vol. I, p. 379; Vol. III, pp. 9–10, 121. Blum, however, talks about depopulation already in the fourteenth and fifteenth centuries. See Jerome Blum, *Lord and Peasant in Russia from the Ninth to the Nineteenth Century* (Princeton: Princeton University Press, 1961), pp. 60–61. It is possible that Kliuchevskii describes the relative position of Moscow among other Russian lands, while Blum refers to the whole country.

times onward, always had a substantial number of slaves. At the time, these were mostly household servants and retainers rather than peasants.[7]

From the middle of the fifteenth century the situation changes drastically. Having become independent from the Tatars (officially in 1480, actually earlier), and having gathered a number of Russian lands, Moscow was confronted with powerful enemies: with Poland-Lithuania and Sweden in the west and northwest, and with the Crimean Tatars in the south. The struggle with the latter went on continuously, while 50 out of the 103 years from 1492 to 1595 were spent in wars against Poland-Lithuania and Sweden, as were the following 30 out of 70 years from 1613 to 1682, not to mention the Time of Troubles, 1598–1613, filled with both civil and foreign wars.[8]

The military proficiency of the Muscovite armies being poor, refuge was sought in large numbers. More than 300,000 men were reported to have been under arms during Ivan the Terrible's Livonian War. There must have been a great increase in the number of servitors. With trade and industry making no significant progress, the government had to assign land to them. This process began on a large scale in the second half of the fifteenth century and was accelerated throughout the sixteenth century.[9]

In the meantime, the central areas of the country became depopulated. The conquest of the whole expanse of the Volga river (begun in 1552) opened up large areas of better soil and attracted large masses of peasants fleeing from high taxes, Ivan the Terrible's oppression (the notorious *oprichnina*) and Crimean invasions. And then came the Time of Troubles which devastated the country once more. Already in the sixteenth century there was fierce competition for peasant hands among the landowners. It must have intensified after 1613.[10]

Thus both ingredients for the development of serfdom – a high land/labor ratio and the government's determination to create a large class of servitors – were present. In addition, there were several other forces working in the same direction. The first was the decline in the power of the great magnates, both at the hands of Ivan the Terrible and during the Time of Troubles. By offering the peasants privileges and protection, these magnates had been quite successful in bidding the peasants away from

[7] Kliuchevskii, Vol. I, pp. 282–83; Vol. II, pp. 182–83.
[8] *Ibid.*, Vol. II, pp. 121, 125, 221–22; Vol. III, p. 135.
[9] *Ibid.*, Vol. II, pp. 221, 229–42, 248; Vol. III, pp. 63–64, 230–31, 257, 283. Blum, pp. 93, 157.
[10] Kliuchevskii, Vol. II, pp. 254–57, 339–44; Vol. III, pp. 182, 244. Blum, pp. 147, 152–54, 157, 160, 252. B. D. Grekov, *Krest'iane na Rusi s drevneishikh vremen do XVII veka* [Peasants in Russia from ancient times until the XVII century] (Moscow-Leningrad: Izdatel'stvo Akademii Nauk SSSR, 1946), pp. 794–96, 849.

the servitors; for this reason the magnates favored the free movement of peasants, while the servitors, quite naturally, opposed it. Now the peasants lost the support of their "friends."[11] The second reason lay in the fiscal interest of the state: peasant migrations, particularly from the center to the periphery of the state, disorganized tax collections.[12] And finally, the peasant communities objected to the emigration of their members because the community carried a collective responsibility for the tax liabilities of its members (until in later years this responsibility was taken over by the masters); the departure of several members would leave the rest overburdened until the next census.[13]

Space does not allow me to give additional details of the process which gradually enserfed the peasants, or to discuss the disagreement between Kliuchevskii, who emphasized the hopeless indebtedness of the peasants to their landlords as the main obstacle to their movement, and Grekov and Blum, who put greater stress on legislative enactments (particularly on the so-called "Forbidden Years," *zapovednye gody*).[14] Let me mention instead two further reflections of the scarcity of labor in Russia: the first manifested itself in the replacement of the basic land tax by a household tax in the seventeenth century, and by a poll tax under Peter the Great.[15] The second is an interesting cultural trait which remained long after its cause had probably disappeared: as late as in the first half of the nineteenth century, the social position of a Russian landowner, as described in contemporary literature, depended less on the size of his land holdings (which are seldom mentioned) than on the number of *souls* (registered male peasants) that he owned.[16]

---

[11] Kliuchevskii, Vol. II, pp. 259, 307. Blum, pp. 253–54. Grekov, pp. 870–71, 903, 909. Grekov, *Glavneishie etapy v istorii krepostnogo prava v Rossii* [Principal milestones in the history of serfdom in Russia] (Moscow-Leningrad: Gosudarstvennoe sotsial'no-ekonomicheskoe izdatel'stvo, 1940), p. 46.

When the leaders of the gentry militia were negotiating a treaty with the Polish king Sigismund regarding the accession of his son to the Moscow throne in 1610 and in 1611, they demanded the inclusion of a provision forbidding the movement of peasants. (Kliuchevskii, Vol. II, p. 349.)

[12] Kliuchevskii, Vol. III, p. 188.

[13] *Ibid.*, Vol. II, pp. 317–18, 336–37, 340. Blum, pp. 96, 234.

[14] Kliuchevskii, Vol. II, pp. 321–23, 331–50; Vol. III, pp. 181–88. Blum, pp. 254–55. Grekov, *Krest'iane* [Peasants], pp. 826, 850. Grekov, *Glavneishie* [Principal], pp. 64–65.

If peasants' debt tied them to their lords as strongly and as hopelessly as Kliuchevskii asserts, it is puzzling that the government had first to limit and then to forbid their movement by law.

[15] Kliuchevskii, Vol. III, pp. 243–46; Vol. IV, pp. 142–48. Grekov, *Glavneishie* [Principal], pp. 71–72.

[16] Here are a few examples. In Pushkin's *Dubrovskii*, the old Dubrovskii is identified as the owner of 70 souls, and Prince Vereiskii of 3000; in *The Captain's Daughter*, the commandant's wife is impressed by Grinev's father's ownership of 300 souls; in Gogol's

2.   *Poland-Lithuania*

On the theory that the length of a report should be proportional to the intensity of research done, this section will be very short. The relevant facts are as follows:

(1)   In the fourteenth century vast, open and very sparsely populated territories in the Ukraine were conquered by the Lithuanians.[17]

(2)   In the fifteenth and sixteenth centuries, Ukraine was repopulated by immigrants from the more central areas of the state. The migration depopulated the central areas to such an extent as to constitute, according to Grekov, a threat to the Polish state.[18]

(3)   By the end of the sixteenth century, the peasants were enserfed.[19]

What is not clear to me is the time sequence of events (2) and (3). In Vol. III (p. 110), Kliuchevskii dates the repopulation of the Ukraine in the sixteenth century; in Vol. I (p. 293), in the fifteenth century. But in both places he attributes the migration of peasants to the intensification of serfdom in Poland-Lithuania. Polish serfdom, according to him, had been established already in the fourteenth century, and Lithuanian, in the fifteenth century.[20] On the other hand, Grekov asserts that according to the Polish legal code of 1493, each peasant could still leave the land, having settled accounts with his landlord. But he also reports that in 1444 the Galician gentry demanded that the government prevent other landlords from interfering with the peasant movements.[21] Evidently, such interference was taking place even then.

In Poland-Lithuania great gaps between legal enactments and the actual state of affairs were quite possible. There were probably considerable regional variations, both in law and in practice as well. I would be happier if it could be established that migration to the Ukraine preceded the development of serfdom, but I am certainly not in a position to settle the matter. It is quite possible that migration and serfdom were reinforcing each other.

The Dead Souls, Pliushkin owns more than 1000 souls; in Goncharov's *Oblomov,* the principal hero owns 350; in his *A Common Story,* a certain Anton Ivanich has 12 mortgaged over and over again...

[17] Kliuchevskii, Vol. I, p. 293.

[18] *Ibid.,* Vol. I, pp. 293–94. Grekov, *Krest'iane* [Peasants], p. 387.

[19] Jerome Blum, "The Rise of Serfdom in Eastern Europe," *American Historical Review,* LXII (1957), pp. 807–36. See particularly pp. 821–22.

[20] Kliuchevskii, Vol. III, pp. 101–02.

[21] Grekov, *Krest'iane* [Peasants], pp. 381–83. There seems to be considerable disagreement among the authorities he cites. He mentions a number of legislative enactments passed at the end of the fifteenth century and in 1510, 1519, 1520, 1532 limiting the freedom of peasants to move (p. 387).

Since I have not studied the development of serfdom in other East European countries, I can make only two brief comments on Blum's well-known and very interesting article on "The Rise of Serfdom in Eastern Europe." His stress on the increasing power of the nobility and on the general depopulation of the area "from the Elbe all the way across to the Volga..." is heartily welcome.[22] But his use of alternating periods of prosperity and depression as important causes of the rise and decline of serfdom cannot be evaluated until he presents an analytical explanation of the causation involved.

3.   Western Europe

We shall deal here very briefly with four events:

(1)   The emergence of serfdom in the late Roman Empire
(2)   The decline of serfdom by 1300
(3)   Its non-recurrence after the Black Death
(4)   The relationship between sheep breeding and serfdom.

The depopulation of the late Roman Empire is, of course, well known. Referring to Byzantium, Georg Ostrogorsky states: "And so ever-increasing masses of the rural population were tied to the soil. This is a particular instance of the widespread compulsory fastening of the population to their occupation which scarcity of labour forced the later Roman Empire to pursue systematically."[23]

This is the clearest statement on the relation between scarcity of labor and the development of serfdom that I have come across in my reading of European economic history.

Similarly, the great increase in population in Western Europe by the end of the thirteenth century when serfdom was declining is also well known. Thus Ganshof and Verhulst talk about "...a considerable and growing reserve of surplus labor..." in France, and Postan discusses signs of overpopulation in England: a growing number of wholly landless men, sub-holdings of many tenants, shortage of pasture, etc.[24] The same information for Western Europe in general is supplied by Smith,

---

[22] Blum, "The Rise of Serfdom," p. 819.

[23] Georg Ostrogorsky, "Agrarian Conditions in the Byzantine Empire in the Middle Ages," *The Cambridge Economic History of Europe,* Second Edition (Cambridge: Cambridge University Press, 1966), I, p. 206. See also pp. 11, 27–28, 33, 66 and 257 of the same volume. Also, W. R. Brownlow, *Lectures on Slavery and Serfdom in Europe* (London and New York: Burns and Oates, Ltd., 1892), pp. 49–50.

[24] François Louis Ganshof and Adriaan Verhulst, "Medieval Agrarian Society in its Prime: France, The Low Countries, and Western Germany," *Cambridge Economic History,* I, p. 294; M. M. Postan in his essay on "England," same volume, pp. 552–56, 563–64, 624; Blum, "The Rise of Serfdom," pp. 810–11.

who adds that: "The problem therefore for western landowners, at any rate before the demographic collapse of the mid-fourteenth century, was not to keep tenants, but how to get the most out of them."[25] Since these facts fit my hypothesis so nicely, let me stop here while I am still winning.

But when we come to the depopulation caused by the Black Death after 1348 (though, according to Postan, English population stopped growing even earlier),[26] my hypothesis is of little value in explaining the subsequent course of events. (See Part I.) Why did serfdom fail to come back after such a sharp increase in the land/labor ratio?

I address myself only to England. Except for one rather strange economic explanation to be discussed presently, I have none to offer and have to fall back on political factors. Serfdom could not be restored unless the landowners were reasonably united in their pressure on the government, and unless the latter was willing and able to do their bidding. But it is most unlikely that every estate lost the same fraction of its peasants. Hence, those landowners who had suffered most would welcome the freedom of peasant movement, at least for a while, while those who had suffered least would oppose it. If so, the landowners could not be united. Postan also suggests the probability that the main pressure behind Richard II's legislation came not from feudal landowners, but from smaller men;[27] English magnates, like their Russian colleagues (see above), could evidently take care of their own interests. Though I cannot judge the "spirit" of medieval legislation, it seems to me that the measures undertaken by Richard's government were somewhat halfhearted.[28] In any case, they were ineffective. So economic forces could reassert themselves and help the peasants.

The strange economic explanation which I mentioned before would delight an economist if only it squared with facts. It is the expansion of sheep breeding, an activity which is land-using and labor saving.[29] Unfortunately such data as I could find do not support the contention that there was an expansion of sheep breeding in the hundred years following the Black Death. The legal exports of English wool, in raw and in cloth, fell from 12 million pounds in 1350 to 8.7 million in 1400 – a drop of 27 percent. Another fall of 12 percent (of the 8.7 million) took place by 1450.[30]

[25] R. E. F. Smith, *The Enserfment of the Russian Peasantry* (Cambridge: Cambridge University Press, 1968), p. 4.

[26] Postan, essay on "England," *Cambridge Economic History*, I, pp. 566–70.

[27] *Ibid.*, p. 609.

[28] Brownlow, *Lectures on Slavery*, pp. 157–83. Smith, *Enserfment*, pp. 4–5.

[29] The idea that sheep-breeding may have had something to do with serfdom was suggested by Nieboer in his book (pp. 371–75) discussed in Part III.

[30] K. G. Ponting, *The Wool Trade Past and Present* (Manchester and London: Columbine Press, 1961), p. 30. The figures are based on a chart facing p. xviii of *Medieval Merchant Ventures* by E. Carus Wilson.

My authorities do not state the proportions of wool consumed at home and smuggled out of the country.[31] Perhaps these were affected by the Hundred Years' War. But as things stand, I certainly cannot claim that an expansion of English sheep breeding took place after 1350 and that it helped to save the peasants from the return of serfdom.[32]

Judging by Thomas More's famous passage about sheep devouring men, by Bishop Latimer's "Sermon of the Plough" (1549), and by other more direct evidence, there must have been considerable expansion of sheep breeding at the expense of crops and of people in the sixteenth century.[33] By that time, however, English peasants hardly needed the help from the sheep in staying free.

But is it possible that the early expansion of sheep breeding which must have taken place sometime prior to 1350 *had* helped the English serfs to gain their original freedom after all?

4.   *The United States*

The American South fits my hypothesis with such embarrassing simplicity as to question the need for it. The presence of vast expanses of empty fertile land in a warm climate, land capable of producing valuable products if only labor could be found, seems to me quite sufficient to explain the importation of slaves. What is not clear to me is the failure of the North to use them in large numbers. Besides social and political objections, there must have been economic reasons why Negro slaves had a comparative advantage in the South as contrasted with the North. Perhaps it had something to do with the superior adaptability of the Negro to a hot climate, and/or with his usefulness in the South almost throughout the year rather than for the few months in the North.[34] I have a hard time believing that slaves could not be used in the mixed farming of the North: much food was produced on southern farms as well, most of the slave owners had very few slaves, and many slaves were skilled in crafts.[35]

---

[31] According to Postan, p. 568, domestic consumption of cloth is not known. Peter J. Bowden arbitrarily assumed it to be 50 percent. See his *The Wool Trade in Tudor and Stuart England* (London: Macmillan & Co., Ltd., 1962), p. 37.

[32] Data on the size of the sheep population, or more correctly on increments in it, would not be sufficient for our problem. We would have to know how many crop-raising peasants were replaced, say, by 1,000 extra sheep.

[33] See E. Lipson, *The History of the Woollen and Worsted Industries* (London?: Frank Cass & Co., Ltd., 1965), p. 19; E. Nasse, *On the Agricultural Community of the Middle Ages, and Enclosures of the Sixteenth Century in England* (London: Macmillan & Co., 1871), pp. 77–78; Brownlow, *Lectures on Slavery*, p. 184; Bowden, *Wool Trade*, p. xvi.

[34] Woodman, *Slavery and the Southern Economy*, p. 7.

[35] Conrad and Meyer, *Economics of Slavery*, p. 80; James Benson Sellers, *Slavery in Alabama* (University, Alabama: University of Alabama Press, 1950), pp. 71, 120, 162–63;

A study of the possible profitability of slavery in the North, along Conrad and Meyer's lines, which could show whether the North could have afforded paying the market price for slaves, would be most welcome.

I have not come across any good evidence that slavery was dying out in the United States on the eve of the Civil War, and I side here with Conrad and Meyer, though, in truth, I am not sure that such a thorough investigation was required to prove the profitability of slavery in the South.[36]

III

In conclusion, let me say a few words about the origin of my hypothesis and about its place in economic history. Although I had discussed it in my classes for a good dozen years, I did not write it up until 1966 because I had been told by an eminent authority that the idea was old and well known. My source was indeed correct because a brief search in the library revealed quite a few predecessors. The most important of them was the Dutch scholar Herman J. Nieboer whose magnum opus of 465 pages under the title of *Slavery as an Industrial System: Ethnological Researches* was published in 1900.[37] The hypothesis which I have immodestly called "mine" was stated by him time and again, and tested against a mass of anthropological and historical data. As you might expect, he was satisfied with his results.

But the hypothesis was not really original with Nieboer. He in turn referred to A. Loria's *Les Bases Economiques de la Constitution Sociale* of 1893, and to E. G. Wakefield's *A View of the Art of Colonization* published in 1834. Some glimpses can be found even in Adam Smith's *The Wealth of Nations.*[38]

I have two disagreements with Nieboer. First, his definition of free land has too much legal and not enough economic content to my taste,

Rosser Howard Taylor, *Slaveholding in North Carolina: An Economic View* (Chapel Hill: University of North Carolina Press, 1926), p. 72; Harrison Anthony Trexler, *Slavery in Missouri* (Baltimore: The Johns Hopkins Press, 1914), pp. 13, 19; Woodman, *Slavery and the Southern Economy*, pp. 14–15.

[36] As the authors practically admit on p. 78. On the profitability debate see Stanley L. Engerman, "The Effects of Slavery Upon the Southern Economy: A Review of the Recent Debate," *Explorations in Entrepreneurial History*, Second Series, IV (1967), pp. 71–97.

[37] It was published in The Hague by Martinus Nijhoff and republished by Burt Franklin, Publisher, New York in 1971.

[38] Adam Smith, *The Wealth of Nations* (London: Cannan's edition, 1922), II, pp. 66–68. There is another book by Wakefield on the same subject: *England and America: A Comparison of the Social and Political State of Both Nations* (London: Richard Bentley, 1833), Vol. II. Other sources: J. E. Cairnes, *The Slave Power* (London: Parker, Son, and Bourn, 1862); J. S. Mill, *Principles of Political Economy*, 1848 (New York: D. Appleton and Co., 1920), I, p. 316.

though he seems to have been unclear rather than wrong. Second, he exaggerated the importance of the hypothesis by claiming, though not in so many words, that free land or other free resources are both necessary and sufficient for the existence of slavery or serfdom: "...Only among people with open resources can slavery and serfdom exist, whereas free labourers dependent on wages are only found among people with close resources."[39] He protected himself with a note on the same page by excluding simple societies of hunters, fishers, and hunting agriculturists, hardly a fit company for the farmers of the American North. He disregarded the possibility that serfdom, once established, could exist for a long time after its initial cause – free land – had disappeared, or that serfdom may be even introduced in the absence of free land. He ignored the role of government. These, however, are minor defects in an important contribution.

On the other hand, my source may have been a bit wrong. If historians have always known about the relation between the land/labor ratio and serfdom (or slavery), they must have tried hard not to scatter too many good, clear statements in places where I could find them, though the students of the American South have been much kinder to me than others.[40] Nieboer could also lodge some complaints. His name can be found neither in the bibliography nor in the index of the 1966 edition of the first volume of *The Cambridge Economic History of Europe*. And it is absent from Blum's classic study of Russian serfdom. I did find Nieboer's name in Genovese's *The Political Economy of Slavery* in connection with some insignificant point, but with a further notation that "Phillips read and referred to this book." Phillips had read it, and confirmed that "hired labor was not to be had so long as land was free."[41]

Perhaps in history this hypothesis occupies a place similar to that enjoyed by economic growth in economic theory not long ago. That place was once described as "always seen around but seldom invited in." If so, why not invite it? After all, the land/labor ratio is readily quantifiable.

---

[39] Nieboer, *Slavery as an Industrial System*, pp. 312, 389.
[40] A clear statement by Ostrogorsky was quoted in Part II. For the American views, see Woodman's collection.
[41] Eugene D. Genovese, *The Political Economy of Slavery* (New York: Vintage Books, 1967), p. 84. Ulrich B. Phillips, "The Economic Cost of Slaveholding in the Cotton Belt," *Pol. Sci. Q.*, XX (June 1905), partially reproduced in Woodman, *Slavery and the Southern Economy*, p. 36.

On the profitability of Russian serfdom

with Mark J. Machina

I. Introduction

Why did the Russian government emancipate the serfs in 1861? Of the
several explanations offered – fear of a serf revolt (Gerschenkron), *raisons
d'état* (Blum), cultural factors (Field), military needs (Rieber), the general crisis of serfdom (several Marxist historians) – the hypothesis most
enticing to an economist was suggested by the Soviet historian M. N. Pokrovskii: the serfs were freed because serfdom had become unprofitable
for the masters.[1] It is enticing because profitability is quantifiable. In contrast to other explanations, this hypothesis can be subjected to a theoretical analysis and, with luck, to an empirical test. This is the purpose of
this essay.

Reprinted by permission from *The Journal of Economic History,* Vol. XLIV, December
1984, pp. 919–55.

Thanks are expressed to Ann Bobrov, Homi Kharas, Ian Ayres, Haim Barkai, Franklin
Fisher, Stephen Goldfeld, Darryl McCleod, Vladimir Shlapentokh, Martin Spechler, Peter
Temin, Martin Weitzman, and two anonymous referees for their helpful comments and
assistance during various stages of this work; to students in several economic history classes
at M.I.T. for their patient (if involuntary) attention; and particularly to William Easterly
(then a graduate student at M.I.T.) for his discovery of a serious error in an earlier version
of the Third Model. The responsibility for the remaining errors is, of course, our own.
Andrea R. Gordon deserves our gratitude for improving our style, and the National Science
Foundation (Grants SES-7709307 and SES-8308165) for its financial support.

[1] Alexander Gerschenkron, "Agrarian Policies and Industrialization: Russia 1861–1917,"
The Cambridge Economic History of Europe (Cambridge, 1965), vol. 6, part 2, pp. 706–
800. Jerome Blum, *Lord and Peasant in Russia from the Ninth to the Nineteenth Century*
(Princeton, 1961), pp. 612–18 (Blum also lists fear of serf revolt among the causes [pp.
552, 616–17]). Daniel Field, *The End of Serfdom: Nobility and Bureaucracy in Russia,
1855–1861* (Cambridge, Massachusetts, 1976), pp. 96–101. Alfred J. Rieber, *The Politics
of Autocracy* (Paris, 1966), pp. 15–58.

The general crisis of serfdom is a well-accepted Marxist doctrine. See, for instance,
P. I. Liashchenko, *Istoriia narodnogo khoziaistva SSSR* [History of the people's economy of the USSR] (Moscow, 1956), vol. 1, pp. 467–510; I. D. Koval'chenko, *Russkoe
krepostnoe krest'ianstvo v pervoi polovine XIX veka* [Russian serf peasantry in the first
half of the nineteenth century] (Moscow, 1967), particularly pp. 378–85; P. Maslov,
Agrarnyi vopros v Rossii [The agrarian problem in Russia], 4th ed. (St. Petersburg, 1908),
vol. 1, pp. 389–91; V. A. Fedorov, *Pomeshchich'i krest'iane tsentral'nogo promyshlennogo*

Pokrovskii attributed the alleged fall in the profitability of Russian serfdom to the *rise* in grain prices following the repeal of the British Corn Laws. To our surprise, this rather implausible explanation made more sense than one would expect: the effect on serfdom of a rise in grain prices, a more or less accidental event, will be shown to be similar to the effects produced by population growth, a much more important phenomenon. Both of these effects are analyzed in the first of our four models. Being free of specifically Russian conditions, the model may be widely applicable. Our next two models, in contrast, deal with two conditions particular to the Russian case: a limit on the serfs' labor obligations (called here "Paul's Law") and the specific rates of exchange between the serfs' land allotments and their labor obligations (the "Inventories") imposed by the government in several Western provinces. The last model is concerned with the effects on serfdom of the substitution of money payments (the *obrok*) for labor services.

These four models are presented in Section II. A report on our attempt to estimate empirically the magnitudes of serf prices as indicators of the profitability of serfdom, as well as some additional observations, are given in Section III and in the Statistical Appendix.

II.   The theory of serfdom

The first three models deal with a single estate which is meant to represent all serf estates in the country. No transactions within the serf sector are recognized. Therefore the owner (or "master" as we shall call him) can obtain additional serfs only from the natural increase in the serf population, although he can free any of his own serfs.[2] The quantity of land is assumed to be fixed in the short run, but variable in the long run because land can be bought from or sold to the free sector (subject to certain legal restrictions in the Second Model). In addition, we make the following assumptions:

(1)   The land of the estate is divided between the master and his serfs in a proportion determined by the master. Land and labor of uniform quality are assumed to be the only inputs, and production

---

raiona Rossii kontsa XVIII - pervoi poloviny XIX veka [Landowners' peasants of the Central Industrial Region of Russia, end of the eighteenth - first half of the nineteenth centuries] (Moscow, 1974), pp. 256–57; and M. N. Pokrovskii, *Russkaia istoriia s drevneishikh vremen* [Russian history from ancient times] (Moscow, 1934), vol. 4, pp. 40–84. Pokrovskii was not the only one to claim that serfdom had become unprofitable for the masters. This view was shared by the other Marxists cited here and by a number of non-Marxist writers. See Blum, *Lord,* pp. 563–64.

[2] In actual fact, a master wishing to free his serfs had to comply with a number of complicated government regulations.

on each part of the estate is subject to the same unchanging production function with constant returns to scale.[3]

(2) All of the land of the estate is utilized, so that (in the short run) an increase in the amount of land for one user implies less land for others.

(3) The total number of hours per week worked by each serf subject to labor services (*barschina*) is constant and independent of the division of his time between his own and his master's land. (The *obrok*-paying serf described in the Fourth Model is on his own.)[4]

(4) Each serf is allotted a combination of land and time sufficient to produce a subsistence level of output for his own use. This level will be treated here as a constant.[5]

(5) The net (of seeds and other expenses) output of the estate and the subsistence output of the serfs can be unambiguously stated in real terms, such as units of grain.

(6) The master seeks to maximize *his own income* from the estate, subject to the constraints imposed by Assumption 4, and by certain legal restrictions in the Second and Third Models.[6]

We are particularly interested in the conditions which would induce the representative master to free his serfs. We assume that, if he did so, he would retain all his land (contrary to the actual terms of the 1861 Emancipation) and that he would operate his estate with free labor under competitive conditions. In all of our models we disregard the existence of house servants, estate craftsmen (the *dvorovye liudi*), and serfs working in manufacturing.

[3] The assumption that serfs did not work harder on their own land might appear strange. But data collected by Koval'chenko, *Russkoe* [Russian], p. 57, for six provinces between 1842 and 1860 show practically equal harvest/seed ratios on both parts of estates. Perhaps the masters appropriated the more productive or more accessible land. Tolstoi's description of how Nikolai Rostov, a model landowner, supervised his serfs on both parts of his estate does not suggest that the serfs displayed any particular ardor when they worked for themselves (*War and Peace,* translated by Leo Wiener [New York, 1968], vol. 4, pp. 370–74). If the serfs had really worked much harder on their own land, it would have paid their masters to use the *obrok* system more frequently than they did (see the Fourth Model).

Koval'chenko, *Russkoe* [Russian], p. 75, confirms that no technological progress was taking place.

No distinction is made in this paper between arable, meadows, waste, or forest.

[4] The fact that the serfs worked much harder in summer than they did in winter is disregarded.

[5] Actually, as Blum describes, there were considerable wealth and income differentials among serfs. See *Lord,* pp. 469–74.

[6] The assumption of income maximization by the masters probably implies a greater degree of rationality than actually existed. From all accounts, it is clear that Russian serfowners were much less efficient than American slaveowners.

Our models present a highly stylized picture of Russian serfdom. For a more realistic description, we refer the reader to Blum's classic work (see footnote 1), which can also serve as background.

List of symbols used in Part II

S Number of serfs on the estate

T Total land area of the estate

T_M Land area of the master's part of the estate (the demesne)

T_S Land area allotted to *each* serf for his own use

L Total labor input on the estate measured in man-hours per week

L_M Labor input on the master's part of the estate

L_S Weekly hours allowed to *each* serf for his own use

H Total number of hours worked per week by each serf

k Fraction of weekly hours worked by each serf for himself $(=L_S/H)$

Y Total income from the estate

Y_M Master's income from the estate

E Subsistence level of each serf

R_L, R_T Marginal product of labor and land, respectively, on the desmesne

Z The price or exchange rate for an hour of serf labor in terms of units of land $(=T_S/[H-L_S])$

Z^* The value of Z imposed under the Inventories in the Third Model

α, β Labor and land exponents of the Cobb–Douglas production function $(\alpha+\beta=1)$

Several other symbols will be explained when they are introduced. All diagrams and numerical illustrations are based on a Cobb–Douglas production function $Y = L^\alpha T^\beta$ with values $T = 1,000$, $H = 70$, $E = 15.618$, $\alpha = .7$, and $\beta = .3$.

The First Model – the effects of population growth

In the absence of legal restrictions, the maximization of the master's income in the short run (with a given number of serfs and a given quantity of land) merely requires an optimal division of the resources of the estate between the master and his serfs. Obviously, this objective will be achieved by equalizing the marginal products of land and of labor, respectively,

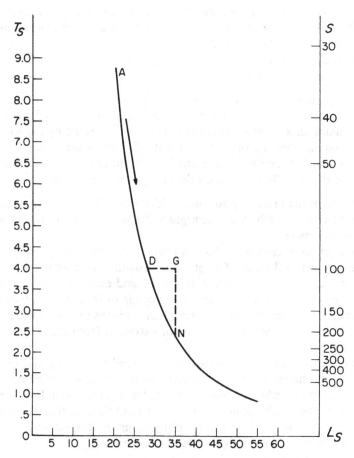

Figure 13.1. The subsistence isoquant. *Source:* See text.

on the two parts of the estate. With constant returns to scale (Assumption 1), this in turn calls for equal land/labor ratios.[7]

The isoquant ADN on Figure 13.1 indicates the various combinations of time and land allotted to each serf to allow him to produce the subsistence

[7] Assuming a given number of serfs on the estate and a constant subsistence level, the maximization of the master's income from the demesne is equivalent to the maximization of total production on the estate. In other words, the estate can be treated like a slave plantation where the slaves work for the master full time and are provided with their subsistence. Although analytically simple, this approach is less satisfactory as a means toward understanding the nature of serfdom and would prevent the use of this model as an introduction to the following ones.

level of output. The right scale shows the number of serfs (on a given estate) which induces the master to choose a particular point on the isoquant, such as point D for 100 serfs.

An increase in the serf population on a given piece of land will require the following adjustments:

(1) A reduction in each serf's land allotment.
(2) A corresponding increase in each serf's free time sufficient to maintain a subsistence output level, as illustrated by the southeast movement along the isoquant ADN in Figure 13.1.
(3) A contraction of the demesne in order to maintain the equality of the land/labor ratio on the two parts of the estate.

The need for the first two adjustments is obvious. That the third is also required can be shown by a simple argument.[8] We shall return to this adjustment process below.

The reduction in each serf's land allotment is likely to be accepted by the serfs as a natural effect of population growth. The master's willingness to reduce each serf's labor obligations, and even to transfer some of his own land to the serf sector, may appear to them as evidence of his generosity. In fact, he will be more than compensated for these concessions by the increased supply of labor extracted from the larger serf population.

Thus in densely populated areas both the land allotments and labor obligations of the serfs, and the fraction of the estate occupied by the demesne, should be relatively small. The evidence presented in Blum's recent work on the whole confirms this conclusion.[9] Foreign travelers were usually appalled by the heavy labor obligations of Russian serfs; they may have failed to note their larger land allotments.

---

[8] Let the number of serfs on a given estate increase by 1 percent. If all of the land for the new arrival is taken from other serfs, the allotment of each will decline by (approximately) 1 percent and their free time will have to be increased accordingly in order to maintain their subsistence. The labor/land ratio on the serf land will then increase by more than 1 percent, but on the demesne it will increase by less than 1 percent, violating the efficiency condition of equal land/labor ratios on both parts of the estate. To restore this equality, the master will have to contribute some of his own land to the new serf's allotment. I. F. Samarin, a liberal landowner highly respected as an authority on serfdom, states that an increase in the number of households (*tiagla*) on the estate always caused the master to contribute some of his own land to their allotments. He adds that a master who refused to do so and yet expected to receive more labor from his serfs would be condemned by public opinion as a violator of the serfs' rights. See his *Sochineniia* [Collected works] (Moscow, 1878), vol. 3, p. 205.

[9] Jerome Blum, *The End of the Old Order in Rural Europe* (Princeton, 1978), pp. 50–59. There was much local variation, however.

A comparison of the magnitudes of these variables between the eighteenth and nineteenth centuries in Russia is very difficult to make because the data for the eighteenth century are sketchy and contradictory.[10] But it is not impossible that the serfs' labor obligations may actually have been lighter in the 1700s (contrary to our model), since Russian serfdom was still developing at that time and did not reach its peak until about 1800.[11]

According to statistical data collected by the government on the eve of the Emancipation the size of serf allotments did vary inversely with population density. But in almost all of the areas outside the Western provinces (which were subject to the Inventories) serfs were reported to owe three days of labor per week, the maximum allowed by law (see the Second Model).[12] To report more would have implied disobedience, to report less would have weakened the masters' bargaining position in the coming Emancipation.

The extent of the demesnes of the masters is less easy to ascertain. For some regions there are simply no data; for others all of the waste and forest, which the serfs were allowed to use under certain conditions, were counted among the masters' land; on the *obrok* estates the demesnes were small or nonexistent. In the two regions having the same fraction of *obrok* serfs – the Volga (23.0 percent) and the more populated Central Agricultural (23.7 percent) – demesnes constituted an average of 64 percent of estate land in the former and 52 percent in the latter, a modest confirmation of our reasoning.[13]

In the long run the master had to decide on the maximum number of serfs that should be employed on his estate. Contrary to the beliefs of Russian intellectuals, serf labor was not free to the owner. Like all workers, serfs had to be paid. However, they were usually paid not in money

[10] See Koval'chenko, *Russkoe* [Russian], pp. 263–81; Fedorov, *Pomeshchich'i* [Landowners'], pp. 19–25; and V. I. Semevskii, *Krest'iane v tsarstvovanie imperatritsy Ekateriny II* [Peasants during the reign of the Empress Catherine II] (St. Petersburg, 1903), pp. 1–100. Unrelated division of land, labor, and output between the masters and serfs in the eighteenth century reported by these authors did not induce them to deepen their investigations.

[11] However, there is some evidence that in the eighteenth century the labor services demanded from serfs were very heavy indeed. According to Kliuchevskii, General Peter Panin, having described the intensive exploitation of serfs to Catherine II, suggested to her that their labor obligations be limited to *four* days a week. See V. Kliuchevskii, *Kurs russkoi istorii* [A course of Russian history] (Moscow, 1937), vol. 5, pp. 128–29, 146–47.

[12] Aleksandr Skrebitskii, *Krest'ianskoe delo v tsarstvovanie Aleksandra II: materialy dlia istorii osvobozhdeniia krest'ian* [Peasant affairs during the reign of Alexander II: materials on the history of the emancipation of the peasants] (Bonn, 1865/66), vol. 2, part 2, pp. 1491–551, and vol. 3, pp. 1227–93. Actually, additional payments in kind were often required.

[13] Ibid.

but in land, and on conditions set not by the market but by the master. *This is the essence of (unregulated) serfdom.* More precisely, the cost of maintaining a serf is the income forgone by the master from the serf's land allotment, or $T_S R_T$. An increasing serf population on a given land area increases the rent per unit of land, R_T, but the ability of the master to reduce the size of each serf's plot, T_S, allows him to control the cost.[14] Even then he cannot avoid the rise in the cost of an *hour* (per week) of serf labor because each serf, allowed more time as a compensation for the reduction of his plot, owes his master fewer hours.

Since each serf works $H - L_S$ hours per week on the master's land, the cost of one hour of his labor to the master is $T_S R_T/[H - L_S]$. The master will desire to own more serfs so long as the benefit derived from an additional hour of serf labor exceeds this cost, that is, as long as

$$R_L > \frac{T_S R_T}{H - L_S}. \tag{13.1}$$

The growth of the serf population weakens this inequality from both sides, raising the cost of an hour of serf labor while lowering its marginal product. Eventually, Expression (13.1) will become an equality and the master will desire no additional serfs. With all serf estates being, by assumption, in the same position, the price of a serf will decline to zero and serfdom will end.[15]

This conclusion, however, holds only in the absence of a free sector. If a free sector exists, and if the marginal product of land in it is lower than in the serf sector, the master can counteract the declining marginal productivity of labor on his estate by acquiring more land. If the wage of free labor (of the same productivity) is above the cost of his serfs' labor, he can hire out some of his serfs either directly or via the *obrok* system (see the Fourth Model). If serfs can be trained for nonagricultural occupations (a common occurrence in the central and northern regions of Russia), new uses for their labor will open up. Thus, the final test of the profitability of serf labor need not take place on the serf estate.

---

[14] If the Cobb–Douglas production function is used, then $T_S R_T$, being that part of the serf's income attributed to land, remains constant because in this production function the relative shares of the factors remain constant and the serf's income is assumed to be constant.

[15] Long before that happens, an old serfowner, observing that the productivity of an hour of serf labor had declined while its implicit cost to him had risen as the serf population increased, might forget about the increasing supply of labor available to him and bemoan the falling profitability of serfdom. Similarly, in a well-organized slave market, the master, operating on the margin, will profess his indifference between free and slave labor long before the marginal productivity of slave labor comes down to subsistence. See Essay 12.

There may be special situations, however, when the master is unable to obtain more land (the Russian gentry was notoriously short of cash), or when employment of his serfs in the free sector is not practical. In that case, so long as the implicit cost of serf labor is below the free wage he will refuse to free his serfs even if he needs no additional ones. At most, he may free a serf if a suitable substitute is found, or retain only one son of a deceased father. In this twilight zone, serfdom may persist for a long time, even with a zero price of serfs.[16]

A fall in serf prices may also be caused by a rise in the interest rate or by noneconomic factors, such as increasing insubordination by the serfs, caused for instance by rumors of a forthcoming emancipation. We shall disregard all such possibilities, and treat a declining or a very low price of serfs as evidence that serfdom was becoming or had become unprofitable for the masters.

We are now ready to deal with Pokrovskii. Except for one brief reference, he said nothing about serf prices. His empirical evidence was limited to a few quotations from "understanding" serfowners and to several examples supposedly demonstrating the superior profitability of free labor which were collected by a liberal government official in 1840, six years before the repeal of the British Corn Laws.[17] None of this evidence need be taken seriously, but his main point that rising grain prices are inimical to serfdom does deserve an examination.[18]

[16] Serfdom may also persist if the master's status is determined by the number of serfs he owns. Many such cases can be found in the Russian pre-Emancipation literature. It is also possible that unfree workers (slave or serf) may be more reliable than free workers.

[17] Pokrovskii, *Russkaia* [Russian], pp. 40–55. The liberal official was A. P. Zablotskii-Desiatovskii, sent by Count P. D. Kiselev to make a firsthand investigation of peasant conditions. This report was included in his major work, *Graf Kiselev i ego vremia* [Count Kiselev and his time] (St. Petersburg, 1882), vol. 4, pp. 271–345.

Actually, the behavior of grain prices, as cited by Pokrovskii, hardly supported his contention. But a more serious recent study made by two Soviet historians does indicate a considerable rise in prices of rye and oats in most provinces during the 1846–1855 (or 1847–1856) period. See Pokrovskii, *Russkaia* [Russian], vol. 4, pp. 44–46, 53; and I. D. Koval'chenko and L. V. Milov, *Vserossiiskii agrarnyi rynok XVIII – nachalo XX veka* [The All-Russian agricultural market, eighteenth – beginning of the twentieth century] (Moscow, 1974), pp. 394–97. But did agricultural prices rise relative to other prices?

[18] We are concerned here with that part of Pokrovskii's argument that is of greatest theoretical interest. We should add that he expected the rise in grain prices not only to make serfdom unprofitable but also to lead to a general reorganization of the serf estates into capitalist enterprises. The serfowners expected to obtain the capital needed for this purpose from the redemption of their serfs by the government on generous terms (pp. 55–84). That such a redemption was in fact carried out after 1861 makes his argument suspect.

Pokrovskii's style is sharp, witty, and partisan. We doubt that his opinion on the profitability of Russian serfdom would have changed had grain prices fallen instead of risen.

Gerschenkron, "Agrarian," p. 726, also spoke about the "sinking profitability of the [serf] estates" without presenting any evidence.

Since a rise in grain prices should benefit all agriculture, free and serf alike, Pokrovskii was obviously concerned only with the relative advantage of using free as opposed to serf labor. A rise in grain prices should make free labor relatively cheaper, at least in the short run, because nominal wages usually lag behind prices. We do not know how long the real wage of agricultural workers in pre-Emancipation Russia might have remained so depressed. With many workers receiving room and board from their employers, their real wage need not have fallen at all. Pokrovskii said nothing about the fall in the real wage and it was not this trivial case that caught our eye.

Several years after the publication of Pokrovskii's book, two economists proved a theorem in the theory of international trade which, when applied to Pokrovskii's assertion, revealed an unsuspected depth in it.[19] Consider an economy consisting of a relatively land-intensive agricultural sector and a relatively labor-intensive craft sector (both exhibiting constant returns to scale), and assume that this economy is currently in equilibrium. A rise in the price of grain (in terms of craft products) will cause an expansion of the agricultural sector and a contraction of the craft sector. The expanding agricultural sector will demand relatively much land and little labor, while the contracting craft sector will release relatively little land and much labor. As a result, there will be an excess demand for land and an excess supply of labor, causing a rise in the ratio of the value of land to the real wage in the free sector. *Since serf labor is paid in land,* the relative cost of serf as compared with free labor will increase. It may rise sufficiently to induce at least some masters to prefer free labor.

If the process just described had taken place, a movement of labor from crafts (and other sectors) into agriculture should have been observed. (The quantity of land used in the nonagricultural sectors was too small to matter.) We have seen no evidence of such a movement and Pokrovskii, innocent of all this theorizing, provides none.[20] Even if some labor had

[19] The two economists were Wolfgang F. Stolper and Paul A. Samuelson. See their "Protection and Real Wages," *Review of Economic Studies,* 9 (Nov. 1941), 58–73. For a more recent discussion of this problem, see Ronald W. Jones, "A Three-Factor Model in Theory, Trade, and History," in *Trade, Balance of Payments and Growth: Papers in International Economics in Honor of Charles P. Kindleberger* (Amsterdam, 1971), pp. 3–21; and Samuelson's "Summing up on the Australian Case for Protection," *Quarterly Journal of Economics,* 96 (Feb. 1981), 149–60.

[20] Between 1840 and 1856 urban population in European Russia increased by 21.8 percent, or at an annual rate of 1.23 percent. It grew more slowly than in the 1825–1840 period (2.25 percent per year), but faster than in the period 1856–1863 (1.02 percent per year). (The Crimean War was fought from 1854 to 1856). As a fraction of total population, the urban population increased from 9.27 percent in 1838 to 9.98 percent in 1863. See

moved back into agriculture – a rather improbable event – the effect on the relative prices of labor and land would not have been large because only a small fraction of Russian labor was employed outside agriculture.

But suppose that this effect had been significant. Would it have undermined the relative profitability of serf labor? This would have depended on how free the masters were to manage their serfs. So long as the masters were able to select the optimal combination of land and time allotted to their serfs, they could readjust the combination in response to a rise in grain prices (by reducing T_S and increasing L_S), just as they must have readjusted it, from time to time, in response to a growing serf population. With two important exceptions (discussed in the next two models), the Russian government left the serfowners almost completely free to deal with their serfs.

But in countries where the serfs' labor obligations and land allotments were fixed by law or by custom, every increase in land values relative to the cost of free labor, whether caused by population growth, rising grain prices, or any other reason, threatened the profitability of serfdom. Although the original arrangements set by the masters must have priced serf labor, in terms of land, below the existing market rates (otherwise serfdom would have been unnecessary), subsequent developments could have raised the value of land so high that eventually the masters would prefer to be rid of their serfs, provided they could retain the land, while the serfs, for the same reason, would wish to remain in servile condition so long as they could use the land originally allotted to them.[21]

The Second Model – the effects of Paul's Law

The limitation of the labor obligation of Russian serfs to three days a week – one of the few important restrictions on the serfowners' powers – originated from a mistaken assertion by Emperor Paul I in 1797. Later

A. G. Rashin, *Naselenie Rossii za 100 let (1811–1913 gg.)* [The population of Russia for 100 years (1811–1913)] (Moscow, 1956), pp. 86, 98.

Urban population, however, is not a good proxy for employment in crafts because many craftsmen resided in villages. See L. V. Tengoborskii, *O proizvoditel'nykh silakh Rossii* [On the productive forces of Russia] (Moscow, 1854), part 2, p. 146.

[21] The fact that in some European countries the inheritance of a serf's plot was not automatic and had to be secured by the payment of a fee (such as the surrender of the best animal) – a custom completely unheard of in Russia, where every additional working serf was always welcome – suggests that these masters were willing to part with their serfs provided they retained the land.

Early in the nineteenth century, the serfs in the Russian Baltic provinces were given their freedom (more or less) without land. According to V. Kliuchevskii, *Kurs* [A course], vol. 5, pp. 299–300, their position became worse at once.

it was incorporated as a law in the 1832 code. We shall call it "Paul's Law."[22]

The purpose of this law was presumably to protect serfs against excessive exploitation.[23] It should have been obvious even to the Russian government, however, that confronted with this restriction alone the master could easily compensate himself by taking back some of his serfs' land; by demanding additional payments in money or in kind, as many masters did; or by abolishing labor services altogether and placing his serfs on *obrok,* which remained completely unrestricted by law.

Leaving the *obrok* method for the Fourth Model and disregarding the possibility of additional payments, we shall analyze the effect of Paul's Law with the help of Figure 13.1. Assume that prior to the passage of the law, the master assigned each serf the combination of T_S land and L_S time corresponding to point D, and that the magnitude of L_S was below the new legal minimum (otherwise the Law would be ineffective). The initial effect of Paul's Law would be to move the serfs off the isoquant to point G and make them temporarily better off, having more time and an unchanged allotment of land. A strong or greedy master might move his serfs back to the isoquant (to point N) right away by taking some of their land. A weaker or kinder one could let the growth of population do the job for him. Such a master would endow new serfs with land taken exclusively from other serfs until point N was reached. In the meantime, the size of the demesne would remain constant or might even increase.

In any case, point N is not yet optimal from the master's point of view. It becomes optimal only after a sufficient increase in the serf population (from 100 to 210 in our example). In other words, Paul's Law merely forces the master to give his serfs a combination of time and land not yet called for by the existing land/labor ratio on the estate. When point N becomes optimal (and thereafter) Paul's Law becomes ineffective, and the results obtained in the First Model hold true again.[24]

---

[22] Blum, *Lord,* pp. 445–47. According to Samarin, *Sochineniia* [Collected], vol. 2, p. 421, the law was very poorly worded. It was not clear to whom this limit of three days per week applied.

[23] But, according to Semevskii, Emperor Paul extended serfdom to several new provinces and raised labor obligations in Little Russia from two to three days a week. See his *Krest'ianskii vopros v Rossii v XVIII i pervoi polovine XIX veka* [The peasant question in Russia in the eighteenth and the first half of the nineteenth centuries] (St. Petersburg, 1888), pp. XIV–XV.

[24] We have no information on the length of time the masters might have taken to move their serfs from point G to N. In the country as a whole, the serf population grew slowly early in the nineteenth century and became almost stationary after about 1830. It is possible that many serf estates remained in a state of transition between G and N until the very end in 1861. See A. Troinitskii, *Krepostnoe naselenie v Rossii po 10-i narodnoi perepisi* [The serf population of Russia according to the 10th population census] (St.

Table 13.1. *The effects of the growth of the serf population on the variables in the second model*

Variable	Between G and N	At non-optimal N (Paul's Law binding)	At optimal N (Paul's Law ineffective)
ΔT_S	<0	0	<0
ΔL_S	0	0	>0
$\Delta T_M{}^a$	0	0	<0
ΔL_M	>0	>0	>0

^{a} As described in the text, T_M may increase, but not because of the growth of the serf population.
Source: See text.

After the serfs are moved to point N, and before this point becomes optimal for the master, the growth of the serf population presents him with few problems. With L_S set constant by law, he merely has to find the corresponding value of T_S from the isoquant and allocate it to each serf. The process is summarized in Table 13.1.

On the basis of the table, it is hard to know what to expect. No wonder some Soviet historians have found that the demesnes were increasing and others found that they were contracting.[25] During the move from G to N, the serfs lose their temporarily acquired gains. Some contemporary observers and later historians who did not understand the nature of the process interpreted the loss as a permanent decline in the serfs' standard of living.

Our main concern, however, is with the effect of Paul's Law on the master's attitude toward serfdom. In particular, we wish to find out what happens to the master's income, to the value of his land, and to the price of serfs. We shall assume that the transfer of serfs to point N has been completed, but that this point has not yet become optimal.

The answer to the first question is obvious: by destroying the equality of the land/labor ratios on the two parts of the estate, Paul's Law

Petersburg, 1861), pp. 54–56 (English translation by Elaine Herman [Newtonville, Massachusetts, 1982], pp. 68–71); and S. L. Hoch and W. R. Augustine, "The Tax Censuses and the Decline of the Serf Population in Imperial Russia, 1833–1858," *The Slavic Review*, 38 (Sept. 1979), 403–25.

[25] See the sources cited in footnote 10. A rise in grain prices, discussed in the First Model, would have little effect on serfdom under Paul's Law. It would merely result in smaller land allotments.

makes serfdom inefficient and reduces the master's income (and hence, of course, the value of the estate).

The answer to the second question is also simple: now that the master has lost some labor but gained land, the marginal product of land on the demesne will fall. He may try to sell or lease some of his land to the free sector; that such actions were restricted by law suggests that some such attempts were made.[26] He may also try to hire free workers or even his own serfs for pay. Finally, the master may solve this and other problems by transferring all or some of his land to the serfs in exchange for an *obrok,* which was not limited by law (see the Fourth Model). Soviet historians give examples of all of these practices, without indicating, however, how widespread they were.[27]

The effects of Paul's Law on the price of serfs are complex. The marginal product of an *hour* of serf labor on the demesne must increase because of the rise in the land/labor ratio. However, each serf now works fewer hours per week. What happens, then, to the marginal product of serf labor per *week*? The answer will be found in Figure 13.2.

The solid curve OWQ indicates the master's weekly income as a function of the number of serfs in the absence of Paul's Law. The dotted curve OW shows his income under the law after the transfer of his serfs to point N. Since Paul's Law reduces the master's income, this curve must lie below the solid one until point W, where the law becomes ineffective. On the assumption that both curves and their derivatives are monotonic, this implies that at the beginning the slope of the dotted curve must be smaller than that of the solid one, but later, if the curves are to touch, the dotted curve must become steeper than the solid one. Since these slopes represent the corresponding net marginal products of labor per week, it follows that in sparsely populated areas Paul's Law reduces the marginal product of a serf and hence his price; in more densely settled areas, it

---

[26] The law, enacted in 1814 and 1827, forbade the alienation of estate land below a minimum of 4.5 *desiatinas* per soul (1 *desiatina* = 1.09 hectares) (Blum, *Lord,* p. 532). It is not clear to us whether this minimum applied to the land allotment of each serf or to the land/labor ratio of the whole estate. Skrebitskii, *Krest'ianskoe* [Peasant], vol. 2, part 2, pp. 1491–539, cites many cases when the land allotment for serfs was less than 4.5 *desiatinas* per soul. In any case, the law merely forbade the alienation of land; it did not compel the masters to acquire additional land to restore the minimum. It was not likely to have been important because the restriction only mattered in densely populated areas where Paul's Law must have been ineffective.

[27] See, for instance, Fedorov, *Pomeshchich'i* [Landowners'], pp. 42–49; E. I. Indova, *Krepostnoe khoziaistvo v nachale XIX veka po materialam votchinnogo arkhiva Voront-sovykh* [The serf economy at the beginning of the nineteenth century according to the materials in the patrimonial archives of the Vorontsov family] (Moscow, 1955), pp. 178–82; and Koval'chenko, *Russkoe* [Russian], pp. 128–57, 177.

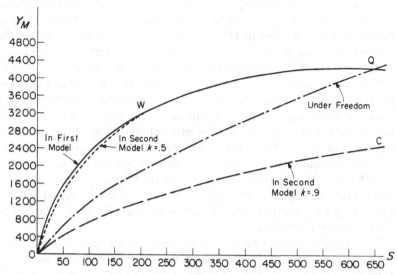

Figure 13.2. The Master's income under freedom and in First and Second Models. *Note:* The curve OQ – Master's income under freedom – is drawn on the assumption that at every point labor is paid the value of its marginal product. *Source:* See text.

raises both; and in very dense areas, where the law becomes ineffective, there will be no change. Since the location of these turning points is empirically uncertain, we cannot make a general statement regarding the overall effect of Paul's Law on the price of serfs or on the duration of serfdom.

All of these assertions are based on the assumption that the restriction on the master's use of serf labor under the law was "reasonable," such as one-half of their total working time. But if the law commanded that the serfs be allowed to work for themselves as much as nine-tenths of their time, then the master would earn less (curve OC) than he would under freedom (curve OQ) and he would give up serfdom right away. This was clearly not the intention of Paul's Law.

The Third Model – the effects of the Inventories

The so-called Inventories were (or were to be) introduced into Western provinces in the 1840s to regularize the obligations of the serfs to their masters and thus to gain the support of the serfs (many of them Greek-Orthodox) against their predominantly Catholic masters, whose loyalty to the Russian state was suspect.[28] The Inventories did not specify the size of the land allotment to be given to each peasant household and the magnitude of labor services to be performed by it; they merely established the rate of exchange between labor and land in reference to a standard land allotment. With some violation of reality, this rate $Z = T_S/[H - L_S]$ will be treated here as a constant.[29] It has already appeared in Expression (13.1) in the First Model, but there it was not imposed by the government; it arose implicitly out of the unregulated maximization of the master's income.[30] As the price of serf labor in terms of land, this ratio was not constant in that model; it was high when labor was scarce and *it must have declined gradually with the increasing density of the serf population.*

To be effective, the Inventories must set the imposed rate Z^* above the implicit rate Z. Thus the price of labor in terms of land is raised to a level which might have existed in the past when the serf population on the given estate was smaller.

To maximize his income in the long run, the master will wish to own additional serfs so long as the inequality in Expression (13.1) holds, just as he did in the First Model. That inequality can be written $R_L/R_T > T_S/[H - L_S]$, or as $R_L/R_T > Z$, but since the Z of the First Model is replaced here by Z^*, it should be expressed as

$$\frac{R_L}{R_T} > Z^*. \tag{13.2}$$

There are two reasons why this inequality will be weakened sooner under the Inventories than it would be without them: first, because Z^* is set above Z; second, because the ratio R_L/R_T, for reasons explained below, will decline faster. Hence the saturation point will be reached here at a smaller number of serfs (in our example, at 128 as compared with 646 in the First Model). But before this happens, several interesting developments will take place on the estate.

The two constraints now faced by the master – the subsistence isoquant and the new price ratio Z^* – are shown in Figure 13.3 by the curve ABCN

---

[28] According to Blum, *Lord,* pp. 460–62, the Inventories were definitely imposed on the three Southwest provinces (Kiev, Volyniia, and Podoliia) in 1848. But in Lithuania and White Russia they were postponed because of the opposition of the serfowners. However, Skrebitskii, *Krest'ianskoe* [Peasant], vol. 3, pp. 1266–73, describes serfs' obligations in Lithuania as being subject to the Inventories. It seems that the same held true in the Minsk province, but not in the rest of White Russia. He warns that the Lithuanian Inventories need not reflect the actual state of affairs (p. 23).

The Russian government did want to improve the welfare of these serfs, but not to the point of arousing the envy of others who lived elsewhere under Orthodox masters.

[29] This is a great simplification. Actually, the serfs' duties were quite complex.

[30] It existed implicitly and was also constant in the Second Model because L_S was determined by Paul's Law and T_S by the subsistence requirement.

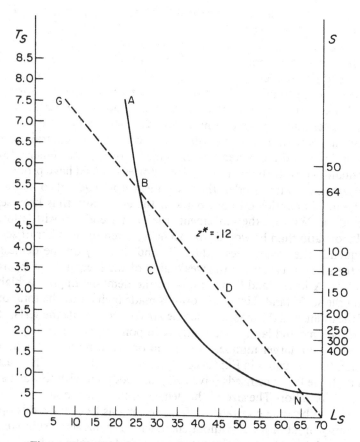

Figure 13.3. The two constraints: the subsistence isoquant and the Z^* ray. *Note:* Different magnitudes of Z^* produce rays emanating from the same point. Note that the right scale, showing the number of serfs, pertains to the isoquant and not to the Z^* ray. *Source:* See text.

and the ray GN respectively. To satisfy both constraints, without being unduly generous to his serfs, the master will place them on the composite curve ABDN, the exact point chosen being determined by the number of serfs on the estate. Depending on that number, the Inventories will affect the incomes of the master and the serfs in several different ways:

(1) If the number of serfs is very small, above point B (less than 64 in our example – see the right scale), the Inventories are completely ineffective because the Z^* imposed by the government is below the optimal Z chosen by the master. An increase in the number of serfs at this stage will

simply induce the master to move them from point A down along the iso-quant until point B is reached.

(2) At point B (that is, with 64 serfs) the Inventories become effective. Point B satisfies both constraints.[31] The serfs will be kept at this point even when their number continues to increase so long as the inequality in Expression (13.2) holds: it will not pay the master to move them down the Z^* ray because the potential gain of moving an additional serf $|\Delta T_S| R_T$ will be smaller than the corresponding loss $\Delta L_S R_L$.[32] So long as the serfs are kept at point B, T_S and L_S will remain constant, in contrast to the reduction in T_S and the increase in L_S which a further movement down the isoquant – now forbidden by the Inventories – would have produced. As we saw in the First Model, this movement was required to maintain equal land/labor ratios on both parts of the estate and thus keep serf-dom efficient. Without the movement, the master ends up with a lower land/labor ratio than he would wish to have, given the number of serfs. Consequently the Inventories reduce R_L and raise R_T on the demesne: this is the second reason for the weakening of the inequality in Expression (13.2). A lower land/labor ratio on the demesne implies a higher ratio on the serfs' land. Hence serfdom is made inefficient: the total out-put of the estate and the master's income are reduced, while the serfs, still allotted the time and land corresponding to point B, gain nothing.

(3) With a still larger number of serfs, at or below point C (128 in our example), the inequality in Expression (13.2) no longer holds. The master now has all the labor he needs (given Z^*) and does not wish to trade any more land for labor. The size of the demesne, the labor input on it, and his income all become constant. In fact, so long as he obtains this opti-mal quantity of labor input without encroaching on his serfs' subsistence (which would occur below point N), the master does not care how many serfs he owns.[33] He can now deal with the serf community as a unit that supplies a constant total labor input on the demesne in exchange for a constant quantity of land, and distributes both the land and the obliga-tions for labor among its members at its own discretion. The efficiency of serfdom is not restored because the land/labor ratio on the demesne re-mains lower than on the serfs' land. Compared with its pre-Inventory

---

[31] The intersection of $Z^* = T_S/[H-L_S]$ with $E = L_S^\alpha T_S^\beta$ (where E is the subsistence level) results in $L_S = H - (T_S/Z^*)$, where T_S is obtained from the equation $H - (T_S/Z^*) = [E/T_S^\beta]^{(1/\alpha)}$, which can be solved by trial and error.

[32] From the definition of $Z^* = T_S/[H-L_S]$, we obtain $T_S = Z^*[H-L_S]$. Hence $|\Delta T_S| = Z^*\Delta L_S$, or $Z^* = |\Delta T_S/\Delta L_S|$. The master will *not* move his serfs down the Z^* ray so long as $\Delta L_S R_L > |\Delta T_S| R_T$, that is, $R_L/R_T > |\Delta T_S/\Delta L_S|$, or, $R_L/R_T > Z^*$.

[33] The minimum number of serfs that allows the master to obtain this maximum income is obtained by solving the equation $(HZ^*S - \alpha T)^\alpha/S = E(Z^*)^\alpha/(\alpha T)^\beta$ for S. The maxi-mization of $Y_M = L_M^\alpha T_M^\beta$ subject to $Z^* = T_S/[H-L_S] = [T-T_M]/L_M$ gives $T_M = \beta T$ and $L_M = \alpha T/Z^*$, both expressions being independent of S.

level, the master's income is permanently reduced, but the position of his serfs may finally improve because, with the inequality in Expression (13.2) gone, the master need not interfere with their movement down the Z^* ray, to a point such as D. Unless his serfs can be used off the estate, the master has no need for additional ones, and serfdom enters the twilight zone described in the First Model.

At this point an interesting development occurs. As we have just seen, the master no longer cares how many serfs live on his estate. But his serfs do. The higher land/labor ratio on their part of the estate results in a higher R_L/R_T ratio as well, and preserves the inequality (13.2) on *their* land. Hence, the serfs will be willing to trade some of their land for labor at the exchange rate Z^* (just as their master did earlier) if they can find new serfs to trade with. Since all estates are assumed here to be in the same position, additional serfs can be obtained from natural increase only, but the serfs might wish to petition the master not to free any of them unless they are all set free.[34]

(4) Finally, when the number of serfs reaches 278, the ratio of the marginal products of labor and of land on the serfs' part of the estate comes down to Z^*, and no additional serfs are wanted.[35] The land/labor ratios on both parts of the estate are equalized, and the earlier inefficiency introduced by the Inventories now disappears. But the serfs do receive a larger part of the estate's total income and each of them is better off. Thus, in relatively thickly settled areas, the Inventories can fulfill the government's objective of improving the serfs' welfare without making serfdom inefficient. Whether this actually happened remains to be investigated.[36]

The Fourth Model – serfs on obrok

Obrok (or quitrent) was the payment made by the serfs to the master, usually in money, in lieu of labor services. On estates where the *obrok* system dominated, most of the land was allotted to serfs.

According to the data submitted by the masters on the eve of the Emancipation, the occurrence of the *obrok* system had a distinctly regional character. The highest proportions of serfs on *obrok* were in the Central Industrial Region (58.5 percent) and in the Lake Region (47.0 percent). Next came the Central Agricultural (23.7 percent) and the Volga (23.0

---

[34] The collective responsibility of peasant communities for tax collection created a similar situation in old Muscovy, where the old-timers objected to the departure of any members. See Essay 12.

[35] The number of serfs that maximizes the income of each serf is $\alpha T/\beta HZ^*$.

[36] Since the Inventories have the effect of reducing the optimal number of serfs on the estate, they make serf agriculture less labor-intensive in the long run. These enactments, or similar ones in other countries, can thus create a class of landless peasants that, strangely enough, can coexist with serfdom.

percent) regions. All of these areas are in Great Russia; outside of it, the *obrok* system was almost nonexistent.[37]

The high fraction of *obrok* serfs in the Central Industrial and Lake regions is easy to explain. The poor soil and harsh climate of these regions had forced peasants from time immemorial to engage in crafts, trapping, fishing, trade, construction, transportation, and other nonagricultural pursuits. By imposing an *obrok* in lieu of relatively unprofitable agricultural labor services the masters were able to tap the serfs' nonagricultural earnings. But why was this system not used more widely? Even in the Central Industrial Region some 40 percent of serfs rendered labor services; in the Lake Region, more than 50 percent. Nor is there clear evidence that the use of *obrok* was becoming more prevalent over time.[38]

And yet, even in the absence of nonagricultural earnings, the *obrok* system had a number of obvious advantages for both sides. It reduced the masters' managerial responsibilities, particularly bothersome for the many civil and military servants among them, and gave the serfs greater freedom and opportunity which, according to traditional wisdom, should have increased their earnings. It would seem that this system should have been dominant even in areas of excellent soil and climate such as the Ukraine, where agriculture was a full-time occupation. But there it was hardly used.

Obviously, many masters must have had good reasons for preferring labor services to *obrok*. We considered a number of possible reasons, such as economies of scale, superior management on the demesne, or the serfs' unwillingness to bear risk, but found none of them convincing. The only explanation to survive our examination was the difficulty of collection. No serf could fall far behind in rendering labor services. In contrast, the *obrok* was collected at stated intervals, such as twice a year. If the serf failed to pay, the master could use threats and punishments, but, judging by the laments of peasant elders and the complaints of professional managers of their inability to collect the arrears, such threats must have been limited in their effectiveness.[39] Perhaps in the industrialized

---

[37] See Skrebitskii, *Krest'ianskoe* [Peasant], vol. 3, pp. 1228–65.

[38] See Koval'chenko, *Russkoe* [Russian], pp. 62–63; Semevskii, *Krest'iane* [Peasants], pp. 48–51, 591–92; and Blum, *Lord,* pp. 394–401. Although there were regional variations between the two periods, the totals for the whole country remained stable.

[39] The difficulty of collection is stressed by Samarin. He also asserts that it is dangerous for peasants used to living and working under their master's supervision to be transferred to the *obrok* system. See his *Sochineniia* [Collected], vol. 3, pp. 44, 233–48. On the master's choice between labor services and rent there exists a considerable literature. See, for instance, Koval'chenko, *Russkoe* [Russian], pp. 163, 207, 212–13, 222; Fedorov, *Pomeshchich'i* [Landowners'], p. 29; Aron Katsenelinboigen, "Disguised Inflation in the Soviet Union: The Relationship Between Soviet Income Growth and Price Increases in the Postwar Period," in Alan Abouchar, ed., *The Socialist Price Mechanism* [Durham, North Carolina, 1977], p. 174, note 2; Folke Dovring, "Bondage, Tenure, and

areas the serfs derived steadier incomes from diversified sources. They may also have been more vulnerable to the master's threat to revoke or not to extend their passports. It is ironic that the institution of serfdom exacerbated this problem: under freedom, a nonpaying tenant could simply be evicted.

Did Paul's Law and the Inventories encourage the shift to the *obrok* system? So one would expect, since these laws made services less profitable while not touching the magnitude of the *obrok*. But Paul's Law was effective only in sparsely populated areas, like the East and the South, where the *obrok* system was uncommon. The Inventories should have been effective in well-settled areas, like the Southwest, and yet labor services completely dominated there. Perhaps the Inventories were introduced too late to produce a change, or the local masters, reputed to be efficient, gained more from labor services.

Whatever the virtues and defects of the *obrok* system were, did it reduce the profitability of Russian serfdom and hasten its end? Soviet historians attach tremendous importance to the supposed shift from labor services to money payments, and see in it the end of feudalism (whatever meaning this term might have in the Russian context), the beginning of capitalism, and evidence of the general crisis of serfdom.[40]

It is possible that in Western Europe the replacement of labor services by money payments did have such an effect: once the level of these payments became fixed, their real value could be destroyed by subsequent inflation.[41] But in Russia the *obrok* levels were not fixed. They were set by the masters and, as Blum has shown, they kept pace with inflation.[42] Nor were the masters precluded from demanding larger payments from particularly prosperous serfs engaged in crafts or trade. Indeed, far from destroying serfdom, the *obrok* system was likely to make it more flexible and long-lived.

The system facilitated the entrance of serfs into nonagricultural pursuits. A serf engaged in such activities would need little, if any, land and hence would cost his master little or nothing. His potential land allotment, in whole or part, could be used by another serf or by the master, thus alleviating the diminishing marginal productivity of labor on the

---

Progress," *Comparative Studies in Society and History* (April 1965), 309–23; and Stefano Fenoaltea, "Authority, Efficiency, and Agricultural Organization in Medieval England and Beyond: A Hypothesis," *The Journal of Economic History,* 35 (Dec. 1975), 693–718.

[40] See the sources cited in footnote 1.

[41] It was shown in the First Model that rising land values could destroy the profitability of fixed arrangements under serfdom.

[42] See Blum, *Lord,* pp. 449–51, and Koval'chenko, *Russkoe* [Russian], pp. 131, 295–97. The latter claims that in the nineteenth century the magnitude of *obrok* was increasing in real terms.

demesne, a potential threat to the profitability of serfdom. There was no limit to the number of *nonagricultural* serfs that a master might wish to own.

This system also had a more direct effect on serfdom. A man on *obrok* remained a serf only to his master. To the outside world, he was almost a free man who could take on jobs, enter into contracts, buy and lease land, hire labor, and even own serfs, all in his master's name. On some large estates such a serf had a dual relationship with his master. As a serf he had to pay the *obrok*; but like a free man, he could take a job on his master's estate or lease his master's land.[43] This remarkable combination of serfdom and freedom allowed him to work as effectively as a free man (if free men indeed worked more effectively than serfs) and still satisfy his master. Admittedly, for the serf it was not an ideal relationship. Besides paying the *obrok* set by the master and obtaining nothing in return, he was subject to his master's whims: his passport could be revoked, forcing him back to the estate; he had to hide his wealth lest his *obrok* be raised; and any property bought in his master's name could be seized by its legal owner.[44]

From the master's point of view, however, it was an excellent arrangement. While the *obrok* contained some agricultural rent for serfs still engaged, at least part-time, in agriculture, for others it was simply a crude income tax imposed on them by their masters, a sort of an old-fashioned tribute. Its magnitude was not restricted by law. It could exist forever if only the masters were able to collect it. So long as they could, the masters had not the slightest reason for renouncing serfdom.

III. An empirical inquiry

An ideal set of data required for investigating changes in the profitability of Russian serfdom would consist of time series observations on receipts, expenditures, and sales values for a suitably representative sample of serf estates. The records left by some large landowners have been examined by Soviet scholars, but to our knowledge, no comprehensive investigation has been undertaken. A somewhat less ideal, but still satisfactory, set of data would consist of time series of serf prices, by provinces or

---

[43] See Indova, *Krepostnoe* [The serf], pp. 178–82; Fedorov, *Pomeshchich'i* [Landowners'], pp. 42–50; and Koval'chenko, *Russkoe* [Russian], p. 151.

[44] Some serfs, particularly those who belonged to wealthy masters, did get some benefits from this arrangement, such as support during famines and protection against other noblemen and government officials. In Turgenev's famous story, "Khor' and Kalinych," Khor', a wealthy *obrok*-paying serf, does not want to acquire his freedom because then "every beardless person would be [his] boss" (noblemen and government officials wore no beards). (*Zapiski Okhotnika* [Sportsman's sketches] (Moscow, 1961), p. 13).

regions, for the several decades preceding the Emancipation. A persistent and widespread fall in these prices could be taken, in our opinion, as evidence that serfdom was nearing its end.[45] We have not been able to discover such a series. Indeed, the most patient scholar would be challenged to construct one from the scattered bits and pieces of data that are available. Most serfs were sold with land; hence, the problem of separately determining serf and land prices, which we are about to face, would remain.

The most important source which has been used by historians consists of data on land sales over the period 1854–1858 (inclusive), published by the Land Department of the Ministry of the Interior in 1859.[46] The data are reported by county (*uezdy*) within each province (*gubernii*), and are divided into sales of populated land (that is, land with serfs) and unpopulated land. For each county and type of land, the report gives the number of sales, the total value of sales, the total area in *desiatinas* (1 *desiatina* = approximately 1.09 hectares), and (for populated land) the total number of serfs, summed in each case over the entire five-year period. In addition, the official prices per *desiatina* and per serf are listed.[47]

We are told in the introduction that the original data had been edited to eliminate extreme and unusual cases.[48] In addition, we are warned that the values of many transactions might have been understated in order to reduce transfer duties, but that the prices of patrimonies might have been overstated in order to protect buyers from possible redemptions.[49] On the whole, it is felt that understatement prevailed. The editor regarded the data to be useful for estimating average land prices, but urged the readers to use other sources as well. The official land and serf prices given for each province were stated to be "almost everywhere below actual prices" (see Table 13.2 below).[50] If so, these official prices might indicate the minimum

---

[45] See the discussion at the end of the First Model.

[46] "Svedeniia o prodazhnykh tsenakh na zemli" ["Data on selling prices of land"], *Zhurnal ministerstva vnutrennikh del* [Journal of the Ministry of Interior Affairs] (1859), book 7, pp. 1–46, book 8, pp. 95–118.

Early in this century, Maslov, *Agrarnyi* [The agrarian], vol. 1, pp. 463–64, used these data to show that serfdom had become unprofitable. But he did not calculate serf prices separately from land prices. Blum did. See *Lord*, p. 372.

[47] Additional details of these data are given in the Statistical Appendix.

[48] The name of the editor is not given, but, according to D. I. Rikhter, he was the well-known statistician A. G. Troinitskii. See D. I. Rikhter, "Zabytyi material po statistike prodazhnykh tsen na zemliu" ["Forgotten materials on the statistics of selling prices of land"], *Trudy Imperatorskogo Vol'nogo Ekonomicheskogo Obshchestva* [Works of the Imperial Free Economic Society] (1897), vol. 2, book 4, pp. 1–28.

[49] According to Blum, *Lord*, p. 81, the redemption period was 40 years before 1830 and three years between 1830 and 1917.

[50] "Svedeniia" ["Data"], p. 3.

Table 13.2. *Prices of serfs obtained by different methods*

	(1) (2) On the assumption that prices of populated and unpopulated land are equal		(3)	(4)	(5)
	By first method	By second method	By regression	Based on *obrok*	Official prices
Major Regions[a]					
Central Industrial	40.8	34.3	122.8[b]	125.2	106.1
Central Agricultural	32.8	22.3	80.8	90.3	120.0
Lake	60.3	29.8	152.8	108.9	97.3
Lithuania	5.5	13.1	47.2	−	119.2
White Russia	7.0	10.8	151.6[b]	−	86.1
Little Russia	36.1	36.7	92.5	−	109.2
Southwest	126.0	62.6	156.5	−	120.0
New Russia	136.4	67.6	113.3	−	120.0
Volga	71.1	32.4	65.7[b]	84.7	120.0
Viatka-Perm'	20.7	44.0	78.3	−	90.0

[a] For the list of provinces in each region see the tables in the Statistical Appendix.
[b] Weighted average of provincial prices.
Sources and methods: Cols. (1) and (2): All data, including the number of serfs used as weights, taken from the sales reports in "Svedeniia" ["Data"]. Col. (3): Prices taken from Appendix Table 13.1 in the Statistical Appendix. The number of serfs used as weights for aggregating the provinces in the Central Industrial, White Russia, and Volga regions taken from Troinitskii, *Krepostnoe* [The serf], p. 45 (English translation by Elaine Herman [Newtonville, Massachusetts, 1982]), pp. 55–56. Col. (4): *Obrok* data taken from Skrebitskii, *Krest'ianskoe* [Peasant], vol. 3, 1228–93. *Obrok* per soul capitalized at 8 percent.

levels of actual prices and thus might provide a useful check on our estimates. Indeed, with only one exception, the official prices of unpopulated land were found to be below the reported prices, and usually with a wide margin. But for populated land (serf estates) the sums of the values of the land and serfs based on official prices exceeded the reported values of the estates in 18 out of 42 provinces. If the reported sale values had a downward bias, why were the prices of populated estates particularly affected? Were these transactions easier to underreport because of their greater complexity? Or did the prices of serf estates suffer a large decline that had occurred too recently to be reflected in official prices? We shall return to the question below.

(6)	(7)	(8)	(9)	(10)

Values of serfs as
percentages of values of the estates

From col. (1)	From col. (2)	From col. (3)	From col. (5)	Real prices of serfs
24.0	20.2	72.3	62.4	42.1[b]
16.9	11.5	41.7	61.9	35.7
32.9	16.2	83.3	53.0	37.6
2.7	6.6	23.7	60.0	9.2
4.7	7.3	102.5	58.2	34.4[b]
19.8	20.2	50.9	60.0	32.7
58.7	29.2	72.9	55.9	45.9
36.1	17.9	30.0	31.8	22.0
42.0	19.1	38.8	70.8	31.9[b]
15.6	33.2	59.1	68.0	39.9

Non-*obrok* serfs are assumed to pay the master two-thirds as much as *obrok* serfs. Aggregation weights are the same as in col. (3). Col. (5): Official serf prices from "Svedeniia" ["Data"]. Aggregation weights are the same as in col. (3). Cols. (6)–(9): Values of the estates taken from "Svedeniia" ["Data"]. Col. (10): From Appendix Table 13.2 in the Statistical Appendix. The deflation method is described there. Aggregation weights are the same as in col. (3).

Comparing the sales data with the official statistics on serf estates we find that, with some regional variation, the sales reports covered 3.6 percent of all land on serf estates in the country and 3.7 percent of all serfs.[51] The near equality of the two percentages suggests that the land/serf ratio in the sales reports must have been reasonably close to the average for all

[51] This implies that on the average some 0.7 percent of all serfs were sold per year. A small fraction should be added to this number to include serfs (servants, craftsmen, and so on) sold without land.

According to R. W. Fogel and S. L. Engerman, 1.92 percent of the slave population of Maryland was sold each year in the period 1830–1840. They accepted this figure as the national average. See their *Time on the Cross: The Economics of American Negro Slavery* (Boston, 1974), vol. 1, p. 53.

estates. However, the average number of serfs and *desiatinas* per sale constituted only some 80 percent of the corresponding averages for all estates, suggesting either that large estates were sold less frequently than smaller ones, or that they were excluded by the editor as "unusual cases." Since large estates usually commanded proportionately lower prices than smaller ones, the exclusion would lend an upward bias to the values in the sales data.

Several historians have attempted to estimate serf prices or the value of the land allotted to former serfs by the Emancipation from these data by assuming that the price of populated land was equal to that of unpopulated land in any given area. (The price of unpopulated land could be easily calculated.)[52] In doing so they disregarded a specific warning against making this assumption recorded in the discussions of some provincial committees prior to the Emancipation, because unpopulated land was bought in small quantities, and usually as increments to estates. Indeed, the average quantity of unpopulated land sold was only some 12 percent of that of populated land, and in some regions this fraction was much smaller.[53]

Even if the two land prices were equal for each province, there would still remain at least two methods of calculating the serf price for a given region: (1) a single weighted average land price for the whole region could be calculated first and then applied to the total (regional) value of the estates, or (2) serf prices could be obtained for each province separately and then averaged for the whole region. (The second method could start at the county level, but we did not undertake such an ambitious task.) The second method, which appears to make a bit more sense, is likely to yield lower serf prices than the first, which is confirmed by a comparison of the figures in Columns 1 and 2 in Table 13.2.[54] Blum must have used the first method; his prices are so close to those in Column 1 that they are not reproduced here.

[52] In addition to Maslov and Blum (see footnote 46 above), this assumption was made by Gerschenkron, "Agrarian," p. 738; Liashchenko, *Istoriia* [History], vol. 1, p. 584; Pokrovskii, *Russkaia* [Russian], vol. 4, p. 93; G. T. Robinson, *Rural Russia under the Old Regime* (Berkeley, 1932, 1960), p. 88; and others who were interested in the fairness of prices charged to former serfs for land allotted to them by the Emancipation.

[53] Skrebitskii, *Krest'ianskoe* [Peasant], vol. 3, p. 17. In some regions, like Lithuania, White Russia, and Little Russia, these percentages were even smaller: 4.4, 2.7, and 5.3 respectively. For the country as a whole, the quantity of unpopulated land sold was some 24 percent of total land sold; in White Russia it was only 8.6 percent, and in the Southwest a tiny 2.8 percent.

[54] Indicating the first and second methods by superscripts, we can express the regional serf prices obtained under each method by

$$P_S^1 = \left(\frac{1}{\Sigma S} \right) \left(\Sigma V_p - \frac{\Sigma P_{Tu} T_u \cdot \Sigma T_p}{\Sigma T_u} \right) \tag{13.1n}$$

The hypothesis of the equality of the prices of populated and unpopulated land in a given area was subjected to a statistical test and rejected (see the Statistical Appendix). It turned out that populated land was much cheaper than unpopulated – much to our surprise, because we have expected populated land to be of higher quality and in better locations. More about land prices will be said below.

Having rejected the hypothesis that the prices of populated and unpopulated land in a given area were equal, we estimated the prices of serfs and of populated land by the regression

$$V_p = c + P_S \cdot S + P_{Tp} \cdot T_p \tag{13.3}$$

where V_p is the total sales value of the populated estates sold in each county over the sample period, S is the number of serfs on the estates, and T_p is the amount of land on the estates, so that the coefficients P_S and P_{Tp} would give the prices of serfs and of populated land (c is a constant term). (The Statistical Appendix gives details.) The results are presented in Column 3 of Table 13.2. In the Central Agricultural, Lake, Lithuania, Little Russia, Southwest, New Russia, and Viatka-Perm' regions the regional serf prices were estimated directly by Regression Equation (13.3). In the other areas, that is, in the Central Industrial, White Russia, and the Volga regions, the hypothesis of a uniform serf price over the region

and

$$P_S^2 = \left(\frac{1}{\Sigma S}\right)[\Sigma V_p - \Sigma P_{Tu} T_p] \tag{13.2n}$$

where V_P is the value of populated estates; S and T_p are the number of serfs and the amounts of land, respectively, on such estates; T_u is the amount of unpopulated land sold; and P_{Tu} is the price of unpopulated land. It is obvious from (13.1n) that in the first method the average price of populated land in each region is the weighted average of prices of unpopulated land in each province weighted by the provincial quantities of unpopulated land. In the second method (13.2n), it is the provincial quantities of populated land that are used as weights, a procedure that seems to us more justifiable than the first.

From (13.1n) and (13.2n) it can easily be deduced that $P_S^1 > P_S^2$ if and only if

$$\frac{\Sigma P_{Tu} T_u}{\Sigma T_u} < \frac{\Sigma P_{Tu} T_p}{\Sigma T_p} \tag{13.3n}$$

A negative relationship between quantities and prices has been found by Gerschenkron and others. See his *A Dollar Index of Soviet Machinery Output, 1927–28 to 1937* (Santa Monica, California, 1952). For a mathematical treatment of the "Gerschenkron Effect" see E. Ames and J. A. Carolson, "Production Index Bias as a Measure of Economic Development," *Oxford Economic Papers,* 20 (March 1968), 12–24. If this effect holds for quantities and prices of land as well, then a negative relationship between the prices and quantities of unpopulated land is more probable than between the prices of the former and the quantities of populated land; hence, this inequality is likely to be true more often than not.

was rejected, and the prices in Column 3 are weighted averages of our provincial serf price estimates.

With the exception of Lithuania (see below) and the unimportant Viatka-Perm' region, the direct estimates of the regional serf prices presented in Column 3 of Table 13.2 are statistically significant (at the 95 percent confidence level), but a more detailed examination of our estimates given in Appendix Table 13.1 in the Statistical Appendix reveals a number of problems. In three provinces (Moscow, Saratov, and Orenburg), the provincial estimates of the serf prices are negative, although not significantly so.[55] In the Central Industrial and Lake regions, the spread of serf prices among the component provinces looks suspicious. In seven provinces and one whole region (White Russia), the estimated land prices are negative, although again none of them significantly so. The generally low significance and high standard errors of these estimates are presumably due to the high degree of correlation (collinearity) between the number of serfs and the quantity of land ($r = .80$).

Further problems are created by the heterogeneous character of labor and land as well as by the practice of reporting the number of serfs solely in terms of males ("souls"), both of which may be shown to be possible sources of bias in our estimates of the prices of land and serfs. In addition, the Russian custom of expressing a serfowner's wealth and status in terms of the number of souls he owned, and thus neglecting the quantity (and quality) of land in evaluating estates, might also have contributed to our comparatively low populated-land price estimates.[56] Finally, two

[55] The negative Moscow price is obviously wrong. In the adjacent province of Vladimir, the serf price was a suspiciously high 211.82 rubles – the highest of all shown in Appendix Table 13.1 in the Statistical Appendix. Sixty-five percent of all serfs in the Moscow province were on *obrok*, paying an average annual sum of 10.84 rubles. Capitalized at 8 percent per year, this would amount to a price of 135.50. Assuming that non-*obrok* serfs were only two-thirds as profitable as the ones on *obrok*, we obtain 120 rubles as the average serf price. Even if the non-*obrok* serfs were completely useless to their masters, the average serf would still be worth 88 rubles. For the Saratov and Orenburg provinces, where the proportions of *obrok* serfs were only 30.8 and 8.6 percent respectively, such an exercise is less meaningful, but, for whatever it is worth, the assumption of two-thirds would yield prices of 82 and 84 rubles, respectively. Of course the 8 percent capitalization rate and the assumption of two-thirds are arbitrary, but it is clear that any reasonable change in these magnitudes would also fail to reduce the serf prices in these three provinces to zero. (Sources are given in Table 13.2.)

The land redemption bonds given to the former serfowners after the Emancipation carried an interest rate of 6 percent per year. Hence the 8 percent capitalization rate used here looks reasonable. Although every serf was mortal, he or she was expected to leave offspring.

[56] See Essay 12, and Blum, *Lord*, p. 367. According to Pokrovskii, *Russkaia* [Russian], vol. 4, pp. 9–10, Nicholas I suggested to one of the committees on the peasant question that it should be forbidden to sell estates or to grant mortgages, unless the number of *desiatinas* was indicated next to the number of souls. In spite of this, published official

special causes might have depressed the prices of populated estates below their normal capitalized values and thus have resulted in lower prices of both land and serfs:

(1) In the middle of our period (1854–1858 inclusive), Alexander II made his famous announcement (on March 30, 1856) that the end of serfdom was in sight. Since the terms of Emancipation were not to be known for several years, the increased uncertainty might well have depressed the prices of serf estates and hence the prices of their land and serfs. In many areas, as noted above, the actual land and serf prices were found, surprisingly, to be below their official prices.

(2) Perhaps the most important reason for the low prices of serf estates was the legal restriction of their ownership to the members of the nobility, who were notoriously short of funds.[57]

Unfortunately, we do not know the net effect of all of these factors on our serf price estimates. Their reliability must be very modest at best. For this reason we also list in Table 13.2 the results of several other calculations, including one based on the official serf prices (Column 5). Columns 6 through 9 give the relative values of serfs as percentages of the total values of the estates to help our readers to form their own conclusions.

It is our impression that in the Central Industrial and Lake regions the main source of the serfowners' wealth was in serfs and not in land, while the opposite was true in the Black-soil areas. If so, our estimates of serf prices in Column 3 look reasonable in the first three regions, completely wrong in White Russia, not unreasonable in Little Russia, overstated in the Southwest, and possibly understated in New Russia and the Volga region (although male serfs in these last two regions constituted only 24

statistics on mortgages of populated estates indicated the number of (male) serfs but not the quantity of land. See "Bankovye dolgi i polozhenie gubernii v 1856 godu" ["Bank debts and the condition of provinces in 1856"], *Zhurnal ministerstva vnutrennikh del* [Journal of the Ministry of Internal Affairs] (1856), part 3, book 2, pp. 199–234. Many other examples can be given.

[57] For the nature of this restriction, see A. Romanovich-Slavatinskii, *Dvorianstvo v Rossii ot nachala XVIII veka do otmeny krepostnogo prava* [Nobility in Russia from the beginning of the eighteenth century to the abolition of serfdom] (St. Petersburg, 1870), pp. 272–86.

In D. Butovskii's note, "Prodazhnye tseny na zemli v Poltavskoi gubernii" ["Selling prices of land in Poltava Province"], *Zhurnal ministerstva vnutrennikh del* [Journal of the Ministry of Internal Affairs] (1860), book 1, pp. 1–8, the author remarks that Cossack lands in that province sold "incomparably" cheaply because only Cossacks were permitted to buy them. He also asserts that land prices in the sales reports ("Svedeniia" ["Data"]) were greatly understated.

Samarin, *Sochineniia* [Collected], vol. 2, p. 121, advocated that personal noblemen, honorary citizens, and merchants of the first two classes be permitted to buy populated estates. As a result of this measure, he expected the prices of these estates to rise. (He also expected the new owners to run their estates more efficiently.)

percent and 27 percent of all males respectively). Viatka-Perm', with its small number of serfs, is of little importance, and Lithuania represents a special case to be discussed below.

Our original intention was to test the hypothesis that serf prices were negatively correlated with the density of the serf or of the entire agricultural population and thus to be able to estimate the population density which would reduce serf prices to zero (if they were positive to begin with). This naive idea had to be abandoned. First, the serf population grew very little during the several decades preceding the Emancipation (although the free population continued to grow). Second, and more important, we found no relationship between real serf prices and land endowment per serf. We should have anticipated that the relationship between these two variables could go either way, depending upon soil, climate, and particularly on the presence of nonagricultural pursuits, such as existed in the Central Industrial and Lake regions.[58]

We did try another experiment – namely, the deflation of serf prices by the local prices of grain (see Appendix Table 13.2 in the Statistical Appendix). The regional results are given in Column 10 of Table 13.2. If our indices of grain prices were less crude and our serf price estimates more reliable, the results of this deflation would be of considerable interest. We shall treat both the grain price indices and the serf price estimates as if they were reliable, but with a clear warning to the reader. Figure 13.4 may help the reader to obtain a quick grasp of the relationship between nominal serf prices and the prices of grain.

The deflation of nominal serf prices by grain prices greatly reduces their variation across regions, lowering the coefficient of variation from .32 to .23. If we remove Lithuania (see below), this coefficient falls almost by half from .29 to .15. The ratio of the highest regional real serf price (in the Southwest) to the lowest (in New Russia) becomes only about 2, and as observed above, the former price was probably overstated and the latter understated.[59]

The results lead to two conclusions. The first is obvious: grain prices must have accounted for a large, and probably the largest, part of the

---

[58] In pre-famine Ireland (1841), village industries were found to be economically important, and the relationship between income and the land/labor ratio was negative. See Eric L. Almquist, "Pre-Famine Ireland and the Theory of European Proto-Industrialization: Evidence from the 1841 Census," *The Journal of Economic History*, 39 (Sept. 1979), 699–718, and Joel Mokyr, "Malthusian Models and Irish History," *The Journal of Economic History*, 40 (March 1980), 159–66.

[59] The ratio of the weighted slave price in the Lower South to that in the Upper South in the United States was 1.82 in 1830–1835 and gradually declined to 1.28 in 1856–1860. See Fogel and Engerman, *Time*, vol. 2, p. 73. The ratio of the highest to the lowest *state* price, however, would be more relevant here.

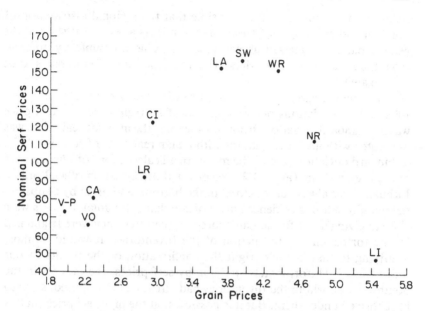

Figure 13.4. The relationship between the nominal prices of serfs and the prices of grain. *Note:* V-P – Viatka-Perm'; VO – Volga; CA – Central Agricultural; LR – Little Russia; CI – Central Industrial; LA – Lake; SW – Southwest; WR – White Russia; NR – New Russia; LI – Lithuania. *Sources:* Table 13.2 and sources of Appendix Tables 13.1 and 13.2 in the Statistical Appendix.

regional variation in nominal serf prices.[60] The second is more interesting. Since in Russia the masters decided where the serfs would live and work, an active interregional serf market would have transferred serfs from areas of low to high nominal serf prices and thus would have brought about a greater regional equality of nominal as opposed to real serf prices. This did not happen. Hence, the regional mobility of serfs must have been insufficient to lead to their optimal geographical distribution *from the masters' point of view.*[61] A high mobility of free workers, however, would have produced a smaller geographical variation of real wages than of nominal wages – a pattern that we did find in the regional distribution of serf prices. This would imply that the serf sector was closely integrated with the rest of the economy. Although plausible, the conclusion

[60] This positive correlation between regional grain and serf prices adds a bit more evidence against Pokrovskii's hypothesis examined in the First Model.
[61] The regional distribution of labor in a country may have several optimums depending on the goals of the decision-makers (such as serfowners or slaveowners, free workers, central planners, and so on).

is far from certain: it is quite possible that the regional distribution of nominal and real wages of free workers in Russia, even if it showed the general pattern suggested above, might have been completely different from the structure of serf prices. This important question remains to be investigated.[62]

Lithuania is clearly a special case. Its estimated nominal serf price was 1.8 standard deviations below the mean of all regions and its real price was 3.3 standard deviations below the mean. If the mean of real prices was calculated without Lithuania, the Lithuanian real price of serfs would be 5 standard deviations below the mean. In all calculations of regional serf prices presented in Table 13.2, except for those based on official prices, Lithuania was always at, or close to, the bottom, and often by a substantial margin. All this evidence may indicate that Lithuanian masters were close to giving up serfdom. Our sources suggest that they were frightened by the forthcoming introduction of the Inventories. It would be most gratifying to find in their fright the confirmation of the results of our Third Model. Unfortunately, judging by serf prices, the masters in the Southwest, on whom the Inventories had already been imposed, seem to have thrived under them. But it is possible that the high serf prices in this region were caused by special local conditions.[63]

Except for Lithuania, we found no other region where serfdom was coming to an end. (We did find that the serf price in Viatka-Perm' was not significantly different from zero, but the number of serfs there was small and was growing at an exceptionally rapid rate – hardly an indication of the end of serfdom.)[64] The assertion would carry more weight if

---

[62] Here are a few straws in the wind: with the exception of the Lake region, the percentage increases (or decreases) in the numbers of serfs and of free males in the period 1835–1859 by regions were positively correlated. The rank correlation between real prices of serfs and the percentage increases in free males by regions for that period would be reasonably high if not for the low nominal serf prices in New Russia and the Volga region obtained by our regression. As observed above, these two prices must have been underestimated.

[63] See Field, *The End,* pp. 80–81; and Blum, *Lord,* pp. 401, 579. The serfowners in the Southwestern region had a reputation for efficiency. Among other things, they cultivated sugar beets on a large scale.

It is, of course, impossible to judge the effectiveness of any particular set of Inventories without knowing local prices, wages, etc.

[64] Between 1835 and 1859 the number of serfs in the Viatka-Perm' region increased by 42.1 percent, as compared with an average increase in European Russia of only .95 percent. But these figures may not be completely comparable since they come from two separate sources and are subject to different definitions. The 1835 figures are taken from P. Keppen, *Deviataia reviziia: izsledovanie o chisle zhitelei v Rossii* [The ninth census: an investigation into the number of people in Russia] (St. Petersburg, 1857), pp. 199–200, and the 1859 figure from Troinitskii, *Krepostnoe* [The serf], p. 49 (English translation, pp. 61–63).

it were deduced from the behavior of time series data, but these we do not have.

If the behavior of serf prices before the Emancipation does not on the whole indicate the end of serfdom in Russia, neither do two other facts frequently mentioned by historians: the absence of growth of the serf population and the heavy indebtedness of the serfowners. It is true that between 1835 and 1859 the number of (male) serfs in European Russia remained practically constant, although with considerable regional variation.[65] But, as was explained by Troinitskii in 1861, and more thoroughly by Hoch and Augustine in 1979, the stagnation was caused not by the absence of natural increase but by other factors, the principal being the transfer of former soldiers of serf origin to the free estate.[66]

It is also true that by 1859 the total debt of serfowners to several governmental institutions had reached what Blum calls the "unbelievable amount" of 425.5 million rubles, involving the mortgage of 42.8 percent of all serf estates and 66.5 percent of all (male) serfs.[67] These figures give an exaggerated impression, however, of the burden of serfowners' debts: the total value of all serf estates in our sales data was 76.3 million rubles, and constituted only between 3.59 and 3.71 percent of the total value of all serf estates in the country.[68] Dividing 76.3 million by 3.65 percent (the mean of 3.59 and 3.71) we obtain 2,091 million rubles as the total value of all serf estates in the country. Of this amount, a mortgage debt of 425.5 million rubles constitutes only 20.3 percent. But Blum also mentions private debt. Although its total amount was unknown, in the Voronezh province it was estimated at almost 17 percent of the total debt. Taking this proportion as the national average (as Blum does), we raise the ratio of the debt to the value of the estates to 24.5 percent. Finally, one source mentions another 5.5 million of a special debt to the government, which was not included in the above figures.[69] This adds an extra 2.6 percent, bringing the total burden of the serfowners' debt to some 27 percent of the value of their estates. This is a very rough estimate, merely giving an order of magnitude. It is surely exaggerated because the values of the estates, as reported in the sales data, were understated. It does not suggest

---

[65] See the sources cited in footnote 64.

[66] See Troinitskii, *Krepostnoe* [The serf], pp. 55–56 (English translation, pp. 68–71); and Hoch and Augustine, "The Tax Censuses."

[67] See Blum, *Lord,* p. 380. The figures are from Troinitskii, *Krepostnoe* [The serf], p. 65, note 2 (English translation, p. 83, note 2).

[68] Calculated from data in "Svedeniia" ["Data"]; Skrebitskii, *Krest'ianskii* [Peasant], vol. 2, part 2, pp. 1492–1551; and Troinitskii, *Krepostnoe* [The serf], p. 45 (English translation, pp. 55–57).

[69] See Blum, *Lord,* p. 381. The magnitude of the special debt was taken from Skrebitskii, *Krest'ianskii* [Peasant], vol. 4, p. 1241.

a light burden, particularly for debtors known neither for their efficiency nor for their business sense, but it does not appear unbearable either, and it is certainly less alarming than the oft-quoted statement that two-thirds of all serfs had been mortgaged.[70]

In any case, the fact that Russian serfowners lived beyond their means – a common trait of the landowning classes – is no evidence that Russian serfdom had become or was becoming unprofitable. It is rather ironic that our only candidate for the termination of serfdom – Lithuania – had the second lowest burden of debt and the lowest percentage of serfs mortgaged.[71]

IV.   Concluding remarks

We have not found that the profitability of Russian serfdom before 1861 was threatened by the rise in grain prices, the growth of population, Paul's Law, or the use of the *obrok* system. The Inventories could have inflicted severe damage and they seem to have done so (or at least were threatening to) in Lithuania, but not in the Southwest or in White Russia.

These conclusions are based on a number of theoretical assumptions and on empirical data of uncertain quality. They should be treated as highly tentative.

Statistical appendix *by Mark J. Machina*

As mentioned in the text, the data consist of five cross-sectional series taken from the cumulative sales data over the period 1854 to 1858. We have for each county: the total value of all populated estates sold during the time period (V_p); the total number of souls (male serfs) on these estates (S); the total amount of land on these estates (T_p); the total value of all unpopulated estates sold during the time period (V_u); and the total

---

[70] In 1980, the ratio of all liabilities to all nonfinancial assets on American farms was 17.8 percent. See U.S. Department of Agriculture, *Agricultural Statistics 1980* (Washington, D.C., 1980), p. 425.

[71] The regional distribution of the serfowners' debts (without that special amount and without private debts) was taken from Skrebitskii, *Krest'ianskii* [Peasant], vol. 4, pp. 1246–49. We found the lowest ratio of debt to the value of serf estates to be in New Russia – 6.4 percent. (That region contained fewer than 400,000 serfs.) In Lithuania it was 12.2 percent. The highest percentage was in the Volga region (29.1), followed closely by White Russia, Viatka-Perm' and the Central Industrial region. A comparison of the burdens of landowners' debts over space and time should be very interesting.

The percentage of Lithuanian serfs mortgaged was taken from Blum, *Lord*, p. 381.

amount of land on these estates (T_u), with values measured in rubles and land measured in *desiatinas*.[72]

On the assumption that arbitrage led to a uniform implicit price of serfs throughout a given market, we would obtain the valuation equations:

$$V_p = P_S \cdot S + P_{Tp} \cdot T_p + \tilde{\epsilon}_p \tag{13.1a}$$

$$V_u = P_{Tu} \cdot T_u + \tilde{\epsilon}_u. \tag{13.2a}$$

for each observation (that is, county) in the market, where $\tilde{\epsilon}_p$ and $\tilde{\epsilon}_u$ are error terms with zero means.[73] If these valuation equations are correct, and if in addition the price of populated land P_{Tp} is equal to the price of unpopulated land P_{Tu}, then the most efficient means of estimating the serf and land prices in each market would be to stack (that is, combine) Equations (13.1a) and (13.2a) and run them over all counties in the market.

To test the hypothesis that P_{Tp} was equal to P_{Tu}, we ran the equation

$$V_p - V_u = c + P_S \cdot S + P_{Tp} \cdot (T_p - T_u) + q \cdot T_u + (\tilde{\epsilon}_p - \tilde{\epsilon}_u) \tag{13.3a}$$

over the whole country, allowing the coefficients P_S, P_{Tp}, and q to vary by province.[74] If the prices of populated and unpopulated land were the same in each county, the q coefficients would equal zero. But a test of the hypothesis that all the q coefficients were zero yielded rejection at the 5 percent (and indeed, the 1 percent) level, with 33 of the 42 provinces having negative q coefficients (8 of these significant at the 5 percent level) and only 9 provinces having positive values (with 1 significant at the 5 percent level).[75] This implies that the price of unpopulated land was generally

[72] Besides listing the above values for each county, the report also gives the provincial sums for each of the five series, as well as listing various ratios of these series for each county (T_p/S, V_p/S, V_p/T_p, and V_u/T_u). While these additional listings are strictly speaking redundant, they provide a means of cross-checking the original series for typographical errors. Such a check revealed about a dozen clearly identifiable typos – that is, where a particular correction in the listed data value served to make both the sum and the ratio(s) correct. However, this check also revealed inconsistencies between the original series, their sums, and their ratios, which could not be so easily corrected. Since the original calculations were in all likelihood performed on abaci, whenever there was any discrepancy, we adjusted (or did not adjust, accordingly) the listed data value on the assumption that the calculated sum rather than the calculated ratio was correct. The large number of counties for which *none* of the reported ratios were correct provides a further justification of this procedure.

[73] Not all counties reported sales of both populated and unpopulated estates.

[74] This equation was run over all counties that reported sales of both populated and unpopulated estates.

[75] The above estimation and test were performed correcting for heteroscedasticity in the manner described below.

higher than the price of populated land, so that in particular, the procedure of stacking Equations (13.1a) and (13.2a), or alternatively, the method used by Blum, *Lord* (see the text), would in general lead to upward-biased estimates of populated land prices, and accordingly, downward-biased estimates of serf prices. In light of this, we did not use the data on sales of unpopulated land in our subsequent estimation, and accordingly took as our sample those counties which listed sales of populated estates.

Estimation of Equation (13.1a) requires both a determination of the size of the "market" in which each county is located, as well as correction of any heteroscedasticity caused by the heterogeneous nature of land and labor and the method of reporting the number of serfs. To see how these latter factors could be a source of heteroscedasticity, note that while S is measured in souls and T_p is measured in physical units (*desiatinas*), P_S and P_{Tp} are most appropriately viewed as the prices per *efficiency unit* of labor and land. Accordingly, our "true" valuation equation is not (13.1a) but rather

$$V_p = P_S \cdot S^e + P_{Tp} \cdot T_p^e + \tilde{\omega}_p \tag{13.4a}$$

where S^e and T_p^e are the number of efficiency units of land and labor sold in each county, and may be expressed as

$$S^e = (1 + \tilde{\eta}_S) \cdot S \tag{13.5a}$$

$$T^e = (1 + \tilde{\eta}_{Tp}) \cdot T_p \tag{13.6a}$$

where $\tilde{\omega}_p$, $\tilde{\eta}_S$, and $\tilde{\eta}_{Tp}$ are random variables with zero means. Substituting (13.5a) and (13.6a) into (13.4a) yields

$$V_p = P_S \cdot S + P_{Tp} \cdot T_p + [P_S \cdot S \cdot \tilde{\eta}_S + P_{Tp} \cdot T_p \cdot \tilde{\eta}_{Tp} + \tilde{\omega}_p], \tag{13.7a}$$

which illustrates why the variance of the error term $\tilde{\epsilon}_p$ in (13.1a) may well vary.

In order to correct for this, we ran Equation (13.1a) (with the addition of a constant term) over the whole country, allowing the coefficients P_S and P_{Tp} to vary by province. If Equation (13.1a) were correctly specified and the market areas were at least the size of a province, this regression would yield consistent estimates of the coefficients, and hence consistent estimates $\hat{e}_p$ of the error terms $\tilde{\epsilon}_p$. We then ran the equation

$$\hat{e}_p^2 = c + \lambda \cdot S + \mu \cdot T_p \tag{13.8a}$$

over the entire country, with results

$$\hat{e}_p^2 = 9.39 \cdot 10^7 + 9.77 \cdot 10^5 \cdot S + 4{,}816 \cdot T_p + \text{error} \tag{13.9a}$$
$$(1.83 \cdot 10^8) \quad (1.91 \cdot 10^5) \quad (22{,}323)$$

where standard errors are in parentheses. Since neither the constant nor the coefficient of T_p were significant at the 5 percent level, whereas the coefficient of S was highly significant, we concluded that the variance of the error term in Equation (13.1a) is proportional to S,[76] and in all the following regressions corrected for heteroscedasticity by weighting each observation by $1/\sqrt{S}$.[77]

To determine the appropriate market sizes for serfs and land, we tested the hypotheses that serf or land prices were equal for all provinces in each of the ten regions of the country. Thus, for each region, we began by running Equation (13.1a) (with the addition of a constant term), allowing land prices to vary by province, and tested the hypothesis that the serf prices P_S were equal for all the provinces within the region. We then tested the hypothesis that the populated land prices P_{T_p} were equal for all the provinces in the region, allowing serf prices to vary or constraining them to be equal according to the outcome of the previous test.[78] Table 13A.1 contains our estimates of serf and land prices for each province, with the appropriate market size determined by the above tests.

The real serf prices reported in Appendix Table 13.2 were obtained in exactly the same manner as were the prices in Appendix Table 13.1, except that the series V_p was initially deflated by our provincial grain price series.

As mentioned in the text, two aspects of our data impinge upon the accuracy of these estimates. The high degree of correlation (that is, multicollinearity) between the number of serfs and the amount of land in the sales for each county ($r = .80$) leads to high standard errors of the estimates. A potentially more important problem is that of bias due to possible correlation of the error term with the regressors S and T_p. Unfortunately, a formal test of such correlation is not possible, lacking any variables to use as instruments. Since the results in (13.9a) suggest that $\bar{\eta}_S$ is an important source of variability, however, any tendency toward equality in the land/labor ratio measured in *efficiency* units in the sales bundles (or even the ratio of land to total serf population) would imply that high

---

[76] We also experimented with adding S^2, T_p^2, and other variables to the right side of this equation, with no change in the results.

[77] That the variance of the error term is essentially proportional to S is highly plausible, since each soul corresponds to a random number of efficiency units of labor (including any attendant women and children), and we might expect this variation to be independent across the S souls in each observation. It is somewhat surprising, however, that the variance of $\bar{\varepsilon}_p$ evidently does not depend upon the amount of land.

[78] All tests were at the 5 percent level. The order of the two tests (equality of serf prices, equality of land prices) was chosen more or less arbitrarily, and upon the assumption that serf prices were more likely to be equalized than land prices (serfs presumably being more homogeneous and more mobile than land). This conjecture is verified by the outcomes of the various tests (Appendix Tables 13.1 and 13.2).

Appendix Table 13.1. *Nominal prices of serfs and of populated land obtained by regression*

Region	Province	Serf price	Standard error	Land price	Standard error
Central Industrial	Tver'	158	27.8	−0.268	2.98
	Iaroslavl'	157	33.4	1.08	3.79
	Kostroma	149	22.7	−0.809	1.12
	N. Novgorod	120	44.4	15.9	6.71
	Vladimir	212	38.2	−6.18	4.54
	Moscow	−1.62	40.2	33.6	6.27
	Smolensk	80.8	60.2	6.65	6.38
	Kaluga	107	38.1	7.80	4.82
Central Agricultural	Orel ⎫				
	Tula ⎪				
	Riazan' ⎬	80.8	17.9	18.7	2.85
	Tambov ⎪				
	Voronezh ⎪				
	Kursk ⎭				
Lake	Novgorod ⎫			1.27	1.08
	Pskov ⎪			−0.313	2.64
	St. Petersburg ⎬	153	29.2	5.18	2.29
	Vologda ⎪			−2.12	2.25
	Olonets ⎭			−2.68	4.29
Lithuania	Kovno ⎫			22.6	2.76
	Vil'na ⎬	47.2	32.2	11.8	3.13
	Grodno ⎭			14.0	3.73
White Russia	Vitebsk	142	16.2 ⎫		
	Mogilev	126	11.8 ⎬	−0.416	0.663
	Minsk	184	13.7 ⎭		
Little Russia	Chernigov ⎫			5.03	3.26
	Poltava ⎬	92.5	25.1	12.2	3.62
	Khar'kov ⎭			15.4	2.64
Southwest	Kiev ⎫			12.8	2.52
	Volyniia ⎬	157	14.3	3.72	1.89
	Podoliia ⎭			9.59	2.27
New Russia	Kherson ⎫				
	Ekaterinoslav ⎬	113	38.0	12.5	1.69
	Tavrida ⎭				
Volga	Kazan'	212	42.6	−0.699	3.34
	Simbirsk	45.2	37.1	18.8	4.22
	Penza	109	49.5	8.75	6.95
	Saratov	−7.29	55.6	18.0	6.35
	Samara	127	15.1	3.74	0.931
	Orenburg	−19.4	71.5	11.0	5.94

Appendix Table 13.1 *(cont.)*

Region	Province	Serf price	Standard error	Land price	Standard error
Viatka-Perm'	Viatka ⎫ Perm' ⎭	78.3	53.8	2.08	2.24

Sources: See Appendix Table 13.2.

values of $\bar{\eta}_S$ would be associated with low values of S (male serfs) and high values of T_p (physical land), implying downward-biased estimates of serf prices and upward-biased estimates of land prices. On the other hand, if it were the case that more productive serfs were sold (or in other words, were bought) more frequently than less productive ones, then high values of $\bar{\eta}_S$ would be associated with high values of S, resulting in an opposite bias.

Appendix Table 13.2. *Real prices of serfs and of populated land obtained by regression*

Region	Province	Serf price	Standard error	Land price	Standard error
Central Industrial	Tver'	50.2	9.46	−0.0834	1.01
	Iaroslavl'	55.5	11.4	0.387	1.29
	Kostroma	54.0	7.71	−0.294	0.379
	N. Novgorod	45.7	15.1	6.05	2.28
	Vladimir	70.5	13.0	−2.05	1.54
	Moscow	−0.381	13.7	10.2	2.13
	Smolensk	25.1	20.4	2.12	2.17
	Kaluga	36.7	13.0	2.66	1.64
Central Agricultural	Orel ⎫ Tula ⎪ Riazan' ⎬ Tambov ⎪ Voronezh ⎪ Kursk ⎭	35.7	7.58	7.77	1.21
Lake	Novgorod ⎫ Pskov ⎪ St. Petersburg ⎬ Vologda ⎪ Olonets ⎭	37.6	4.94	0.496	0.235
Lithuania	Kovno ⎫ Vil'na ⎬ Grodno ⎭	9.24	6.06	3.77 2.30 2.80	0.520 0.590 0.703
White Russia	Vitebsk Mogilev Minsk	31.3 30.8 40.2	3.71 2.70 3.13	−0.0880	0.151
Little Russia	Chernigov ⎫ Poltava ⎬ Khar'kov ⎭	32.7	8.90	2.46 4.96 4.22	1.15 1.28 0.935
Southwest	Kiev Volyniia Podoliia	67.2 21.2 43.3	3.65 4.10 3.23	1.83	0.473
New Russia	Kherson ⎫ Ekaterinoslav ⎬ Tavrida ⎭	22.0	14.3	3.33 2.95 1.76	0.600 0.903 0.492
Volga	Kazan'	100	19.7	−0.334	1.54
	Simbirsk	21.4	17.2	8.85	1.95
	Penza	57.6	22.9	4.55	3.21
	Saratov	−3.06	25.7	7.59	2.94
	Samara	52.0	6.99	1.53	0.431
	Orenburg	−8.13	33.1	4.53	2.75

Appendix Table 13.2 *(cont.)*

Region	Province	Serf price	Standard error	Land price	Standard error
Viatka-Perm'	Viatka ⎤ Perm' ⎦	39.9	27.4	1.06	1.14

Sources to Appendix Tables 13.1 and 13.2: "Svedeniia" ["Data"]. The deflator consisted of a weighted average of prices of rye, oats, and wheat only. The prices of rye (for 1846–1855) and of oats (for 1847–1856) were taken from Koval'chenko and Milov, *Vserossiiskii* [All-Russian], pp. 394–97. Prices of wheat were calculated by us from materials published in a number of issues of the *Zhurnal ministerstva vnutrennikh del* [The Journal of the Ministry of Internal Affairs] for the period 1846–1856. The numerous gaps in the data were filled by us in a "reasonable" manner. The production figures of rye, oats, and wheat for the period 1870–1874 used as weights were taken from Iu. E. Ianson, *Sravnitel'naia statistika Rossii i Zapadno-evropeiskikh gosudarstv* [Comparative statistics of Russia and of West-European countries] (St. Petersburg, 1880), vol. 2, pp. 308–09, 419–21.

Were Russian serfs overcharged for their land by the 1861 Emancipation? The history of one historical table

> Ah, don't say that you agree with me. When people agree with me I always feel that I must be wrong.
>
> Oscar Wilde, *The Critic as Artist*

> It were not best that we should all think alike: it is difference of opinion that makes horse races.
>
> Mark Twain, *Pudd'nhead Wilson*

If five economists are said to express six opinions about a current event, how many opinions should be expected from five historians about an event that took place over a hundred years ago? I am referring to the allegedly excessive prices charged the former Russian serfs for the land allotted to them by the provisions of the 1861 Emancipation. That these prices were found excessive by several historians is not surprising – what else could have been expected from the gentry-dominated tsarist government of the time? – but that these historians would agree on the *exact magnitude* of the overcharge does appear a bit strange. The data shown in Table 14.1 (taken here from Gerschenkron) have been presented time and again.[1]

The reasons for this unusual unanimity are not far to seek: the historians took these figures from the same source, a paper published by A.

Reprinted by permission from the proceedings of the Conference on the *Agrarian Organization in the Century of Industrialization: Europe, Russia and North America,* held in Montreal in 1984 and published by JAI Press, Greenwich, Conn., 1989.

The two epigraphs were added, the first and the last paragraph were rewritten, and a few minor changes were made in the original text.

Thanks are due to Marina Goldberg, then an undergraduate student at Yale University, for her assistance in the early stages of this essay, to the National Science Foundation (Grant No. SES-7709307) for financial support, and to Professor Mark Machina for helpful comments.

[1] Here are a few examples: G. T. Robinson, *Rural Russia under the Old Regime* (Berkeley, 1932, 1960), p. 88; M. N. Pokrovskii, *Russkaia istoriia s drevneishikh vremen* [Russian history from ancient times] (Moscow, 1934), Vol. 4, p. 93; A. G. Mazur, *Russia Past and Present* (New York, 1951), p. 164 (he cites the figures in the text instead of using a table); P. I. Liashchenko, *Istoriia narodnogo khoziaistva SSSR* [History of the people's economy of the USSR] (Moscow, 1956), Vol. 1, p. 584; A. Gerschenkron, "Agrarian Policies and Industrialization: Russia 1861-1917," *The Cambridge Economic History of Europe* (Cambridge, 1965), Vol. 6, Part 2, p. 738.

Table 14.1. *The basic data*

	Allotment land in thousands of dessyatinas (1)	Value of allotment land at free market prices in millions of roubles		Value of allotment land at redemption valuations (4)	Column 4 as percentage of column 3 (5)
		1854–8 (2)	1863–72 (3)		
Non-black-earth provinces	12,286	155	180	342	190
Black-earth provinces	9,841	219	284	342	120
Western provinces	10,141	170	184	183	100
Total for the three zones	32,268[a]	544	648	867	134

[a] For some reason the total of column 1 (32,268) is missing from his table.
Source: A. Gerschenkron, "Agrarian Policies and Industrialization: Russia 1861–1917," *The Cambridge Economic History of Europe* (Cambridge, 1965), Vol. 6, Part 2, p. 738. One *desiatina* (spelled by Gershenkron as *dessyatina*) = 1.09 hectares.

Lositskii in St. Petersburg in 1906. They accepted his figures on faith, without examining the origin of his data and the nature of his assumptions. They did not even check his arithmetic.[2]

Obviously, to calculate the alleged overcharge for the allotted land, we must establish the correct magnitudes of three variables: (1) the quantity of land allotted to the peasants, (2) the amount they were charged for it, and (3) the amount that they should have paid at "free market prices." The Emancipation was an extremely complex operation lasting some twenty years. The quantity of land allotted to the peasants and the amounts charged for it in the various areas were adjusted and readjusted many times. Therefore, any composite figure, even as simple as the quantity of land or the charge for it, may be subject to a good margin of error. Although my own research in this area has been confined to market land prices, I shall make a few brief remarks about the other two variables.

Lositskii gave very few sources of his data. All I could do with the quantity of the allotted land was to correct his additions and to compare

[2] A. Lositskii, *Vykupnaia operatsiia* [The redemption operation] (St. Petersburg, 1906). Actually, he was more concerned with the excessive interest rate charged the peasants for the money lent to them than with the inflated prices for the land.

Table 14.2. *The quantity of allotted land (thousands of* desiatinas*)*

	(1) From Lositskii (corrected)	(2) From Zaionchkovskii (adjusted)	(3) Percentage difference between col. 2 and col. 1	(4) Recalculated col. 5 of Table 14.1
Non-black-earth provinces	12,286.5	13,002.6	5.8	181
Black-earth provinces	9,876.9	10,771.1	9.1	113
Western provinces	10,141.1	10,113.5	−0.3	98
Total for the three zones	32,304.5	33,887.2	4.9	128

Sources: Lositskii, op. cit., pp. 38–39; Zaionchkovskii, op. cit., pp. 431–43. Additional explanations of these figures are given in note 3.

his figures with those published by the Soviet historian Zaionchkovskii in 1958. In cases of disagreement, I decided to use the latter's figures because Zaionchkovskii knew of Lositskii's work and seemed to have done a more thorough job. But as Table 14.2 shows, the differences turned out to be small.[3]

I have been unable to check Lositskii's figures on the total cost of land charged the peasants;[4] hence, for the purposes of this essay they are ac-

[3] P. A. Zaionchkovskii, *Provedenie v zhizn' krest'ianskoi reformy 1861 g.* [The actual conduct of the peasant reform in 1861] (Moscow, 1958), particularly pp. 431–43. In eight provinces, the data for one county each is missing. I added the missing figures by assuming that the quantity of land allotted to the peasants in each missing county was proportional to the quantity of populated land (serf estates) in that county.

Lositskii's work is rather sloppy, and his assumptions are not always consistent. He might have used the wrong weights in obtaining provincial land prices from county data. My experiments with alternative sets of weights changed some provincial figures but had little effect on regional totals. The details of my corrections and adjustments are not discussed here because they are not important for this essay.

[4] Lositskii mentioned the *Report of the State Bank* for 1893 as the source of his data, but the search in the 1892 and 1893 reports turned up nothing. It is likely that he referred to a special publication of the State Bank in 1893, but no such report was found in the Widener and the Union catalogues.

According to him, the financial records of the redemption operation were kept so badly that two ministers of finance (S. Greig and N. Bunge) left office before they could get an exact report.

cepted. Of the several totals he gave, I chose the ones that looked most reliable.[5]

Our next task, of greater interest to an economist, is finding those "free market prices" that the peasants should have paid. Table 14.1 evaluates the land allotment in two sets of prices: for the periods 1854–58 and 1863–72. Gerschenkron's use of the 1863–72 prices for the calculations presented in column 5 of Table 14.1 suggests that he considered them more relevant than the 1854–58 prices. He was probably right, but unfortunately the reliability of the 1863–72 prices does not support the trust he placed in them. They were described by D. A. Rikhter, the author of an important paper on land prices and a recognized expert on the subject, as fragmentary and incomplete:

... The number of statements relating to [land sales in] the 1863–72 period is insignificant and the statements themselves are subject to doubt because there is no indication that they are based on concrete cases [of land sales]. It can be surmised that they are recorded on the basis of accidental recollections of the correspondents.

He also mentioned that the data were assembled in 1883 and 1889, that is, some ten or twenty years after the land sales had supposedly taken place.[6] On reading this evaluation of the 1863–72 prices, I lost further interest in them.

Having rejected the 1863–72 land prices as unreliable, Rikhter then proceeded to bring to his readers' attention another set of price data – for 1854–58 (published in 1859) – that he regarded highly and that, judging by the title of his paper, must have been forgotten by that time (1897).

Because these data were described and analyzed in considerable detail in Essay 13, I can be brief here.[7] They consist of reports of actual land

---

[5] In the text of his paper (p. 12), the total amount charged the peasants is 897 million rubles; in his summary table (p. 16) (from which our Table 14.1 must have been derived) it is 866.6, and a recalculation of the addition in his detailed table (by provinces, pp. 38–39) produced 870.2. No explanation for these discrepancies is given. Fortunately, they are small. Until a professional historian skilled in archival research finds something better, I shall use the corrected figures from that detailed table, but because some of the relevant data are lacking for three provinces (Don, Ufa, and Astrakhan') both the quantity of land allotted there and the charges for it are excluded from figures used in the subsequent discussion and in Table 14.3. This omission is of little importance.

[6] D. I. Rikhter, "Zabytyi material po statistike prodazhnykh tsen na zemliu" ["Forgotten materials on the statistics of sale prices of land"] *Trudy Imperatorskogo Vol'nogo Ekonomicheskogo Obshchestva* [Works of the Imperial Free Economic Society], 1897, Vol. 2, Book 4, pp. 1–23.

[7] See Essay 13 which gives a detailed list of sources. The report on the 1854–58 prices "Svedeniia o prodazhnykh tsenakh na zemli" ["Data on selling prices of land"] was published in the *Zhurnal ministerstva vnutrennikh del* [The Journal of the Ministry of Internal Affairs], 1859, Book 7, pp. 1–46; Book 8, pp. 95–118.

sales classified by provinces (*gubernii*) and counties (*uezdy*) for that five-year period and divided into sales of populated land (with serfs) and of unpopulated land. The main obstacle to deriving prices of populated land is the difficulty of separating the value of land from the value of serfs. Lositskii attempted no such separation; he simply assumed that prices of populated and of unpopulated land (in each area) were equal.[8] A formal statistical test rejected (on the 5 percent level) this assumption. Rather surprisingly, populated land turned out to have been much cheaper than unpopulated land. If so, the peasants might have been overcharged much more than Lositskii and his followers have suggested.[9]

To find the prices of populated land, we ran a regression of the values of the populated estates against the number of *desiatinas* and the number of serfs on them in each area. Unfortunately, the rather high correlation between these two variables may have made the estimates of them imprecise, and the heterogeneous character of land may have imparted a downward bias to the estimated land prices.[10]

Perhaps a rough idea of the magnitude of the overcharge imposed on the peasants can be obtained by other, less sophisticated, methods. It has been estimated that the total value of all serf estates in the country amounted to some 2,100 million rubles and that they contained about 98 million *desiatinas* of land.[11] The 33 million *desiatinas* received by the peasants thus constituted some 34 percent of land owned by their former masters, and the payment of some 856 million rubles about 41 percent of the value of the estates. A sizable overcharge is already in sight. But the estates contained not only land but also serfs. (The peasants were not supposed to buy their freedom.) If we could find the fraction of the market value of the estates embodied in land, we could easily calculate the market price per *desiatina,* compare it with the price charged to the peasants, and thus estimate the magnitude of the overcharge.

The sales reports also contain the official prices of land and of serfs (by provinces) used by the government for granting loans secured by the estates. The editor explicitly warned the users of the reports that these official prices were set below market prices, but said nothing about the *relative* understatement of land and of serf prices.[12] As an experiment, let us assume that these prices were understated in the same proportion so that

---

[8] This assumption was made by several historians in spite of a specific warning against it. See Essay 13, pp. 264–65.

[9] Ibid., pp. 272–79.

[10] Ibid., pp. 265–66.

[11] The sources and methods are given in ibid., p. 271. All these figures exclude the provinces mentioned in note 5.

[12] Ibid., pp. 261–62.

the *ratios* between the prices of land and the prices of serfs in a given province remained reasonably correct. Now by evaluating the estates in the sales reports at these official prices (in a given area), we can find the fraction of the values of the estates represented by land. The results are presented in column 1 of Table 14.3.

They are a bit surprising. According to the traditional view, land constituted the major part of a serfowner's wealth in the South (the black-earth zone), but not in the North (the non-black-earth zone) because in the South the combination of soil and climate favored agriculture, while in the North a good part of the master's income came from the nonagricultural pursuits of his serfs.[13] My calculations do not confirm this view; the fractions of the values of the estates in the sales report represented by land turned out to be very similar in the several zones; if anything, the non-black-soil figure is a bit higher than the others.[14] It is possible that the official prices of land and of serfs were set by the governmental lending institutions so arbitrarily that even the price ratios used in the present experiment make little sense. On the other hand, grain was cheap in the South and expensive in the North, particularly before the construction of railroads, and it is the value of the harvest rather than its quantity that is reflected in the price of land.[15] These results are certainly insufficient to reject the traditional view, but they may be good enough to plant a seed of doubt about it in the reader's mind.

The combination of the figures in columns 1 and 2 gives the value of land on the serf estates, and its division by the number of *desiatinas* produces an estimate of the market price of a *desiatina* of land (in each zone) that the peasants should have paid (column 4). The last column gives the ratio between the actual price paid by the peasants and this calculated market price. These ratios, whether taken by themselves or compared with Lositskii's estimates in Table 14.1, are amazing, to put it mildly: on the average, the peasants were overcharged more than three times; in both black-earth and non-black-earth zones they overpaid more than four times, and only in the West were they lucky to escape with a modest double price!

That the overcharges in the first two zones were nearly the same again contradicts the accepted view that the peasants in the North suffered more.[16]

---

[13] See Gerschenkron, op. cit., p. 730.

[14] There was also little variation in this ratio among the several regions comprising each zone. The two highest ratios were in White Russia (47.7 percent) and in the Lake Region (46.4 percent), neither region belonging to the black-earth zone. In the other regions, the ratios were around 35 percent.

[15] The weighted average official price of land (in the sales reports) in the black-earth zone was only 3 percent above that in the non-black-earth zone.

[16] See Table 14.1 and Gerschenkron's discussion, op. cit., pp. 739–40.

Table 14.3. An estimate of the overcharge

	(1) Value of land on serf estates as percentage of their total value at official prices	(2) Estimated value of all populated estates in the country in millions of rubles	(3) Total value of land on serf estates in millions of rubles (1) × (2)	(4) Total land area on serf estates in thousands of desiatinas	(5) Average market price per desiatina on serf estates in rubles (3) ÷ (4)	(6) Price per desiatina of allotted land charged to peasants in rubles	(7) Overcharge ratio (5) ÷ (4)
Non-black-earth provinces	37.9	570.1	216	35,211	6.14	26.30	4.28
Black-earth provinces	32.1	850.6	273	35,992	7.57	31.75	4.19
Western provinces	36.5	671.4	245	27,048	9.07	18.09	1.99
Total and weighted averages for the three zones	35.4	2,090.9	740	98,251	7.53	25.58	3.40

Notes and sources:

Column 1: From the reports on land sales by the method described in the text.

Column 2: Estimated by the method described in Essay 13, p. 271.

Column 3: By multiplying column 1 and column 2. The zonal values do not add up to the total exactly because each was estimated separately.

Column 4: From Essay 13, p. 261.

Column 6: From Tables 14.1 and 14.2.

The data in this table differ from those in Tables 14.1 and 14.2 because of the exclusion here of the three unimportant provinces of Don, Ufa, and Astrakhan', for which full data were not available.

A different method of estimating land market prices, although still based on official prices, gave somewhat more conventional results: the overcharge ratio was *at least* 4 in the North, 3.3 in the South, and 1.9 in the West.[17]

But it is unlikely that even the tsarist regime, acting as it did in the interests of the serfowners (the *pomeshchiki*), could have perpetrated such a fraud. There must be some other explanations of these fantastic ratios. Indeed, there are.

First, as mentioned above, the official prices, even if used as price ratios, might be completely wrong.

Second, our basic source of information is the reports of land sales. How good a sample do these reports constitute?

Third, the reported sale values of serf estates must have been grossly understated (to reduce transfer duties). In fact, in a number of provinces the values of estates as reported were below those calculated on the basis of official prices.[18] If the reported prices had been correct, it would have paid some enterprising members of the gentry (if there were any) to buy up serf estates, mortgage them, and never repay the loans. But if the values of the serf estates were so understated, is it likely that the prices of unpopulated land used by Lositskii had been reported truthfully?

---

[17] Perhaps a bit of simple algebra will clarify the nature of both methods. For every serf-owning unit (an estate, a country, a province, etc.) there is the identity

$$V = P_S S + P_T T, \tag{14.1n}$$

where V is the value of the unit, P_S and P_T are market prices of serfs and of land respectively, S is the number of serfs, and T is the number of *desiatinas* of land. To find the magnitude of P_T, we need a second relationship between the two prices. The first method provides it by the assumption that

$$\frac{P_S}{P_T} = \frac{P_{SO}}{P_{TO}}, \tag{14.2n}$$

where P_{SO} and P_{TO} are official prices of serfs and of land respectively, so that the ratio P_{SO}/P_{TO} is a given constant for a certain unit (or area). The substitution of (14.2n) into (14.1n) quickly determines the magnitude of P_T.

The second method also starts with the identity (14.1n), but instead of using (14.2n) it assumes (as asserted by the editor of the sales reports) that $P_{SO} \leq P_S$. Therefore

$$P_T \leq \frac{V - P_{SO} S}{T}. \tag{14.3n}$$

In other words, the use of the official price for serfs gives us the *maximum* magnitude that the price of land can attain.

The lower overcharge for the West obtained by all three methods undoubtedly reflects the desire of the Russian government to earn the support of the peasants, many of them Greek-Orthodox, against their Catholic masters.

[18] To complicate things further, we note that the values of certain estates, the patrimonies, might have been overstated.

Fourth, a sharp recent drop in the values of serf estates, not yet reflected in the official land and serf prices, might have been caused by the rumors of the forthcoming Emancipation.

Fifth, there might have also been more permanent reasons for the depressed prices of serf estates. Probably the most important one was the legal restriction on their purchase and ownership to the members of the nobility (*dvorianstvo*), a class notorious for lack of cash and absence of business sense.

It is also likely that the Russian habit of evaluating an estate in terms of the number of serfs on it (which determined the owner's social status) rather than in terms of its land area contributed to the low market prices of populated land.

So far I have not considered the possibility that the land allotted to the peasants might have differed in quality, broadly defined, from the rest of the populated land. There is much anecdotal evidence that some masters contrived to allot their former serfs poorer land. On the other hand, the law required the allotments to consist of "serviceable" land (*udobnaia zemlia*) only.[19] This would imply that the peasants received their farmstead, arable, and some meadows, to the exclusion of waste, pasture, and forest. Was a *desiatina* of allotted land more or less valuable than the average *desiatina* on the serf estates?[20]

There is one more qualification. The market prices of land (like most prices) are the results of marginal transactions involving small fractions of the total stock of land (only 0.7 percent per year in the present case). Do these market prices really apply to the giant land transfer engineered by the Emancipation? Suppose that the compulsory transfer of land from the masters to the former serfs had never taken place, and that instead the peasants had been lent the same 870 million rubles to buy land on the free market. What prices would they have paid, and how much land would they have acquired?[21]

What conclusions can we draw? Were the peasants overcharged for their land? They most probably were. Perhaps they were overcharged much more than anyone has ever suggested. And perhaps much less, or not at all. The five historians with whom my story began could well afford to express six opinions. And even more than six.

[19] See Zaionchkovskii, op. cit., pp. 142–45.
[20] There is also a point made by Gerschenkron (op. cit., pp. 740, 745–56) that the restrictions imposed on the ownership and use of the allotted land made it less valuable for the peasants.
[21] When one American corporation takes over another, the stockholders of the latter are usually paid some 20–30 percent more than the market price of their shares. See M. C. Jensen and R. S. Ruback, "The Market for Corporate Control: The Scientific Evidence," *The Journal of Financial Economics*, Vol. 11 (1983), pp. 5–50.

Index

Abramov, F., 187n
Abramovitz, Moses, 50
aggregation, 58–63, 108, 113; *see also*
    integration
agriculture
    growth of labor productivity in, 95
    Soviet policy for, 190
    technological progress in, 105
Allen, R. D. G., 212
Almquist, Eric L., 268n
Ames, Edward, 130n, 207n, 265n
Antonov, O. K., 20n, 138
arithmetic index, to compare Soviet and
    U.S. economic efficiency, 128–31
arithmetic measurements of productivity,
    50, 87–90
Arrow, Kenneth J., 53n, 75n
Augustine, W. R., 251n, 271
Aukrust, Odd, 50n
Averch, H., 177n

Baran, Paul, 16n
Baron, Harold, 16n
Baumol, William J., 177n, 216n
Becker, Gary S., 22–23
Bellamy, Edward, 27, 39
Bergmann, Barbara, 23n
Bergson, Abram, xiv, xv, 36n, 43n, 77n,
    90n, 126–27, 131–37, 147n, 153n, 157n
Berliner, Joseph, 41n, 42n, 90
Bishop, Robert L., 29n, 46n
Blum, Jerome, 230n, 231n, 232, 233n, 234,
    238, 239, 240n, 241n, 242, 244, 250n,
    252n, 254n, 258n, 259, 261n, 264,
    266n, 270n, 271, 272n, 274
Board of Governors, Federal Reserve
    System, 114n, 115n, 123n
bonus, 205, 207, 209–16
Bornstein, Morris, 202n, 203n
Bowden, Peter J., 236n
Bowles, S., 18n
Brown, William H., Jr., 175n
Brownlow, W. R., 234n, 235n, 236n

Burns, A. F., 114n
Butovskii, D., 267n

Cairnes, J. E., 237n
Campbell, Robert W., 158n
Canada
    growth of capital productivity in, 98–101
    growth of labor productivity in, 95–98
    growth of output in, 93
    rate of growth of Residuals, 101–6
capital
    formation in Soviet Union and U.S.,
        147, 150
    formation of, 58, 65
    productivity in Soviet Union and U.S.
        for, 153, 156–57
    rates of return in Soviet Union and
        U.S., 133
    see also inventory
capital goods prices, 150
capitalism, 5–7
    components for analysis of, 16
    defense of, 18–27
    demand under, 34–35
    economic power and risk under, 32–38
    objections to and evils of, 7, 15–17, 25–26
    power under, 35–38
    worker and consumer under, 19–21
capital stock
    depreciation charge against, 133
    in determining depreciation, 57–58
Carolson, John A., 130n, 265n
Carter, Anne P., 119
Carter, C. F., 115n
Chamberlin, Edward, 35n
Chenery, Hollis B., 75n
Cheung, Steven N., 42n
China, 9, 10
Cole, G. D. H., 31n
collective farms
    as producer cooperatives, 176–90
    system of, in Soviet Union, 190–92
    see also producer cooperatives

Collier, Irwin L., Jr., 46n
common markets, 12
communism, 13–14, 113
competition
    for labor under serfdom, 225–27
    perfect and monopolistic, 33–34
Conrad, Alfred H., 229n, 236n, 237
consumers, 40–41
    in capitalist countries, 19–21, 35
    comparison of, under capitalism and
        socialism, 45–46
    power of, 36–37
    under socialism, 38–42
    in Soviet Union, 19
Creamer, Daniel, 150n
Crosland, Richard, 30n
Crowe, W. R., 115n

Davis, Hiram S., 50, 87
decision making, economic, 3–6
demand
    under capitalism, 34–35
    effect in socialist countries of excess,
        40–44, 203–4
    elasticity of, in compensation model,
        208–12
    excess, 43–44
Denison, Edward F., 78n, 87n, 130n
depreciation
    of capital stock, in Soviet Union and
        U.S., 133–34
    treatment in geometric index, to identify
        Residual, 57–58, 64–65, 69
De Witt, Nicholas, 144n
Diamond, Peter A., 219n
Dich, Joergen, 31n
disaggregation, 108, 113
discrimination, racial, 22–23; see also
    sexism
Domar, Evsey, xin, 147n
Dovring, Folke, 258–59n

economic development, 3, 10–12, 146; see
    also underdeveloped countries
economic growth
    comparison of, between Soviet Union
        and U.S., 152
    effect of technological change on, 49
    measurement of "effort" in achieving,
        144–45, 150
    of output, in selected countries, 93
    see also capital; technological change
economic power
    under capitalism, 35–38
    as criterion to compare capitalism and
        socialism, 31

of excess demand, 40–44
    under socialism, 38, 42
    see also monopoly power
education, 11
Edwards, Richard C., xiin, 15–27, 29n, 39n
efficiency, 135–40
"effort," see economic growth
Ellman, Michael, 203n
emancipation of serfs, in Russia, 239, 281
Engels, Friedrich, 31n
Engerman, Stanley L., 237, 263n, 268n
engineers, 165, 170
Ernst, Maurice, 123n
excess demand, see demand

Fabricant, Solomon, 76–77, 80n, 85, 86,
    111, 115
Fedorov, V. A., 239n, 252n, 260n
Fel'dman, G. A., 146n
Felker, Jere E., 202n
Fenoaltea, Stefano, 259n
Field, Daniel, 239, 270n
firms
    government-owned, 31
    privately-owned, 31, 33–34
first-in-first-out accounting, see inventory
Fisher, Irving, 114n
Fogel, Robert W., 263n, 268n
foreign aid policy, 12
free trade areas, 12
Frickey, E., 112
Friedman, Milton, 26
Fusfeld, Daniel R., 202n, 203n

Galbraith, John K., 35n, 215–216
Ganshof, François Louis, 234
Geary, R. C., 115
Gehman, Clayton, 115, 123
Genovese, Eugene, 238
geometric index
    compared with arithmetic index, 79–80
    to compare Soviet and U.S. economic
        efficiency, 132–35
    to measure Residual, 54–69
    preference for, 127
    Rules I and II for, 55, 58–63, 65–66
    value-added, 67–69
Germany
    growth of capital productivity in, 98–101
    growth of labor productivity in, 95–98
    growth of output in, 93
    rate of growth of Residuals, 101–6
Gerschenkron, A., 10, 108n, 112, 130–31,
    239, 247n, 264n, 265n, 280, 283, 285n
Gerschenkron Effect, 130–32, 153n
Gintis, Herbert, 19

Gogol, Nikolai, 232n
Goldman, Marshall I., 159n
Goncharov, Ivan, 233n
Gorbachev, M. S., xviii
Gordon, Robert A., 86n, 145n, 152n
Gorz, Andre, 18n
grain prices, effect of rise in, 240, 247–49, 268–69
Gray, Lewis C., 229n
Grekov, B. D., 231n, 232, 233
Griliches, Zvi, 57n, 137n
Grousset, René, 30n

Hagen, Everett E., 49n
Harney, M. P., 22n
Harrod–Domar model, 53
Heckman, James J., 37n
Hicks, John, 180
Hirschman, Albert O., 29n
Hirshleifer, Jack, 215n
Hobsbawm, E. J., 16n
Hoch, S. I., 251n, 271
Hodgman, D. R., 108n, 114n
Hogarth, C. J., 225n
Holzman, Franklyn D., 41n
Horwitz, Bertrand N., 203n
human problems, in economic development, 10–12
Hunnius, C., 18n
Hymer, Bennet, 16n

Iadov, V. A., 18
imperialism, 24–25
income distribution under capitalism, 21–22, 25
index, value-added of "pure" type, 111
index numbers, construction of, 126–28
index of domestic material inputs, 112–13
index of final products, 111–12
index of imports, 112
index of industrial production
    comparison among theoretical indices, 110–24
    "pure" Soviet-type, 109–13
    of Soviet Union, 107
    theoretical problems of aggregation in, 108–9
index of output with value-added weights, 113, 115
Index of Structural Change, xiii, 4, 69–72, 116
Index of Technical Change, 4
Index of Total Factor Productivity, xiii, 4, 76–78, 85–87, 116, 127, 137, 145
Indova, E. I., 252n, 260n
industrial capacity, 93

industrialization, 144, 146
inequality, 21–22
inflation, 204
input, in Kendrick's Index, 80–81, 83
input–output method
    comparison among systems for, 63
    techniques of Soviet planners for, 3
    use of tables for obtaining empirical results, 118–19, 122
integration, in geometric index, 58–63
Inventories system, 245, 253–57, 259
inventory
    comparison of, in Soviet Union and U.S., 157–58
    gross and net, 66

Japan
    growth of labor and capital productivity in, 95, 98, 101
    growth of output in, 93
    rate of growth of Residuals, 101–6
Jasny, N., 108n
Jencks, C., 18n
Jenkins, D., 18n
Jensen, M. C., 288n
Johnson, L., 177n
Jones, Ronald W., 248n
Jonung, Lars, 209n
Jorgenson, Dale W., 137n

Kahan, Arcadius, xin
Kaplan, N. M., 108n, 111, 114n, 115n, 156n, 163
Karlin, Samuel, 53n
Katsenelinboigen, Aron, 258n
Kendrick, John, xiv, xv, 4, 49n, 50, 73–87, 92, 93n, 98n, 101n, 103n, 105n, 116, 127, 131n, 145n, 153, 165n, 170n, 171, 175
Kendrick's Index, see Index of Total Factor Productivity
Keppen, P., 270n
Keynes, John M., 34
Kirkpatrick, Nora, 49n
Klein, Lawrence R., 54–55n, 59n
Kliuchevskii, V., xvii, 225–26, 230n, 231n, 232n, 233, 245n, 249n
kolkhozes, see collective farms
Kornai, Janos, 29n, 34, 46n
Korol, Alexander, 144n, 165
Kosygin, Alexei, xvi, 202–3, 205, 209
Koval'chenko, I. D., 239n, 241n, 245n, 252n, 258n, 259n, 260n
Kravis, Irving B., 86n
Kuh, Edwin, 63n
Kuznets, Simon, 21, 73, 77n, 98n, 112, 150, 153, 156, 157n

labor force
   distribution of, in Soviet Union and
      U.S., 158–59
   in Russia, as a cause of serfdom, 225–27
labor input, *see* productivity
labor market, effect of excess demand in,
      41–42
land allocation
   effect of population growth on, 242–49
   under Inventories system, 253–57
   under *obrok* system, 257–60
   under Paul's Law, 250–252
   in Russia after Emancipation, 281
   see also Inventories system; *obrok*
      system; Paul's Law
landowner, *see* serfowner
land prices, in Russia
   after Emancipation, 280, 282–85, 287–88
   data for, 261
   statistical analysis of, 272–77
Lange, Oscar, 5, 29n, 40n
last-in-first-out accounting, *see* inventory
Latimer, Hugh (Bishop), 236
Lebergott, Stanley, 81n
Leontief, Wassily, xiii, 4, 50, 69–72, 116,
      118
Liashchenko, P. I., 239n, 264n, 280n
Lipson, E., 236n
Lithuania, serf market in, 270, 272; *see
      also* Poland-Lithuania
Loria, A., 237
Lositskii, A., xviii, 280–87
Lutz, F., 177n
Lutz, V., 177n

Machina, Mark J., 272–77
machine building, comparison between
      Soviet Union and United States,
      170–75
manager, *see* socialist manager
Markowski, S., 21n
Marris, Robin, 115n
Marshall, Alfred, 36n
Marx, Karl, 5, 30, 35, 36–37, 38n
Maslov, P., 239n, 261n, 264n
Massell, Benton F., 50n
master, *see* serfowner
materials, exclusion in indices of, 83–84,
      92
Mazur, A. G., 280n
Meyer, John R., 229n, 236n, 237
Mikoyan, Anastas I., 40n
Mill, John Stuart, 237n
Mills, F. C., 115n
Minhas, B. S., 75n
Mokyr, Joel, 268n

monopoly power, in socialist countries,
      204–5; *see also* competition
Moorsteen, R. H., 108n, 111–12, 114n, 115n,
      126, 146n, 171, 174
More, Thomas, 236
Mudgett, B. D., 115n
Musgrave, Richard, xi*n*

Nasse, E., 236n
Nieboer, H. J., 228, 235n, 237–38
Niitamo, Olavi, 50n
Nimitz, Nancy, 158n
Nixon, Richard M., 22, 37n
Nutter, G. W., 108n, 114n, 139, 171, 174

obrok system, 240, 245–46
   advantages and disadvantages of, 258–59
   effect of Paul's Law and Inventories
      system on, 259
   see also serfs; serfowners
Okun, Arthur M., 30n
Osipov, G. V., 18
Ostrogorsky, Georg, 234, 238n
output
   growth in selected countries of, 93
   of industry, and depreciation, 58
   in Kendrick's Index, 80

Parks, Richard W., 222n
Paul's Law, 249–53, 259
perestroika, xi, xviii, xix
perfect competition, 32, 35
Persons, Warren M., 114n
Phillips, Ulrich B., 238n
planner, *see* socialist planner
planning, government, 4, 40–42
Pokrovskii, N. M., 239, 240, 247–48,
      264n, 266–67n, 269n, 280n
Poland-Lithuania, serfdom in, 233–34
political change, 13
Ponting, K. G., 235n
population growth, and profitability of
      serfdom, 242–49
Postan, M. M., 174n, 234–35, 236n
power, *see* economic power
prices, *see* capital goods prices; grain
      prices; land prices; serf prices
price setting
   under perfect and monopolistic
      competition, 34
   by producers, 204–5
price system, and excess demand in Soviet
      Union, 203–4
producer cooperatives
   model with varying supply of labor,
      184–90

Pure Model of, 177–84
see also Pure Model
producers
under capitalism and socialism, 35–38,
45–46
price setting by, 204–5
productivity
analyses of, 74
arithmetic measurement of, 87–90
growth of capital in selected countries,
98, 101
of labor in Kendrick's Index, 80–81
of labor in selected countries, 95, 98
of labor in Soviet Union and U.S., 170
rate of growth in Soviet Union and U.S.
for total factor, 158
profit motive, under capitalism, 20
Pryor, F. L., 21n, 46n, 204n
Pure Model
of hypothetical producer cooperative,
177–90
mathematical appendix for, 192–99
Pushkin, Alexander, 232n

quitrent, *see obrok* system

Rashin, A. G., 249n
raw materials, as input, 56–57; *see also*
materials
Reddaway, W. B., 50n, 58n, 82n, 115n
Reich, Michael, xii*n*, 15–27, 29n, 39n
research and development, in Soviet Union
and United States, 165
Residual
comparison of growth of output and,
103, 105
correlation with rates of growth of other
variables, 105–6
definition and composition of, xiii, 49–50
geometric index method to express,
54–69
methods to obtain, 66–67
rate of growth of, 92, 116
role in analysis of arithmetic (value
added), 101
Solow expression of, 50–52, 53
see also Index of Total Factor
Productivity
Ricardo, David, 226
Rieber, Alfred J., 239
Rikhter, D. I., 261n, 283
risk
as criterion to compare capitalism and
socialism, 31
under perfect and monopolistic
competition, 32, 35

Roberts, Paul Craig, 37n, 38n, 40n
Robinson, G. T., 264n, 280n
Romanovich-Slavatinskii, A., 267n
Rozhin, V. P., 18
Ruback, R. S., 288n
Rule I, 55, 63
Rule II, 58–63, 65–66
Russia, 9, 10
development of serfdom in, 230–32,
245
emancipation of serfs in, 239–40
see also Soviet Union

Samarin, I. F., 244n, 250n, 258n, 267n
Samuelson, Paul A., 248n
Schmalensee, R., 20n
Schmookler, Jacob, 49n, 50
Schroeder, Gertrude E., 202n
Schumpeter, Joseph, 7, 32, 72
Scitovsky, Tibor, 30n, 34n, 177n
Sellers, James Benson, 236n
Semevskii, V. I., 245n, 250n
serfdom
development in Russia of, 230–32
in Poland-Lithuania and Western
Europe, 233–36
serfowner, 240–41
effect of Paul's Law on, 251–53
maximization of income of, 242
serfowners, debt of, 271–72; *see also* Paul's
Law
serfs
effect of Inventories on, 253–57
effect of *obrok* system on, 257–60
effect of Paul's Law on, 249–53
effect of population growth on, 242–49
emancipation of, 281
payment for labor, 248
prices for, 252, 272–77, 284–85
services, 134
servitors, *see* serfowners
Seton, F., 108n
sexism, 23–24
Shabad, T., 123n
Shkurko, S. I., 203n
Siegel, I. H., 115
Skrebitskii, Aleksandr, 245n, 252n, 254n,
258n, 264n, 271n, 272n
slavery
in Russia, 230–31
in United States, 236–37
see also serfdom
Smith, A. D., 50n, 58n, 82n
Smith, Adam, 36, 237n
Smith, R. E. F., 235n
Smith, Vernon L., 175n

socialism, 6
  as economic system, 138
  existence of, 16–17
  power and risk under, 38–44
socialist enterprises, organization of,
    18–19; *see also* firms
socialist manager, effect of bonus offer on,
    207–9
socialist planner, role in deciding profit
    and sales, 4, 40–42, 205, 207
Solow, Robert, 4, 50–53, 75n, 87n,
    92–93n, 150n, 173n
Solow method, to measure technological
    change, 50–52
Soviet Union
  capital productivity in, 153, 156
  collective farms as producer
    cooperatives, 178
  economic development in, 146
  economic reforms of 1965, xvi–xvii, 202
  index of industrial production, 107
  planners use of norms or coefficients,
    3–4
  price system and excess demand in,
    203–4
  workers and consumers in, 18–19
Spence, Michael, 222n
Stalin, Joseph, 40n
Starovsky, V. N., 190n
Stephenson, Matthew A., 37n, 38n
Stolper, Wolfgang F., 248n
Stone, F., 115n
Suppes, Patrick, 53n

Taylor, L. S., 20n
Taylor, Rosser H., 237n
technological change
  effect on economic growth, 49
  role in economic growth, 103
  see also geometric index; Index of
    Structural Change; the Residual;
    Solow method
Tengoborskii, L. V., 249n
Terborgh, George, 175n
Terleckyj, Nestor E., 87, 165n
Thornton, Judith, 34n, 46n
Tinbergen, Jan, 50n
Tolstoi, Leo, 241n
Trexler, Harrison A., 237n
Troinitskii, A., 250n, 270n, 271
Tucker, Robert C., 31n
Tugan-Baranovsky, M. I., xvi, 177n
Turgenev, Ivan, 260n

underdeveloped countries
  assistance for, 10–12
  choice of governmental system for, 5–10
  problems of economic change in, 13–14
United Kingdom
  growth of capital productivity in, 98–101
  growth of labor productivity in, 95–98
  growth of output in, 93
  rate of growth of Residuals, 101–6
United States
  capital productivity in, 153, 156
  economic development in, 146
  growth in capital productivity in, 98–101
  growth of labor productivity in, 95–98
  growth of output in, 93
  rate of growth of Residuals, 101–6
United States Department of Agriculture,
    272n
United States Department of Health,
    Education and Welfare, 18n, 37n

value-added Index, 89–90
value-added weights
  compared to value-of-output weights,
    108
  in geometric index method, 67–69
Verhulst, Adriaan, 234
Vetter, Heinz-Otto, 37

Wakefield, E. G., 237
Ward, Benjamin, xvi, 177, 180–83, 192
Weisbrod, Burton, 29n
Weiserbs, D., 20n
Weisskopf, Thomas B., xii$n$, 15–27, 29n,
    39n
Weitzman, Martin L., 30n, 127, 133, 217n
Westfield, F. M., 177n
Wiles, Peter J. D., 21n, 33n, 36n, 40n
Wilson, E. Carus, 235n
Wolfle, Dael, 143n
Woodman, Harold D., 229n, 236n, 237n,
    238n
workers
  alienation of, 18–19, 37, 39
  in capitalist and socialist systems, 18–19,
    45–46
  unemployed, 134
  see also consumers; producers

Yugoslavia, 18–19

Zaionchkovskii, P. A., 282, 288n
Zdravomyslov, A. G., 18